Sustainable Non-Profit Management

Build and run a hundred-year charity
Save a struggling non-profit

By R. A. Williams

Amazon Paperback Edition
ISBN: 9781520408217
ISBN issued by Amazon KDP

I would like to thank my parents, Ron and Olga Williams, who showed me what intelligent and practical volunteer work and charity administration looked like. Without your example, I would not have been able to codify the sustainable management principles in this book. Some people study charity and philanthropy; others grow up fortunate enough to be immersed in it. Your willingness to include me in this aspect of your lives is one of the reasons I've been able to participate as much as I have in charitable activity.

To my author friends Wendy Donges and Tracey Rollin, who explored the eBook publishing idea and shared their tips and tricks: thank you very much for your advice. Thank you also for the good, swift kick in the pants when I needed it.

I would particularly like to thank the online reviewers at mrmoneymustache.com, who kindly reviewed the draft version of this book and provided feedback. Your commonsense, ultra-frugal advice is appreciated and I thank you for your hard work. So, thank you to DeepEllumStache, mewseido, missbee, and all those who chose to remain anonymous.

The cover design for this book is by Tatiana Villa.

Table of Contents

Dedicated to my daughter, Erica

Introduction

This book is for people who want to run a not-for-profit business in a responsible, sustainable way.

You may be a new member of a Board of Directors, or you may have just been elected as an officer of your local Parent-Teacher Association. You might be an experienced volunteer or administrator whose church is struggling, or you may even wish to set up a tax exempt charity of your own.

I'm assuming you already have some basic knowledge, such as what a Board of Directors is and what kind of information should be contained in an annual report. You most likely already know what a volunteer is and have participated in some fundraising. I will review the basics, but if you want detailed instructions as to how a meeting should be run or what kind of information should go in an annual report, I recommend Robert's Rules of Order or any introduction to business management.

Most of my advice is directed at small, local charitable ventures. If you manage part of a large-scale not-for-profit venture such as a global church, a national chain of charity hospitals, or a major political party, then you most likely already have a law degree, a business degree, or both. If so, the chapters on corporate structure, budgeting, and cash flow will be mostly review. You may, however, benefit from the chapters on social capital and also the various analysis techniques I present throughout the book. They scale well.

Organization of the book

This book is divided into four sections. The first is an introduction to some of the basic principles and business concepts you must understand in order to lead a charitable venture. The second focuses on two of the three charitable domains, program and fundraising, The third section focuses on administrative techniques and strategies, and the last section touches on some special cases and concerns for particular types of charities.

Terminology

I use the phrase "not-for-profit" and "non-profit" interchangeably, and prefer the phrase "non-profit" because it's shorter. As anyone who has been in the field for any length of time already knows, the fact a business has no owners or shareholders doesn't mean it can't make, and spend, a substantial amount of money. It can have contractors and employees as well as volunteers, and it can own assets.

If you run into an unfamiliar word, check the back of this book. It contains the common definitions of the special terminology related to the field.

My background

I have experience as a volunteer, and later an administrator and founder, for small and mid-sized charities in Canada and the United States.

As a child and young adult I participated in charitable ventures in Alberta, Canada. There, several types of fundraising not considered tax exempt by the US tax code are quite common. Charity raffles, bingo, and even casino activities are very popular fundraisers. The rules for fundraising under Canadian and US laws differ enough for me to justify explicitly targeting this book to the US market.

Since 1999, I have been active in various charities in the state of New Mexico. My contributions range from volunteer work to fundraising to management.

Over the years I have done volunteer work for charities related to youth mentoring, education, sports, fine arts, elder and veteran care, animal welfare, medical research, food banks, and children's charity. I have been employed as a seasonal part-time contractor by non-profit groups to teach youth sports.

I grew up in a family that valued volunteer work. It was part of our family culture. As a child, I participated in fundraising for churches and community centers. As an adult, I served on four different not-for-profit Boards of Directors, and have held the office of Treasurer three times. Most recently, I was a founding member of the New Mexico Brazilian Jiu Jitsu Competitor Sponsorship Program in 2012. As of 2016 I continue to serve as President.

Through my involvement with different charities, I have organized, planned, and participated in every kind of legal fundraising that exists. These activities have ranged from labor based activities such as stadium cleanup or car washes to social capital based activities such as sales and sponsorship based activities I fondly refer to as "thing-a-thons". I have written proposals and obtained grants, and I have successfully solicited businesses and individuals for donations of goods and services.

Although nearly all my experience in the not-for-profit sector has been with tax exempt charities as opposed to lobbying or political action groups, I have working knowledge of other not-for-profit organizations. I am also a member of a credit union, for example, and have served as Treasurer of a homeowner's association and a local branch of a fraternal order.

Through my involvement with non-profit companies, I have seen both good and bad management. I have been privileged to have been part of some great things, but I have also been part of a few disasters. Much of this book contains experience gained from the problems and the disasters.

Over the years I noticed that the successful, sustainable charities I've been involved with have several things in common. There are specific things their administrators do to help promote health and longevity in all aspects of the charitable venture. I have collected these patterns of decision making and presented them here so that they can be examined by other people who want to build or run a hundred-year charity.

One thing that I have never done is accept money to administer a charity. I therefore do not consider myself to be a professional grant proposal-writer, donation solicitor, or charity administrator. Although I have done the work, I have never accepted payment for it. Frankly, I don't need to. I have enough income from other sources to meet my family's needs.

My philosophy

When it comes to managing a non-profit company, I am very conservative and risk averse. This is because I have seen too many cases where ill-advised program expansion or poor spending decisions have burned out a charity's volunteer base or left it unable to cope with routine challenges. The key values that drive my approach are as follows.

Accountability

I believe that a non-profit company is accountable not just to the community it serves, but also to the people who support it through labor and donations. It is also accountable to the people it employs, who deserve to be treated in a manner that makes long-term employment worthwhile.

Community

A charity that fails after a period of unsustainable operations damages the community it was created to serve. Many people get hurt in the process. Not only is a needy community deprived of the resources the non-profit used to provide, but the people who worked to make it happen also suffer. Employees are out of a job without a way to collect back pay. Volunteers are burned out and demoralized. Their families are suffering the consequences of months or years of neglect. Donors are disgusted and cynical, and those who raised money from friends and family often find that they have permanently damaged their relationships with their loved ones.

By contrast, when a charity shuts down cleanly the job losses still occur, but employees are not left with pay in arrears and the donor and volunteer bases are not damaged.

Sustainability

I believe that the only ethical way to run a non-profit company is to ensure it is sustainable: that is, run in such a way as to not exhaust its people or resources. This requires a fiscally conservative management strategy, and it limits the growth rate of the program to the resources available.

Pragmatism

I believe that a well-run non-profit company must select fundraising strategies appropriate to its existing resources, such as the size and capabilities of its existing donor and volunteer pool.

Fiscal conservatism

I believe that the amount of money or resources that can be safely and sustainably raised from a given pool of people is extremely predictable, and that the amount raised from a community using network and labor based fundraising represents the total commitment of that community to the charity at that time. The dollar amount is invariably less than you are hoping for.

My fiscal policies are very conservative because I believe that a responsible non-profit must scale its program and administrative spending to fall within the amount of money that can be sustainably raised. This belief is not shared by the majority of the non-profit community.

Integrity

I am against waste, fraud, dishonesty, and abuse in all its forms. I refuse to work with or help non-profit companies that will not operate within the law, or that are interested in pushing the limits of what the law allows them to do.

Risk management

I believe that the volunteers, donors, and employees of a charity are best served when their corporate culture respects and emphasizes the physical, mental, and emotional health of the people whose labor and resources sustain it. This is possible only with a conservative risk management strategy. Later in this book I discuss some of the forms of insurance available to mitigate certain types of risk.

Cash flow management

There is a direct relationship between deficit spending, debt, risk, cash flow, cash reserves, and organizational flexibility. Excessive debt burdens an organization the same way it burdens a household. Therefore, I believe that responsible debt management and cash flow management is a critical part of running a non-profit company.

Over the years I have noticed that non-profit companies that are under financial stress become far more vulnerable to organizational stress such as interpersonal rivalries or grudges. As a result, I refuse to work for charities or non-profit ventures that refuse to adopt and follow sound fiscal policies. I can and do perform turnaround consultation when I have the time, but I have also noticed that when you lead a horse to water and it refuses to drink, you can only hold its head under for a short while before you have to have a conversation about glue.

Balance

I believe that healthy non-profit companies maintain a balance between what they provide to their community and what they receive in terms of labor and donations. When this balance is upset, the company exhausts its donors, volunteers, and employees. Eventually it reaches a tipping point beyond which it is impossible to recover. This tipping point is impossible to predict accurately, but there are ways to tell when it's happened.

Giving shouldn't hurt

There are people who believe that giving to the point of discomfort is spiritually beneficial. I believe that if giving causes you significant discomfort, you're taking it too far.

Charity and non-profit work can be hard, and sometimes it is thankless, but it should never be endless or exhausting. If you find yourself sapped of energy because of your charitable work, it means you're overreaching.

Avoid the temptation to compete with others to see who's the most dedicated. There will always be someone else with a bigger bankroll, more free time, or a better list of contacts.

Emergencies should be rare

A well-run organization doesn't have a lot of emergencies. Unless you're literally battling a forest fire or filling sandbags to try to hold back a flood because your charity provides natural disaster response, you shouldn't be experiencing fear or significant stress. Furthermore, when the fire is out and the flood has passed, so should most of your stress. *A properly run charity should never remain in crisis mode.*

If your non-profit company is bouncing from one social or financial emergency to another, if you're losing people due to burnout, if you can't see a positive return on your invested work and money, or if you're constantly scrambling to raise enough money to cover necessities, what you have is a management problem.

Enough war metaphors, already

War—as Sun Tzu once said—is a serious business. So is running a not-for-profit venture. But they aren't the same. Anybody who says that they are is trying to sell you something.

Americans, as a group, like to use war metaphors to describe business activities. Books that try to apply military strategies or leadership secrets to business sell well. But there's something fundamentally stupid about using war analogies that way.

If you're constantly "fighting a battle", "dodging bullets", or "under fire", then if you're not working for the Red Cross or Doctors Without Borders in an actual war zone, you've either got delusions of grandeur or an unhealthy work environment. Either problem should make you reconsider your involvement.

Sitting around a table and deciding what to do about next year's budget is not quite the same as being shot at. So, pretending to be in a life-or-death situation just to squeeze a few more bucks out of a donor or a little more effort out of your volunteer pool is one of the most obviously manipulative things you can do.

Even if all the above reasons weren't more than enough, I have one final reason for disliking military metaphors in the context of non-profit management: *they are already so overdone as to be meaningless.*

Short term ventures

Not all not-for-profit corporations need to be sustainable. If you're trying to get somebody elected or if you're raising money for specific disaster relief, your organization is only going to operate for about three years. So it doesn't make sense to plan for the next thirty. The information about buying real estate or investing in income producing assets doesn't apply to you, however there are parts of the book that will.

Even if your current venture is strictly short-term, pay special attention to the chapters on social capital and cash flow. People who plan a long-term career in election fundraising or charity management need to be mindful of how they manage the people who support them. So although it's OK to push your volunteers and donors hard in the short term, make sure you do not exhaust their forbearance.

Disclaimer

This book is offered for sale in the United States and elsewhere, however it emphasizes US tax and liability laws and makes frequent references to government agencies and financial products unique to the United States. Although some of the principles that relate to human nature and logistics apply all over the world, the specific laws governing charitable ventures vary from one nation to the next. So do insurance products and business structures. Business techniques that are appropriate in the United States may not necessarily work elsewhere.

Within the United States, individual states sometimes regulate fundraising raffles or games of chance differently, and have different standards for tort prosecution. Some states municipalities offer exemption from property tax for certain kinds of charities, but others do not.

This book is not intended to serve as a substitute for professional legal or tax advice.

Warning

I speak and write bluntly, and I call things the way I see them. At times, I use expressive language to drive home an important point. It's because I've noticed that when people have an emotional reaction to one of my analogies, they take the concept behind it more seriously.

Over the years, I have developed extreme contempt for some attitudes and behaviors that are fashionable in the non-profit world. I have seen the bad decision making that comes from those imbecilic world-views, and I have also seen the devastation caused by those bad decisions. So, in order to help you learn from bad mistakes others have made, I am not shy about pointing them out or discussing why the mistakes are bad.

Some of the material in this book may shock or upset you. Most people who get involved in volunteer work have deeply held convictions about human nature and charity. Some of the things I say in this book may contradict these convictions or offend you.

People punish the messenger

The advice in this book will provide you with the tools to analyze a non-profit that is struggling or failing. It will help you identify and correct persistent cash flow problems or resource allocation conflicts. That does not mean that the conclusions you draw or the corrections you suggest will be welcomed by others. If you're trying to turn around a struggling charity by using the principles in this book, expect resistance.

Nobody likes to be told their services are not needed

At times, I have made myself unpopular with professional grant-writers, fundraising experts, and paid non-profit administrators. I have done this by saying that people with those job descriptions should confine their efforts to mid-sized or larger charities where they can be sustainably employed.

It's unfashionable to point out the fact that size matters, or that some fundraising or administrative options are simply inappropriate for a given charity based on the volunteer and fundraising base it actually possesses. I say it anyway.

No growth for growth's sake

I always recommend that a charity try to maintain an optimal size for its program and purpose. Sometimes that means giving up growth opportunities. This flies in the face of most business textbooks, which pay lip service to economy of scale but generally present growth as an inherently good thing. I find that most charitable ventures have an optimal size in terms of both head count and geography.

Windfall management

When your charity gets a large amount of money, especially if it all arrives at once, people get little dollar signs in their eyes. People are willing to manage cash flow responsibly when money is tight, but if it becomes temporarily plentiful the temptation to spend that money and expand the program is immense.

This book contains a chapter on grants and how to use grant money. At times, people will pressure you to use grant money for other than its intended purpose. Don't succumb to the temptation.

Not all problems are solvable

It's fashionable to pretend that there's no such thing as an unsolvable problem. In the real world, you're limited to the resources you've got. There's always going to be a finite amount of labor, money, space, and other resources available.

Within reason, you can turn labor into money or vice versa, but the rules about how money works are constant. If your liabilities are greater than your assets, you've got a negative net worth. If your income can't cover your expenses, you're insolvent. If you've borrowed so much and are so insolvent that you can't cover your contractual liabilities such as the service on your debt and you're unable to borrow any more, you're bankrupt.

No matter how optimistic you are, there is such thing as a debt that's too big or a disaster from which an organization can't recover. You may also be outnumbered by people who are addicted to crisis management or who are committed to driving their charity into the ground instead of solving the problem.

Nobody likes to give up

This book contains many examples of unrecoverable problems, where a not-for-profit company simply cannot be saved. When the debt, scandal, or other problems are too great to be overcome, it is often better to close down the existing venture and start another. Also, no company can be saved if its administrators are committed to mismanagement.

There are people who, if you pull them out of the hole they're in, will immediately start digging a new one and jump into it. They will pull you in alongside them if you allow it. Don't let yourself be drawn into codependent nonsense.

It's always best to shut down a doomed venture cleanly. But if for some reason you're not in a position to force a shutdown, at least have the sense to resign.

You don't need my permission—or anybody else's—to save yourself from damage to your personal reputation or from legal or financial risk. If you find yourself in the middle of an unsolvable problem, leave.

Section I: Charitable Basics

This section contains eight chapters that cover the fundamental aspects of what a not-for-profit corporation is, how it works, and how it interacts with the rest of the world. If you have taken courses in business administration or accounting before, some of the information will be familiar to you.

At times, you will hear people use the words "non-profit", "tax exempt", and "charity" interchangeably. Please don't do that. This section will explain the distinction between these terms and introduce some of the rules governing how charities must operate in the United States.

Maxims and Equations In This Section

Maxim #1: Human "need", as expressed by the demand for your charitable offering, expands to consume and then exceed the available supply.

Maxim #2: There are ideas and social theories that can never work because they are based on models of human behavior that are completely wrong.

Maxim #3: Law trumps ideology every time.

Maxim #4: When more than a third of the people are burned out for any reason, the group itself is toxic.

Maxim #5: Social capital is a finite resource.

Maxim #6: Never sell off an asset, which has long-term value, to get rid of a short-term problem.

Maxim #7: You cannot solve a cash flow problem by making it bigger.

Equation 1: $$Net\ Worth = Assets - Liabilities$$

Chapter 1: Charities Are Not Magic

People are drawn to non-profit management because they see a problem and want to help solve it. They tend to be smart, hardworking, ethical, and successful in other parts of their lives. So they set out to improve the world.

Unfortunately, sometimes when these capable and well-intentioned people start actually working for a charitable cause, something weird happens. They abandon their good judgment and common sense. Pretty soon they start making bad decisions that affect the long-term health of the organization.

Few people really set out to exploit the non-profit company they create, or to get into legal trouble. Nobody sets out to drive their church into bankruptcy, or to make a mistake that costs someone else his or her job. But it happens every day. It happens because too many people treat the non-profit world as if it were a vacation from reality. This chapter discusses some of the specific misconceptions people tend to have about non-profit ventures.

The magic bubble

Wouldn't it be nice to have a small alternate universe you could set up any way you want? Where anything is possible? Where the world and the people in it function exactly the way you think they should?

Founding a charity is a heady, empowering experience. It's one of the few ways ordinary people can feel as though they're changing the world for the better. They can write down a mission statement and compose bylaws that reflect their most deeply cherished beliefs. They can choose people for their Board of Directors who share their ideals and vision. They even get to come up with their own name for the venture.

With all of this creative power floating around, it's easy to feel like the normal rules have been suspended. But don't get so caught up in figuring out how your charity should work that you lose sight of how the world operates. If you do, you'll run into problems, because outside your magic bubble the rest of reality doesn't care whether you agree with it.

The world won't change all that much

People don't start charities, or volunteer to run them, unless they truly believe they can make a difference. They're confident enough to believe that if they get personally involved, they have the power to change things around them. It's good that they're confident, because they'd never step forward otherwise, but the confidence becomes a liability if they start thinking they can change the basic laws of physics, economics, or human nature.

It really is possible to improve the world through a charity. The March of Dimes, for example, eradicated a dreaded disease. Achieving medical or artistic breakthroughs is very possible, and it's one of the reasons charities exist. But while it's possible to correct some of the environmental or social problems caused by human error or shortsightedness, it's not possible to rewrite the basic laws by which the universe works. No matter what we do, ice will always float on water, hot air will always rise, the words "yes" and "no" will have opposite meanings, and market trends will always reflect the aggregate buying and selling decisions of large numbers of people.

Universal laws really are

The world we live in, charitable bubble and all, is governed by some basic physical, logical, and economic laws. These are not arbitrary rules that human beings made up. They did not come from our culture, religion, or level of spiritual enlightenment. They are simply facts of life that people eventually figured out, and that became part of our collective knowledge.

Deciding that "things are going to be different now" does not give any of us the ability to suspend universal laws. We can suspend social conventions or customs that are made up by other human beings, if we wish. Or we may invent new ones. We can create secret handshakes or new business structures. But we cannot change the basic facts of life. Here are a few examples.

Physics

Gravity doesn't stop working simply because you've stepped into a room full of people who are convinced they can levitate. Regardless of how you word your mission statement, you cannot cause the planet to spin more slowly so that there are more hours in a day. Also, reading an inspiring book or hearing an awesome motivational speech can't actually give a human being the ability to be in two different places at the same time. Please remember this when you work out your volunteer schedule.

Mathematics

Three will always be more than two. Subtracting a large positive number from a smaller positive number will leave a negative number. If the number in question happens to reflect your bank balance, that means you owe someone money.

Reformatting a spreadsheet or altering the layout of your balance sheet won't change the fact that fifty percent of five is two and a half, but a hundred percent of zero is still zero.

Cause and effect

The rules of formal logic say that if "A" causes "B", then when you have "A", "B" will necessarily follow. This is particularly important when it comes to predicting other people's responses to negative behavior.

Human beings limit their contact with folks who make them uncomfortable. If you're cruel and rude to someone, he or she will find reasons to not be around you. If you're dishonest to someone, he or she will not trust or respect you.

A charity environment, for the most part, is made up of volunteers. They can leave whenever they wish. So you can't expect them to absorb the kind of abuse that can be dished out to an employee or a co-worker.

There are entire industries and branches of government where shouting, name calling, cursing, threats, and sarcasm are considered customary or even necessary ways to manage subordinates or to conduct a negotiation with peers. This approach will not work in the non-profit world, where the victims can walk away.

Like attracts like

Emotionally healthy people withdraw from unhealthy environments. If you allow toxic or irresponsible behavior to flourish, if you fail to eradicate corruption or wink and nod at bad behavior, the people who don't like it will eventually understand that they must also tolerate it as part of the cost of doing business with you. If they find it intolerable, they will leave. Over time, only toxic or irresponsible people and their enablers will be left.

Fit happens. When it doesn't, walk away and look for something that works better for you.

Supply and demand

Charitable ventures are exercises in supply-side economics. The entire purpose of a charity is to provide human beings (or the animals and environment around them) with something they either can't or won't seek out or pay for themselves.

In a typical market economy, the price of scarce goods will increase until supply and demand are in a state of equilibrium. If the supply of goods increases beyond that level, the price must fall when suppliers are forced to compete for customers. But the price cannot fall too far: nobody can stay in business if they sell or give away products for less than they cost to make or get.

However, if you are providing a charitable service for free or at low cost, you will notice that the demand for your charitable service always expands to consume, and then exceed, the available supply. No matter how much you expand your charitable program, you will never reach a state of equilibrium where the market is satisfied.

This is not an exception to the laws of supply and demand. It is what happens when a useful and valuable good or service is delivered at a cost substantially below what the customer would expect to pay. High prices deter people from over-consuming or taking more than they really need. There is no such deterrent when the item is free or heavily subsidized.

That's one of my maxims, in fact:

Maxim #1: Human "need", as expressed by the demand for your charitable offering, expands to consume and then exceed the available supply.

Magical thinking

Magical thinking is the notion that people can change reality simply by wishing, thinking, hoping, vibrating, or believing strongly enough. The idea behind this notion is that people "attract" luck or opportunity simply through the force of their beliefs and their positive mental attitude.

It doesn't actually work.

Think and Grow Rich by Napoleon Hill was an international best-seller, but every single person Hill wrote about in the book had to actually get up off of his or her duff and *do* something in order to become successful and wealthy. Simply having a positive mental attitude wasn't enough. It was just the beginning: the first step on a road to success that sometimes took quite a while to accomplish. Sadly, popular culture remembered the book as having advocated fantasizing and dreaming as an effective substitute for planning and action.

Don't get me wrong: wishing and thinking are good ways to inspire people to focus on the results they want and to take the kind of action that will produce the results. But when fantasy is used as a substitute for action, the things that can only be accomplished through hard work simply don't occur.

One of the great things about reality is that you always get the results of what you do. You can compare those results against what you intended to accomplish, and learn whether or not your strategy worked. Armed with this knowledge, you can improve your approach and become more effective.

Unfortunately, people who engage in magical thinking generally misinterpret the results of their decision making. Any positive occurrence is interpreted as a sign that the strategy is "working", but negative occurrences are either overlooked or explained as being the result of insufficient faith or incorrect implementation of the strategy. This results in no improvement.

Victim-blaming is a common symptom of magical thinking. Far too many people believe that a person who gets sick, has an accident, or is the victim of a crime somehow attracted the bad luck or consensually willed the disaster to occur.

Under most circumstances, if a business experiment fails, the organizers take a look at what happened and why. But in a charity where magical thinking is practiced, the fact that donations are slowing down is frequently blamed not on factors that could be studied and improved, but on someone's "lack of commitment" or else outright sabotage. This is a problem, because although reality just delivered a very clear message that your local economy has changed or your fundraising approach isn't working, if you're unwilling to use the new information to correct and refine the approach, you're never going to actually fix the problem.

Vive la baloney: magical thinking in groups

When people succumb to magical thinking in groups, it becomes taboo to suggest a change in approach even if a plan isn't working. People start to confuse commitment to the cause with commitment to the plan or approach. So people who suggest a change in approach are often accused of disloyalty. For an illustration of how this works, here's a simplified account of the French Revolution and the Reign of Terror.

Spurred on by some over-educated optimists, the French peasants and working class *sans-culottes* became convinced that they could improve the bad economy, create jobs, and feed themselves by killing all the priests and aristocrats in France, dividing up their wealth, and creating a classless society. So that's what they did. Yet they didn't achieve their goal. Bread failed to appear, the weather was still nasty, crops were still failing, the economy got worse because everyone was suddenly too good to do manual labor, and the streets were even filthier.

A strategy is "good" only if it is suitable to the existing conditions and forgiving of minor error. An excellent strategy produces decent results even when the circumstances and resources are less than ideal, or when there are small errors in implementation. But when a strategy produces poor results, there's something wrong with the strategy. Either it's unsuited to the conditions and resources, or it's fundamentally unsound.

Under normal circumstances, political leaders back away from a losing strategy. But that's impossible in an environment where dissent comes across as disloyalty. Rather than admit they were wrong, leaders commit more. In the case of the French Revolution, politicians asserted that the only reason the plan hadn't worked was because not enough counter-revolutionaries had died. The result was the Reign of Terror, in which even tiny children were executed for the "crime" of being related to someone who complained about an unjust execution. France's economy didn't improve until its citizens came to their senses and got rid of the homicidal wing-nuts who were in office. At that point, nobody had to pretend that decapitation was an effective form of weather control, and people were able to return to work.

Charities seldom literally execute people, possibly for fear of losing their tax exempt status. At most, they fire employees or make volunteers uncomfortable enough to quit. Still, nothing about a charitable mission or a noble cause makes magical thinking work.

Conflation

Every once in a while, charity organizers *conflate* problems. This means they decide that two phenomena are related even though they aren't, and try to solve one problem by addressing another.

Suppose the Mud Hockey Society is in debt, and also suffers from a shortage of volunteers. These problems aren't necessarily related. But if the organizers decide that they can get rid of debt by signing up new volunteers to do fundraising, it won't work if the debt is due to ongoing embezzlement by a corrupt Treasurer.

One of the best cures for conflation is fact. The more you know about the inner workings of your charitable venture, such as where money goes and what work is done by whom, the better you will be able to identify what is really causing your organization's problems. Also, if you're able to arrange for an occasional independent audit or work assignment exchange you will often flush out problems like the one afflicting the fictional Mud Hockey Society.

Many times the visible problem is actually a response to another more serious but hidden concern. The Mud Hockey Society, for example, will never know its Treasurer is embezzling money unless it has an independent audit of all the receipts, expenses, and revenues.

Risk management and "doubling down"

In the game of blackjack, the goal is to get a group of cards worth twenty-one points, or as many points as possible without going over twenty-one. When a player has two cards that add up to thirteen or fourteen, the odds of the next card being a ten or a face card (worth ten) are high if few have been dealt. Instead of taking another card and risking a loss, or deciding to not take another card and accepting a guaranteed loss, some players "split and double down". They split their hand into two hands and double their bet so that they now have two hands of cards on the table and a better chance of winning at least one.

Splitting and doubling down can make sense in blackjack, where the player is actually redirecting commitment from a losing hand and doing something that increases his or her odds of winning. The player is at a table where somebody has to be a winner, and the winner takes all the money including what is put on the extra bet. Having two chances to win, instead of one, can make mathematical sense depending on what cards are on the table and in the deck. But in real life, when people dramatically increase their material personal stake in something they often aren't abandoning a losing strategy in favor of a potentially better one. They're clinging to a losing strategy without doing anything to change it into something that stands a chance of working. This is often called "doubling down on a losing bet". All it creates is a waste of resources.

Never increase your investment in an organization that asks you to double down on a bad bet.

"Faith" based solutions

Faith is at the core of every effective ministry and every well run church or religious institution. It's a good force in general, so long as it's not confused with magical thinking.

Magical thinking can look and feel a lot like faith, especially if you've ever had something good happen after praying for it. Investing attention and emotion in something feels a lot like work, and therefore like progress toward a goal. The entire "slacktivist" movement, in which people genuinely feel as though they have helped cure a deadly disease by clicking on an icon on a Web site, is a perfect example of magical thinking. Expressing verbal or electronic agreement should never be treated as an acceptable substitute for concrete, tangible effort.

Another way you will see magical thinking masquerading as faith is in the realm of cause and effect. I'm astounded by the number of people and organizations who believe that they can pray their way out of the very predictable consequences of their own bad decisions, *without first correcting or changing the bad decisions that got them into trouble in the first place.* For the record: *it doesn't work.*

People who pray for rescue from the consequence of their own bad habits or bad decisions without first correcting what they're doing wrong sometimes receive a windfall or "lucky break" of some sort. Perhaps their church or charity gets an unexpected donation that allows them to pay off debt or cover operating expenses. But if the debt is the result of years of overspending and borrowing, and if the overspending and borrowing does not stop, the charity will blow through the windfall almost immediately. It's the same with a charity as it is with a household: if you habitually spend more than your income, it's only a matter of time before you burn through the extra and end up right back where you started.

Visualization

Professional athletes, dancers, and musicians who have already mastered the basic skills of their craft have a trick called visualization. They fantasize about the perfect performance, and imagine every detail as they go through it. *For a person who already has the necessary skills*, it's frequently just as good as getting in a bit of extra practice. The key to the technique, though, is that the person practicing through visualization has already gone through the learning process and put in enough real practice to have mastered the skills. That's why I italicized the phrase that mentioned necessary physical skills: there is a craft that goes along with each sport or artistic activity. Without it, visualization doesn't help.

The visualization technique has unfortunately been co-opted by people who think they can use it as a substitute for acquiring the basic skills of their craft or for doing necessary work. Too many people, including charity organizers, go straight to the advanced visualization technique without first having mastered basic fundraising. Naturally, they fail. It's like deciding to perform a complicated Beethoven sonata without having studied or memorized the piece, and without having mastered basic scales or position transitions.

There's nothing wrong with sitting around a boardroom table brainstorming or playing "what if". It's good to look at fresh ideas once in a while. But fantasy sessions can't be used as a substitute for genuine planning or effort.

It's possible that there is indeed pie in the sky. But it will only be yours by and by if you do things that will result in you getting your hands on it. Hype sessions are great for coming up with a goal, but they do not create actual progress toward it.

Not all ideas or ideologies are created equal

One of the reasons people start charities is because they have ideas about how things *should* work. These ideas are often grounded in ideology or politics instead of observation. But a charitable venture is one place where people like to try out a new way of thinking or of doing things. Unfortunately, as has already been noted, people love their ideologies even when strategies based on them don't actually work. Sometimes the strategy is at fault, but at times the ideology itself is part of the problem.

Here's another of my politically incorrect notions: there are ideas and social theories that can never work because they are based on notions of human behavior that are completely wrong.

Communism, for example, fails in every situation where participation is mandatory, the natural rewards associated with extra effort are removed, and the natural penalties associated with freeloading no longer apply. Why is this? Well... it turns out that human beings respond to incentives. The insight sounds obvious now, but we wouldn't have figured it out as a society unless somebody, somewhere, experimented with a system that removed the incentives related to work.

Maxim #2: There are ideas and social theories that can never work because they are based on models of human behavior that are completely wrong.

There's nothing wrong with using a not-for-profit to conduct a social experiment. Overall, it's probably cheaper than taking over a country. Unfortunately, social-experiment charities seldom prosper, chiefly because their organizers are seldom willing to admit that their charity is a social experiment.

Making decisions on how you *would like* for human beings to behave or reality to work, or how you believe human beings *would* or *ought to* behave in a less constrained environment is a form of experimentation. Much of addiction treatment, for example, is still in the experimental stage. There are lots of theories about why people practice addictions and on what they will, or should, do when separated from their drug of choice. So far, there is no universal approach to addiction treatment because what works for one patient may not work for another. So if you have a charity that provides addiction treatment resources, one of the most important things you can possibly do is to keep records of both successes and failures. You use information about the people you couldn't successfully help to refine your approach or to proactively identify patients that have a high probability of success.

What you must not do, under any circumstances, is ignore evidence that your approach is failing. If your new addiction treatment approach is a bust, or your lobbying program is failing to produce any changes in how legislators vote, acknowledge it and try something else.

Not an extension of the ego

It's impossible to ignore the role of arrogance in non-profit mismanagement. Administrators tend to be a confident lot. However, when an organization becomes dominated by one person who runs the group as an extension of his or her ego or identity, that person is very likely to start using the charity to advance his or her personal agenda. This doesn't always involve dishonest or illegal behavior, but it turns the charity into a life support system for its chief member and his or her pet projects.

The only remaining alternative

Since charities aren't magic, what are they?

A charity is, first and foremost, a business. They call it a "not-for-profit corporation" for a reason. Sure, it's structured a bit differently from some for-profit businesses. If the charity has tax exempt status, it also has a few extra rules to follow to keep the IRS happy. But the rest of reality doesn't change just because you're devoting yourselves to some noble purpose in the public interest.

As a business, every charity inhabits reality. It is subject to the same rules of reality as any other collection of people.

If you drop a pencil or pen on the table during a Board meeting, you will notice that it falls toward the ground. The law of gravity is still in effect. (Try this sometime if you don't believe me). Similarly, the criminal laws of your country or state are still in effect. If you were to strangle someone or steal his wallet during a Board meeting, you would still face the same criminal charges that would apply if you did it in your own living room.

Laws against embezzlement, fraud, and every other kind of white-collar crime apply in the non-profit sector. Liability rules apply too: if you run over somebody while driving a vehicle owned by your church's youth group, both the church and the driver are liable, just the same as if you'd been driving a vehicle owned by a for-profit employer.

Businesses have assets, liabilities, and cash flow. Your program—the goods or services you provide to your community—takes the place of a for-profit company's products. The system you have for developing your product and delivering it to the public takes the place of a for-profit company's market research and logistics. Your fundraising team takes the place of a for-profit company's sales and marketing staff.

All the basic facts of life that apply to a for-profit business apply to you as well. This means that, like it or not, you have to do some basic things in order to survive, such as:

- Bookkeeping
- Maintaining receipts
- Keeping track of your resources
- Performing the minimum necessary reporting required by the IRS and by your state (which will vary depending on the size of your charity and how much money you bring in)
- Budgeting
- Goal setting
- Disaster prevention
- Fundraising
- Measuring your progress toward your goal
- Following reasonable procedures for meetings

27

- Managing people
- Providing training
- Enforcing standards
- Hiring and firing both employees and volunteers
- Filing necessary government paperwork, and
- Operating within the law

The sooner you accept the fact that your charity is a business, the sooner you can become objective about your resources, personnel, and options.

Chapter 2: There Will Be Paperwork

As Hyman Roth said famously to Michael Corleone in *The Godfather, Part II:* "This is the business we have chosen." Michael was whining about how one of his friends had been killed by a rival, and Hyman, the older and wiser of the two gangsters, explained that the risk of assassination was simply part of a career in organized crime, and that both he and Michael had been completely aware of that risk and accepted it willingly when deciding to get into the business in the first place. Hyman was explaining that Michael had to learn to accept the bad along with the good, and to stop whining about it.

Hopefully, your not-for-profit company isn't a branch of the fictional Corleone Mafia family, and assassination is not a major threat. But the underlying principle is the same: because you have chosen to be in business, there are going to be some basic facts of life that apply to you. This chapter will illustrate them.

For the most part, the down side of deciding to run a tax exempt charity is that there's going to be some paperwork and some jumping through hoops.

You must answer to legal authorities

Buying, selling, and providing services to the trusting public is a privilege, not a right. In order for human beings to move beyond barter and to start using currency and credit, and in order for them to be willing to do business with strangers, there has to be a basic level of trust. So, no matter where you go on the planet, if you want to do business with other people or other businesses, you have to show that you're worth trusting. You do this by following the same standards, laws, and credential systems as anybody else in your business. You let the appropriate authorities know you exist, and you pay the same kinds of taxes and license fees as everybody else in your business.

Human history has shown us repeatedly that a purely libertarian economy that has no regulation, quality control, or external audit system makes it easy to go into business, but it is also susceptible to the kind of public health and safety nightmare described by Upton Sinclair in The Jungle. People stop trusting each other. Simply to keep the abuses in check, and to provide some accountability for businesses that harm or cheat people instead of helping them, every nation and state has instituted different kinds of weights, measures, standards, and laws for people who provide their services to the public.

Incorporate and register with your state

Before you raise money in any state, or before you engage in any business transaction that involves money or something of value, you need to register with the Attorney General in that state. As part of the first registration process, you must "incorporate" or set up a corporation.

A corporation is a legal entity that can open a bank account, pay taxes, own assets, hire employees and sign a contract in its own right, without necessarily relying on the assets of its owners or shareholders (if it has any). It is founded and administered by human beings, and follows specific tax rules.

A not-for-profit corporation is structured differently from a regular corporation: for example, it has a Board of Directors instead of shareholders. For this reason, you cannot form a for-profit company and later "take it non-profit". Whether you are a not-for-profit venture must be decided before you incorporate.

Prior to incorporation and registration, you don't legally exist as an organization. So you can accept donations, and you can hand out money or goodies, but you're doing it in a personal capacity. You don't have the right to do business. This means you don't have the right to solicit the public, hire employees, or exchange goods and services for money. You can't open a bank account, buy insurance, or rent space as an organization. You can still do all of these things in a personal capacity, of course, but then as far as the law is concerned you're simply performing a free service for your friends and neighbors, and there's no distinction between your assets and your business's assets.

If you want to solicit donations, charge money for goods or services, advertise your services to the public, or enter into a contract, you must incorporate and register.

Registration and solicitation

If you register as a not-for-profit corporation in a given state, you may solicit donations there. Where you spend the money isn't important. You can spend it outside the state or even outside the country if you like:

disaster relief charities do it all the time. But to conduct business in a particular state, you must register there. If you wish to sell advertising space in a newsletter printed in the state of Arizona, you must be registered in Arizona. If you want to solicit donations in Tennessee, you must be registered in Tennessee.

If you plan to do business in more than one state, there's more than one way to deal with the requirement to register in every state where you do business. Some charities register separately and establish regional offices. Others, such as the United Way, incorporate and are administered separately in every state, and operate independently.

No need to over-register

Generally speaking, if you're setting up a new charitable venture, it's wise to register in as few states as possible. A museum, hospital, or nature preserve, for example, serves only the immediate geographical area. The vast majority of your solicitation is going to occur where you operate. Similarly, if you're raising money for missionary travel or overseas hunger relief, the vast majority of your solicitation is going to occur where you and the rest of the volunteers or employees live and work. That's where you should register.

There's no benefit to registering in any state where you're not able to also have some infrastructure. You need a registered agent: a resident of the state willing and able to act as the agent for your organization. He or she will have to have a physical mailing address (a post office box won't do), a phone number, and the wherewithal to answer official correspondence and to file annual reports on your behalf. You may be able to find a law office where, for a fee, you can arrange to have someone open your mail and act as your agent.

Conduct a cost/benefit analysis before registering in each new state. Every cent you spend on registration or on maintaining an in-state agent is administrative overhead, not a program expense. Unless you bring in enough revenue to justify keeping a branch office open and running a program in the new state, it doesn't make financial sense to expand. It's a far better idea to keep your administrative overhead low.

Consequences to not registering

If for some reason you decide to not incorporate and register, the legal authorities of any state in which you're operating can force you to turn over every cent you raise even if you've been providing goods or services in exchange for what you receive. Since you don't exist in any official corporate capacity, the state has no choice but to go after you as an individual.

If you incorporate and register in one state but do business in another and are caught, the jurisdiction that applies is the state in which the offense occurred, not where you live or do business. So, if you're based in Maine but are being sued by the state of Texas, you're going to have to travel to Texas to defend yourself. If you don't show up or pay somebody to represent you, you lose automatically. Overall, it's far cheaper to simply go through the registration process.

Following up

After you have registered, you are responsible for filing regular reports with your state. You must also keep your banking and contact information up to date. If your fundraising strategies change or if the address of your not-for-profit corporation changes, you must inform the state.

The bigger and more complex your charity becomes, the more detailed your reporting requirements become. Many small charities therefore confine their fundraising operations to just their home state.

If you do not wish to incorporate or register with any state, feel free to operate as an independent individual. You have the right to give away your own money and resources, and you have the right to perform services for others provided you do not charge money for these services or advertise them to the public.

Register with the IRS

If you accept donations of money or goods, or if you wish to hire a contractor or an employee or open a bank account, you must register with the Internal Revenue Service (IRS) and obtain an Employer Identification Number (EIN). By doing this, you are acknowledging their authority and agreeing to operate under the tax laws that govern your specific type of business.

You register your not-for-profit corporation with the IRS after you incorporate and register within at least one state.

Once you have registered with the IRS, you will get your unique EIN. This is like a Social Security number for your not-for-profit corporation.

You may identify your company as a not-for-profit corporation with the IRS if, and only if, you have incorporated as a not-for-profit corporation at the state level. The designation you choose for the IRS must match the type of organization you registered with your state.

The fact you register as a not-for-profit corporation does not mean that you are tax exempt. Unless you apply for, and receive, a letter of determination from the IRS that says your not-for-profit is tax exempt, by default you must file and pay taxes.

There are a few select categories of not-for-profit business that qualify for tax exempt status. If you have a church, charitable venture, trade union, or other kind of business that fits this model, you can apply for and receive a letter of tax exemption. The kind of taxes for which you will be exempt will depend on the category for which you qualify. However, unless you apply for tax exempt status and receive approval from the IRS, you are not tax exempt.

If you're reasonably sure your application will be approved, the IRS permits you to operate as if you were tax exempt. For a 501(c)(3) charity, this means you will have the option of issuing tax deductible receipts in exchange for donations. However, if you are not approved or if you abandon your application, you are responsible for tracking down all your donors and explaining that they can't use that deduction after all.

Keep employment records

If you hire employees or contractors, you must keep track of hours worked, and payment, even if you are tax exempt. Employees and contractors aren't the same when it comes to withholding income tax or Social Security, but hiring only contractors doesn't get you off the hook when it comes to tax reporting.

You are responsible for ensuring you comply with all federal and state laws concerning the employment of non-citizens. If you are hiring a specialist of some kind from outside the country (which is very common in sports or the fine arts), it's up to you to ensure he or she has the appropriate documentation. The fact you're a not-for-profit business will not protect you if the Immigration and Naturalization Service investigates you for hiring undocumented employees.

The minimum information you must collect for all your employees and contractors includes:

- Full name
- Current address and contact information
- Social Security Number

- Date hired
- Date terminated
- Hourly wage (or yearly salary)
- Hours worked
- Amount paid
- Value of any additional taxable benefits (which might include health, dental, or other forms of insurance)
- Any deductions made from the payment such as for pre-tax savings plans such as 401(k) plans

Obtain a municipal business license

If you advertise services to the public or offer products for sale, even for a charitable purpose, you must register with your city or town and get a business license. If you want to open an ethnic dance school and give dance lessons to the general public, you usually need a license even if no money is exchanged.

There is generally an annual fee associated with getting or maintaining a business license. This sort of fee can be considered a business expense.

Obtain all other appropriate licenses

Some kinds of services are subject to inspection to make sure they meet safety and quality standards. Most municipalities require special licensure for restaurants and food production plants, to aid in the inspection process. Elder care, physical and mental health care, and child care are subject to licensing and inspection. Schools must generally be accredited by your state and follow a minimum curriculum.

If your operations require the use of a vehicle, you're allowed to buy one using your not-for-profit corporation's money, but that vehicle still needs to be registered and insured. You need a license plate, and you also need to make sure the person who drives it has the appropriate license and credentials.

There's more than one class of driver's license for motor vehicles. A tractor-trailer rig is not the same as a motorcycle, and a three-axle bus with air brakes is not the same as a passenger van. Before you buy a vehicle, it's a good idea to make sure you know who's going to be driving it. Whereas a regular driver's license allows a person to drive any two-axle vehicle and to pull a trailer, a vehicle with more than two axles (such as a bus) generally requires a different kind of license.

Alcohol and gambling are special cases

If your facility serves alcohol, you must obtain an appropriate liquor or beer and wine license, or use a licensed caterer as a subcontractor.

The United States has special laws for businesses that are, or were, considered potentially immoral. Chief among these laws is a stipulation that money earned from non-sanctioned business activities is never tax exempt. Indeed, when the US federal government wants to discourage a specific kind of business, such as medical cannabis dispensaries in the early 2000's which were legal in some states, the IRS simply decides that no expenses related to the activity are tax deductible. Such a business, regardless of its for-profit or not-for-profit designation, is then required to pay tax on all of its revenue as opposed to on its profits after expenses. This administrative measure has forced many companies out of business.

Although revenue from gambling or alcohol sales is not tax exempt, and must be declared to the IRS, some not-for-profit businesses or charities do it. Raffles, for example, are a way to draw people over to a charity's booth at a fair or public event. Depending on the value of the prize and the ratio of the prize value to the ticket cost, if the winner ends up more than $600 ahead you will generally have to file the appropriate tax paperwork on the declarable income.

State law, or in very rare cases municipal law, may restrict raffles and games of chance. Not all states permit bingo, Keno, or 50/50 draws to occur outside of licensed establishments, regardless of who is running the games. Before organizing a draw or raffle, you should check the laws in your area.

Door prizes and other raffles in which tickets are given away for free are legal in every state. You may, if you wish, solicit donations to go along with tickets you distribute. Money earned in this way is considered a donation, however you should make sure to keep the prize value under the IRS limit for declarable income.

Many community theaters and stadiums serve beer or wine to people who are attending the show, and there's such a thing as a fundraising gala where alcohol is served. But in all of these cases, the income from alcohol sales or gambling is a trivial part of the organization's total income. At the stadium, people pay far more for their tickets than they do for their beer. Likewise, at a fundraising gala people generally do not pay for their beverages at all because they are included with the cost of the ticket and regarded as a type of operating expense. It is still a good business practice to account for alcohol sales separately, and the ethical thing to do is to either "sell" it at cost so that there is no profit at all, or to declare the income and to pay tax on it, no matter how trivial the amount may be.

Volunteers and employees must be licensed

Depending on the kind of services you offer, there may be licensing requirements for your employees or volunteers. Lack of these credentials may affect your charity's ability to get specific accreditation as a school or childcare facility.

The general rule as to whether an employee needs a license to perform a specific service through your charity is easy: if you would need a license to do the same work as an employee, or in a private capacity, you need it to perform your charity work too. If you're running a concession for fundraising purposes and the venue requires you to sell hot food, you must have the same food preparation permit that you would need if you were an employee of the venue. If you're cutting hair to raise money for charity, you must be a licensed hairdresser.

Make sure that everyone who is driving a vehicle for activities related to your not-for-profit venture is appropriately licensed and insured, *even if it's their own vehicle.*

Law and medicine are two industries that are heavily regulated by state licensing authorities. If your charity is set up to provide legal services, then the people giving legal advice should be actual lawyers who are licensed to practice in your state. If you're diagnosing diseases and writing medical prescriptions, the person doing that work had better be a doctor.

If for some reason you want to heal people or give them legal advice without going through the process of becoming a doctor or passing the Bar exam, it's vital that you not register yourself as a business of any kind, and that you not advertise your services to the public. Perform healing and give legal advice in the privacy of your own basement, don't lead anybody to believe you're considered qualified to do it, and don't provide services to anyone who doesn't know you. There may still be massive consequences to you if things go wrong, but at least you're only affecting other consenting adults. The second you set yourself up as an organization that serves the public, you're required to follow the same standards as everyone else who serves the public.

Zoning laws apply to you

Towns and cities generally have rules as to what kind of business can be run in a residential neighborhood. Some neighborhoods also have homeowner's associations that are given the authority to fine property owners or to place liens on their property for violating rules about what kind of business can or cannot operate there. The kind of business you're allowed to operate out of your home may be restricted based on where you live. You won't necessarily be prohibited from using your home address as a place to collect mail for your non-profit company or to conduct an occasional administrative meeting, but if you're conducting program activities that bring people to your home in large numbers you may eventually run into a zoning conflict.

Many residential homeowner's associations do not allow business advertising to be visible from the street, and they restrict the extent to which you can create extra vehicle traffic or parking in order for customers to come to your door. Any for-profit activity that would not be allowed in your neighborhood based on zoning laws or homeowner's associations is equally forbidden for a non-profit company.

Zoning laws often limit the size, location, and type of building that can be set up on a piece of real estate. There are generally restrictions against selling or renting out housing space in a retail or industrial area, just as there are rules limiting the kinds of business that can be conducted in a residential area.

Depending on where you live and what kind of concessions you need, you can sometimes request a change to the zoning for a piece of property, or to obtain an easement which is an exception to the rules that would otherwise apply. Just because you request an easement or change doesn't mean you will get it.

Overall, the practical thing to do is to carefully consider the type of space your not-for-profit corporation needs to occupy, and look at how it fits into the zoning of your town or city.

You must submit to inspection

From time to time, if you have a building that is open to the public it will have to be inspected to make sure it complies with the local fire and safety codes.

Food service is different from food preparation. In order to prepare and serve food in a soup kitchen or shelter, your business must have a commercial kitchen that meets or exceeds health code standards. Expect an initial inspection followed by random unscheduled inspections.

If you are remodeling or building a new structure, it must meet building codes especially if plumbing or electric work has been done. Fire codes also apply, and may specify a maximum number of people your business is allowed to serve. Building codes often require restrooms, fountains, and wheelchair access features. The way you use the space will affect which standards apply: living quarters have different standards from light industrial facilities, and kitchens are inspected differently from storage areas. Sometimes inspections are required for relatively simple activities such as installing a new furnace or replacing an air conditioner.

The fact that your business is non-profit in no way affects how the health or building codes apply. If you do not want to submit to inspection or regulation, it is best to not try to run a business. Operate out of your home if the zoning allows it, and operate in a private capacity.

Regular reporting is required

Most states require annual reports from all their registered non-profit corporations even if fundraising or other activities are not underway and the organization is in a dormant state. It is important to ensure that the Attorney General's office is kept up to date with the latest version of the Bylaws, a current list of officers and Board members, and of course the address and phone number of the registered agent.

Federal and state tax reporting

The IRS currently requires that all companies file income tax returns every year. Tax exempt companies are no longer an exception to this rule.

Luckily, the filing process is not burdensome for a small charity with gross receipts of $50,000 per year or less. Such small charities need only fill out an electronic postcard called the Form 990-N confirming the EIN, address, and contact information. The entire process takes less than a quarter of an hour for an unskilled person, including the time necessary to locate your EIN if you've filed it away somewhere.

For charities that gross more than $50,000 per year, the paperwork burden associated with tax reporting is roughly on par with doing the taxes for an individual who itemizes deductions. Only the largest and most complex charities, which operate in multiple states and have budgets of several million dollars, have a tax structure that can be considered truly complicated.

If you have employees, you must collect withholding tax and pay it on time. If you have paid contractors who earn more than the annual minimum, you need not collect withholding tax but you must report the amount earned by each person. Failure to report this can cause trouble for your employees or contractors when they file their own personal tax returns.

Consequences to not filing federal tax returns

Failure to file federal returns for three years in a row, even for a tax exempt not-for-profit charity, results in automatic revocation of your tax exempt status. It is a stupid way to lose tax exempt status, but thousands of charities manage it every year by failing to file three years in a row.

The IRS revokes tax exempt status automatically to help guard against the corporate equivalent of identity theft. Also, whether or not you have filed a return is a matter of public record..

Failure to report employee or contractor income, or failure to collect and pay withholding tax, will subject your business to fines. The fact you're a tax exempt charity in no way protects you from an audit. Indeed, if your company's oversights are serious enough, the officers of the company can be fined or even face criminal charges in a personal capacity.

Consequences to not filing state tax returns

Most states require that you file an annual tax return or report every year. If you don't, you cannot expect any benefits related to having tax exempt status in that state. Many donors or grantors routinely check for both federal and state level tax exempt status. If you are not in good standing with your state Attorney General's office, many grantors will scratch you off the eligibility list and discard your application.

Forgetting something fairly simple such as filing a tax return is a symptom of extreme disorganization, lack of attention to detail, or inability to spread duties fairly across the executive team or the Board. It happens occasionally when members of a charity are slacking off and causing their duties to devolve onto others, or when one somewhat codependent member of the executive team is scrambling around trying to do everybody else's work while some members coast along and do not contribute.

Not filing a state tax return gives the impression of instability, incompetence, high turnover, or other problems with the executive team.

Your EIN and tax information are public information

Every company's EIN, although similar in some respects to an individual's Social Security number, is public domain. The IRS offers a Web site and electronic lookup service that can be used by anybody who wishes to look up your charity and to determine whether it is tax exempt. Companies, charities, and government agencies routinely do this before giving out grant money, and sophisticated major donors check the EIN as part of their due diligence research before committing themselves. Even banks look up the EIN when someone representing your company opens an account. Keeping track of which EINs represent a viable, active charity, and making that information available to the public, helps anyone who may wish to do business with your organization to ensure that he or she isn't being conned

Taxes often still apply

"Tax exempt" does not mean that no taxes apply to you, ever. There are some kinds of tax that you simply can't avoid.

Income tax for employees

Employment related taxes apply to everyone. You must always pay and withhold Social Security, Medicaid, federal income tax, and state income tax for every employee. It's not a well-known fact, but even priests and ministers pay income tax.

Social Security and Medicaid are matched: one half is paid by the employee, and the other half is paid by you (the employer). The employee's half is generally withheld from his or her paycheck and remitted to the IRS along with the employer share. As the employer, it's your job to keep track of whether the appropriate tax was withheld. If for some reason you don't collect this tax, it's not unusual for the IRS to treat you as though you did collect it but decided not to turn it over.

Employment tax isn't money you own or can use for other purposes. It's supposed to be money you are collecting on behalf of Uncle Sam. If for some reason you choose to not save the employment tax, or if you dip into it to cover other expenses such as payroll, you're violating tax law. The fact you're a charity won't matter to the IRS one bit.

Non-exempt income is taxable

If your charity is engaging in a kind of fundraising that is not tax exempt, such as a raffle or a bingo game, you owe tax on the portion of your income that you made that way.

Many charities own property that isn't needed or used for its program activities. If your church receives a bequest of a house, or land, or other real estate you may be able to put the property to work making money for you. You can sell it, of course, and be exempt from capital gains tax the same way you are exempt from income tax on a stock dividend. But if you use the asset to make money by renting it to a third party, or to conduct an unrelated business such as a used bookstore, those business activities are often not tax exempt. Depending on your location, if you're using property that belongs to the charity to earn an income, such as by leasing a vacant lot to a cellular phone company, that income may also be taxable. You can generally deduct business expenses related to the income, but the onus is on you to make sure you keep records of any non-exempt activities.

You can't use the charity to make tax free money for yourself or your cronies

If for some reason your charity functions as a pass-through, with donations directed to a specific individual, this is not a tax exempt activity and depending on how much of it you do and whether there's a private benefit to an insider, you may be on shaky ground with your federal tax exempt status. Furthermore, inurement transactions wherein money is set aside for a specific individual, private benefit transactions that provide financial benefit to insiders, and "self dealing" transactions in which you use the charity to buy or rent out property you own in a personal capacity, are not tax exempt activities. You must pay tax on all such transactions, and the recipient of inurement or private benefit transaction is also on the hook for income tax.

There are several aspects of using a charity for personal benefit that violate the IRS standards for tax exempt activity. The first, and the most common, is the private benefit transaction. Other examples, such as earmarking funds for the use of specific individuals, is called "inurement" or the creation of a "private instrument". Insider benefits that are available to the management team and their friends and family but not to outsiders are equally inappropriate.

Directed donation, where a donor dictates when and how a donation will be used, cannot be used to specifically benefit a specific individual. Nor can the funds be set aside for expenses related to that individual. This, which is called using a charity as a "pass-through", is not a tax exempt activity. Any money received that way is taxable as income, and the donor may not claim the donation as a deductible expense at income tax time. Donations can be directed toward a specific program or a specific activity or category of expense (such as a new sound system or a building upgrade), but they cannot be directed toward specific individuals.

Sales or gross receipts tax

Not every state has a sales or gross receipts tax. The states that have them sometimes provide partial relief for federally recognized tax exempt charities, but the rules vary from one state to the next. Some states require tax exempt charities to file and declare the income even though taxes don't apply. Others exempt charities from having to collect sales or gross receipts taxes. Still other states don't have a transaction based tax at all.

If you live in a state where gross receipts tax applies to non-profits, and if the tax applies to some particular goods or services you're providing as part of a fundraising venture, you have a choice in terms of how you collect it. You may collect it on top of your regular transaction, or you may build it into your price structure. Either way, you're obligated to collect the tax and forward it to your state.

For example, suppose your state has a 7% gross receipts tax and it happens to apply to your particular sale. A $10 transaction now costs your customer $10.70, but you keep the 70 cents separate and remit a payment to your state, along with all the other gross receipts from all your other transactions. Another option, and one more favored by fundraisers, is to build the tax into the end product. So if you sell something to your customer for $10, the actual price is only $9.35 because 9.35 x 1.07 = 10 and you have to set aside 7% of the base price for tax.

If for some reason you aren't collecting gross receipts tax even though it applies, your state generally decides that you're building it into your pricing structure. In some states, gross receipts tax applies to barter income as well.

A sales or gross receipts tax isn't money your organization owns. It is money you collect on behalf of your state government. If your state law requires you to collect sales or gross receipts tax, do it. Set the money aside, and forward it as part of your usual filing process. Don't forget to check the laws in your state and to keep up with changes in the rules related to gross receipts tax on goods and services.

Property tax

Property tax is a municipal tax imposed by a local city, town, or village. Each person or company that owns property is assessed an annual dollar figure that represents a share of the municipal expenses such as firefighting, public schools, and law enforcement.

Not all property is within a municipal incorporated area. If you set up your program office in a rural area, in an unincorporated part of your county, municipal property taxes most likely won't apply.

It's a popular myth that charities and churches are completely exempt from property tax. Each state sets its own rules, even though property taxes are collected at the municipal or county level. Although every state provides at least some measure of property tax exemption for charities, you generally have to apply for the exemption letter which is generally handled at the state level because so many charities hold property in more than one county or municipality, and because the state already keeps track of registered not-for-profit corporations. The process for applying for the exemption is generally managed at the county or occasionally the municipal level, but the standards for obtaining exemption from property tax are generally the same throughout the state. Approval is not automatic. Furthermore, until you have approval, property tax must be paid although sometimes there is a process whereby you may be reimbursed.

Most states restrict the kind of charity that is eligible for tax relief and also restrict the kind of property for which tax relief is available. When the property is used primarily or exclusively for making money, property taxes frequently apply. If it is used primarily for program activities such as education, worship, administrative space, or providing services in a charitable fashion, the property is frequently tax exempt.

Many states require that a not-for-profit company seeking exemption from property tax be a "public charity" that provides all or most of its services for free or at a low cost, that benefits a disadvantaged group, and that relieves the government of at least some of its obligation to help the poor or less fortunate. A charity hospital would meet this goal, as would a soup kitchen. A church might meet this goal, if there are significant community support ventures such as clothing drives for the poor. But a yoga school or a tennis club may not qualify, and a credit union or social club that restricts its benefits to its own members most likely won't.

If you have a charity that your state deems worthy of property tax exemption, congratulations: you don't have to pay property tax on the real estate you own if it is being used primarily for your program activities. So you don't have to pay tax on your synagogue or mosque, and if you keep a building for "parsonage" to house your religious leader that building might be tax exempt too. But this exemption is limited to property that's being used to provide your program.

Property used for a side business is often still taxable. If you also own property used for a for-profit subsidiary business such as a religious publishing company, a wind farm, or an apartment complex, those properties usually aren't tax exempt.

It's your job to keep track of each property owned by your charity. You must determine whether property tax is owed for the real estate, and whether income tax or sales tax apply to the money it makes.

Chapter 3: Other Facts of Life

You now know that there are all kinds of reporting and tax laws that apply to your non-profit simply because it's a business. But, if you want to do business in the United States, there are some other rules governing how you have to treat people during the regular course of your business operations. There are also some expectations and facts that come from operating in a market economy. This chapter will discuss some of them.

Labor and non-discrimination laws apply

Relying on volunteers instead of paid workers does not make you exempt from having to provide a safe workplace. Safety standards as enforced by the Occupational Safety and Health Agency (OSHA) apply to you. If you have paid workers, you need to obey the laws regarding breaks, wages, and overtime.

As a result of the civil rights movement, businesses no longer have the right to dictate who gets to sit at the lunch counter. If you sell goods or services, you must serve every customer regardless of age, gender, national origin, veteran status or anything else. You must offer the same price to every customer. If sales, loyalty programs or bulk discounts are part of your pricing structure, they have to be available to anyone who makes the appropriate purchase.

If you extend credit, such as through a micro-loan company or a credit union, you may evaluate customers' credit-worthiness, but you must apply the same selection standards to all customers.

Limits to non-discrimination laws

Non-discrimination laws do not require you, or your volunteers or employees, to tolerate abuse. You can legally refuse a customer who is drunk, belligerent, stealing, or a risk to employees or patrons. If an individual does something *to you* that justifies a ban, the law supports you. The law does not support refusal to do business with entire categories of people who aren't breaking the law, making trouble, or harming you.

You have the right to ban drugs, tobacco, and alcohol from your premises. You may limit whether firearms or outside food or drink are brought in, and you can also enforce a dress code and safety standards on your property. Testing for illegal drug use is fine provided you have a printed anti-drug policy and you can prove your employees, volunteers, and recipients of charity understand that submitting to a drug test is a condition of employment or of receiving your services. Most organizations that test for drugs accomplish this by printing out a copy of their drug test policy and getting everyone to read and sign it.

Defining the charitable class you wish to serve

If your program provides goods or services to people, you are allowed to specify the "charitable class" of people who will receive a private benefit through your charity. Although the IRS is not fond of private benefit to individuals who do *not* need charity, they recognize that charitable service to people who need it is the entire reason why your charitable program exists. So, while you're setting up your Bylaws, figure out who needs your help.

It is OK to limit your services to a specific gender, age, or ethnicity provided that group of people is a "charitable class", meaning there's a measurable disadvantage to being in it. This is one of the reasons you see so many scholarships for visible minorities but relatively few restricted to able-bodied white men.

Some of the most obvious charitable classes include sick or elderly people, children, crime victims, and people with a disability or low income. People from groups that generally earn less than average (such as women or visible minorities) are generally considered to be of a charitable class, as are people who are minorities within their field of study. Scholarships for male nursing students or female engineering students can be gender-limited this way.

A narrowly focused program is perfectly legal

Many charitable programs have a narrow focus in order to provide the maximum benefit to their recipients. Disease research and aid programs are a classic example. Raising money to research sickle cell anemia (a genetic disorder that primarily affects people of recent African descent) does not mean you're prejudiced against other ethnic groups. Providing aid to prostate cancer victims does not mean you're anti-female.

Separation by age and gender is legal

It's reasonable to separate people by size, age, or gender for activities involving sports or physical contact. Sports programs routinely separate adults from children.

It's OK to limit your program recipients by age if your facilities can only accommodate one group at a time, or if the introduction of someone from a non-qualifying age group would affect the experience of your charitable class. There's no reason you should be forced to accept a normal, able-bodied 25-year-old into a senior citizens' pickle ball league or a 3-year-old into a midnight basketball program for young adults.

If your program provides shared housing, it is legal to separate unrelated adults by gender. This is to ensure the safety and comfort of the people you serve. So if you operate a barracks style homeless shelter or a halfway house for recently paroled sex offenders, it is reasonable to limit your program to men only. It doesn't mean you're anti-family or anti-female. It means that the program you can provide with the resources available to you provides maximum benefit and safety when it is narrowly focused.

Exclusivity is legal but may affect your tax status

If you run a private club and being of a particular gender is a criterion for admission, you can keep your gender restriction and still qualify for a 501(c) designation that provides partial tax exemption. It will not be the full 501(c)(3) exemption, and donations will not be tax deductible, but that's not due to the gender restriction. It's because a private club operates solely for the benefit of its members as opposed to providing a charitable service for society.

When it comes to hiring, churches have a little bit more slack than other kinds of businesses: they can require that their employees follow their religion. This makes sense especially when they hire clergy: it would defeat the purpose for a congregation in need of ministry to hire somebody from a different sect. Religious based discrimination is not permitted to any other type of charity. A faith-based soup kitchen can't hire based on religion, but a church can.

If you're a church and you're hiring people for, say, a school or sports center that is an outgrowth of your church, you are entirely within your rights to make hiring decisions based in part on the applicant's religion, however if you require membership in a faith for even one employee besides your minister, you must require it for everybody. You can't be selective and insist that your janitorial staff must be baptized members of your religion but your youth sports director doesn't have to. Also, if you have standards of conduct based on your religion and want to make those standards a condition of employment, you must apply and enforce the standards equally for everyone. If you don't, the employee you fire or refuse to hire has grounds for a discrimination suit and the fact you're a church will not protect you.

Laws of supply and demand apply to you

You operate in a market economy, so your company's long-term survival depends on whether the community you serve thinks you're worthwhile. If you stop providing the program the public wants to receive, or if the public's needs change, donations will dry up.

Sometimes the supply of the kind of program you offer exceeds the demand. Churches with empty pews compete for parishioners. Community theatres that charge for admission compete with other kinds of live and recorded entertainment. Arts programs, zoos, or providers of intangible benefit must therefore always make sure to do two things: stay relevant to the communities they serve, and budget at least a little bit of money for advertising.

Sometimes the demand for charitable services outstrips the supply. This applies chiefly to hardship relief charities. During a cold winter in a poor city, homeless shelters do not compete for people to fill the beds. They compete for the volunteer and donor resources necessary to meet the increased demand. When times are tough, and demand for charity services are highest, there will be fewer donations to go around because people will be focusing on their own survival. Charities that specialize in hardship relief are often financially strapped due to the same external problems that create pressure for them to expand. Food banks and homeless shelters must therefore set aside a rainy-day fund, while managing their debt and cash flow intelligently.

You have a target market

The following people can be considered "customers" of your charity or not-for-profit venture:

- The recipients of your charitable activity
- Your donors, including organizations that distribute grants or people who contribute to your fundraising ventures by buying sale items

48

- Your volunteers, including people who work on your administrative team
- Your employees or prospective employees, who need exciting work and a rewarding work environment, and
- Anyone who pays for the program services you provide, such as by attending your church or your museum, buying a copy of your documentary DVD, or buying the publication in which your research articles appear

If your program does not directly benefit human beings, but is focused on environmental preservation or animal welfare, the first point is not relevant to you. Nor is the last point, unless you're in a position to operate a wilderness preserve or a facility that can be visited by the public. If you're performing bald eagle rescue, doing an archaeological dig, running a captive breeding program to save a frog species that is extinct in the wild, or funding research to study colony collapse disorder in honeybees, you can't allow the general public into your facility. Archaeological dig sites are kept secret for a reason.

It makes sense to figure out who your target market is as early as possible. This will help you make intelligent decisions about whom to recruit for your Board of Directors and how to best spread the word about the good work you do.

You have competition

No matter how big your community is, it contains a finite amount of resources that can be directed to charitable ventures. You are therefore competing for donor dollars and volunteer hours. You are competing against other charities that operate in the same area, or that offer a similar program. You also compete against online fundraising initiatives, recreational spending opportunities, and even your donors' needy relatives and friends.

When the need is big enough, redundancy doesn't matter. After Hurricane Katrina, the Joplin tornado, and the tsunami that hit Japan, there was a massive global outpouring of help. But charities that form for a specific relief project appear, do their work, and then close. They don't need to operate sustainably because they aren't around for the long term.

Similar charities can coexist when nobody has the capacity to handle the load. Long-term, other charities can be a mixed blessing. You might be able to save time and resources by teaming up with them for specific projects. But you don't want to be mistaken for each other, and competing for donor dollars can be difficult if the other charity is better established.

If you're the new kid on the block, it's your job to differentiate your program from others. If you want to offer a youth mentoring program, it should have features that make it different from the Big Brothers/Big Sisters program. If you want to run a food bank in an area that already has one, it should either serve a niche market or do something that complements the existing facility. Serve as a collection or distribution center, or specialize in perishable products.

The issues discussed by your founders should include:

- Should this be a temporary effort (such as disaster relief) or do we want this charity to be here for a hundred years?
- What other groups and resources are in place already to serve our target market?
- How does our program differ from the others?
- Is it possible to cooperate with existing groups to meet our joint goal more efficiently?

Swallowing your pride and teaming up with another group that's working toward the same goal can often help you get there faster and more reliably.

You have a maximum capacity

If you provide any kind of tangible benefit to people, animals, or the environment, there's an upper limit to the number you can serve. Because your endowment fund is finite, will support a specific number of thousand-dollar scholarships per year. Because there are twenty-four hours in a day and seven days in a week, there's an upper limit to the number of signatures you can collect on a petition and to the number of children's baseball teams you can outfit. There's even an upper limit to the number of hot lunches you can serve at your soup kitchen and the number of beds you can fit in your homeless shelter.

Even if your work provides more of an intangible benefit by providing cultural, spiritual, or intellectual stimulation, there will still be limits on the number of people who can benefit from your program. The fire department limits the number of people who can be inside your church or museum, and your book publisher limits the number of copies in every printing.

Growth seldom scales smoothly

Mathematicians use the word "linear" to describe costs that increase uniformly with capacity, so that your cost per unit remains the same no matter whether you distribute one unit, a dozen, or ten thousand. In the real world, a business's operating costs are seldom linear. You will have fixed costs that are necessary for you simply to keep your doors open, even if you serve nobody at all. You will also have variable costs that apply to each person served. But your fixed costs will only be fixed within a specific range, because eventually you have to expand again by ordering a new run of books, or adding a wing to your hospital. Instead of increasing with a smooth slope, your operating costs relative to size looks more like a staircase. So the increase in fixed costs associated with expanding sometimes make it more economical to stay relatively small.

There will be people who oppose you

One of the hardest things for charitable people to accept is when an intelligent, well-informed, powerful member of the community speaks out against them. It's easy to ignore the yapping of random, ill-informed wing-nuts. But when criticism comes from a well-respected media source or when people show up at your facility with picket signs, it's a shock at first.

Most people who disagree with you aren't actually ignorant, wrong, mentally ill, or evil. Outside of Hollywood movies and badly written fiction, there's no such thing as clear-cut "good" and "evil" people. Nor is there such thing as a hero so noble and pure that the only people who dislike him or her are morally corrupt. Even Jesus Christ had detractors: the money-changers in the temple, for example, are not recorded as having appreciated the sudden need to find another place to open up their businesses so that they could feed their families.

In fiction, a hero who is always right, who makes no mistakes, and who is loved by all except some totally unreasonable detractors or rivals is called a "Mary Sue" or a "Gary Stu". It's not a complimentary term. Real people, heroic or otherwise, screw up sometimes. Also, if you can't make an omelet without breaking a few eggs, the person whose eggs they are will object.

Aesop wasn't kidding when he said that one person's meat is another person's poison. No community ever has perfect alignment of ideology or interests. Personality conflict is real, and sometimes good people leave good charities on bad terms. Anyone who has a negative experience with you cannot be expected to donate or to speak well of you.

People who have never met you in person and who have no inside knowledge of your organization will still object to your specific program for any of the following reasons:

- They have reason to believe the services you provide are not helping the community you purport to serve
- Your program, or one like it, harmed someone they know
- They have reason to believe your particular charity is not well run or does not execute its program well
- The program you are providing violates one of their deep ethical, ideological, or cultural values, or
- They are antagonistic toward the people your charity serves, and do not believe they are worthy of aid

A person who is radically opposed to what you are doing isn't necessarily uninformed or malicious. He or she simply prioritizes things differently or has interests that don't align with yours. The construction you're opposing for environmental reasons might be what's providing his or her job. The relief packages you're proposing to drop into his or her neighborhood may undercut local food prices and force local farmers out of business.

Personal ideology can conflict with a program

If your convictions are strong enough, there may be work that is so badly out of step with your ideals that it's impossible to do the work and still think well of yourself. You may find yourself unable to offer high interest loans to needy people, or you may find yourself unable to help in the legal defense of a violent criminal you know is guilty.

The only solution to ideological conflict is to avoid it. Choose fundraising and program activities that suit your ideology, and you will be happier and more effective.

If you truly do not wish to enable the use of addictive drugs, do not open up a needle exchange. If you do not wish to perform an abortion even in cases of medical need, do not open up an obstetrics practice specializing in high-risk pregnancy. If you think cold-calling is annoying or wrong, don't buy somebody else's contact list and use it for solicitation.

Before you accept an invitation to the Board of Directors, make sure to volunteer with the organization for a while first. This will help you assess whether the charity aligns with your values. When founding a new charity, seek out Board members who either share your vision or are willing to accept your leadership and standards.

It is unwise to join a charitable organization and then try to redirect it. It is equally unwise to hire someone or accept a new Board member whose values are radically out of step. You will spend most of your time fighting with people who have no problem doing business in a way you despise.

Commitment to sustainable management is itself a personal ideology. I once resigned as Treasurer from a charity when I realized the rest of the management team was so committed to providing a life support system for a clique of professional speakers that they were willing to take on high interest debt and skirt the law to do it. I was, at the time, inexperienced enough to truly believe what the other Board members said about wanting to turn their organization around and run sustainably within the law. It turned out that what they really wanted was a well-heeled person to write check after check to enable the charity to continue to avoid the otherwise predictable consequences of fiscal mismanagement.

Before I left, I tried everything I could think of to convince them to obey the law and to act with fiscal responsibility. It didn't work. I eventually resigned on extremely bad terms. I think it's safe to say that the rest of the executive team was happy to see me leave. Up until that point, I was the odd person out. My objections had become so consistent that they came across as an attempt to undermine the charity and the other members of the Board. The charity in question later collapsed as a direct result of bad fiscal management and unethical behavior, but by that point I was long gone.

If you feel strongly enough about it…

As any craftsman will say, it's important to use the right tool for the job. If you're trying to get laws changed or get specific people elected, you need to make sure you're doing it through the appropriate non-profit structure. You may not use a church or a 501(c)(3) charity to do any significant amount of lobbying without losing your tax exempt status, and trying to influence the outcome of an election is the kiss of death for a charity.

What happens when you start a fight you can't win

There are people who like to deliberately push the limits of the law and get away with as much as possible. Some want the attention that comes from publicly breaking the law in as belligerent a way as possible. Others are acting out a martyr fantasy, so they try to bait people into responding negatively to their own belligerent conduct in order to claim "persecution". Still others engage in magical thinking, and declare that the fact they haven't been caught or charged yet is evidence of their moral rectitude. These people are dangerous to have around, especially if you allow them to represent your charity.

Getting sued satisfies someone who's spoiling for a fight—they get their fifteen minutes of fame—but it comes at the expense of all who benefit from the charity's program. Lawsuits are expensive and they divert necessary resources away from your program. They create bad publicity that often turns away good and reliable donors while attracting positive attention from negative people. Bad publicity sometimes attracts belligerent donors who appreciate the fact you're willing to be the lightning rod, but these new donors will seldom be there for you in the long term. When the dust settles and your charity has returned to normal operations or is gone completely due to mounting legal fees, the belligerent donors will see that you are no longer providing them with the drama they crave. So they will drift off to support another charity or business that is in conflict. They don't want to support you because of shared principles... they want the conflict. That's their agenda, and when it no longer aligns with yours they will leave. But the original donors who were scared off by the bad publicity won't necessarily return.

You definitely don't want to start a fight with the IRS because you decided to use your charity to push the limits of what the law allows you to do through your particular kind of tax exempt entity. Losing tax exempt status is a serious blow to any charity, which must now pay property taxes plus federal and state income tax. Donations are no longer tax deductible and the organization is generally no longer eligible for government or corporate grants. Income drops and expenses take a huge leap. Even if the charity is not forced out of business (and many are), less money is available to run the program or do charitable work.

I've always believed that the expenses associated with defending a lawsuit, and the damage done to a charity if it loses its tax exempt status, does far more damage than can be justified by fifteen minutes of fame. So I always advise people to operate within the law and to not go out of their way to harass others. The kind of charitable venture that lasts a hundred years or more tends to avoid extreme measures and situations. It also tends to maintain cash reserves and to create lasting public benefit in exchange for the donor dollar. You can't do these things as well when you're dealing with a lawsuit.

For the dedicated nonconformists

Always pursue the *minimum* necessary certification or organizational formality necessary to accomplish your goal. The more complicated the business structure, the more effort it takes to keep it going, and the more paperwork is involved. A nonconformist has trouble toeing the line at the best of times. Seeking out tax exempt status, or registering as a business at all, carries with it a bunch of expectations and restrictions that not everyone likes.

It's possible to accomplish a charitable goal in a personal capacity without hanging out a shingle. If you want to educate children, offer free tutoring to families in your neighborhood. If you want to give to the poor, set aside money from your family's monthly budget and start giving. You will have full control over your program and clientele so long as you operate in the privacy of your own home, using your own money and resources.

If you do not like the restrictions associated with tax exempt status, don't apply for it and don't try to operate tax exempt. Paying extra taxes may be worth it if you feel the need for more freedom.

When it comes to your employees, make sure you select people who aren't in love with the idea of pushing the legal limits. You can't afford the kind of expense they create.

Depending on the kind of charity you have, you may be eligible for government funding if you are working toward poverty relief. If you are a food bank, a soup kitchen, or a homeless shelter money is often available from federal or state governments to supplement what you raise yourself. But beware: there are strings attached. As a condition of receiving the help, you may not be able to require the people who benefit from your program to, say, perform work in exchange for accommodations or attend religious services before or after meals. I know one ministry that operates a homeless shelter, but that refuses any form of government help because the administration team believes the compromises involved in order to secure government funding would detract from the efficacy of its program. It takes guts to turn down free money, and the decision to go it alone has kept the shelter from growing as much as it might otherwise have grown, however the shelter is still considered to be one of the best in the region.

Ideological entitlement

Charitable ventures attract people who are strongly committed to improving the world. It's normal for such people to be committed to some ideology. However, when it comes to business, learn that other people don't necessarily follow your ideology when interacting with you. Never get the idea that your particular ideology puts you above the law, and try not to hang out with other people who do.

I'm not trying to scare you away from lobbying or from trying to change a law you believe is bad. I'm not even trying to deter you from civil disobedience if you have already exhausted all the other legal remedies. The civil rights movement owes much of its success to peaceful, nonviolent civil disobedience. But be wary of people who truly believe that their ideology will, or should, protect them from the predictable consequences of antisocial behavior. They are wrong.

Maxim #3: Law trumps ideology every time.

If someone trips on a crack in your sidewalk and breaks his or her wrist, that person is entitled to payment for the resulting medical expenses. It doesn't matter how much good you do in the world, or whether you're tax exempt: the law requires you to be responsible for what happens on your property.

If you run a business that serves the public, you must serve the entire public. You don't get to decide which members of the public are or are not entitled to your services. If you try, you'll eventually attract the attention from someone on the other side of the ideological fence who's as eager for a fight as you are. When that person seeks you out and files suit because of your biased or discriminatory practices, don't pretend you're a victim. You had the opportunity to open a private club instead, and you made your choice.

Some people want a conflict of interest

As a non-profit administrator, you're likely to make sure your operations don't conflict with your own beliefs. You're also in a position to steer your organization clear of unnecessary legal trouble by ensuring you stay within the law and treat other people well. But you also have to watch out for the other people working with you: employees, donors, volunteers, or your fellow administrators.

There have been cases where someone with an axe to grind goes out of his or her way to find a job in which they can create a big ideological stir on someone else's time and dime. There are also cases where people are so hungry for attention that they're willing to ignore the best interests of their charity in order to get their fifteen minutes of fame. None of this attention-seeking behavior is good for an employer. You don't need for other people to use you, and your work, in order to make a name for themselves by sabotaging what you hold dear.

Not all conflict of interest is ideological. There are people who work for you and with you not because they wish to serve, but because they wish to profit personally. Perhaps they want money, so they overcharge for services or skim a few hundred dollars out of the till at your concession fund-raiser. This, in its own way, can be just as dangerous. Having someone get caught with their hand in the cookie jar damages your charity's credibility.

Wise administrators plan for conflict of interest the same way they plan for fires or computer crashes. Here are the ways smart non-profit administrators prepare for conflict of interest problems.

- Study and understand the laws that apply to your business, and structure your bylaws and business processes to follow the law
- Communicate your expectations to your employees and supervisors in advance, and in writing
- Supervise your employees and contractors to ensure laws and your organization's policies are being followed
- If you believe that there are other people who would like to improve their reputation at your charity's expense, have written policies about the kinds of donation you are willing to accept
- Have a written disclosure process for conflict of interest
- Recuse people with conflict of interest from decision making
- Keep records of your decision making, in case someone later has reason to question what you did, or why
- Have regular audits of your accounting books

- Listen to whistle-blowers, prevent retaliation against them, and conduct timely and diligent investigations where needed, making use of unbiased outside investigators
- If one of your business practices creates a serious public relations problem, consider abandoning it even if you're within the law
- Never elevate any person, or group of people to a position of so much authority that the rest of the non-profit acts as a rubber stamp for its decisions

Conflict of interest is a major problem for all businesses, but because of ideological entitlement in the general population, charitable or non-profit organizations are far more vulnerable to it. Also, because so much of your business depends on the public trust, it is important to watch out for conflict of interest, prevent it as much as possible, and have a plan for dealing for it when it occurs.

Cause, effect, and abuse

The laws of cause and effect apply to you. Specifically, you can expect people to respond to how you treat them. Whether the people you treat well remain loyal to you is not always up to you, because sometimes people react to things that are beyond your control. But people definitely respond if they believe you're treating them poorly or disrespectfully.

You cannot expect to retain the support of people you abuse, or to whom you deliberately show disrespect. This rule applies not only to your own conduct, but to the people you hire or allow to otherwise represent you. It's in everyone's best interest to promote a culture of respect.

Verbal abuse

Healthy people respond to abuse by distancing themselves from it as much as possible. If you address someone in a way they find objectionable, and they object to it, and you keep using the very language you have just been told is derogatory or offensive, expect the person you're verbally degrading to find ways to avoid interacting with you. This is not "punishment" or "retaliation". It's normal human behavior.

For people whose adult life experience is in the military or who have had special training to supervise government contractors, tantrums and tirades may be the way they have been taught to do business. Screaming at somebody who is not behaving exactly the way you want them to behave, or who disagrees with you, is presented as normal and customary during basic training. Publicly accusing somebody of theft, dishonesty, and incompetence is something government representatives are taught to do as a matter of course or as a negotiation technique. These behaviors work well in the military or in government because the people you abuse aren't able to get away from you. There are no real consequences to verbally abusing somebody, sabotaging them, or even physically attacking them provided you stay within the rules on the book or there are no witnesses. But once you get out into the real world, you will learn that there are consequences to belittling or denigrating people, and to doing things that make you come across as a very immature person.

If you persist in addressing an adult man as "boy", adult women as "girls," or using words like "loser", "honey", "idiot", "dumbass", "bitch", or "asshole", please understand that this kind of speech is very degrading to others. Human beings don't like to be degraded. It isn't fun for them.

Although you have the legal right to speak in an extremely derogatory way toward or about others, they also have a legal right to freedom of association. Volunteers vote with their feet; donors vote with their wallets.

You may hear people bleat about how their husband or wife considers the word "idiot" to be a form of endearment, how they personally don't mind being called the N-word, how they heard a racial slur in a song the other day, or how their friends call each other names all day long and understand they're just kidding. All these statements may be true. But please don't confuse one person's standards or an inside joke with a universal standard of what other people think is appropriate in a business environment.

Good intentions don't go very far if they are poisoned with careless behavior, especially if it creates a bad first impression. Very few people who meet you for the first time are going to stick around to find out whether you meant the vicious thing you just said. They will simply conclude that you're representing the official position of the company, and that if they want to receive your program services or work with you to as volunteers, they will have to submit to degrading behavior as a condition of participation. Most will just find somewhere else to work or volunteer.

It's true that, in the first half of the 20th century, people who were in positions of power and privilege could use any kind of derogatory language they liked, and nobody dared to object. Indeed, many people declared that they "didn't mind" being referred to in dismissive, derogatory terms simply because they were afraid of losing their job or their financial security if they said otherwise. This led to a sense of exaggerated entitlement in a fairly small set of people who were so privileged that they really did have the continued support of the people they abused, simply because their targets had no other option if they wanted to stay employed, married, or out of the emergency room.

In this day and age, people are free to leave abusive spouses, employers, and co-workers. If you find that people are pulling away from you because of things you say, it's not necessarily because there's a vast politically correct movement trying to stifle your oh-so-important right to self-expression. It's because you're allowing toxic waste to spew out of your mouth, and other people are exercising their equally important right to avoid it.

If you call somebody by a name they dislike, even if it's a nickname or a variation of their own name as opposed to some unrelated word, it's reasonable to expect them to ask you to stop. If you choose to continue despite their protests, expect them to do whatever it takes to reduce their discomfort. This may involve limiting their contact with you, or even breaking it off entirely.

There are people who assert that they "can't" stop using fake terms of endearment such as "hon" or "baby", or that they are so accustomed to using hated nicknames or belittling language toward specific people or categories of people that they are just incapable of stopping. Therefore, they assert that people who object to their language are being unreasonable. Astoundingly, the same people, when stopped by a police officer or when speaking to their bosses or their landlords, develop a miraculous ability to refrain from mocking or degrading that person. This is why you won't be able to get anyone to believe you if you try to get away with passing degrading speech off as a vital part of your culture or your personality.

If you're so committed to what you describe as your habits, culture, personality, or Constitutionally protected right to freedom of expression that you simply can't find the wherewithal to interact positively with someone, please understand that you're putting your right to run your mouth the way you want ahead of the best interests of your charity. You won't be able to do that very long if the other administrators on your team are mentally and emotionally healthy people, or if they understand cause and effect. Charity is a team sport: it is not possible to found and run a charity by yourself. To register your not-for-profit corporation requires at least *two* founders. Also, to accomplish your program goals you will eventually need the cooperation of other people.

It's wise to pick your verbal battles if you are the one who has to correct someone else's speech. Using your sense of persecution as a club to beat other people into line and control how they communicate is just as toxic as unrestricted hate speech. First, make sure you're not correcting that person constantly, and make sure that your complaints are reasonable according to some objective standard. If you find yourself correcting everybody around you, and if you find yourself responding to other people's derogatory speech on a daily basis, then unless you're going out of your way to interact with bigoted people there's a good chance you're the one with the problem. If you insist on nit-picking everyone else's speech so as to find something to criticize on a daily basis, do you expect other people to stick around for long?

Harassment

Be careful when it comes to teasing, flirting, ribbing, prank playing, or other kinds of horseplay. It's all fun and games until somebody doesn't want to participate or to watch it occur. If at any point the nonsense starts to interfere with productivity, it's your duty as an administrator to stop it.

If someone asks you to stop what you believe is harmless fun, because they don't think the teasing, flirting, or pranks are funny, then please take their objection seriously. If you don't, you are very likely to lose the person you're abusing. Unlike employees, volunteers don't lose income when they quit: in fact, they gain free time. There are always charitable ventures clamoring for help and for donors, and from a volunteer's perspective they have very little to lose.

After someone objects to unwanted physical contact or verbal harassment, it doesn't really matter what your intentions are. You might think you're being friendly by demanding a hug or by touching or patting people on the shoulder, head, or rump. But many people interpret those gestures as extremely unfriendly violations of their personal space.

Be wary of allowing anybody, even a trusted and honored founder, to behave as though he or she is above reproach. No matter how solvent you are, you cannot afford the legal trouble and bad press that comes simply because someone powerful decides he or she deserves to use the charity as a personal forum for creative self-expression or "fun" at someone else's expense.

Immunity

One of the easiest ways to lose volunteers, donors, and supporters is to allow a small number of high-status people to exercise their egos at other people's expense while being immune to the consequences.

Making excuses for bullying behavior simply because the bully is a founder or a key donor is penny-wise but pound-foolish. Too many charities become toxic simply because Boards are unwilling to confront or correct people who abuse their authority.

It's the same with a charity as it is with an apartment complex: the bad tenants (or in the charity's case, the bad volunteers, employees, or customers) invariably drive out the good ones. When exposure to verbal abuse or harassment is a condition of participation, people who don't like it will eventually vote with their feet. Eventually, the only people you will have left will be the ones who are willing to tolerate abusive behavior or who secretly like it and approve of it.

Chapter 4: Social Capital

The phrase "social capital" was not coined by me. It's been growing in popularity, though, and I'd like to take this opportunity to discuss what it is and how it affects charitable ventures.

Social capital is an invisible social currency: a combination of credibility, respect, trust, and a feeling of obligation toward the person or organization that has it. A person with lots of it is known and respected by peers, subordinates, and superiors. His or her actions are interpreted in the best possible light.

The more social capital you have, the better people tend to trust your judgment and your word and the more willing people are to help you if you need something. They don't necessarily do it out of a sense of guilt. Whoever helps a person with lots of social capital generally has a sense of repaying that person on behalf of the whole community.

Companies can have social capital too. It's often called "goodwill" and it refers to a company's public reputation as a result of years of business. Brand loyalty is an example of social capital in the corporate world.

Not-for-profit companies require more than just money to get by. In-kind donations of space, equipment, and items for resale are common, and very few charitable ventures could get by without volunteers. But surely by now you've noticed that some individuals, and some companies, are better at attracting donations and volunteer work than others. This is because charitable ventures run on social capital, and some people have more of it than others and know how to use it.

The benefit of the doubt

People with social capital tend to be given the benefit of the doubt when things go wrong. A person with whom you have social capital forgives you if you goof up, tolerates your eccentricities, and is willing to go out of his or her way to help you. There is enough trust to allow the two of you to exchange major favors, and to rely on one another in an emergency. Of course, this is only true up to a point: social capital can be lost or exhausted, as this chapter will show.

The modern form of honor

During the Middle Ages, the word used for social capital was "honor". At that time, the concept was reserved for people who, due to an accident of birth, were part of a wealthy and powerful social class. Although it was supposed to be synonymous with honesty, humility, morality, and personal worth, "honor" ended up being just one more privilege of the elite. But in society as a whole, the hunger for what the word "honor" represented remained and grew stronger over time.

Social capital is the modern equivalent of honor, and the best news of all is that it's for everybody. You don't need money, connections, or privilege. All you need to do is to find a healthy community and support it.

Social capital is not rank or status

There is no conservation of social capital. Just because one person has more of it doesn't mean another has less. Just because somebody gains social capital doesn't mean someone else loses it. It's not a zero-sum game.

People play rank and status games all day long, but they seldom compete with each other to see who has the most social capital. Indeed, the people with the most social capital in a community often do not have a high place in the social hierarchy. It's because people who have social capital understand that the social capital of others is not a threat to their own. It's not necessary to determine who has "more". The only thing that matters is whether or not you have "enough" to get help if you need it.

How to get social capital

The only way to get social capital within a community is to have a history of presence in it and service to it. People must know and value you based on what you've done for them. They must also trust you because they have seen you treat other people well and because you've shown yourself to be reliable. Those whose judgement they trust must have a high opinion of you.

The desire human beings have to help people of higher social capital is not just an individual obligation. It's a combined social debt for which the entire community feels responsible. This is part of human altruism.

When you have a friend or a social group and spend time with them regularly, social capital gradually builds up between you so long as your interactions are positive. This is great, because every once in a while somebody makes a mistake and needs forgiveness or aid. If what you need does not tax the social capital your friend has for you, the occasional debits will be replenished over time.

Three ways to support others

There are three ways to support other people. You can reach down and help pull somebody else up to your level. You can let someone on the same level as you lean against you for support or comfort. Or, you can stand beneath somebody and boost him or her up to a higher level of achievement.

In a healthy community, all three of these activities produce social capital for the person who does them. Social capital is therefore a byproduct of service and of considerate behavior toward others.

Spending or losing social capital

The social capital you have is the result of thousands of tiny social transactions. Every time you benefit somebody, help somebody constructively, or are present when it counts, you gain social capital in the eyes of the person or people who benefit from having you around. Similarly, if you do things that are destructive or harmful, you lose social capital.

You can spend social capital by asking somebody for a favor or for help. This is different from losing the social capital, because you get something in exchange provided the request is reasonable. As long as you have enough social capital to cover the value of the favor you're asking of somebody, if that person has the resources and ability to help you, he or she will do it gladly, without feeling resentment. The lack of resentment is key, by the way. If you find yourself feeling resentment toward someone who is asking you for (yet another) favor, you are interacting with somebody who has exhausted the social capital he or she has with you. Either he or she has asked for a favor that is too big—as in, something you cannot afford to do or give—or that person has asked too much of you for too long.

If you ask for something that's too big and your friend has to turn down your request, it's important to understand that even though you didn't receive any benefit you have still dipped into the well and withdrawn some social capital. Nobody enjoys the experience of saying "no", and when altruistic people find themselves unable to help, they experience mild disappointment or even feelings of inadequacy. Those negative feelings, and the stress they might experience from trying to help you and then failing, is what withdraws from the social capital account.

Running out

It's sometimes hard to recognize when your social capital is exhausted or overdrawn. There's no Web site where you can check your balance, and you won't receive regular monthly statements. Your first sign that your social capital has run out is often that your relationship with the other person isn't as good as it used to be.

If someone who has helped you in the past is now avoiding your company, it means that something about being around you is creating a negative experience for that person. Chances are that you've been asking too much for too long, and your friend is not able to give you what you need.

The source of your friend's stress may not be obvious. It could be that his or her personal or emotional resources are less extensive that you believe. Or he or she may have committed those resources elsewhere: a person with a sick child or who has just had a major financial setback seldom has the time or money available to donate or volunteer. Your friend may in fact be in need of help. If you've got a give-and-take relationship with that person, this is your opportunity to hold up your end of the social contract. Be that impartial listener, or babysitter, or extra pair of hands.

The most likely reason why your social capital runs out is because at some point in the past you've been more of a burden and more of a one-way street than you realize. If your friend has had to either give up something important or take from somebody else in order to help you, you've been asking a lot. Social capital is finite, and it's possible to exhaust even the people who love you the most.

Social capital versus money

I have referred to social capital as an "invisible currency" because it behaves a little bit like money. For example, earlier in this chapter there are ways I discussed earning or spending it. A person can also lose social capital, lend it to others, or exchange it for other things. Indeed, one of the most popular fundraising activities for a charity is to ask volunteers to monetize a little bit of their personal social capital for the charity's benefit. Done in moderation, this is not harmful. Unfortunately, very few struggling charities know what moderation looks like.

A person, family, company, government, or other organization loses social capital when it engages in or condones activities that hurt or prey on the community they are supposed to serve. Although a person with a lot of social capital is often given the benefit of the doubt if they are charged with something truly depraved such as child molestation, the social capital disappears if the accusations turn out to be true.

People will seldom socialize with, share with, recommend, or hire a person who has lost his or her social capital. They may still maintain social and family ties, but they entertain the disgraced person individually, making sure to keep them out of sight of their victims, and they do not expect other people to share a table with them.

Your social capital can be lent to others. Suppose you ask a friend to hire your son or daughter for a summer job. Your kid may not be qualified and might not have an ounce of job experience, but if you have enough social capital, your friend will give your kid a chance simply as a favor for you. This is an example of lending social capital: your friend is giving your kid the benefit of the doubt because you have the social capital to justify the risk. If your kid turns out to be a good employee there is no permanent loss of social capital because your friend didn't lose anything.

Any time you ask somebody to help a third party as a favor for you, you are either lending your social capital or giving it away to the third party. Codependent people do this all the time. They use up their credibility and social capital by calling in for their spouses at work or asking angry relatives to forgive yet another slight from their bratty child "for my sake".

The comparison of social capital to money breaks down when we consider that money is quantifiable, fungible and mobile. Social capital is less so.

Money is quantifiable because it can be counted. Social capital cannot. Since you can't truly tell how much you can ask of your friends before they start to resent you (and often they have trouble telling this themselves) it's impossible to say, at any given moment, how much social capital you have. Also, social capital with a rich, generous friend will produce a bigger loan than social capital with a poor, struggling one, simply because what your social capital can bring you depends so much on what the other person is able to give.

Money is fungible. One dollar will serve the same purpose as any other. But there is nothing interchangeable about friends, relatives, or the respect and regard we have for one another. Human beings are not fungible (regardless of what management textbooks say), and therefore neither is social capital. The person who replaces an employee who leaves is not necessarily as trustworthy, friendly, or outgoing as the one who left, so social capital won't necessarily accumulate as readily.

You will always have some people to whom you're closest, and some people you love more than others. Human beings are almost always willing to give more, and share more, with their favorites. No matter how many people come into or out of your life, you really can't replace your mother, your father, or your first love. So, how much social capital you have with someone may depend on the type of relationship you have with them. Yet, as many unhappy families learn, it is possible for a person to behave egregiously enough as to exhaust the patience, tolerance, and love even of the closest relatives.

The last major way in which social capital differs from money is the extent to which money can be moved around from one community to another. A dollar earned in one community can be easily spent in another, but the same cannot be said of social capital. When a well-respected, well-liked, well-trusted person leaves one city and moves to another, he or she must prove himself or herself all over again to a brand new set of people.

Monetizing social capital

It's possible to convert social capital into money. Every time you ask somebody to give you something, without giving something of equal value in exchange, you're basically selling off a bit of the social capital you've built up over the years. When you hit up a friend for a loan or a gift, you're turning a bit of social capital into money.

A lot of charitable fundraising requires the charity to monetize social capital of some sort. Either it trades off of its own reputation, by running a mail or ad campaign or by asking its volunteers to perform labor, or it trades off the social capital of its volunteers, who monetize their own social capital by soliciting donations or selling overpriced items to people in their social network.

No matter how well known and well trusted an individual or institution is, social capital is not infinite. There eventually comes a point of diminishing returns, where an organization has solicited its donor base or volunteer pool too much and alienated it in the process.

If you want your non-profit to last more than a couple of years, you must learn to manage social capital by using your fundraising team, your volunteers, and your other resources in a sustainable way. It's far easier to sell social capital than it is to build it up, and often people don't realize that they've seriously overtaxed their volunteer or donor base until it's too late.

The well

The picture on the cover of this book is an old engineering diagram of an artesian well. I believe the well, and the aquifer that feeds it, are the most important symbols in this book. The ideas of the well and the aquifer can be applied in more than one way.

I think of a person's social capital reserves, with respect to each other person or group, as being like a well. A well draws its water from an aquifer that is replenished by rainfall, much like a person's reserves of social capital are replenished through ordinary positive human interaction. The amount of social capital you have with a person or a group can go up or down depending on whether you're taking more out of the relationship than you put in. The same can be said of a well. If you take a small amount of water out with a bucket or a pump, the level of the water won't change because the aquifer is big and healthy enough to easily replenish it.

The more water you take out of the well, the longer it takes for the aquifer to replenish it and get back into the condition it was in before you started dipping. If more than one well is drawing water in the community, it will stress the aquifer. The amount of money or social capital available for charitable work, within any community is finite in the same way the resources of an aquifer are finite.

Many small demands made on the well have the same effect as one large demand. Consider, for example, a time in your life when someone has consistently chiseled small amounts of money out of you: asking you to fill the parking meter or lend a couple dollars here and there, but never repaying what is owed. You eventually get just as frustrated as if that person borrowed a significant sum of money or a necessary item from you, but failed to return it. The friendship is noticeably damaged, and will not return to its former state until the debt is repaid.

Running the well dry

Compassion fatigue is when a person's well of caring runs dry. Too many people have asked too much for too long, and it's impossible to give anything more.

It's possible to run someon else's well dry by making requests that exhaust your loved one's resources or patience. It doesn't matter what you're asking for or why you're asking: when you run out of social capital with somebody, that person starts thinking of you as a drain on their resources. They begin to resent you for it, and they avoid you.

When the well runs dry, the friendship is ruptured. Your loved one will avoid you as much as possible, and that creates a problem because it deprives you of the chance to make contributions to the well again. A well, once run dry, may therefore stay dry for a long time. But as long as there's a little bit of positive social contact, and perhaps some reciprocation from you, the well will eventually start filling up again because the aquifer that feeds it is not completely exhausted.

When somebody sinks an extremely deep well and overtaxes an aquifer, the water table in the immediate area drops. This means that other wells in the area may go dry despite not being used excessively, simply because one person is milking the aquifer as much as possible. The human equivalent is easily visible in families with addiction or alcoholism: one individual makes such big and ongoing demands on others that there are no resources left if anybody else in the community needs help.

Running the well dry is a very serious threat to your social connection, because it damages the system of relationships that replenishes your social capital. But it is not automatically fatal to the relationship so long as a relationship or emotional bond still exists. Over time—and it may take years—if you make no demands and interact with the person you exhausted in a positive way, social capital will trickle in the way rainwater does into an aquifer. You may never have as much as you did before you ran the well dry, because you did permanent damage to the relationship, so you may never be able to ask this person for anything ever again. But you do have a relationship of sorts.

Exhausting the well, and the aquifer

The most serious problem you can have with social capital is when you make demands on a relationship that are so big, so ongoing, and so oppressive that you destroy the emotional bond the other person has with you. You not only run the well dry, but you exhaust the aquifer that feeds it. This is not simple social insolvency. It's outright bankruptcy. You no longer have a relationship with the person you've exhausted, and you damage your relationship with the whole community.

If you exhaust a friend, he or she does more than avoid you. This person will seldom think highly of you. Since people occasionally talk to one another, other people in your community will eventually find out how you treated someone they love and respect. When you exhaust the well with one person, understand that you've reduced the level in the whole aquifer. You can't just move on to the next person in the community and expect everyone to act as though nothing happened. This is one of the reason an acrimonious divorce or breakup does so much damage in a group of friends.

People who exhaust the well by deliberately stealing from someone or screwing a particular person over are sometimes surprised when they go to the next person thinking that they can take some more. Although they often take steps to make sure their first victim doesn't warn others, they often discover that there's just not as much available to take from the rest of the community. That's because they're confusing the well with the aquifer.

The well versus the aquifer

The well is a very good analogy for your social capital account with someone else. Although you may draw from the well with various requests, you are not the owner of the well: the other person is. Only he or she can see the water level or know for sure whether there's a lot to spare. Also, other people are drawing from their well. It's a shared resource, but you can't necessarily see how much other people are taking or receiving, or whether they are also giving back. If one person takes too much from you, you will necessarily have less available to give others until your resources recover from a big depletion.

The aquifer is a good way to think about your social capital in the community at large. Whereas the well represents your social capital account with one person, the aquifer represents how the community as a whole feels about you. Take too much from too many people, or take an exorbitant or abusive amount from one, and the entire water table drops. A community that has one person taking far too much has little or nothing left for anyone else.

Just as your actions contribute to how full the aquifer is, so do the actions of others. The topology of the aquifer varies as people enter and leave the community. When someone leaves permanently, the community can no longer make social capital transactions with him or her. This is great news if the person who leaves was a heavy user of other people's resources. But if the person who leaves was a net contributor, there is less charitable work being done in the community, and people of great social capital take their reputations along with their material resources with them when they leave.

Institutional social capital

Groups of people, or organizations, can have social capital just the same way as people do. When people talk about a brand they trust, or a charity they respect, they're making social capital statements.

Unsolicited donations are the ultimate acknowledgment of social capital. When someone whips out a wallet and gives money, he or she is expressing respect for your group's program mission and confidence in your group's administrative competence and integrity.

An organization receives or loses institutional social capital at the points where it is directly in contact with the public. The people who put on the program and provide services, the people who raise money from the general public, and the administrators who sign contracts on the company's behalf, and make decisions visible by people who have no direct connection to the organization, are its public face. Employees of a charity that work entirely behind the scenes doing data entry or running the accounting department do not affect the organization's social capital one way or another unless they do something that draws public attention, such as embezzling the payroll or winning the lottery and giving the proceeds to the charity that employs them.

Social capital and charitable work

Charities run on social capital. Donations, volunteer labor, and everything else a charity needs to run comes from a pool of donors and volunteers. If a non-profit loses some aspect of its social capital, such as by being involved in a scandal that destroys its reputation, donations dry up pretty quickly. Similarly, if a non-profit doesn't regularly prove its worth by regularly being seen improving the world and accomplishing its mission, people forget it exists, and they don't write checks anymore.

When raising money, a charitable venture can monetize either its own social capital or the social capital of part of its volunteer base. Both resources are renewable but finite. If pressed beyond their natural limits, they will lose their ability to regenerate. If you continue to demand or gouge more time, money, or resources out of people they will eventually take whatever action is necessary to save themselves. Maybe they'll stop opening your direct-mail pleadings, or maybe they'll just stop answering the phone when you call.

Burnout and institutional social capital

Burnout is what happens when you've been giving so much for so long that you have nothing left. It can occur at work, or in an overtaxing family relationship. It can also occur through your involvement in church or charitable ventures. When you're burned out, not only are you not useful to others, but you start to have trouble caring for yourself. You're starting to see other people, or your charitable venture, as nothing more than a bunch of demands being made on you.

Human beings can only function at peak potential for a short period of time. The rest of the time, we have to rest. If we don't, we get burned out and have to recover.

A burned out person's emotional and psychological reserves are depleted to the point where he or she is in distress. For your own sake and for that of your organization, such a person needs to be taken off of fundraising or high stress duties for a while and given light duty until he or she is in a state of balance again. Nourish them socially and care for them emotionally, demanding very little of them until they recover. This means you should involve a burned out person in fun activities to the extent they are able to participate, but require no significant work. Treat them like a person receiving chemotherapy or some other debilitating but hopefully temporary setback: show them the honor they deserve as a worthy and valued member of the community, and give them the space they need to heal.

Requires a healthy community

There is such a thing as a family or community so toxic that people who work to support it are treated with contempt instead of respect. In an alcoholic family or a codependent workplace, the people who accomplish the most and who are the pillars of support for the entire organization are treated as oppressors or control freaks.

Maxim #4: When more than a third of the people are burned out for any reason, the group itself is toxic.

If for some reason you are in an organization where hard work isn't acknowledged or rewarded, or where people are routinely pressured to sacrifice family ties or their own health in order to contribute to the organization, this isn't a group in which it's possible to earn social capital.

Toxicity can build up in a community like poison can build up in the bloodstream: slowly enough to be hard to detect at the time. But if you're feeling badly burned out or stressed, and everyone around you seems to feel the same way, the problem is not you. You're in a bad situation.

It doesn't matter where the toxicity came from. If it's wrecked more than a third of the people in the community, then it's reached critical mass. You can't singlehandedly fix the problem.

Leave this community if you value your health. Do this no matter what it costs you. If you do this, you *can* get your emotional health back.

Threats to institutional social capital

When your non-profit loses enough social capital, you will not be able to attract enough donors or volunteers to keep the program going. There are many ways in which charities have wasted or exhausted their social capital. They can all be summarized as "killing the goose that lays the golden egg".

Failure to respect donor privacy

Selling your donor list and contact information is one of the worst things you can do. The second worst is to not respect a donor's request to be left off of the mailing or E-mail list.

Nobody likes to be solicited by strangers, especially in the privacy of their own home. Although you might be able to make a quick buck by selling or sharing your donor list with similar charities, it's an act of extreme hostility toward your donors.

Aggressive fundraising

Pressuring people to give by physically grabbing them, approaching them in public, and trying to bypass answering machines or systems they set up to protect themselves is not OK.

The federal Do Not Call list exists for a reason. Unlisted phone numbers and spam filters exist for a reason. People do not like being dunned or harassed. If somebody asks to not be put on a mailing or E-mail list, or if someone does not explicitly opt into solicitation E-mails, leave them off.

Anti-spam and privacy regulations restrict what you can do with electronic and snail-mail contact information. It's presently legal to buy and sell contact lists, but savvy donors have ways of figuring out who sold them out and inflicting punishment. This is an area of law that changes rapidly, and it's reasonable to expect further restrictions on the use of your donors' contact information for fundraising activities.

Although the law allows you to solicit people who have done business with you in the recent past, that doesn't apply when they explicitly ask you to not call or ask for more, more, more. When they ask to be removed from a call or E-mail list, remove them.

Respect "no soliciting" signs on doors and apartment complexes. People already get an avalanche of advertisements, pitches, and touting every time they step into a public place. They can't even buy groceries without enduring a pitch to donate "the extra" to some charity or another. Workplaces often have charitable campaigns and people frequently bring sign-up sheets into the office. Home is the only refuge from the feeding frenzy. If for some reason you or your volunteers are going door to door in your neighborhood canvassing for an election or soliciting donations, please respect people's desire to be left alone.

People prefer to give when they are able. From the outside looking in, you have no way to tell who just had to pay a large property tax or medical bill, or who is short of cash. If you pressure them, you might get an occasional five to twenty dollars out of people whose backs are against the wall, but you're not going to get thousand-dollar donations from individual philanthropists. Even very wealthy people sometimes have short-term cash flow problems. Nobody likes to be hit up when they are unable to give. So creating artificial time limits related to donations is an extremely bad idea.

Scandal

Every time someone gets caught with his or her hand in the cookie jar, it reflects badly on the people who employed him or her. When a religious leader gets caught molesting children, or when financially predatory behavior gets covered up or enabled, the entire organization loses credibility and social capital.

Failure to screen

Conducting background checks of employees and volunteers is important if those individuals will be handling money or interacting with the public. It is important to screen out people whose past conduct makes them a legal or financial risk. Regardless of your ideology, you cannot afford to put the interests of any individual before the interests of your charity or the community it serves.

If you believe that it's important to provide felons with a means to earn an honest living, you can accomplish that goal without employing a convicted child molester in a day care. While you have the Constitutional right to expose yourself to as much risk as you see fit, you do not have the right to impose that risk on others who do not consent to it.

Most people consider it morally repugnant to knowingly provide a known predator with a new opportunity to offend. Depending on your ideology, you might not feel the same sense of disgust. But your donors will.

Becoming a life support system for insiders

If the majority of the money that comes in gets paid back out to an Executive Director, or spent on tasks that do not tie directly to your program, your charity is no longer focused on the program. It now exists solely to keep someone employed.

People won't work for free so that someone else can be employed. Nor will they donate: they work hard for what they earn, and they resent it when they are donating the results of their labor simply to pay someone else to work toward the same goal.

No perception of need

Get caught wasting money, and people will quickly decide you don't need theirs.

Hypocrisy

People hate hypocrites. They may forgive you for having an employee who steals (if you fire him or her), but they won't forgive you if the offense has something to do with your program. If the president of a medical charity is charged with animal neglect it's unfortunate but survivable. If the abuse happens at an animal shelter, it's a public relations disaster.

Clique behavior in the program

One of the worst things you can do to people who are in need is to set up the perception that other people with similar problems are somehow beneath them. Anybody who is on the receiving end of blame, shame, or denial of medical treatment due to the specific type of cancer they have will remember that bad experience for the rest of their lives. They, and their families, will then become your enemies.

One example of clique behavior is the hierarchical way cancer patients are treated. Breast cancer, and women's breast cancer in particular, has been elevated above all other form of cancer not just in terms of publicity but in terms of how patients are treated by doctors, nurses, and medical practitioners in the cancer community. A person suffering from lung cancer is frequently shamed or criticized for having caused the cancer, even if he or she has never smoked. Women suffering from cervical cancer are shamed for having unclean sexual practices despite the fact that not all cases of cervical cancer are related to viral infection. People with bone, facial, or other cancers often cannot get treatment or support because all available resources are focused on the breast cancer patients. Not only do they get snark from some of the breast cancer patients who have been taught to believe that their cancer is more serious and horrible than anyone else's, but they get flak from the medical staff too. Soft-science and alternative medicine providers get in on the act too, and sometimes accuse patients of having deliberately caused their cancer.

The fact that science has been able to find some links between environmental triggers and cancer doesn't change the fact that we live in an inherently unjust, random world where even a small child can develop cancer. Not all lung cancer victims have ever smoked, and only a committed magical thinker would believe that it's possible to actually avoid disease simply by making all the "good" and healthy choices.

Woe betide anybody who dares to show up at a cancer support walk having beaten something besides breast cancer. Other forms of cancer just aren't cancer-y enough to be included despite the fact that the chemotherapy is just as vicious. But saturating the available market by "pink-washing" all sorts of products in order to get one to two percent of the sales revenue may actually be contributing to declines in other kinds of cancer awareness. Also, by over-identifying breast cancer as a female problem, the breast cancer community has succeeded in stigmatizing the male breast cancer patients who make up perhaps a tenth of the patients.

If you run a charity that serves people, please remember that they are human beings who are fully aware of status and stigma. Make sure you don't elevate one clique above another.

Symptoms of social capital exhaustion

You can tell whether you, or the organization you represent, are running out of social capital based on other people's change in behavior toward you. Any of these behaviors represent a dangerous drop in your social capital.

- You have had more than two social capital based fundraisers (see the fundraising chapters for details) in the past year, and they have involved the same people
- The last three social capital based fundraisers have brought in progressively less money
- Volunteers are quitting or refusing to return phone calls
- People who used to do fundraising are now refusing or no-showing in significant numbers
- More than one person on the Board is not returning phone calls
- You have had to fire, lecture, or reprimand at least one Board member or volunteer for criticizing your deficit spending
- Your organization has a negative net worth
- You've had to make a personal donation to cover payroll or routine operating expenses
- Board members are resigning
- You've been in the newspaper for something very bad
- In response to another solicitation, a major donor has told you to go do something biologically impossible
- Somebody is suing you
- More than one member of your Board or management team is experiencing insomnia or marital trouble because of the non-profit

Social capital is a resource that can be renewed if a group of basically healthy and functional people interact normally with each other in a way that promotes trust. But if the group becomes unhealthy, to the point where interactions decrease trust instead of promoting it or increase stress instead of building ties, then people in the dysfunctional group are gradually chewed up and worn out just by being there.

Maxim #5: Social capital is a finite resource.

How to (re)build social capital

Like money, social capital is far easier to spend, waste, or throw away than it is to accumulate. It's possible to rebuild your social capital, but it will not be an overnight process. It takes decisive action and discipline. Here are a series of steps you can use to rebuild social capial if you need to do so.

Step 1: Issue a major public apology to all you have wronged, and apologize personally and in private also.

Step 2: Stop the activities that burned through your social capital in the first place. If the social capital loss was due to illegal or unethical behavior by an employee, fire him or her. If you're borrowing money to cover operating expenses, stop all non-contractual spending. *This may require temporarily shutting down program operations.*

Step 3: Meet any contractual commitments that you have, but cancel all other spending and resource-intensive activities. You will have to reduce or even eliminate some of your program activities. This may require you to cut expenses by laying off some or even all of your employees.

Step 4: Cancel the next fundraiser that can feasibly be canceled. This sends a very strong message to your volunteers that they are valuable and worth caring for. It will allow them to rest and to step away from constant fundraising activities. It will also show them that they, and their time, are valuable and important.

Step 5: If you have unsecured debt in excess of 100% of your sustainable annual income from fundraising, either begin bankruptcy proceedings or dissolve the charity. Otherwise proceed to the next step.

Step 6: Sell off any assets that you can. Nothing is exempt from the axe. If this means you lose your church building or capital equipment, so be it.

Step 7: Write up a new budget and spending plan in which your program is scaled to less than 90% of your sustainable annual income from fundraising. This 90% must include service on your debt. This is the size of charity you can afford to run. It includes ten percent margin for error and for savings that can become your cash reserves.

Step 8: Present the new budget to your Board. If they accept it, restructure with the smaller program and prove your worth to the community all over again. Otherwise, dissolve.

If you follow these steps, you will be in a position to start building again. Begin small, as though you were a brand-new charity, working within the limits you've got. As you expand, gradually begin to re-hire key people if they are available. But make sure you never use a volunteer with the exact same job title and description as a former of current employee.

Chapter 5: Assets and Liabilities

This chapter deals with money and things that can be exchanged for it. It deals with what your organization owns, and also what it owes.

By the end of this chapter, you will be able to distinguish between different kinds of assets and liabilities. You will be able to construct a balance sheet for your not-for-profit business. You will also be able to ask intelligent questions about a charitable venture you're being asked to help run.

Assets

Everywhere in the financial world, an *asset* is defined as something that is either money, or a thing that could potentially be exchanged for money.

Money is an asset regardless of whether it's in cash, an uncashed check, or a bank account.

Anything that is denominated in US dollars, or the currency of any other nation, is an asset. Stocks, bonds, commodity futures, and other securities are assets.

Commodities and material goods are assets. Jewelry, office supplies, and gravel are assets. So is clothing or food that is legal for sale.

Intellectual property in the form of patents or copyrights are assets. The goodwill of a business (otherwise known as its institutional social capital) is an asset, but it is not quantifiable or tangible unless it is monetized.

Land, real estate, vehicles, and anything where ownership is determined by title or registration is an asset. Back when it was legal for human beings to be owned, bought, or sold by others, slaves were considered an asset, however since slavery is illegal everywhere human beings are no longer assets in a financial sense.

Regardless of what you might have heard from somebody's "rich dad", an asset is NOT defined as "something that makes you money". It's true that some assets (such as dividend producing stocks) make you money, but the real definition of an asset is something that has monetary value. If you could legally sell an item at a stock exchange or flea market, it's an asset.

There are plenty of assets that cost you money. A 30-year-old car that doesn't run but that you're paying to insure is still technically an asset. A heavily mortgaged building is also an asset, even though you're making payments on it once a month. Although the building is an asset, the mortgage against it is a liability.

Limits to the definition of "asset"

You don't get to count things as "assets" in a financial sense unless they can potentially be sold.

If it's illegal to sell a thing, it cannot be listed as an asset. There are laws against selling makeup or food that has been opened, food that has spoiled or that is incorrectly labeled, or secondhand mattresses. Things like these cannot be listed on your balance sheet.

A bald eagle feather, a kilogram of cocaine, or a human kidney might have a dollar value to some unscrupulous buyer, but they cannot be listed as assets.

Things that are not *transferable* cannot be sold to anybody else, and they therefore cannot be considered an asset. The software license for your organization's computer, for example, or the Web hosting service you pay for, can't be sold to anybody else if you decide for some reason you no longer want the product or service. So your computer is an asset, but the licensed software on it is not.

If you've got something for which you cannot find a buyer at any price, what you have is not an asset but garbage. Your grandchild's finger painting might have a lot of sentimental value to you, but nobody's going to pay money for it unless your kid grew up to be Frieda Kahlo, Frank Lloyd Wright, or a serial killer.

Income producing assets

The kind of asset everybody likes best is the sort that makes the owner money. This is the sort of asset every charity needs.

Securities and similar passive investments

Stocks, bonds, and other income producing securities provide the easiest way to accumulate wealth or income. Even an interest bearing savings account yields a few dollars per year that you didn't have to work for.

Mature charities almost always have investments of some kind. They serve three purposes. First, they produce a small amount of income for the charity through interest or some other return on the investment. Second, they act as cash reserves. Should the charity have a sudden need for money due to an emergency, they can dip into cash reserves for the money to deal with the problem, instead of having to borrow. This allows far more flexibility, because borrowed money has to be repaid and creates an ongoing monthly burden on the charity's cash flow. Unlike a loan, which has fixed monthly payments that are mandatory, cash reserves can be replenished at whatever pace makes sense. Finally, money that has been set aside is available to take advantage of opportunities and good deals.

An extremely healthy, mature small or medium-sized charity maintains investments, including cash reserves, of six months to one year's worth of operating expenses. Larger charities with annual budgets of several million dollars often get by with less, because their income is steadier and more predictable.

Endowment funds

Many charitable foundations are started with a large donation made by one or more wealthy people. This donated money, known as an endowment fund, is invested in stocks, index funds, or some other income producing financial vehicle so that it yields a return every year. The money returned by the investment is enough to pay not only the administrative costs of running the charity, but the majority of the program expenses.

The Bill and Melinda Gates Foundation is an example of a charity based on an endowment fund. It was started with money donated by a couple who, at the time, were the wealthiest people in the world. As a result of their sizable donation, they are no longer at the top of the list due to having given so much to their foundation.

Endowment fund charities seldom or never need to do fundraising, although all of them are required to have a designated agent who is capable of responding to communication and cashing a check should someone send in an unsolicited donation. Such charities generally pay for the services of an investment advisor or manager to look after the endowment fund so that, over the years, enough of the interest or profit is added back to the invested *principal* to compensate for inflation. This is seldom a full-time task except for accounts worth hundreds of millions.

Endowment fund charities always have someone to administer the program. The largest ones hire somebody for the purpose, but for most family trusts or memorial endowments the work can be done on a volunteer basis. The program always involves giving away money, either to individuals or to other charities. So, the administrator(s) might select scholarship or bursary recipients, review applications for grants for film documentary projects, or identify other charities in need of one-time or ongoing grant donations.

Properly run, an endowment fund based charity can operate indefinitely because the administrators never spend the principal. Each year, they spend only part of the interest generated by the return on the invested money. Only after administration fees are paid and enough interest to compensate for inflation is added back into the principal are any dollars available to conduct the program.

For example, suppose your million-dollar endowment fund requires a quarter of a percent in management fees, and the rate of inflation is half of one percent per year. In a very good year, your investments might yield a ten percent return, or $100,000. Subtract half a percent for inflation ($5,000) and a quarter of a percent for management fees ($2,500) and you still have $92,500 to play with. Not bad!

Now suppose it's not such a good year, and your investments generated only a one percent return ($10,000), with the same rates of inflation and the same management fees. You now have only $2,500 for your program expenses. Can you scale your operations to fit within that budget? Well... sometimes. If you keep your expenses low and don't whip up too much public expectation of an ongoing source of grant or scholarship money, you can get away with it.

This of course is a very simplified example of how to manage an endowment fund. Appropriate investment strategies vary depending on how much money is available and what kind of other assets, such as patent royalties or real estate, are included. The largest endowment funds often have more than one kind of asset. Similarly, not all the gains from unusually good years are spent right away. Most are reinvested into the index fund or into other investments. Administrators often limit themselves to only about 4% of the total invested principal no matter how successful the market has been. This is frequently called "the 4% rule", which is used often by individual people who achieve financial independence and live off their invested assets. The 4% rule works just as well for a not-for-profit corporation especially when the dividends and capital gains are tax exempt.

Bequests

A *bequest* is a one-time donation of assets, generally made as part of a deceased person's will or trust. A bequest may be in the form of money, stock, or items such as paintings or art.

Conditions may be attached to a bequest. For example, people who leave their art collections to museums frequently stipulate that no part of it is to be sold or given away. Some donors require that their collections be displayed as a group, or separately from other items. Should the charity close or else not be able to meet the terms of the agreement, the items must be returned to the deceased person's estate, representative, or next of kin.

Intellectual property

Intellectual property produces *royalties*, which are fees for the use of the intellectual property, payable to the person or company who owns the rights to it.

Authors receive royalties from the books they publish. Songwriters and composers receive royalties when their music is used in a film or performed in public. However, authors can sell the rights to their work to others. Because of the current international copyright law, the rights to the work persist for many years after the creator's death. It's not unusual for an author's next of kin to continue to receive not only royalties for what their deceased relative wrote, but for entirely new books based on his or her characters and ghost written by another author who works only for hire. When the rights to a piece of literature or music have been sold, the new owner is the one who collects the royalties.

Inventors receive royalties when they patent an invention and license the use of their patented idea to someone who makes use of it. Patents expire earlier than copyrights, usually within 20 years after the patent is registered. Also, unlike copyrights, patents filed in one country are not often automatically honored in another. When patent or copyrights expire, the intellectual property goes into public domain and can be used by anyone. But until that happens the rights to the intellectual property can be good income producing assets.

Obviously, intellectual property doesn't license itself. People who create it frequently hire an agent who, in exchange for a portion of the royalties, markets the intellectual property to prospective licensees. If you have by chance inherited intellectual property in a bequest, you perhaps are already represented by such an agent.

Income producing real estate

Residential real estate can be leased to people who need a place to live, and commercial real estate can be leased to business occupants who require retail or light industrial space. Empty land can frequently be leased to oil or mineral companies (if you don't mind a bit of damage). Or, if you're more ecologically minded, you may be able to lease land to a small organic farmer. Ranchers particularly value grasslands with surface water readily available.

All real estate requires management. It takes effort to find a tenant if you don't have one. It takes money and effort to maintain buildings, or to repair fences on open land. It even takes effort to get rid of a tenant who's damaging your property. Residential tenants are by far the most high-maintenance. So, if you do not wish to be bothered with the daily hassle, you will most likely need to hire a property manager of some kind. Depending on the kind of property your organization owns, if you are renting it out for income you may have to pay property tax even if you are tax exempt.

Loans made to others

Many businesses lend money to other businesses, or to people. It's an extremely bad idea to lend money to any of your officers or business insiders, because it creates a big conflict of interest and is a reportable activity. It can also violate the self dealing laws of your state or the self dealing prohibitions in your Articles of Incorporation that are necessary to secure tax exempt status. But if you're a credit union, it's normal for you to offer mortgages and car loans to other people. In fact, it's one of the reasons why you're in business.

If your organization lends money to somebody else and receives interest, the loan is an asset. The interest on that loan is the income produced by that asset.

If you have provided goods and services to somebody but have not yet been paid, you have effectively made a loan to that person. Depending on whether you use the accrual method or the cash method of accounting, things delivered but not paid for may show up differently.

Certain insurance policies

When a person with life insurance dies, the company that sold the insurance policy must make payments to the deceased person's beneficiaries. It's possible to name a charity as a beneficiary of a life insurance policy.

There have been cases in which a charity, named as a beneficiary of somebody's life insurance, has been able to borrow against that insurance. I do not recommend this strategy. It's in astoundingly poor taste and it can't be done without the owner of the policy noticing. Besides, the insured person can always change the beneficiary on the insurance policy, or cancel the policy. Sometimes, they simply stop paying the premiums. If you are borrowing against the policy and it suddenly stops existing, generally the lender will "call" the loan or force you to refinance it.

Depreciating assets

Although some assets like bonds or patents can make you money, not all assets do. Some *depreciate* or go down in value over time. A vehicle, for example, is worth a little bit less every year. So is a building, because over time they do eventually wear out. But a patent that suddenly expires is worth nothing. All of a sudden, its value goes to zero.

Fluctuation in value (which is what happens when the stock market or the real estate market goes up and down and people's opinion of the value of an asset changes) is not the same as depreciation.

White elephants and sacred cows

The phrases "white elephant" and "sacred cow" became part of the English language when British travelers to Siam (present-day Thailand) and India noticed some local customs that gave them a better insight into universal human nature.

Throughout southeastern Asia, kings kept white elephants as a form of conspicuous consumption. Since the animals were very expensive to maintain and not usable for labor, the cost of maintaining one would ruin all but the most wealthy people. Although having one as a status symbol was awesome, it often wasn't worth the expense. So, every time a courtier would become obnoxious, the king would give him a white elephant as a passive-aggressive sign of "royal favor". So a figurative "white elephant" is an asset that not only requires money to maintain, but is so expensive that it takes necessary resources away from the rest of the organization. The value it adds to your venture doesn't justify the expense of maintaining it, and it's hard to get rid of.

In parts of India, cows were (and still are) sacred to Durga, the Hindu goddess of wisdom. They were not slaughtered for food, and were allowed to roam wherever they liked, even into stores and public buildings. The nuisance and property damage they caused was considered an acceptable tradeoff for having them around. Even if they were destructive, nobody would consider getting rid of one. In business, a figurative "sacred cow" is something that is considered exempt from sale, budget cuts, or even criticism. It is not necessarily a money-consuming asset, nor is it necessarily productive or vital to your charitable program.

In the not-for-profit context, it's easy for organizational sacred cows to develop. It happens when people get so fixated on a mechanism that they're using to accomplish a program objective that they decide the mechanism is the program. It happens when a very senior or well respected member of the group has a pet project, or when a conflict of interest causes an important insider to rely on the not-for-profit corporation for personal income.

If your organization is devoting disproportionately large amounts of money to an activity that's not mentioned in the program statement, that's a sacred cow. If you're paying more than market rate for goods or services, the company or individual from whom you are buying them is a sacred cow. If you're being pressured to categorize an expense as being "program" when in reality it is being used toward fundraising or administration, that's a sacred cow.

Small charities often fail because they turn into life support systems for sacred cows and white elephants. When times are tough, you have to be willing to do more than just kill these expensive mammals. You have to barbecue the critters and sell the burgers for operating capital.

Value of an asset

The value of a bank account is very easy to calculate. Simply look at the account balance, subtract any checks that have been written against that account but not cashed, and the result is the value of that asset. But other assets change in value over time.

Calculating the value of a depreciating asset

A depreciating asset generally follows a predictable pattern. *Straight-line* depreciation assumes a product loses all of its value over a period of time, such as a specific number of years from the date of its acquisition. You simply divide the amount you paid by the number of years over which it depreciates, and that's the amount of value it loses per year.

Non-linear depreciation is a situation in which an asset loses more of its value in the first years you own it, and less value later on. A new car is a perfect example of this kind of depreciation. Some new cars have been known to lose as much as a third of their value the year after they are sold. But after that, the depreciation tapers off. Generally, objects that depreciate this way follow some kind of industry standard. For cars, the Kelly Blue Book is considered as being the go-to authority for the reasonable asking price for a used vehicle based on its condition, mileage, and age.

Appreciating assets

Bonds are an excellent example of an asset that is expected to increase in value over time. When a government or company issues a bond, the rate of interest is fixed. This yield rate is permanent and does not change once the bond has been issued unless for some reason the issuer agrees to adjust it for inflation.

Bonds mature after a specific number of years after issue. Once a bond matures it generally stops accruing interest or increasing in value.

Some bonds are sold at a discount from their *face* value, which is their value at maturity. Others are sold at an initial price, to which the interest is added at maturity.

If for some reason a bond needs to be sold before it matures, it's usually not sold back to the issuer but to someone else who wants a partially matured bond. The selling price will be at or above the initial sale price, but below the price at maturity. How close the price is to the mature value of the bond depends on how much time remains before the bond is mature.

Book versus market value

Stocks, bonds, and many other things that go up and down in price only really have a value when they're sold. If you bought a piece of land twenty years ago for $100,000 then the *book value* is $100,000. Today, similar plots of land in the same area might be selling for $150,000 but you don't earn a profit until you sell. The price you get depends on what the buyer thinks your land or building is worth. This decision will be based on at least some conditions you don't control, such as whether oil has been found close by, whether someone built a meth lab in the basement of a house they were leasing from you, or whether your industrial park is now downwind from a new chemical plant.

If you buy a stock today for $10, and the value goes down so that the stock is only worth $8, you don't get to count the loss until you sell that stock. But, if you look at the going rate for the stock on a real-time stock market Web page, you can see the *market value* of your investment, which is what it would be worth if you sold it today.

Liquidity

Liquidity is the ease with which an asset can be converted into cash. Money in a bank account is the most liquid possible asset. It's available pretty much on demand. You can write a check. You can transfer money electronically. You can even walk into a bank, withdraw a hundred thousand dollars in cash, and walk back out again, but I don't recommend it. First, it's physically dangerous to walk around with that amount of money because the world is full of gun-toting idiots who will kill for far less. Second, the bank has to report cash transactions above about $10,000 or so because they have a high probability of being related to some kind of organized crime. Third, cash is a pain in the neck to count and verify. If you're simply strolling down to the local Lamborghini dealership to do some cash shopping, everyone would prefer that you pay with a cashier's check or a wire transfer, simply to avoid making some poor schmuck check all of those bills to make sure they're not counterfeit. Some of them probably are, no matter how carefully your bank checked them. Finally, banks don't keep a ridiculous amount of cash on hand. If you need large amounts of cash, they prefer to have at least a day or two of advance notice.

Money market accounts are less liquid than checking or savings accounts, because the money isn't available in cash. It is transferred into your checking account, so as to be available the next day or possibly even later.

Stock accounts are less liquid than money market accounts. Stocks can be sold immediately at the going rate, but if you want to sell at a particular price you have to wait until someone puts in a buy order at that price. Either way, once you sell a stock the money is available one to three business days later depending on how your brokerage works.

Bonds are less liquid than stocks because it's often difficult or impossible to sell a bond before it matures. Commodities are more difficult still, especially if you have the actual product on hand and not just a certificate stating that you own a thousand gallons of airplane fuel. If you've got ten thousand pounds of pig iron sitting around, the only way you can sell it is if you can find someone who wants to buy pig iron, and who can work out how to transport it. A system exists by which you can sell your iron, but it's still going to take time for the buyer to pay you and come pick it up.

There are other kinds of securities such as futures, options, and more sophisticated investment vehicles. These are suitable for institutional investors or extremely wealthy and sophisticated individuals. Although the rate of return is higher than it would be on, say, an ordinary stock or a bank savings account, the risk is much higher and often cannot be accurately assessed by a less sophisticated investor. There's a good chance that the investment will collapse, and that investors will lose everything.

In the past, unscrupulous dealers sold high-risk investments to people who didn't understand the risk and who weren't able to withstand the loss. The trouble it caused was bad enough for the federal government to pass laws regulating investment sales. It's now illegal to offer high-risk investments to buyers who aren't wealthy enough to tolerate the loss of the investment, who aren't used to managing high risk investments, or who aren't financially sophisticated enough to understand the risk. So, whereas any average person can open up a discount brokerage account and buy stocks, the *qualified* buyers capable of taking a high risk security off your hands are harder to come by. High risk securities are therefore less liquid than stocks, bonds, or commodities.

Real estate is far less liquid than stocks, bonds, or any other security: it requires not just a buyer, but a series of inspections and frequently a long process of negotiation and financing before the deal can close. Also, if you're selling a piece of real estate such as a building, you have to sell the whole thing, and that's a major purchase. Not all prospective buyers are qualified to buy: they may lack the money, or the ability to get a loan. Before you succeed in selling an unwanted house or apartment building, you might have to go through offers from two or three unqualified buyers.

The least liquid assets of all are unique items such as art, jewelry, coin collections, or intellectual property. All of these require experts to appraise their value, find a buyer (such as an auction house), ship the product to the buyer, or in the case of collections find multiple buyers. These things take time. Just because you've inherited a painting and want to put it up for auction at Sotheby's doesn't mean it's going to happen right away. First it has to be seen by an expert who verifies that the painting is what you say it is. They check the *provenance* or the history of the painting. Then, if Sotheby's accepts the painting and it's in line with what the auction house usually sells, it has to be advertised to potential buyers. Nobody cruises by the major auction houses for fun. People generally only go if there's a product that interests them. Auction houses generally group related items together for sale because they appeal to the same prospective buyers. So it could take weeks or months before your auction house puts your item on display.

Liabilities

A negative asset, or money you owe to somebody else, is a *liability*. Another definition for liability, in the financial sense, is the legal obligation to repay money that has been borrowed.

Every time you buy something on credit, you accrue a liability as well as gaining an asset.

Although a car is an asset, if there's a loan against it the entire amount of the loan is a liability.

If you borrow money to buy a building, the mortgage is the loan a bank gives you. This mortgage is also a liability.

Secured versus unsecured debt

A *secured* loan is one that is guaranteed or backed by some kind of asset. Generally this is the asset that was purchased using the loaned money. A car loan is secured by the title to the car. A mortgage is secured by the title to the real estate.

If for some reason you stop making payments on a secured loan, the organization that gave you the loan reserves the right to *foreclose* on the loan or *call* the loan, indicating that it is due in full immediately. If you do not pay, the lender may then *repossess* the asset by taking it back.

There's a specific legal process that the lender must go through in order to repossess your asset and liquidate it by selling it to someone else to get their money back. If you've nearly paid the asset off and the lender makes more on the sale than you owe, then after they've deducted all their expenses they have to pay you back whatever is left over. There's generally not much.

Obviously, not everything bought with credit can be taken back. If you borrow money to cover operating expenses, for example, the person or company that lent it to you can't repossess the utilities you paid with it. A loan or liability that is not backed by any specific asset is called unsecured. For example, credit card balances, student loans, and medical loans are all unsecured debt.

Legal judgments or settlements

Debt is the most common kind of liability, but there's a special kind of debt if a person or company has lost a court case or settled out of court. If there's an unpaid judgment against the company, it owes money to somebody because of a court's decision or because of a legal agreement made with some plaintiff's lawyer.

A legal judgment might consist of a large lump sum payment, or of several smaller payments spread over a long period of time. Settlements for an injury lawsuit might require months or even years of payment. The judgement is an ongoing debt that must be paid. Even if you close down your not-for-profit company and liquidate all the assets, payments of judgements and debts comes first.

Leases, licenses, and royalties

If you've signed a lease for a vehicle or an office, or if you've licensed intellectual property and are making royalty payments, the entire amount of your outstanding lease is a liability. The same goes for the value of the licensing or royalty agreement. If you've agreed to pay a million dollars a year for the next five years in exchange for the naming rights at the local ball park, that naming agreement created a five million dollar liability.

At some point, somebody with the authority to commit your company made an agreement to pay in the future. That agreement is what creates your liability. You can't necessarily walk away from that agreement just because you've had a change in management.

Term contracts

If you've signed a year-long gym contract or a two-year cellular phone contract, the total value of the contract is a liability. It's money you're on the hook to pay out. Even if you're not actively using a building, or a cellular phone line, or some other thing that you've paid for, you generally have a legal duty to keep on paying. Furthermore, in many states service contracts "auto-renew" unless you go through a complicated multi-step process to avoid renewing. This is how many shady alarm companies, gyms, and service providers stay in business.

Liens

A *lien* is a special kind of responsibility that encumbers the title to an asset but is not secured by the title to that asset. The lienholder can't take the asset and sell it to pay off what the asset owner owe, but the owner also can't sell the asset until the debt is paid and the lien is taken off.

A mechanic's lien, for example, can be placed against a building by a person who performed repairs on it. If you own an office condominium and have not paid your dues to the owners' association, the owners' association may place a lien on your property. If you owe city property taxes, municipal governments routinely place liens on property so that the taxes can be recovered before a property is sold. Depending on where your property is located, unpaid water and utility bills can also result in liens against the property.

Liens themselves are not debt, but they indicate the presence of a debt against the asset. If you own real estate and there's a lien against it, the debt represented by the lien is a liability. However, if you are a homeowner's association and have placed a lien on one of the homes in your condo complex for failure to pay dues, the debt represented by the lien is a kind of asset because it represents money owed to you. But it's not a very liquid asset. You aren't guaranteed the money until the unit sells.

One of the reasons people hire title companies (or lawyers) when buying real estate is to make sure that the title to the real estate is clear, to ensure there are no liens against it, and to force the seller to deal with liens if they exist. Title insurance, which is available in some states but not others, is another way to protect against liens or other title defects.

Being a not-for-profit corporation will not protect your group against a lien due to an unpaid bill. You are just as accountable as you would be if you failed to pay the bill as a for-profit company or in an individual capacity.

Net Worth

The net worth of a person, or a company, is the difference between its assets and its liabilities. If you add up everything you own, and subtract everything you owe, the difference will be your net worth.

Equation 1

$$Net\ Worth = Assets - Liabilities$$

The Balance Sheet

One of the most important parts of your annual report is the balance sheet. Prepared by the Treasurer, it consists of two columns.

The first column lists your company's assets. This may include real estate, long-term investments like your endowment fund (if you have one), bank accounts, and the money in the till from last week's bake sale.

Many accountants and treasurers like to group assets by type. For depreciating assets, they generally list both the book value and the current estimated value after depreciation.

The second column lists your company's liabilities. All the debts are here: mortgages, car loans, and unpaid bills.

Many accountants and treasurers like to group debt by type. One useful technique is to separate the short-term debt from long-term debt.

Short-term debt is debt that is normally paid off within three months or less. Revolving credit card debt that is paid off every month, or payment for shipments of products or supplies that are due less than three months after delivery, are definitely short-term debt.

Long-term debt is the sort that takes years to pay off. Most long-term debt is secured by an asset of some kind. A mortgage is secured by the title to the mortgaged property. A car loan is secured by the title to the car. Debts to contractors that result in mechanic's liens are secured by a lien against the building that makes it impossible to legally sell the property until the debt is paid. The same goes for liens from utility companies, public utilities such as water or sewer providers, and from the city if there is a lien for unpaid property tax.

At the bottom of the balance sheet, you subtract the liabilities from the assets, and the result is your organization's net worth. The balance sheet can be therefore regarded as a snapshot of your not-for-profit company's financial status at a particular moment in time.

Things to know

Here is a short list of asset and liability questions you should ask before committing yourself to joining the Board of Directors for any not-for-profit company, or before accepting employment with that company.

If you are a member of the Board of Directors for a not-for-profit company, you should also be able to answer all of these questions either off the top of your head or after glancing at your last annual report. If you can't answer these questions, get a copy of your annual report and read it until you can answer all the questions:

- What is this organization's net worth?
- What kind of income producing investments does this organization own?
- What kind of cash reserves does this organization maintain?
- Does this organization own any real estate or vehicles?

- Does this organization own any art, collections, or other less liquid assets? (This is relevant to museums in particular)
- What kind of debt does this organization have?
- How much of the debt is secured, and by what assets?
- How liquid are the assets of the organization?
- Are there any outstanding legal judgments against this organization?
- What kind of long-term leases, contracts, or agreements has this organization signed?

Chapter 6: Cash Flow

This chapter deals with money in motion. Money flows into your charity every time you receive a donation or perform fundraising. Money flows out of your charity every time you buy something, pay someone for a service, or give something away.

The movement of money or assets into and out of your organization is called *cash flow*. It is measured as the change in your organization's net worth, over time. By the end of this chapter, you will have a basic understanding of how cash flow works. You will also have some principles you can apply to your not-for-profit company.

You can have cash flow within your organization too. If you have a checking account, a savings account, and a petty cash box, then every time you hold a bake sale cash flow occurs. When you exchange money for an asset (such as by purchasing a computer or selling a stock), that's cash flow too. Not all of your cash flow will necessarily be in the form of cash. Checks, electronic transactions, and money orders are part of your cash flow too.

Learning to track and predict patterns in your cash flow is an important part of business management, and the rules that govern cash flow in non-profit companies are no different than the ones that apply to your own household.

Figure 1: Cash Flow

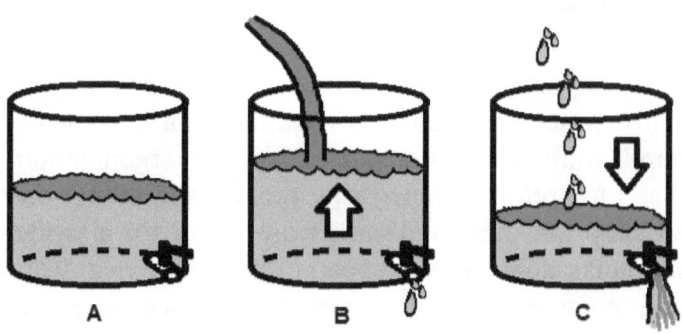

In Figure 1, image A shows a water tank. This bucket has a drain at the bottom. When you open the drain valve, water flows out of the bucket. The wider you open the valve, the faster the water flows out.

Image B shows what happens when water comes into the tank faster than it is leaving. Over time, the water level in the tank gets higher.

Image C shows what happens when water leaves the tank more quickly than it is added. Over time, the amount of water in the tank gets lower. Eventually, the tank will run dry, and water will barely drip out of the faucet, even if it's all the way open.

If we were to suppose that the tank represents your company, and the water represents money or assets, the picture of the tanks would be a pretty good analogy as to how cash flow works. The water pouring or dripping into the tanks represents income in the form of money or other assets. The water pouring or dripping out of the tanks represents money or assets leaving the company.

If you're not earning any money but you're also not spending any, your net worth will remain the same, just like the water in tank A. The same thing will happen if you are spending money at the same rate you're earning it. The amount of money or assets you have won't change because enough is coming in to cover your expenses.

If you take in money faster than you spend it, your charity's net worth will rise much like the water level in tank B.

If you spend money faster than you make it, your charity's net worth will fall much like the water level in tank C.

Using water tanks as an analogy for cash flow is very common in the business and personal finance community, but the analogy isn't perfect. Every water tank in the world has a maximum amount of water it can hold before it overflows. But there's no upper limit to the amount of money or assets an individual or company can accumulate. There are also ways in which money can be invested to provide interest as a source of income, so that the level in the "water tank" would increase if none was taken out.

The most important difference between water tanks and net worth is the fact that a water tank can't go negative. If a tank of water goes dry, the outbound water flow stops. But if your organization runs out of assets, it has the option of borrowing money and taking on debt liability in order to keep the outbound cash flow going for a while. Finally, the water in the tanks doesn't ever expand or produce new water, but there's such a thing as an asset that can create more income, such as the stocks and interest bearing savings accounts discussed in the previous chapter.

Balanced cash flow

Cash flow is said to be balanced when the amount of money coming in is roughly equal to what's going out. Look at the five diagrams in the following figure. Which of them represent balanced cash flow?

Figure 2: Cash Flow Balancing

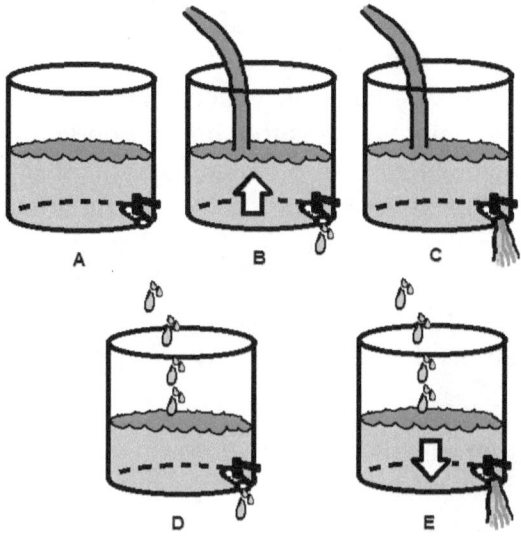

Tanks A, C, and D represent balanced cash flow, because the amount of money coming into and out of the account are roughly equal. In the case of Tank A, no money is coming in but none is going out.

If you spend more than you make, you will either have to sell off assets or accumulate debt, so your net worth will go down. If you make more than you spend, you will retain assets and your net worth will increase.

Inbound cash flow

There are only three possible sources of money for a non-profit. They can be divided into the following categories:

- Income from fundraising, including donations
- Income from passive income generating assets
- Income from sales of assets

99

Each source of income can be referred to as an income stream, particularly if it is regular or ongoing. Fundraising has its own domain and there will be several chapters devoted to it later on. This chapter emphasizes the kinds of income that aren't related to normal fundraising.

Interest

Interest is a fee that is paid for the privilege of borrowing money. If you park your money in an interest-bearing savings account, the bank may pay you interest for the privilege of using your money until you need it again. Or, if you're a credit union that's in the business of lending money to others, it's reasonable to expect interest payments along with payments of the *principal* which is the money you lent out. You can even lend money to another business or to an individual if you're not in the business of lending money out, however be careful about making loans to Board members, employees, and relatives of insiders. Such transactions represent a conflict of interest, and depending on the kind of not-for-profit corporation you have they may represent an illegal form of *self-dealing* in which an insider uses the charity for personal financial gain.

Windfalls

A windfall is an unexpected one-time donation or money that very seldom has conditions attached. A large grant may be considered a windfall, as may a big gift from a formerly minor supporter who won the lottery. If an apparently worthless asset becomes suddenly valuable and you can sell it at a gigantic profit, that's a windfall too. Maybe a small-cap stock skyrockets in value due to a lucky break or to inventing something that changes the world, or maybe the odds and ends left behind at a garage sale include a genuine Stradivarius.

Like bequests, windfalls cannot realistically be predicted or planned for. They are a nice bonus, but cannot be relied upon as a source of operating capital.

The best way to use a windfall is as a small endowment fund: stash it and save for something special. The second best way is to use it to get rid of debt. Pay off the mortgage on the church building, or pay off the computer equipment loan. This takes a large contractual or mandatory expense out of each month's outbound cash flow, and frees that money up for other purposes.

The third best way to use a windfall is to use it to buy capital equipment or for activities that sustainably expand your program in a way that doesn't require you to raise even more money.

Never, ever spend a windfall in a way that requires you to commit to more ongoing payments.

Bequests

Sometimes, a charity receives a large amount of money as a bequest from someone's will. This is a special kind of windfall, because by definition it happens only once per donor.

You can't predict the timing of a bequest, so it's unwise to try. Also, human beings are indecisive creatures at times. It's normal for a person to suddenly have a change of heart near the end of his or her life, and to change his or her will. Just because you've been told to expect a bequest doesn't mean you will receive one.

Later in this book, I discuss different forms of fundraising and categorize donors by type. A bequest might come from more than one kind of donor, but like an inheritance it's a bittersweet gift, because somebody who loved you had to die in order for you to receive it. Given a choice between a good friend and that good friend's money, most people would rather have their friend.

Asset sales

There are four times a healthy charity sells off or gives up assets:

- As part of a side business, where donated items or sold online, in a silent auction, or as another form of fundraising, where the assets collected are intended to be sold
- To liquidate assets that are not directly useful to the program, that are not money makers, or that have high maintenance costs. This frees up the money for investment in something more useful
- To exchange one asset, such as bank account money or an unusable old vehicle, for a higher value asset that is more useful to the company, or
- To pay off higher-interest debt

The asset isn't always exchanged for money. It can be swapped or bartered for other things. Land and real estate exchanges are the most common examples.

Maxim #6: Never sell off an asset, which has long-term value, to get rid of a short-term problem.

A healthy charity never sells off assets to pay operating expenses, to make payroll, or to solve a cash flow glitch when the income isn't quite enough to cover the expenses. If you find yourself tempted to sell off assets for this reason, or to make an unscheduled dip into your charity's savings account, pay attention: it's a sign that your charity is unhealthy.

The exception to Maxim #6 occurs when an *unhealthy* organization is selling off assets to avoid bankruptcy. When this occurs, the charity has usually been run in an unsustainable way for a long time, and is in crisis. If you see an organization selling off valuable assets without any other visible explanation, it's often a sign that they are in trouble.

Investments

Investment income is some of the nicest income to have, because it doesn't require labor and it doesn't affect the social capital of your organization or the people in it. You can have one dollar, a thousand dollars, or a million dollars in a bank account or a certificate of deposit, and they all require the exact same level of effort to manage.

If you are a disciplined investor, the return on your invested money can be re-invested over and over. This will allow your assets to accumulate over time. While making money and investing it should never be the primary goal of your not-for-profit corporation, the income produced by investments has to be factored into your overall cash flow.

Long-term investors often say that the correct time to sell a blue chip stock is "never": it's better to collect the dividends year after year and watch the value of the stock increase over time.

You can tell a charity is in trouble when it starts selling stock or long-term investment in order to cover operating expenses or to pay service on a debt.

Outbound cash flow

Every time you spend money, you create outbound cash flow. If you pay cash for postage, or if you write a check for the utility bill, that's outbound cash flow.

Every time you commit to paying money in the future, you create a future expense or liability for yourself. These liabilities affect your future cash flow.

The following list has examples of things a typical not-for-profit corporation might spend money on in the average month.

- Rent or mortgage

102

- Utilities
- Purchase of capital equipment
- Repair fees
- Wages and salaries
- Fundraising materials
- Postage and stationery
- Licensing fees for computer software
- Accounting services
- Program expenses
- Insurance
- Vehicle payments
- Debt service

Flexibility of expenses

If you look at the above list, you will notice that the expenses can be described in four different ways. A regular monthly expense comes at the same time every month, but the size of the expense may vary. Your heating and electric bill are examples of regular monthly expenses.

Not all expenses necessarily occur each month. Some liability insurance policies, for example, are paid only once a year. So you can classify expenses based on their *regularity*. You will have expenses that are monthly, semiannual, annual, or else completely *irregular*.

A second way to classify expenses is based on whether the expense is *reducible*. Not all expenses will vary in size. An electricity payment, for example, might be very high in the summer when the air conditioners are running, but it will be lower in the spring or fall. It's therefore possible to reduce the electric bill by turning out lights and by using less electricity. So I think of these expenses as reducible.

Not all expenses can easily be scaled back simply by using less. You can't easily reduce the size of your mortgage payment one month by only using half as much space. So your rent or mortgage is an example of an expense that is regular but not reducible.

A third way to classify expenses is based on whether the expense is *delayable*. Utility and rent bills are due on the same day every month and it's very difficult to renegotiate the timing. But it's relatively easy to postpone renovations or the purchase of a new computer. Consider the following expense list for an imaginary not-for-profit corporation.

Table 1: March Expenses by Category

Expense	Regular?	Reducible?	Delayable?
Rent	Yes: monthly	No	No
Heating	Yes: monthly	Yes	No
Fix gas leak	No	No	Emergency
Wall paint	No	Somewhat	Yes
Stamps	Annual	No	Yes

Regular expenses that are ongoing commitments, and that can't be reduced or delayed at need creates a drain on your cash flow. The more regular monthly spending commitments you have, the less flexibility you've got. If you're already paying $500 per month for rent, that's $500 you can't cut back or redirected to something else. However if you have a $100 heating bill, you may be able to trim the expense by lowering the thermostat.

Contractual expenses, such as mortgage payments or debt service, are the most difficult kind of regular expenses to get out of. There are generally penalties if you don't pay on time, or if you seek to exit the contract early. It therefore pays to think carefully before you make a lasting financial commitment. Before you sign your lease, think carefully. Are there things that could interfere with your ability to pay? If so, is there a buyout option or an early termination penalty? Where is the money to pay the lease coming from? If donations or side business revenue suddenly took a dive, how long could your charitable organization hold out?

A business with predominately flexible expenses—expenses that can be reduced or delayed at will—can weather tough times better than one with predominately regular, fixed expenses. Postponing a major purchase by saving money until you can afford it is an excellent, conservative strategy that saves your business from the burden of ongoing monthly debt payments.

Debt

Many companies borrow money to take advantage of an opportunity or to solve a short-term problem, and pay it back over a longer period of time. This is not necessarily dangerous (in fact it's one of the only practical ways to buy real estate).

Debt is risky because it creates a drain on your future cash flow. The regular payments must be paid, and that means there's less money left over to run the rest of your program. Debt service is also a category of spending that cannot easily be reduced or postponed when income is lean. If you take out a loan to buy a van for your senior citizen transport service, those monthly payments are extremely regular but not reducible or delayable.

The kind of cash flow commitment created by debt is among the least flexible. Not only are the payments usually fixed in terms of size and quantity, but if for some reason you miss a payment or make only a partial payment, interest accrues and you end up owing even more.

This doesn't mean your organization should *never* take on debt. If you need a building, a vehicle, or other expensive purchases to run your program, it's reasonable to borrow provided your charity can afford it.

Some hard and fast debt rules

Here are some rules that you simply must follow if you want to run a financially sustainable organization. Some of these might look familiar if you've ever read books on personal money management. The principles are the same.

- Borrow money chiefly for appreciating assets such as real estate, because these things can be expected to hold their value
- Do not borrow from banking institutions for the purpose of investing in securities such as stocks, bonds, or commodities
- Never borrow money for a depreciating asset unless that asset generates income greater than the amount of the payments
- Never borrow money for an expense not related to your program
- If you must borrow money, secured debt has a lower rate of interest than unsecured debt and is easier on your cash flow
- Never borrow money without a clear repayment plan, or without having a stream of income in place to repay it
- Never borrow money unless you have the ability to pay off the loan immediately should the need arise
- Absolutely never borrow money to cover normal operating expenses; it simply postpones the reckoning and makes your cash flow problem worse
- Never take on debt that amounts to more than twice your organization's annual income

I should probably clarify a couple of the points in this list. There's an old notion about "good debt" versus "bad debt", with "good" debt being the kind of debt that allows you to make money in the long term. That

105

idea isn't good enough for modern life in the not-for-profit sector. *All* debt has an impact on your cash flow.

Before borrowing money, you should ask yourself how you'd repay the loan if for some reason it became due immediately. A mortgage, for example, is secured by the title to the property. But a credit card loan or other unsecured loan isn't backed by anything.

It's possible to get into trouble borrowing from vendors or service providers, because many people don't think that ordering merchandise on net-30 terms (meaning that payment is due 30 days after delivery) is borrowing. But it is. Once you order the merchandise, you've accepted the terms of the agreement. That's a contract.

Money is *fungible*, which means that any one dollar can replace any other dollar. So, since any given dollar could potentially be used as part of a debt payment, most charitable organizations are reluctant to explicitly set money aside for debt service. This is a mistake. Anyone who manages a household knows to set money aside for the mortgage (or rent) and utilities before going shopping for anything else. There's no reason to not do the same in a not-for-profit organization.

You're not here to take risks

If you're in the charitable field, you're here to serve humanity, or the environment, or your deity of choice. It's about doing something worthwhile in the service of something bigger than yourself. You're not here to serve yourself by promoting your own ego. Taking financial risks in order to make your organization bigger or more impressive solely for growth's sake is inappropriate if you want to build or run a hundred-year charity. Therefore I recommend a financially conservative, risk-averse strategy especially where debt is involved.

We've all heard stories about entrepreneurs who mortgage themselves to the hilt, maxing out their cash advances on their credit cards and borrowing or *leveraging* against every possible asset in order to put their money into a business opportunity that turns out to be a massive success. The stories about people who do that and *fail* are less fun to read, but for every runaway success there are many people whose investments do not pan out and who end up bankrupt because of it.

If you want to take risks with your personal assets, go for it. Go ahead and invest your 401(k) money in penny stocks or mortgage your house to start a business. You have the legal right to do that: it comes under "pursuit of happiness". What you do not have the right to do is to risk other people's resources. As a not-for-profit administrator, you have a fiduciary duty not just to the company and its Board members, but to the community you serve.

Just because you can be approved to borrow money doesn't mean you should borrow every cent available. Asking a banker how much you can afford to borrow is stupid: it's like asking a bartender whether you should buy another drink. The bartender has a financial interest in serving you as many drinks as you're willing to buy, right up to the point where you become a legal liability due to being too drunk to drive home. So long as the bartender stops short of making you drunk enough to present a risk to him or her, he or she is going to serve you another drink if you want to buy one regardless of whether it's good for your health or whether buying one more drink will mean you no longer have enough money to pay your rent. Likewise, the bank has a financial interest in lending you as much as it can, at as high a rate of interest as possible, so long as it does not actually drive you out of business.

When you ask a banker how much you can borrow, the figure you will be quoted is the maximum the bank is willing to lend you before the loan puts *the bank* at risk. Whether the loan puts *you* at risk is not a blip on the banker's radar screen except to the extent that you may not be able to keep up with the payments. Depending on how stable your organization is and how much you have in terms of cash reserves, you may become very uncomfortable with payments on a debt just half the size of what a lender is willing to offer you.

Organizations that leverage themselves to the gills inevitably change their operating focus. All it takes is one minor glitch: the death of a major donor, or a sizable insurance claim. Then, instead of being in business to execute their programs, they are in a struggle for survival. The entire purpose of sustainable non-profit management is to *avoid* being in a struggle for survival. It is therefore necessary *to not over-leverage yourself to begin with.*

Cash flow problems

A *cash flow problem* occurs when your spending outstrips your income to the point where you no longer have enough money on hand to cover your financial commitments. Even if the problem is temporary, your only options are to borrow money, liquidate other assets, or delay or defer payment of other debt. It isn't pretty, and it's a sign of bad money management.

A cash flow problem is not a simple matter of making a big purchase using money already saved, or of dipping into cash reserves to cover a temporary shortfall and then replacing those cash reserves. A cash flow problem occurs when you either have no liquid savings or reserves, or have exhausted them due to unexpected expenses, deficit spending, or both.

There are only three reasons for cash flow problems to exist.

Possibility #1: you're spending too much

Overspending is the most common reason for a cash flow problem to occur. If you spend more than you earn, then no matter how big your cash cushion is or how large your bankroll might be, you're going to run out of money eventually. The solution is to spend less. Find some aspect of your business operations that can be done more cheaply or postponed until a later date. You can often free up cash flow by using volunteer labor instead of employees or consultants, donated space instead of rented space, and in-kind donations instead of donated money. This allows your money to be used for things that can only be accomplished with money, such as paying the electric bill.

Sometimes, extra spending is in response to an unexpected expense that wasn't in the budget. A wise administrator budgets with a *contingency* for unpredictable but expected expenses. For a small or new charity, I like a 10% contingency. Once you've been running a few years and are better at predicting expenses, or once you've expanded to the point where an unexpected expense somewhere may be offset by an unexpected surplus or windfall elsewhere, you may be able to drop your contingency to 5% or even less.

The contingency goes "above the line": it is a predicted expense, not something "below the line" representing money you hope not to spend.

If you have a new venture and aren't building contingency into your budget, you're doing it wrong. There's no way you can accurately predict every single expense throughout the year, so set aside a portion of your budget to deal with expenses that are *unpredictable, but expected.*

Nobody can predict a car accident, the sudden death of a major donor, or a freak hailstorm that destroys their building's roof. Even if you have insurance (which you should), you will still have to pay the deductible. But life happens, and it's reasonable to expect that *something* will happen over the course of the year that will require money.

Too often, I hear well-meaning administrators say they thought they planned for everything, but they "just didn't expect" whatever black swan just came along and ate their cash reserves. Guess what: it's your job to *expect.* You may not be able to predict, but it's your job to understand that unpredictable bad or expensive things happen sometimes. That's why you set money aside in each year's budget so that you can deal with them. This money, by the way, can be banked with your cash reserves but it is not part of your cash reserve that you hope to not have to spend. It is money that you *will* need to spend. You just don't know what you're going to need it for.

The contingency budgeting technique—which, incidentally, I got from my father, who picked it up during his decades of experience in construction management—works just as well for charities as it does for lump sum bids. It's also a brilliant thing to build into your grant proposals if you are expanding your program. Use contingency budgeting even if you aren't having a cash flow problem, because it will save you from developing one later.

Possibility #2: your cash reserves are too lean

If an occasional surprise like a bounced donation check or an unexpected bill of some kind can keep you from being able to make payroll, then you don't have enough in cash reserves. Cash reserves provide a financial "cushion" that can allow you to pay for emergencies without impacting your usual business operations.

Emergencies should be temporary. If they aren't, you have a serious management problem. Something beyond your control has changed to create a new normal standard of operations, but your leaders have failed to adjust. So the "emergency" is now the new normal and you operate in permanent crisis mode.

If you immediately stop overspending and are not too deeply in debt, you may be able to wrap up the immediate crisis. Once you do, your organization's first priority should be to rebuild its depleted cash reserves. The cash reserve is like a cycling helmet for your organization: if you've run into something large and solid, before you get back on the road you need to replace that helmet with something that will withstand the next impact.

Possibility #3: you overestimate your income

Many organizations believe that their fundraising team "should" be able to bring in more and more every year. That's only true if you're expanding into new communities and acquiring additional people to raise money. If you've got the same core group that you've had the last five years, or if you're a parent-teacher association that relies on parents from the same neighborhood year after year, then the community you've got is the only one you're going to get. You've got an aquifer that can produce a finite amount of social capital and a finite amount of money.

Any group of people or set of resources will gradually become more efficient over time, if efficiency depends on mastering a skill or going through some kind of learning process. But after this occurs, there's still a maximum amount of money that a concession stand or a charity gala will bring in. Expecting the profits to be bigger and bigger every year is unreasonable once people hit their stride and become basically competent.

Economic downturns that affect your donors affect you too. Too many charitable ventures continue to make demands on the communities that support them even when the communities are themselves in need of help. When their fundraising ventures start producing fewer returns on their invested time, their solution, instinctively, is to have more fundraisers. This is the exact opposite of what is required for a sustainable approach: organizations that increase the pressure on a dwindling resource simply ensure the resource is exhausted faster.

Failure to examine patterns in fundraising while putting a budget together, or insisting that the fundraising produce enough money to satisfy the budget despite changes in the economy that affect your volunteer or donor base, will cause cash flow problems.

When it gets ugly

Negative cash flow by itself isn't bad, provided it's a planned expense that you have already saved for. Spending or using some of the money raised after a big pledge drive or fundraising initiative is normal. Most charities have seasonal or cyclic variations in the donations they receive and their expenses, and any organization can spend more than it earns in a given month simply by making a big purchase. Paying off an outstanding debt, or buying capital equipment, or making planned renovations can cause you to spend a lot. But they should not generally put you into unplanned or high-interest debt.

There are special words used for companies or individuals whose spending exceeds their resources for too long. In the interest of decency, I'll omit the ones that aren't printable, and focus on the ones you might hear in the news.

Negative cash flow is when your spending exceeds your income. It doesn't necessarily represent a problem. For example, you may spend six months saving money toward a particular purchase of equipment. When you buy the equipment, in that month you will spend what you saved toward that goal, which may represent more money than you brought in that month. This is negative cash flow for the month in which you're doing the spending. But if the spending is predicted and you have enough money to afford it, it's not dangerous and in fact it's a normal part of doing business especially for a small charity.

Cash flow problems occur when you don't have enough money on hand to pay your bills or meet your existing financial commitments, and are forced to either sell off assets or borrow money to continue operating. Then of course there's insolvency and bankruptcy, which require more explanation because there's more than one kind. Some people use the word "bankruptcy" to describe certain types of insolvency.

Two types of insolvency

Negative net worth is when your debts exceed your assets, however you may still have operating capital. This is sometimes called "legal insolvency", but if you still have operating capital and can pay your bills as they come due you do not meet the definition of "technical insolvency". To avoid confusion, I use the phrase "negative net worth".

Negative net worth is not the end of the world, and it can happen for reasons completely beyond your control such as if a major asset such as real estate purchased with a loan suddenly loses most of its value. Buying a new van for a mobile ministry, for example, may cause technical insolvency if it's your only major asset, because a new vehicle loses substantial value the moment you drive it off the lot. The same goes if you just used a mortgage to buy a building for your new shul, temple or mosque and the economy suddenly takes a dive so that the resale value of your building is less than what you owe for it. It doesn't mean your charity can't afford the payments, however it is a sign that you're putting all your financial eggs in one basket.

A new charity may go through a period of negative net worth, but it's a dangerous time and you should strive to build up cash reserves and reduce debt. It is not generally a good time to spend more or make long-term financial commitments. No charity with a negative net worth is sustainable.

Do not expand your program if your organization has a negative net worth. Raise the money first, then sign the lease or hire the employee. How much money should you raise? A good general rule is that you should have at least a few months' worth of operating capital on hand, but if you happen to have a negative net worth I recommend increasing that amount until your net worth is no longer negative. Then you can selectively reduce debt or acquire income producing assets as you wish, and you also have cash on hand to deal with unpleasant surprises.

Insolvency, or more properly "technical insolvency", is when you don't have enough money on hand to pay your bills, and you've sold off or liquidated all the assets that can be easily sold. You may still have a positive net worth (or not), but you cannot pay your debts or meet your financial commitments without borrowing money. This is a more uncomfortable situation than simple negative net worth. Insolvency is the kind of financial trouble that keeps people awake at night.

Bankruptcy

The word *bankruptcy* is used to describe two things. The legal use of the word describes a procedure for liquidating or shutting down your business when you can no longer pay your debts out of your assets (negative net worth) and when you are also insolvent and lack the operating capital to continue making payments on your debts or financial commitments. In practical terms, we speak of people or companies as being *bankrupt* when they have painted themselves into a financial corner, and have no way to cover their debts. A company becomes insolvent when it runs out of operating capital, but bankrupt when it has a negative net worth and cannot raise enough money to cover the service on its debts.

Bankruptcy happens in the not-for-profit sector all the time, but since not-for-profit companies don't have owners you are more likely to see the organizations shut down than to see them go through the legal bankruptcy process. Furthermore, bankruptcy creates a permanent blot on a charity's image so that it will be difficult to attract or keep donors. Many charity organizers therefore prefer to shut down and start over after a major financial setback.

Three paths to bankruptcy

There are three main paths to bankruptcy for not-for-profit organizations. Organizations that are run by thundering imbeciles can sometimes bounce back and forth from one path through another before finally dying. But these are the three most common paths to disaster.

The "expensive mammal" path: negative cash flow, then insolvency, then bankruptcy

If you're on the expensive mammal path, your company gradually exhausts its resources caring for white elephants or sacred cows such as the ones discussed in Chapter 5. It's possible for a particular item on your budget to be both a white elephant *and* a sacred cow: expensive to maintain, but hard to get rid of and immune from budget cuts.

With this business model, you bleed to death slowly. First, you acquire the expensive mammal. Next, you notice it requires more resources than you expect and is not as productive as you hope. Instead of improving your cash flow, you experience the financial equivalent of a slow leak. Every month, you spend a little bit more than you take in. Pretty soon, there's nothing in the checking account, but Flossie still needs her kibble and will die without it. You might sell off assets, but pretty soon they too run out, and Flossie's still hungry.

If the expensive mammal is a white elephant (such as a building that's more expensive than you can afford), your charity generally starts by cutting other program areas to afford to pay service on the debt. Eventually, you stop focusing on your program and become a life support system for Flossie. The real estate fetish displayed by most American churches and religious organizations, as evidenced by the "need" to have exclusive use of a building for worship, can lead churches to commit to expensive leases or mortgages that can easily become white elephants.

If the expensive mammal is a sacred cow (such as an employee or a high-cost program activity), your charity will borrow money to keep the cow going. Eventually, the debt service on the borrowed money will start to affect the rest of your cash flow.

While your organization is bleeding to death, instead of trying to stop the bleeding you will attempt to give the patient the financial equivalent of a transfusion. It's bad medicine and worse management, but in order to raise money to pay for the expensive mammal you will exhaust your employees, donors, and volunteers. If your organization has assets (such as a white elephant) it may be briefly possible to borrow money, but there's no way to repay what you're borrowing.

Some of the volunteers will exhaust their personal social capital, and others will quit in disgust when they realize that all their hard work is going solely to support the expensive mammal.

The "field of dreams" path: negative cash flow, then negative net worth, then bankruptcy

This path takes its name from a movie title. The original movie was about an idealistic person who took a leap of faith that was rewarded. The reality, however, doesn't work out as well.

If you're on the field of dreams path, you believe that if you build "it", people will come. In other words, you believe that if you expand your program, people will automatically support it with money and labor. In the real world it's the other way around: first you build a foundation and then you erect your castle.

The field of dreams path to bankruptcy starts with a bang but ends with a whimper. It's because the management team has decided to do everything backwards. It builds a huge castle in the air, then tries to move in and live there, assuming they will be automatically and magically supported by the community. When they inevitably fall through the floor, it's a long way down to the ground, but the impact always seems to come as a surprise.

It takes money to build an "it". In the beginning that isn't a problem, because someone with more money than sense writes a check. Maybe you bring in a large grant. Maybe you receive an unexpected gift from a friend who wins the lottery. Regardless of how it happens, your organization is now awash with money. Remember all those wouldn't-it-be-nice-if conversations you had with your fellow idealists? You're now in a position to act on at least some of them. Indeed, expanding your program might be mandatory. Grants frequently must be used to make an existing program bigger, by expanding into a new territory or offering your services to more people. But what if your organization is exactly the size its donor and volunteer base can support?

Outgrowing your donor base and your fundraising team is an extremely poor idea. Without the income necessary to continue supporting your expanded program, you'll have to spend your savings (if you have any). The only question is when. Your initial windfall will be spent very quickly, because cost overruns are a normal part of construction even when you're building an air castle. Indeed, you'll find that the expenses expand to consume, and then exceed, all available resources.

Maxim #7: You cannot solve a cash flow problem by making it bigger.

It's easy to get caught up in the excitement of having lots of money. Organizations often financially overcommit themselves when times are good, and make long-term agreements or commitments with the assumption that the cash flow to cover them will simply appear out of nowhere. They fail to scale back spending to match available capital.

Then, all of a sudden, the money is almost gone but there are a bunch of bills to pay and more coming in.

Seemingly overnight, your organization is plunged into the red. Like a celebrity who loses a major endorsement, you end up with a few illiquid assets, very little cash on hand, and very little to show for your period of splendid solvency. It's not that you intend to borrow: it happens when bills come due and you can't pay them.

This isn't the slow bleed like the expensive mammal path to bankruptcy. It's a financial embolism. You probably won't be able to liquidate assets quickly enough to cover expenses, so when you can't borrow anymore, you fold.

The "Pied Piper of Hamelin" path: debt, then bankruptcy

Do you remember that old story about the Pied Piper of Hamelin, who was hired to cure a rat problem and who found a creative way to retaliate when he wasn't paid?

The Pied Piper of Hamelin path to bankruptcy begins when an organization fails to understand why it doesn't have as much money as it wants or needs, and why fundraising efforts are producing diminishing returns. Despite its best efforts, the organization just isn't raising enough money.

If you've read the earlier chapters of this book, you can instantly recognize the symptoms of exhausted social capital and burned out volunteers. You also know the solution. But suppose your Board doesn't want to restructure financially, or doesn't recognize or accept that they have a problem. Instead, they decide to hire a fundraising expert who declares that he or she can whistle up far better returns on your fundraising efforts. In other words, you hire the Pied Piper.

One of the exercises I introduce in this book to assess your organization's fundraising capability is called the Rat's Butt test. Basically, the extent to which your community cares about you or your program is reflected by the amount of money you're able to raise from it. If you collect a rat's butt from everyone who's willing or able to give one, the resulting pile of fuzzy hindquarters represents the community's entire investment in you. That's not a reflection of the number of rodents running loose in the community, so much as a reflection of how much you can expect to realistically collect.

There will always be money and assets floating around that aren't being directed your way. Some of them stay in the pockets of donors. Some are directed to different charities. Most families, and most individuals, have a maximum amount of money or resources they can give to charity. No matter how important you think you are, you generally aren't going to get *all* of it.

In the old story, the Pied Piper of Hamelin had a magic flute that, when played, caused all the rats in the town to follow the piper and obey his commands. What better way to collect even more rodent tails, than to hire someone who can lure every last one out of hiding?

Finding ways to get more out of your existing donor and volunteer base sounds like a good idea at first. But if you've read the chapter on social capital, you know that there's a finite amount of money you can extract from your community before you permanently damage it. Frequently, by the time your organization gets around to hiring the Pied Piper, you've already run several wells dry and damaged the aquifer that feeds them. But, never fear: the Pied Piper has a solution.

The Pied Piper generally teaches you to manufacture an emergency of some kind, so as to manipulate or guilt-trip bigger donations out of your personal social network. That's the secret to his or her success: the ability to get more out of people in the short term by making a personal plea for help. You generally do this by taking your fundraising "to the next level" by attempting something far more difficult, expensive, and risky than anything you've tried before. To draw in help from your personal network and also the charity's network, you have to overextend. Overextending is the act that stimulates other people to respond altruistically by rescuing you. Or, at least that's the goal.

The first time you try the new techniques, they work brilliantly. The money flows in, at the expense of your credibility, and you continue on your merry way without correcting the behaviors that got you into financial trouble in the first place. But there's a hidden cost: it's obvious to every single person you ask for "emergency" aid that the trouble you're in is self inflicted. After all you aren't asking for money to cover a personal emergency such as car trouble or medical expenses. You're asking for it on behalf of somebody else. So you go to the well, and you withdraw an awful lot more than you think, especially if the amount you're asking for is more than trivial. You get what you want in the short term, but there's a long-term impact on your credibility and your social capital.

Invariably the followers of the Pied Piper decide that the new fundraising technique was so successful that it ought to be repeated. They describe it as "better" and "more effective" than anything they have tried before, and they decide that the results they got using emergency tactics will be the new normal. They do not see, or do not care about, the damage to their reputation or their social capital.

The second time you try the new technique of voluntary overreach, it doesn't go so well. When you contact your friends and ask them to bail you out of a second self-inflicted emergency, you will hear a lot less "yes" and a lot more "no". You may also hear some cruel words and unkind estimates of your mental acuity. Depending on how frank your friends are, you may be compared unfavorably to a donkey or a female dog. You won't bring much money in. In fact, you may not even be able to pay the Pied Piper. "It takes money to make money", at least the way the Pied Piper does things, so there's a good chance that you've spent a lot of money for a fund-raiser that ends in disaster.

There's another story about a boy who cried "wolf" to deliberately raise a false alarm. Eventually people started to ignore him, and then one day a real wolf came but nobody paid attention to his pleas for help. If you have enough false or self-inflicted emergencies, your community will stop responding. This means that the strategy proposed by your hired Pied Piper will eventually stop working.

You and the Pied Piper will part ways, and generally not on good terms. Hopefully you can do it without violating your contract, because if you operate in bad faith, breach a contract, and get sued in a personal capacity, commercial liability insurance won't help you. Guess where that metaphorical flute ends up?

Risk taking behaviors

An advertising or fundraising budget of zero is impractical, but so is any investment where the risk is out of proportion with the reward. In any fundraising operation or other venture, your initial and ongoing expenses can generally be calculated, but before setting your plan in motion it's wise to consider the worst case scenario in which your venture creates no income at all, but you are still obligated to pay the expenses.

If your charity could not survive the expense of a failed investment or fundraiser, that initiative is too big. Proceeding with it anyway is an extreme risk, and if you want to run sustainably you should avoid that sort of risk taking behavior.

Things to know

Before deciding whether to get involved in an existing charity, try to find out what the cultural attitude toward money is. If there's an overall culture of fiscal irresponsibility, you cannot make a difference by yourself.

Ask the existing charity administrators the following questions:

- Has this organization ever been cash flow negative?
- Is the organization currently in a negative cash flow position?
- Has this organization recently borrowed money for program activities?
- Has this organization ever tried to spend its way out of a cash flow problem?
- How liquid are the organizations assets?
- Has there been a liquidity problem in the past?

Chapter 7: Non-Profit Versus Tax Exempt

As I mentioned in the introduction to this book, I use the phrase "not-for-profit" and "non-profit" interchangeably, and prefer "non-profit" because it's shorter. But taken literally, "not-for-profit" is actually the more appropriate description, because it points out that the business is not run in a way that distributes profit to owners or shareholders. The phrase "non-profit" can be taken to mean the same as "not-for-profit", but it can also be construed as proof that a charitable business cannot, or should not, have or spend significant amounts of money. That's a very inaccurate perception and it leads to bad spending decisions by inexperienced not-for-profit administrators.

This chapter will further illustrate what it means to be a not-for-profit corporation, and what it means to be tax exempt.

A not-for-profit corporation is one that has no owners or shareholders, and that cannot pass profits (or losses) back to them. They pay out no dividends, and profits and losses don't pass back through to anybody. So the corporation is operating for some other reason besides creating profit. Hence "not-for-profit".

No profit directed to shareholders

A charity, by definition, is set up as a not-for-profit company. While many for-profit companies do aspire to help humanity and to make the world a better place, the key factor that distinguishes a charity and an ordinary company is the issue of ownership.

For-profit businesses have owners or shareholders who have some financial stake in the company, and who receive a portion of the profits. They might be set up as a sole proprietorship (with one owner), a partnership (with multiple owners), or a corporation (with multiple shareholders). But a not-for profit corporation has no owners or shareholders. The Board of Directors handles long-term decision making, and there is an Executive team, or a group of Officers, who handle the day-to-day business.

Default status is for-profit

The default status of any businesses is "for profit" unless it is set up and incorporated as a not-for-profit corporation. An existing for-profit company cannot switch over to not-for-profit status. It must actually dissolve and reincorporate as a not-for-profit. The reverse is not true. It is possible for a not-for-profit corporation to give up its tax exempt status, as the National Football League (NFL) did in 2015 to retain more assets and pay bigger executive salaries than were plausible under the limitations for tax exempt organization. It is also possible, but more difficult, for a not-for-profit corporation to become for-profit by changing its designation with the Attorney General's office, and by becoming a for-profit company by issuing shares to private shareholders or else offering them for sale to the public by listing them on a stock exchange.

Implications of self-dealing

Self-dealing is a business transaction in which a not-for-profit corporation or charity, often a private foundation as opposed to a public charity, does business with an insider or decision maker in a personal capacity so that the insider makes a profit in a personal capacity. Certain individuals are "disqualified" from doing business with their foundation. Anyone who has the ability to influence a decision made by the foundation, and the immediate family members of such a person, are disqualified from doing business transactions with that particular foundation. Likewise, government officials are disqualified.

It's illegal to use a not-for-profit corporation as a way to transfer money or assets to yourself, to a government official, or to anyone in the immediate family of someone with decision making authority in the not-for-profit corporation.

An example of self-dealing is when a charity rents space in a building owned by a member of its Board of Directors, or if a political campaign rents space in a building owned by a member of the candidate's immediate family. Another example would be if a member of the charity's Board makes a loan to the charity and receives interest payments. Such transactions are taxable and must be declared, even if the transactions are beneficial to the foundation.

There are exceptions to the prohibition against self-dealing. If the business relationship predated the decision by which a person becomes disqualified, such as if you're renting space in a building owned by a person who later gets involved with your charity and joins your Board or is elected to public office, it's not considered self-dealing if you continue the business relationship. Also, transactions related to bequests from the estates of individuals closely involved in your charity are not considered to be self dealing. If your charity receives, for example, half the value of a piece of real estate left to you in your founder's will, with the responsibility of selling that real estate and returning the remainder to the estate, it's legal to sell that bequest and return money to the estate without the transaction being considered self-dealing. You're allowed to donate to your own charity or foundation, and you're also allowed to receive or make use of benefits from it if and only if the same benefits are available to members of the general public who go through the same process.

Self-dealing transactions are restricted in some states but not all. Depending on where you live, you may have to add a special section prohibiting self-dealing to your Articles of Incorporation in order to qualify for tax exempt status.

Non-profit versus no money

The shorter phrase, "non-profit", is sometimes misconstrued as meaning "no money". It's related to the belief that raising money for charity and holding some back as cash reserves or spending some of it on things besides the program is somehow bad, dirty, or inappropriate. (In reality administrative and advertising expenses do happen, and maintaining cash reserves is a prudent and appropriate way to prepare for emergencies.) While some charities do operate on a shoestring budget, it's a mistake to think that non-profit automatically means there's no money involved. Non-profits can make a lot of money, spend a lot, and save a lot from one year to the next.

Emergency first responder services are a classic example of a non-profit organization that knows how to raise and spend money. New ones are created every year in response to natural and human-made disasters. Established organizations like the Red Cross or Doctors Without Borders spend hundreds of millions of dollars every year on global disaster relief. Not all of it goes directly for food or medical supplies, either: a substantial amount of money is spent maintaining the infrastructure that allows relief organizations such as the Red Cross to move large numbers of qualified people, quickly, into the places where the need is greatest. They have the well-deserved reputation of being the very first people to provide meaningful aid anywhere on the planet, without regard for politics or military conflicts. One thing the Red Cross is not, is broke.

It's true that retaining "excess" profits from one year to the next, beyond what is justified by cash reserves or savings toward capital equipment, can be regarded as uncharitable. Certainly you should not make a habit of setting aside more than is necessary to run your organization for a few months, and if retaining excess capital is part of a pattern of behavior that resembles for-profit business more than it resembles charity, your tax exempt status may be revoked. But that should never prevent you from having savings, investments, or cash reserves sufficient to run your organization.

Registration

Every non-profit corporation has to be registered with the Attorney General of the state (or states) in which they do business or solicit funds. The names of the founders (or people who start up the non-profit) are recorded. The corporation must also have a registered address and agent. The founders' identities and addresses are public record. As part of the registration process, you will generally be required to upload or file a copy of your Articles of Incorporation and your Bylaws.

The use of the Attorney General's office to register corporations is one example in which the business laws and structures in the United States differ from those in other countries. In other nations, different mechanisms exist to register a not-for-profit or charitable organization, however there is always some kind of registry available at either the provincial, state, or national level. You must register in every region where you do business, solicit donations including by mail, or engage in fundraising.

Unless you are actually offering goods or services to the public you will not necessarily need a business license. This is particularly true if you do not have a brick-and-mortar address devoted to the exclusive use of your venture. If you are a booster club operating out of a local public school or a small charity operating out of its founder's home, avoid paying for a business license unless you have to in order to accomplish your necessary program and fundraising activities.

Simply registering as a non-profit corporation in a state does not entitle a charity to start soliciting funds or doing business. It must also register itself with the Internal Revenue Service and obtain a unique identifying number. This registration entitles the corporation to begin soliciting business. However, obtaining tax exempt status requires an extra step. Tax exempt status must be explicitly applied for. There is an official form, a fee, and a series of steps and processes to follow.

Approval is not automatic. Although there is an expedited process wherein disaster relief charities are moved to the front of the line, and where some basic kinds of charities receive approval in only a few months, a charity that provides money or goods directly to individuals receives additional screening and oversight to ensure that tax exempt status is not being abused.

Depending on the kind of charity you are running, it may take eighteen months or more to obtain tax exempt status.

Non-profit does not necessarily mean tax exempt

Just because a company does not have shareholders or owners does not mean it meets the standards for tax exemption.

In order to be tax exempt, a business must be structured as a not-for-profit company, it must exist for one of a handful of tax exempt purposes as defined by the Internal Revenue Code, and it must operate as a charity (as opposed to for the private benefit of key individuals). In order to be tax exempt, a not-for-profit corporation must fit into one of three general categories.

501(c)(3) Charitable Organization is the most desirable tax exempt designation. It is exempt from paying income tax, donations are tax deductible, and donors can remain anonymous.

A 501(c)(3) corporation must be set up as a public charity or private foundation, but public charities have the most operational latitude. To be tax exempt under Section 501(c)(3) of the Internal Revenue Code, the company must be organized and operated exclusively for the specific exempt purposes set forth in that Section. None of its earnings may inure to any private shareholder or individual. In addition, it may not be an "action organization" that seeks to influence legislation as a substantial part of its activities. Nor may it participate in any election campaign activity for or against political candidates.

501(c)(anything else) is not quite like a 501(c)(3), because it is either defective in some aspect of its organization, or it is allowed to engage in lobbying. For example, a credit union, trade union, or social club operates only for the benefit of its members. These organizations are exempt from paying income tax, but donations are not tax deductible.

527 Political Organizations exist solely for political purposes. They pay no income tax, but donations are not tax deductible and they must declare who their donors are.

Unless a non-profit meets the specific standards for inclusion under Section 527 or Section 501(c), it may be set up as a not-for-profit, but it does not meet the standards for tax exemption. This means that donations to the business are not tax deductible, they must file business income tax returns and pay tax on their profits, and they are not eligible for any of the special perks or benefits that go along with tax exempt status. These perks might include exemption from municipal property tax, or the opportunity to receive grants from businesses, government, or tax exempt organizations.

Many legitimate charities do a lot of public good, but cannot meet the standards for tax exemption. It's because some aspect of how they are organized or run is deemed "defective" by IRS standards. Perhaps they provide private benefit to specific individuals, or perhaps a portion of their income inures or is given to specific people.

For example, suppose a non-profit corporation is set up to provide a source of income to police officers injured in the line of duty. The income from donations is directed or earmarked for specific individuals. So, even though there aren't any owners making a profit, the non-profit is still not tax exempt.

Non-profit or tax exempt does not necessarily mean charity

A "charity" is a special type of non-profit organization dedicated to improving the lives of human beings and animals. The IRS has a list of activities it considers to be charitable. These activities include providing services to the needy, providing medical aid, education, or disaster relief, helping animals or the environment, or even providing intangible benefits such as religious services. Promotion of amateur and professional sports competition, for example, is considered a charitable purpose. Under some circumstances, donations to recognized or "registered" charities can be tax deductible.

Not all non-profit corporations have a charitable purpose. A credit union, a labor union, and a private golf and country club are all run as non-profit institutions. So are political action committees and special interest advocacy groups. Many of these examples may qualify for limited tax exempt status, but donations are not tax deductible.

Just as not all non-profit corporations are necessarily charitable, not all charitable ventures qualify for tax exempt status. The following diagram illustrates how the concepts fit together.

Figure 3: Types of Not-For-Profit Category

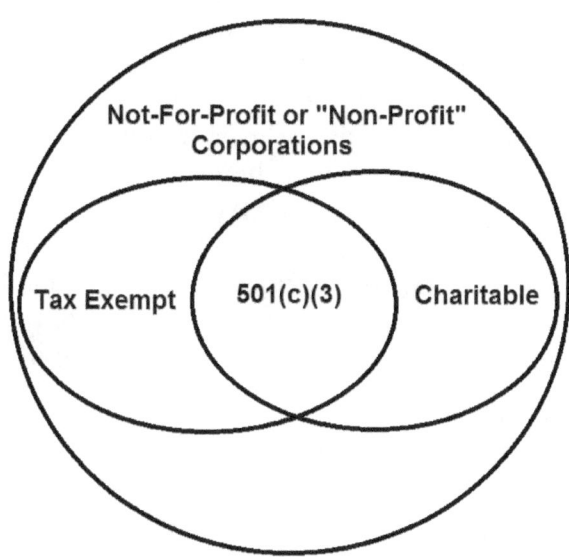

The highly desirable 501(c)(3) status is reserved for charitable not-for-profits that meet the standards for tax exemption. It's possible to be a charitable not-for-profit corporation without being tax exempt, and it's possible to be tax exempt without having a charitable component.

From time to time, non-profit businesses lose their tax exempt status completely, or are downgraded from the 501(c)(3) category into a different designation so that donations are no longer tax deductible.

There are some taxes you must pay even if you are tax exempt

Tax exempt doesn't mean you never pay another cent of tax. Sorry. All it means is that your charity doesn't have to pay tax on anything it makes through donation or fundraising.

Property taxes

Some municipalities or counties waive property taxes for tax exempt charities such as churches, if the property is used for conducting the charity's program. Depending on your location, the church building itself, its related buildings such as parsonages or recreation centers, and everything related to the charitable program might be exempt from property tax.

You can't just ignore a property tax bill. The exemption must be applied for and authorized, and approval is not automatic. Most states have laws specifying the process for obtaining approval for property tax exemption, although the mechanism for getting the approval is sometimes delegated to the county or (rarely) the municipality. Once you have the exemption letter, exactly what that exemption entitles you to do occasionally varies by municipality.

The general rule is that if the primary purpose of the building is to conduct your program, no tax applies, however if you're using the land or building primarily as a source of money from a side business or as a rental, tax generally applies. A very few municipalities offer additional exemption for specific kinds of charities conducting side businesses. But if the property is leased to someone else, or if it is empty land donated or bought for speculation purposes, property tax may indeed apply.

Vehicle related taxes

You will still have to pay to register your vehicles, and if your municipality requires evidence that your vehicle meets emission standards, there are fees associated with testing.

Employment taxes

If you have an employee, you must pay the employer's half of the Social Security and Medicare, and withhold the employee's half from his or her paycheck. Basically, you match the employee's payment cent for cent. Federal income tax must be withheld, and if your state has income tax you must withhold this too.

You are not exempt from having to pay employment taxes even if you are a church. Members of the clergy who receive wages or salaries must likewise pay income tax just as if they were employed in some secular business. Certain types of housing, known as "parsonage", may sometimes be provided for them tax free.

Income taxes for employees

People who are employed by a charity, including ministers, pay income tax. For employees, you must withhold income tax and Social Security. For contractors that supply their own tools and uniforms, where you do not control the work being done, you can use Form 1090, in which case the contractor is responsible for paying the self-employment tax.

Hiring a contractor means that you do not need to deduct Social Security or income taxes and you do not pay employment tax. However, if you are supervising the worker and calling the shots to the point where the "contractor" is basically an employee, you cannot use Form 1090 to get around having to pay and deduct tax. There has to be a contractor agreement that specifies the type and duration of work to be done.

If your charity pays money out to individuals such as for a scholarship, individual grant, or bursary, the people who receive it have to declare it as income for tax purposes.

The only time you are allowed to give money to people and not declare it is if you can prove the money is reimbursement for some expense related to the charity, or if you are paying somebody for services rendered but the total annual amount is less than the reporting threshold for a Form 1090. This is sometimes the case for temporary, casual work such as refereeing or scorekeeping at a sports competition.

Hidden sales taxes

Although tax exempt charities are generally exempt from state or municipal sales tax, luxury taxes built into the price of commodities such as gasoline cannot be avoided.

Income tax on non-exempt activities

Not all fundraising activities are tax exempt. Although you are allowed to operate a business for fundraising purposes, and although you generally do not have to pay tax on investment income, any part of your revenue that comes from gambling, alcohol sales, or any other activity that is not tax exempt is taxable. It must be reported and declared every year.

There are types of transactions that are not tax exempt. If your charity functions as a "pass-through" wherein donors designate a specific individual to receive the benefit they provide, or if a portion of your income or profits automatically inures to a private individual, what you have is called a "private benefit transaction".

Crash and burn offenses

There may be fifty ways to leave your lover or a million ways to die in the West, but there are only eight ways to lose 501(c)(3) tax exempt status once you've gotten that little letter which confirms you have it. That little sheet of paper is worth more than its weight in platinum, but the benefits it provides disappear if you do anything on this list.

(1) *Fail to file your annual 990 or 990-N for three years in a row.* It takes about fifteen minutes' worth of effort, for a small charity. After three years of not filing, you will automatically have your tax exempt status revoked

(2) *Do something blatantly illegal, or against the public interest.* Examples include using a charity to launder money from illegal activities, using a charity as a cover for an illegal Ponzi scheme, or in the case of a charity hospital, being uncharitable enough to sue poor or uninsured patients

(3) *Operate for the benefit of private interests such as the founder, the founder's family, an employee, or any other insider.* Examples include allowing a founder or insider to use the charity's bank account or credit cards for personal or family expenses, or allowing a select group of people to use the charity to promote a book, to sell artwork, or to otherwise benefit financially, while retaining the profits for themselves. Other examples include any system in which fundraising done by one person is earmarked for that person's or family's use is a private benefit transaction; such transactions may never be more than a trivial amount and there has to be some means to provide for needy recipients. Private benefit also covers nepotism that is undisclosed, or that results in overpayment for services, or that results in charity benefits being unfairly directed to relatives of insiders

(4) *Allow "inurement", which is when money is set aside for the sole benefit of a specific individual.* Any system in which an individual can accrue money, property, or other things of value that may be used in a private capacity is inurement. So is any form of directed donation or "pass-through" giving wherein a donor specifies the recipient of the donation

(5) *Allow excessive focus on for-profit activities.* This includes retaining excess capital instead of spending it on program, excessive executive salaries or benefits, and allowing more than half of the charity's resources to be tied up in a fundraising business activity

(6) *Provide commercial-type insurance* such as life or property insurance as a fundraising activity

(7) *Lobbying* activities intended to influence legislation, if they are more than a trivial part of the charity's activity

(8) *Electioneering* activities intended to influence the outcome of an election

Some surprisingly legal activities

Because of the eight crash and burn offenses, and the difficulty some people have in understanding what is or is not a legitimate expense for a charity, there is a lot of confusion in church and charitable communities as to what is or isn't allowable. This section discusses activities that are perfectly legal for a 501(c)(3) tax exempt corporation, as of 2015.

It is perfectly legal for a tax exempt organization to provide money or goods directly to individual people. For example:

- You can pay your employees
- You can pay administrators (within reason: if you are grossly overpaying somebody, that constitutes a private benefit transaction and is not allowed)
- You can reimburse people for receipted purchases made on the charity's behalf
- You can write a check directly to an individual who benefits from a charity (scholarships or bursaries often work this way)
- You can hand out products or merchandise to individuals (food banks work this way)

It is legal for a tax exempt organization to hire relatives or friends of the founders. However, family relationships and conflicts of interest must be disclosed. The charity must also have a policy in place to recuse people from any financial decision-making process who stand to benefit from it.

It is perfectly legal to operate a charity that does nothing but raise and distribute money. For example, booster clubs raise money for arts or athletics programs all the time. Endowment and private operating foundations raise money and distribute it to other charities. Some private operating foundations distribute money to businesses or corporations, such as by funding the production of educational films or by supporting fine arts productions

It is legal for a tax exempt organization to own large amounts of stock, bonds, or other income producing assets. These may be given to the charity in the form of a bequest, such as in somebody's will or as in a large donation made by a wealthy person or family. Or, they may be the result of strategic investment done by the charity. For example, some Ivy League schools, particularly Harvard, have massive endowment funds thanks to generations of big gifts from alumni. They use these funds to provide scholarships and tuition aid to many of their students. Likewise, endowment foundations typically have large trusts that contain a portfolio of trusts, stock, real estate, or other income producing assets. The interest produced by these assets is used every year to fund the program.

It is perfectly legal for a tax exempt charity to make billions of dollars a year promoting professional sports, and by selling advertising and merchandise. For example, most national professional sports promotions are tax exempt, despite the impressive amounts of money they make and the big salaries they pay. The NFL was tax exempt until 2015. Professional major-league baseball players pay income tax, as do the individuals or businesses that own the teams, but MLB is a not-for-profit corporation as is the NBA.

It is completely legal for an executive of a tax exempt charity to retain air miles or hotel points earned while traveling on charity business, and to use them later for personal or family travel. In fact, the charity cannot keep these travel incentives since they are tied directly to the individual and not to the company.

It is totally legal for a church or charity to hire a lobbyist or to lobby elected officials directly. But the lobbying activity may not take up more than a trivial portion of the charity's resources.

It is legal for a church or charity to spend money on issue related advertising to raise awareness about an issue, provided they never try to tell people which way they should vote, or which candidate they should or should not support. The general rule is that raising awareness is OK, but outright endorsement or condemnation is not allowed under tax exempt rules.

It is perfectly legal for a church or charity to publish election guides, to mention the election, to encourage people to vote, or to host debates or guest speakers who happen to be politicians running for elected office. All candidates must be given equal time and resources, and no publications or speeches from the pulpit should ever attempt to tell readers which way to vote.

Chapter 8: Non-Profit Business Structure

There are many ways to set up a for-profit business, but they differ from the structure of a not-for-profit business, which must be set up as a corporation. There is no such thing as a non-profit sole proprietorship or limited liability company (LLC). As I mentioned in the previous chapter, not-for-profit corporations cannot have shareholders or owners.

A *corporation* is a business where the day-to-day management of the company is done by officers or executives that may or may not be paid for their work. These officers report to the *Board of Directors*, which is the chief governing body of the corporation, and which has the authority to appoint or dismiss any or all of the officers or executives. The Board of Directors meets regularly to discuss the long-term goals of the corporation and to monitor the progress and approach being used by its management team.

Your corporation will have its own legal identity that is separate from you, from the Board of Directors, or from any employees or officers of the company. This is one of the reasons why you must register it. Your corporation can, with a little bit of paperwork, open its own bank account, sign a contract, or hire an employee.

Whereas a for-profit corporation is owned by multiple *shareholders* or owners who purchase a slice of the business and who vote for members of the Board of Directors, you may have members at large. These are people, typically members of the public for a public charity, who have an interest in your charitable venture. They will be your donors, your volunteers, and anyone who has a stake in the long-term health of your venture. They will not receive profits in a year where your organization's income exceeds its expenses, but they will also not be individually liable for the organization's debts unless they have committed some sort of fraud, gross mismanagement, or other behavior for which they are culpable in a personal capacity.

Your not-for-profit corporation offers liability protection to its Board and members at large just like a for-profit the corporation offers liability protection to the owners. The debts of the corporation are limited to the assets of that corporation, and shareholders, employees, or executives of the corporation are not individually liable for the corporation's commitments. Corporations have their own bank accounts and financial instruments, and these are separate from the accounts used by their directors, employees, and shareholders.

The legal separation between corporate and individual identity depends on keeping all money, bank accounts, and assets separate. If you, as a Board member or representative of your not-for-profit corporation, fail to keep the money separate than your protection disappears. For example, if you keep your personal money into the corporate account, obtain a loan or mortgage in a personal capacity for the company's benefit, or write a company check for a personal expense, you lose your protection. Should your corporation lose a lawsuit, your personal assets may be taken by creditors or seized by the authorities to cover the corporation's commitments. For this reason, it is customary for people who sue a for-profit company to also sue the owners in a personal capacity. If a not-for-profit corporation is being sued, the plaintiff frequently names the officers of the corporation and possibly the Board of Directors as defendants. Insurance is available to help protect those individuals against a frivolous suit, but if the defendants did in fact use their corporation commit fraud, breach a contract, or otherwise behave in an illegal fashion, a court can and will hold them financially accountable in a personal capacity.

Not-for-profit means no shareholders

The only distinction between whether a corporation is for-profit or not-for-profit, besides the way it is registered with the state Attorney General, is the presence of shareholders.

A for-profit corporation has shareholders. Its shares may not necessarily be publicly traded, and in fact many wealthy families set up corporations to protect family assets from one generation to the next.

A not-for-profit corporation has no shareholders. It therefore cannot pay out dividends or pass through a profit or loss at any given time. The fact that there are no shareholders is the key distinguishing feature of a not-for-profit corporation.

All not-for-profit companies are corporations

All not-for-profit companies must register as corporations. This means that every single tax exempt or not-for-profit company is a corporation with a Board of Directors and executives or officers that manage the charity on a day-to-day basis. For an extremely small not-for-profit corporation, these roles may be handled by the same person.

The corporation is the only business structure legally available to a not-for-profit company. The LLC business structure is not available, and no not-for-profit business may register as a sole proprietorship, because by definition a sole proprietorship's profits go to the individual who owns it.

Not-for-profit corporations behave like C-corporations and are allowed to retain assets or profits from one year to the next. Over time, this has allowed some well-established not-for-profit corporations to accumulate a great deal of wealth. But none of it can be paid out to shareholders in the form of a dividend, because there are no shareholders.

Board of Directors

All corporations are guided by a Board of Directors. For a not-for-profit corporation, these individuals are almost always volunteers. They meet a few times a year to discuss long-term goals, and they are responsible for directing the overall direction of the non-profit. Hence the name "director". It is the Board of Directors that is responsible for the long-term direction or goals of the corporation. This is the group of people responsible for determining whether or not a corporation survives a hundred years or more.

A hundred-year charity has Board members who are committed to responsible management of their foundation or organization. They are acquainted with the major employees and administrators of the charity. They participate actively and pay attention to changes in the economy and society. They do far more than meet once a year to rubber-stamp decisions made by the Executive Director, the President, or other decision makers they appoint.

For large charities, Board members are generally either major long-term donors, former high-ranking employees of the non-profit who have since retired, or executives from businesses in some other related industry. Organizations sometimes swap: present high ranking members of one company may serve on the Boards of two or three more. This guarantees a large and ongoing network of people who share the same administrative vision.

Large non-profits generally seek out Board members who have experience in non-profit administration in general, and also in the specific industry related to the non-profit. The expectation is that each Board member will bring either a unique skill or perspective, or some marketing or public relations benefit, or some sizable donation either directly or through a business or foundation that member represents.

Small or medium sized non-profits will seldom turn down a Board member who is a skilled administrator, but they tend to be biased in favor of major donors. They seldom acquire a new Board member solely for public relations. For this reason, they sometimes have difficulty growing.

A hundred-year charity will generally deliberately draw Board members from as many different professions and social circles as are useful from a fundraising perspective, but new charities are limited to the social and business circles of their founders. Unless the Board is willing and able to move beyond the clique approach, it will eventually start drinking its own bathwater. At that point, it risks losing touch with the community it serves or with changing conditions in the outside economy or society.

To show how the different groups of people work together and are related to each other, here is a Venn diagram showing the structure of a hypothetical medium-sized charity we'll call "Imaginary Futures".

Figure 4: Typical Non-Profit Structure, "Imaginary Futures"

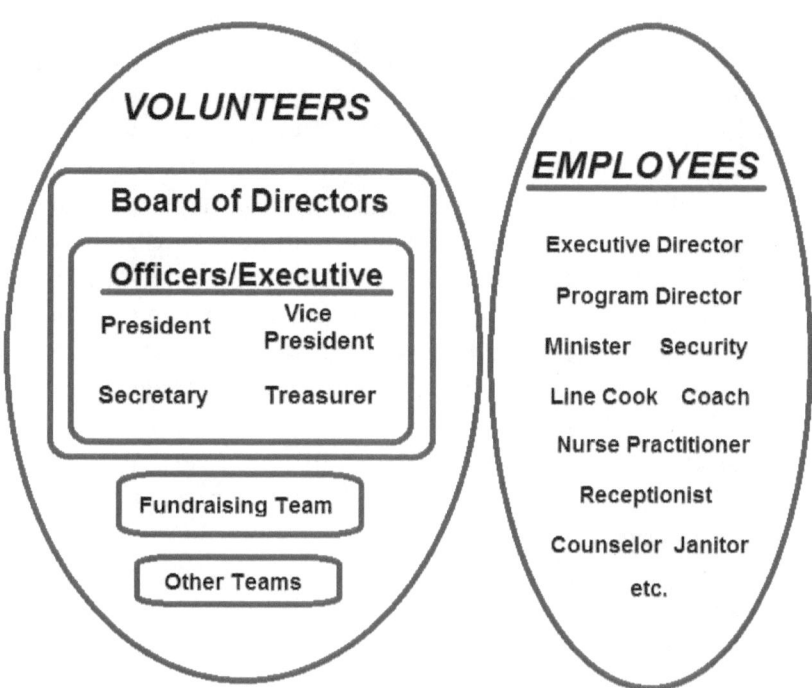

"Imaginary Futures", an imaginary charity, is an adult day care for people with physical and mental disabilities. It was spun off from a large, well established church that is still a major source of donations and volunteer labor. "Imaginary Futures" provides heavily subsidized services to working-class people who are too poor to afford private care, but too well off to qualify for government subsidies. It provides lunch and snacks every day for fifty adults, along with a structured environment featuring physical education, one-on-one occupational therapy, medical supervision, and group activities. Accordingly, it has about a dozen employees, a handful of whom are higher-functioning people with disabilities from the greater community.

Corporations, even charitable ones, retain characteristics that reflect their founders' priorities. Since "Imaginary Futures" was founded by members of a church, it includes an in-house ministry. But it is big enough to need independent fundraising that goes far beyond the church population. It also requires paid administration. The annual budget is about $1.2 million, which is quite low, but it is sustainable because most of the group leaders are volunteers.

Notice that the Volunteer and Employee circles *do not overlap*. This is a very important management principle that you must remember later. A sustainable nonprofit that has employees is able to *pay* these employees out of its operating budget. If for some reason the non-profit is having trouble making payroll, or if the employees are feeling pressured to help out in a volunteer capacity beyond their paid scope of work, it's generally a sign that the charity's program or administrative structure has expanded beyond its healthy and sustainable size. There are serious legal problems with using employees to perform volunteer work. The volunteer work must be totally unrelated to their regular jobs, performed outside business hours, and preferably in a different location from their usual workspace. Likewise, the volunteer work must not be identical to work done by any paid employee. Fixing a budget shortfall by asking people to work off the clock is illegal.

Note that the Board of Directors is all-volunteer, including some special Board members who are elected by the rest of the Board to perform specific tasks.

Note also that there is a box labeled "Other Teams" in the volunteer circle. These individuals may include cleaners, drivers, assistant receptionists who fill in while the regular one is on vacation, and other volunteers whose duties overlap those of paid employees. It is OK to have paid and unpaid workers.

Officers or Executive team

There are four people responsible for handling the day-to-day business of running "Imaginary Futures". The President, Vice President, Treasurer, and Secretary, known collectively as the "executive" or the "officers" of the non-profit, are elected by the Board of Directors. Like Board members, these officers are volunteers. In fact, these officers technically are Board members who are elected to their positions by their peers.

The officers of the non-profit are the people who have the authority to commit the company. They may sign checks, sign contracts, and make deals on the non-profit's behalf. But they answer to the rest of the Board.

The ***President or Chairperson of the Board*** can be considered the head of the Board of Directors. The title "President" is generally preferred, because "Chairperson" is a bit cumbersome to say, while "Chairman" is a very outdated, old-fashioned term that does not take into account the fact that the majority of charity administrators are female.

"Chair" is sometimes used as a shortened term that is also gender neutral, but some people find it too informal.

The President organizes meetings and comes up with ways to implement the strategy set out by the Board. He or she generally is generally the external face of the charity, and focuses on representing the charity when dealing with external organizations such as the press, legal authorities, or major donors. Often considered the "chief volunteer", the President should be seen at all fundraisers and should interact regularly with the volunteer pool.

The *Vice President* is focused on internal charity matters, such as organizing fundraisers and building the volunteer pool. He or she generally doesn't solicit donations as much as the President will, but will be more focused on the program itself.

For a small charity such as a mobile needle exchange, the Vice President will most likely be the person who buys a van, purchases needles in bulk, and signs up volunteers to drive around and swap. For a soup kitchen, the Vice President may hire a cook, sign a contract to rent a building, or put together an annual donation drive.

In the case of "Imaginary Futures", which is a medium-sized charity, the daily management duties are taken over by the Executive Director. So this Vice President focuses on fundraising, and on writing grants to cover occasional large purchases.

The *Treasurer* is considered, by some, to be more powerful than the Vice President, because it's the Treasurer who signs the checks and keeps track of the money. If the charity has income producing assets, the Treasurer keeps track of them. This individual needs bookkeeping skills, and is often a current or retired accountant.

The *Secretary* is responsible for making sure the decisions of the Board are recorded. Taking the minutes of every meeting and recording the results of votes can be critical later if there's a major change in the direction of the charity, or if something goes wrong. Many times, if the charity is the victim of fraud or embezzlement, it's the Secretary's notes that allow the wrongdoer to be caught and brought to justice.

The *Executive Director*, despite the name, is not a member of the Board of Directors. He or she is hired by the small charity's Board of Directors to perform some or all of the day-to-day administrative activities required by the charity. This might include volunteer training, hiring, or conducting a fundraising campaign. This is invariably a paid position. For many small charities, the Executive Director is the first and only person hired. In the case of "Imaginary Futures", the Executive

Director attends a portion of each Board meeting to deliver a report and also attends the annual meetings and most of the meetings of the executive team to keep everybody up to date with what is going on.

The **Program Director**, like the Executive Director, is an employee of the charity and not a member of the Board of Directors. He or she is responsible for the ongoing program activities. In the case of "Imaginary Futures", the Program Director is responsible for ensuring that the adult daycare facility runs properly and in compliance with the law.

Alternate Titles

The exact titles given to people who work for a not-for-profit company vary depending on how they are defined in the organization's Bylaws. Extremely large corporations, regardless of whether they are for-profit, generally follow the for-profit business model when it comes to describing their officers or employees. These titles are similar to the roles that exist in a publicly held for-profit corporation.

Generally, in a large charity, the *Chief Executive Officer (CEO)* does the same kind of work performed by the Executive Director of a smaller organization. Sometimes roles and titles are combined, and one person can be "President and CEO". This is the position of greatest authority.

The title *Chief Financial Officer (CFO)* applies to someone serving in the role of Treasurer. Some regard this position as the one with the most actual power.

Large non-profit corporations typically have multiple Vice Presidents, each of whom is in charge of a different region or a different activity. A major charity might have Vice Presidents for fundraising, marketing, program development, and even public relations.

Paid versus unpaid roles

Who gets paid, and how much they earn, becomes a matter of public record for any corporation that is not tax exempt, or for any tax exempt organization that earns more than $50,000 per year. For smaller charities, the people getting paid are far more likely to be contractors than employees, simply because there's less tax paperwork and fewer legal barriers should the charity wish to end the arrangement.

If your organization is large enough to consider having a paid employee or contractor, one of the wisest things you can do is to make sure your Bylaws spell out which positions are paid and which ones are not. You will almost always have more work than you can afford to pay for, and that means you'll always need volunteers. But it's best to separate paid workers from volunteers in terms of their job duties, hours, or location of service.

Suppose you run a food bank that provides emergency food hampers to needy people. You will need people to unpack and check donated food, to sort and store different kinds of food, to assemble food hampers, to deliver them if necessary, and to make sure the perishable food is stored at a safe temperature. You will need office workers to answer telephone or online applications from people who are applying for services. You will even need people to collect cash and in-kind donations, do the banking, solicit donations, pay the bills, train other workers, and advertise your food bank. Even with an outstanding executive team, that's a lot of labor.

Volunteers tend to be part-time as opposed to full-time, seasonal as opposed to year-round, and temporary as opposed to permanent. That's not to say that you'll never find a volunteer willing to put in a 40-hour work week for years on end. Every once in a while, you'll luck out and get someone who meets that description. Some are retired or financially independent; others are married to a primary household breadwinner but have no significant child or elder care responsibilities. Most volunteers aren't going to be able to put in a full eight-hour day every day because they have other things to do. If you need someone to be available for a full third of their waking hours, and if you need day-to-day continuity so that they can work on long-term projects, you're simply going to have to pay that person.

Most charitable ventures try to use volunteers for the repetitive work and fundraising, and paid specialists for the kind of work that requires advanced training or special licensure. This is an intelligent decision provided you always have enough volunteers to do the grunt work. For an imaginary food bank, you will most likely want to use volunteers for the food checking, food storing, and hamper assembly. It doesn't matter if John Doe stocks shelves one day and Mary Roe does it the next: you can train that person in an hour or less. So it doesn't matter if the work is done by five volunteers working one day per week, or ten volunteers working half a day each. Indeed, for simple tasks volunteers can be pretty fungible. It doesn't matter if John and Mary swap shifts, or if one covers for the other. That situation changes if Mary is the only one who knows all the health code rules about how meat should be stored.

Any activities that require long-term commitment or a higher level of trust or authority are better suited to paid employees than to volunteers.

Your banking, your bill paying, and any financial activities not done by the Treasurer are good activities to assign to a paid employee. Similarly, the person who trains the volunteers and who hands out job assignments is an authority figure.

Volunteers seldom object to receiving direction from a paid employee of the charity, or from a volunteer. The reverse is not true. Employees don't like being directed by volunteers, and volunteers get frustrated when they see somebody else being paid to do work they do for free.

If you've got two people with the same title, job description, or duties, you can get in serious trouble if you pay one but keep the other in a volunteer capacity. First, it violates the Fair Labor Standards Act. Second, the moment the volunteer needs money or is in any way dissatisfied, he or she can sue for back pay and overtime. Such suits are almost always successful, and if the volunteer has been putting in twenty hours a week for you for the last five years, you will suddenly owe that person a lot of money. You may also not replace paid employees with volunteers to do the same tasks.

Employees may volunteer, but only outside of their normal working hours doing work that differs substantially from their paid work. It is a violation of the Fair Labor Standards Act for any employee to volunteer in a capacity similar to his or her ordinary work.

Section II: Program And Fundraising Domains

Everything your charity does falls into one of three categories or charitable domains: program, fundraising, and administration. Every expense you have can be classified as belonging to one of these domains, and classifying expenses, activities, and personnel based on the domain in which they spend most of their time can be a useful exercise. This section contains only five chapters, but it discusses the first two domains.

Most people consider program activities to be the important part of charitable work, and it's certainly the most visible because it provides the purpose for which the charity exists. But it will receive only one chapter in this book. Why? Because it's relatively easy to design a fantastic program. Raising money for it is harder, and administering the charity so that it runs smoothly and sustainably is more difficult still. That's why the third charitable domain, administration, receives its own section.

Maxims and Equations In This Section

Equation 2: $\quad Total\ program\ costs = Fixed\ costs + Variable\ costs$

Equation 3: $\quad Variable\ costs = Per\ unit\ cost \times Units\ of\ service$

Equation 4: $\quad Per\ unit\ cost = \dfrac{Total\ program\ costs - Fixed\ costs}{Units\ of\ service}$

Equation 5: $\quad Profit = Income - Expenses$

Equation 6: $\quad Spending\ Limit = Total\ Operating\ Budget - Contingency$

Chapter 9: Program

There are three key charitable domains: program, fundraising, and administration. The next few chapters will explore the definitions, issues, and challenges associated with each domain. This particular chapter is devoted to the program, which is the specific product or service provided by your not-for-profit corporation.

By the end of this chapter, you will have the skills necessary to tell whether a non-profit has a clear collective vision or goal. You will have the skills to distinguish between program and non-program activities. You will know how to analyze a program's various costs, and you will be able to draw intelligent and informed conclusions about how well a non-profit's program operations match its stated goal. Using nothing more than basic arithmetic, you will even be able to quantitatively assess the effectiveness of your program. You will even be able to identify which operations give your non-profit the most "bang" for its buck, and which operations might be costing you more than they're worth, such that it might be worth considering other less costly ways to accomplish those particular activities. In short, you will be able to perform a full professional analysis of your non-profit's program strengths and weaknesses.

By the end of this chapter, you will also start to see some things that most other people can't. If the leaders of your non-profit cannot clearly spell out what their goal is in one sentence, or if you have a major discrepancy between your non-profit's stated goals and the way it actually spends its money and resources, the problem will pop right out at you. So will some solutions.

Definition of "program"

A non-profit's program consists of the goods and services it delivers to its recipients, and the particular way it makes the world a better place. Your program is your reason to exist. It's the stuff that you deliver to the community around you.

If you run a church, your program will most likely involve ministry. If you run a youth camp, your program is to provide camp services to a specific set of young people who would not otherwise receive them. If you run a wildlife protection charity, your program may purchase land to provide habitat or advertise to raise awareness about endangered species.

A non-profit company's program is the place where the rubber meets the road. You actually plant the baby trees or clean sludge up after an oil spill. You comfort a crying baby in the hospital, or you set an eagle's broken wing. Maybe you teach a child to read or discover a genetic marker that accurately predicts a dreaded disease. Perhaps you make quilts for cancer patients or build houses that will allow homeless families a safe place to live. Maybe you feed hungry people or restore eyesight to the blind. Perhaps you have a religious message that you are delivering to people who want desperately to receive it. Possibly you provide the means for collective bargaining to protect the rights of workers.

Overall, program activities are where the big drama is. If your program requires significant technical skill, the people who provide it will undoubtedly be dedicated and competent professionals. However, program activities are also the public face of your organization.

Blurt it out in one sentence or less

People in creative fields often talk about having an "elevator speech": a pitch that you can give to people in one minute or less, if you ever happen to be in the same elevator as a person who has the ability to hire you, produce a movie you wrote, or provide venture capital to develop your new invention. The non-profit field is simpler. When someone asks you what your group does, you had better not need to take an entire minute to say it.

It should always be possible to state what your organization does in one sentence. This is useful for recruiting volunteers, soliciting donations, and setting up your Articles of Incorporation. The Articles of Incorporation is one of your two key organizing documents (your Bylaws are the other). What sort of things should go into your organizing documents will be discussed more thoroughly in a later chapter.

If for some reason you, or more particularly your Board of Directors, cannot state your organization's reason for existing in one sentence, you have a serious problem. Either you all lack adult communication skills, or you disagree about why you exist. Yogi Berra once said that if you don't know where you're going, you're certain to get there. This is doubly true when people make decisions in groups.

An organization that cannot clearly articulate its goals often does not have a common vision as to what it should be doing, or how it should accomplish its goal. This leads to long, rambling discussions and kum-ba-yah sessions that go nowhere. While every group of people who work closely together should sometimes have a few such sessions, preferably under the influence of appropriate food and drink, eventually the team bonding has to be focused.

When discussing your program, either to set up a new non-profit or to accurately describe it to a prospective Board member or donor, it is vital to start with a general description. Always move from the general to the specific. Being able to summarize your organization's overall goal in one sentence is the first step.

The program statement

Your Articles of Incorporation must include a statement describing the purpose for which you are incorporating. The same sentence, or a slight variation of it, usually makes a pretty good mission statement as well. However, I prefer to think and speak of it as a "program statement" because it helps reinforce the idea that program activities are only one aspect of what a non-profit does.

The program statement, mission statement, or purpose sentence from your Articles of Incorporation describes your purpose overall. It is basically a "what" question, as in "what do you do?" Everything your organization does should support this goal, either directly or indirectly. So how do you justify your existence? Here are examples of some possible program statements.

- Our animal shelter provides food, shelter and medical care for abandoned cats and dogs.
- Our karate club provides low-cost martial arts instruction to low-income children and adults in the community.
- Our legal aid society provides free or low-cost legal advice to disabled people, elderly people, and low-income people in the community.
- Our high school sports booster club raises money to help pay for student athletic activities.

One of the best mission statements ever created was NASA's famous goal: "landing a man on the moon and returning him safely to the earth" before the end of the decade. The statement was part of the "Special Message to the Congress on Urgent National Needs" as delivered in person by President John F. Kennedy before a joint session of Congress on May 25, 1961. It was clear, precise, and easy to understand. So it caught not only Congress's attention but the imagination of the entire public. For a while, it appeared that everyone involved was clear as to how his or her activities contributed to that goal. There's a famous story about a conversation between President John F. Kennedy and a NASA janitor during a presidential tour of NASA in 1962. Supposedly the President asked the broom-toting janitor what he was doing, and the janitor replied: "Well, Mr. President, I'm helping to put a man on the moon."

The Board of Directors is the governing body of your non-profit corporation. Their duty is to control the overall direction of the charity. If they are unable to come up with a clear, one-sentence mission, the organization as a whole does not have a direction. You most likely have two or more groups of people with irreconcilable differences in opinion as to what your non-profit should be doing. Some of them may have an undisclosed conflict of interest. Others may be hung up on the mechanism by which they expect to achieve the goals. Stop what you're doing until you get a consensus everyone can live with.

If you lock the Board of Directors up for two or three hours, they can generally brainstorm a viable program statement. If they cannot, take note of whether there is a serious disagreement in the direction the charity ought to take. If you have only a handful of dissenters, you may be able to settle for a mission statement supported by the majority of the Board. However, notice who the dissenters are, and if you notice a pattern of opposition to even reasonable and sustainable decisions, you may ask for their resignations or you may call a meeting of the Board to vote them out.

If you cannot reach a quorum without the dissenters present, your group is having an identity crisis and is very likely to split no matter what you do. If you are a member of the Board yourself and you see that the group is incapable of arriving at a consensus, consider leaving and joining an organization that has a clearer view of where it needs to go.

Having a program statement is vital, because it allows you to easily determine which activities are necessary to your program and which are not. Every year at budget time, you will be better able to classify goals and expenses as "needs", "wants", or "nice-to-haves" if you know what the program mission is. You will also be better able to accomplish the goals of your program if you are clear about which activities are actually part of the program statement and which are not.

List of program operations

Within the overarching umbrella you now have described as "program", you should also be able to point to several specific programs or initiatives that your non-profit venture does to advance your overall goal. If your overall goal as described in the mission statement is the "what", you must also be able to direct your attention to a "how".

The difference between "what you do" and "how you do it" can be subtle, but it's important. Sometimes there's more than one path up the mountain: more than one way to reach a particular goal. In engineering, the "what" might be a list of product and interface requirements, and the "how" is a detailed design. In transportation, the "what" might be a list of destination cities and the "how" is a detailed description of your airline routes showing which plane flies where, on what date and time.

You cannot make intelligent progress on a list of program operations without a program statement. But once you have your program statement, you are ready to create a list of key activities your group performs, or wants to perform, in order to accomplish its program goal.

I find it easy to begin by repeating the mission or program statement, adding the word "by", and listing the specific activities undertaken in the support of that program. For example, consider the imaginary animal shelter with the program statement described earlier in this chapter. The Board of Directors has determined that it provides food, shelter and medical care for abandoned cats and dogs by:

- Renting out and maintaining a free-standing building containing 175 cages of various sizes, appropriate for housing cats and dogs
- Maintaining facilities appropriate for outpatient animal surgery
- Making animal beds out of donated material
- Storing donated pet food and distributing it to the animals every day
- Providing trained volunteers to feed, bathe, and interact with each animal every day, and to clean cages
- Providing a facilitator to conduct the animal adoption process, and

- Providing a veterinarian and assistant to perform medical care, including shots and sterilization, for all the animals brought in

Now you can clearly see seven separate areas of importance related to this particular charity. Other non-profit ventures may have more points, or fewer, depending on what their program is intended to accomplish. You can also see some of the details about how the charity goes about accomplishing its purpose. For example, this particular animal shelter happens to provide in-house veterinary care and even surgery as opposed to taking the animals to a vet as outpatients. It maintains in-house lodging for the animals instead of distributing them among, say, volunteer foster homes. Different animal service charities make different program choices.

Your list of program operations should deal only with the services you provide to the community you serve. It shouldn't include anything related to raising money, balancing the books, advertising, or running the company.

Make sure to ensure every single activity your non-profit does that causes it to provide a service to its target market. Suppose the animal shelter were to provide basic obedience training to all the dogs that came in, to improve their odds of being adopted by somebody in the community. That activity should be on the list of program operations, even if it doesn't relate directly to the program statement.

As you read through the above list of activities, perhaps you will notice that our hypothetical animal shelter has a few program activities that don't directly relate to its program statement. This occurs naturally in non-profits that have been around a while, but if the activity consumes more than a trivial portion of the resources, then either the program statement needs to be updated or the charity has allowed itself to deviate from its primary mission.

It's actually all right to change your program radically provided you communicate fully with the Internal Revenue Service about the reason for your change in direction and purpose. Making a major change of course, such as by changing from a medical research charity into a tax return service, can sometimes result in the revocation of your tax exempt status. However, if it is a simple matter of adjusting the beneficiaries of your charity from one charitable class to another simply because the dread disease you set out to cure has been cured, you will not get much resistance. The March of Dimes, for example, started out as the National Foundation for Infantile Paralysis, with the goal of eradicating polio in children. It succeeded so well that it needed a new goal. Now, its mission is to prevent birth defects and infant mortality. This change, however was not an accident and it occurred as a result of deliberate management decisions. It was not an example of program drift.

Program drift

Program drift occurs when what you actually do deviates substantially from what you're supposed to be doing. When I consult for a charity that's in trouble, one of the first things I do is to make them categorize their budget line items based on whether they belong to program, administrative, or fundraising activities. Then I march through the "program" items and compare them with the program statement.

I once read the mission statement of a charity that said it provided year-long structured mentoring programs for at-risk teens. Yet despite constant fundraising, they were chronically broke. It turned out that the majority of their annual budget was spent to hire public speakers to provide an intensive offsite course lasting three to five days at the start of the year-long program. These professional speakers were not listed in the program statement, yet the vast majority of the charity's income was being spent on their speaking fees even though the volunteer pool was exhausted from the constant fundraising. So the Board sat down and wrote a new mission statement that also failed to mention the professional speakers. Accordingly, guess what was first on my list of things to cut?

Grouping assets by program operation

Now that you have your list of program operations, you can start to list equipment, assets, and personnel related to each operation. Every operation in your Program Operations list now becomes a category.

Make an asset list for each program operation. The animal charity, for example, would have lists for its housing program, its surgical program, and perhaps others. The housing program list would include the cages, food dishes, food, and everything the animals use on a day-to-day basis. It would also include the portion of the building, and the portion of the utilities needed to heat, light, and clean the animal housing space.

There will most likely be some assets that are shared. Split them up by percentage. For example, in the imaginary animal shelter described above, suppose one building houses the animals and the veterinary facilities, and has both office space and a reception area where people can meet animals for adoption or drop them off. Just divide up the building based on square footage, and assign a percentage to each program operation that requires a portion of the asset. These percentages will most likely not add up to 100%, because administrative office space and fundraising resources are not included in program related calculations.

Human labor belongs on these asset lists (just not necessarily on the balance sheet of your official annual report). In a small non-profit it's common for one person to wear many hats, but there's a specific amount of work per week that goes into running the program. You will generally be able to break this down into hours of labor, or fractions of a full-time worker.

Do not differentiate between paid or unpaid workers at this point of the exercise. Even if your program operation clearly says "volunteer" because that's how you happen to accomplish your program operation at the moment, set aside how you pay for the labor and focus simply on how much work is needed, what type of work is required, and whether it has to be done by a specialist or professional of some kind. After all, the animal shelter's veterinarian is perfectly capable of cleaning cages in a pinch, and can probably be trained to process animal adoption paperwork, but the receptionist would need a veterinary license and years of education before he or she would be qualified to spay or neuter a cat or dog.

Estimating true costs for program operations

This is the second-to-last step in quantifying the value of your program. It's time to make a series of tables, one for each program operation asset list. This can be done by hand, but spreadsheet software makes the process faster, neater, and easier to distribute.

For each operation asset list, make a table with five columns. The columns, in order, will be:

1. Item: the name of the asset or resource (example: 15% of the building)
2. Replacement Cost: The total replacement cost, in dollars, if you had to buy the asset or percentage of the asset described in column 1. For personnel, this figure will be zero, because this column is strictly for material assets that can be bought or sold
3. In-Kind: The dollar value of the portion of the column 2 figure that was provided by in-kind donation. Again, for labor related assets this cost is zero

150

4. Annual Cost: The annual expense associated with maintaining this asset. Include debt service related to the asset or portion of the asset described in column 1. For labor, include the total you would spend every year if you were hiring a part-time employee contractor to do the work. On an hourly rate, this will be more than minimum wage because it must include the income taxes, training expenses, and other overhead. For items that are purchased once and that do not need to be refreshed or maintained, this cost is zero. But for items like vehicles that need maintenance, registration, and other expenses, there must be a number in this column

5. Volunteer: The dollar value of the portion of the column 4 figure that is provided through volunteer labor instead of through an employee or contractor. Clearly, for paid labor or purchased items, this value will always be zero.

When all your table entries are complete for a program operations asset list, add up the values in columns 2 through 5, and they will reveal the true cost of the program operation. Here is an example of what the table for our imaginary animal shelter might look like:

Table 2: Program Operation Cost, Animal Shelter Feeding

Item	Replacement Cost	In-Kind	Annual Cost	Volunteer
Rent, 5% of space	$0	$750 (5% of $15,000 rent/yr)	$750 (5% of $15,000 rent/yr)	$0
Utilities 5% of total	$0	$0	$240 (5% of $400/mo)	$0
Food, 175 animals	$1,000 food on hand	$21,000 per year + $1,000	$21,000 ($120 per animal)	$0
Labor	$0	$0	$29,200 ($20/hr, 4 hr/day)	$29,200
Total	$1,000	$22,750	$51,990	$29,200

The above table shows that 5% of the space is used for the animal shelter's food related activities: just what is used to store, prepare, and clean up. Compared to the amount of space needed for a veterinary clinic and the animal cages, food storage space is almost trivial. But it is necessary to the program. If the animals were housed somewhere else, or if for some reason the feeding program was moved offsite, this is the amount of space that would need to be replaced in order for this particular program operation to continue. Animals have to eat.

If the feeding operation had to be replaced or rebuilt from scratch, such as after a fire, it would cost a thousand dollars to replace the food currently on hand. Over the course of a year, the operation consumes nearly a thousand dollars a week to run. The annual costs are also impressive, requiring half of a full-time employee for labor and a great deal of cat and dog food. But notice that the labor comes exclusively from volunteers, and all the food is being donated. So, it appears, is the storage space. In fact, the only out-of-pocket expenses, at present, are related to the utility payment. So although the program consumes a lot of resources, it has a very small impact on the shelter's cash flow.

If your non-profit operates at more than one site, it is very useful to perform similar calculations for each location or building.

Comparative analysis

If you fill in the tables for each of your program operations, you will be able to compare the costs for each. This will tell you exactly where your money, donations, and volunteer labor is going, at least with regard to program activities.

Column 2 with its replacement costs contains information that be partially gleaned from your annual report, or that can be re-used for your annual report if this is your first year in business. These figures will reappear in the "asset" portion of your balance sheet, where you list all the assets and liabilities for the entire company, however the balance sheet contains the value of an entire asset and gives no indication as to how it is being used.

Comparing columns 2 and 3 will show what portion of your assets that have come from in-kind donation. This is vital information, because it helps you understand what kind of non-profit you are, and what portion of your operating expenses come from in-kind donation as opposed to donations of money or things that can be turned into money.

Most small charities grossly underestimate how heavily they rely on in-kind donations such as loaned space. This leads to the people who donate space or resources being undervalued or not properly acknowledged, and so when the donors inevitably lose interest or find a higher-priority use for their resources, the charity is in trouble. So, treat your in-kind donors the same way you would treat people who write checks. If you are not issuing receipts for in-kind donations, you need to start.

Column 4 shows the total amount of labor consumed by a specific program operation, and column 5 shows how much of the work is being done by volunteers. This process can reveal whether your non-profit has any volunteers who are critical to the operation.

Keeping track of how many volunteer hours are worked and how much each person is doing will help you understand whether or not the amount of work you're requiring of each volunteer is sustainable. The chapter on volunteer management will discuss how to do this.

You now have an intelligent way to start tracking your resource flow. This is slightly different from cash flow, since it involves things besides money. It may help to think of your non-profit's program operations as several different channels into which you put resources every year.

Units of service

Each time your program serves somebody, you can count one unit of service. If your charity delivers three scholarships per year, you have three units of service. If you house a thousand homeless animals per year, you have a thousand units of service.

Fixed and variable costs

You will notice that some of the costs associated with running your program remain constant regardless of the number of people or animals you serve. The rent for an animal shelter doesn't depend on how many animals are inside. The rent for a commercial kitchen doesn't depend on how many meals are prepared there. If you have a full-time employee, you pay him or her the same regardless of whether he or she is providing counseling to one person per day or to eight.

Variable costs increase with the number of people you serve. If you run a meal delivery service for shut-in veterans, there's a relationship between the number of meals you serve and the cost to provide them.

Equation 2

Total program costs = Fixed costs + Variable costs

Each meal has a per-unit cost. That's what it costs to provide one more unit of service (assuming you're not already operating at full capacity, such that you'd have to get an additional building).

Your variable costs are the sum of all your per-unit costs. You can calculate them like this, if you know how many units of service you achieved.

Equation 3

$$Variable\ costs = Per\ unit\ cost \times Units\ of\ service$$

So, if you know how many people your program serves and how much it costs to serve each you know your variable costs. Similarly, if you know how many people you served and how much you spent on the fixed cost part of your program, you can figure out your per unit cost. As long as you have at least two out of three of the costs you need, you can use basic algebra to get the third.

Starting from the total program cost, you can calculate per unit cost this way.

Equation 4

$$Per\ unit\ cost = \frac{Total\ program\ costs - Fixed\ costs}{Units\ of\ service}$$

Your per unit cost is a very important way to measure your charity's effectiveness. It won't always be the same from one year to the next, because sometimes you'll buy things in bulk, have goods or products left over, or have to throw things away. Then you will know how much it costs to provide each unit of service. Add in your fixed costs, and that's your total program cost.

The lower your fixed costs are compared to your variable costs, the more flexible your program is.

White elephants

The analysis described in this chapter reveal whether there are program operations that are costing a disproportionate amount of money, volunteer time, or other resources.

As described in Chapter 5, a "white elephant" is something that's more trouble than it's worth, but almost impossible to get rid of. There are a lot of white elephants in the non-profit world, because people get emotionally attached to their pet projects and the various special activities set up to accomplish the program.

Earlier in this chapter, I described a mentoring charity that spent a disproportionate amount of its money on paid speakers. In that particular case, the paid speakers were a white elephant. There was a clique of them who specialized in putting together the kind of presentation or kick-off course required by the mentoring charity. For a variety of reasons, the Board of Directors and the executive team had used the speakers so long that they were unwilling to consider conducting a mentoring program in any other way. They were so anxious to pay the professional speakers that they were willing to go into debt, destroy their volunteer base with ceaseless fundraising, engage in deficit spending, and ultimately sign a contract with a Pied Piper who purported to be able to teach them how to make their fundraising more effective, but who instead cost them their credibility.

Having a labor-intensive or material-intensive program is not dangerous, so long as you understand the extent to which your program relies on that resource. If you have, for example, a very volunteer-heavy program, your volunteers are your most important resource. You must therefore make sure to train them, appreciate them, and manage their workload so that they do not burn out.

If your organization is having trouble retaining volunteers or is developing cash flow problems, the kind of analysis described in this chapter will show you which program activities are out of control. You don't necessarily have to cancel them, but they must become a candidate for cutbacks or restructuring.

If it wasn't for the in-kind donations and the volunteer work, the animal feeding problem at our imaginary animal shelter would be very expensive to run. Deciding to not feed the animals simply isn't an option: if they aren't fed, they die. Luckily, the management of our imaginary animal shelter has already found a way to get free food, space, and labor. So there are almost no out-of-pocket expenses. If the animal food being provided is of a reasonable quality and obtained through legal, sustainable means (nobody is chopping up corpses and using them for kibble *Little Shop of Horrors* style), then this particular aspect of the program is healthy and well run. There's no room to cut costs to address cash flow problems elsewhere in the organization, should they exist.

If you have a program operation that is costing more than your company can afford, it is very practical to start by comparing the operation to your company's mission statement. If there is a gap, it's reasonable to ask why the program operation exists, whether it should continue at all, or whether the goal can be accomplished more cheaply.

Tailoring your dreams to suit what you've got

Given infinite money and resources, most of us could pull off some pretty impressive results. But, in the real world, we have limited time, personnel, and money.

The hardest part of program management is delivering reasonable services with the resources you've actually got, and resisting the temptation to expand. One common mistake is to commit to an ambitious program without having the resources to make it happen. While it makes for watchable made-for-TV movies, most of those movies are "based on" real stories, and there's been a lot of dramatic license taken to present the hero as an underdog. In reality a program that is not well supported by funding burns people out and frequently also fails to deliver the promised level of program quality.

Chapter 10: Types of Fundraising

Fundraising is the second of the three key charitable domains. The other two are program and administration.

This chapter will define fundraising and identify two different ways to classify fundraising techniques. It will introduce the concept of sustainability as it pertains to raising money. By the end of this chapter, you will be able to look at a fundraising technique and determine whether it is labor based or social capital based, and you will be able to identify whether or not the labor or social capital is being drawn from your organization, or from your people.

Definitions of fundraising

Most people define fundraising as the process by which people collect money for some purpose. After years of doing it, I no longer see it that way. I define fundraising as the process by which the people who care about a charity monetize either their labor or some form of social capital for the charity's benefit.

Nobody ever simply collects money. As one of your parents no doubt told you, money doesn't grow on trees. It isn't just lying around waiting to be picked up by some deserving person or non-profit venture.

The only way to get money legally is to get somebody else to give it to you voluntarily. You can do this either by convincing that person to trade it for something of equal or greater value, or by convincing the person to accept something of lesser value, or even no value at all, in exchange.

Donors

Your *donor pool* is the set of people who have given to your non-profit before. For a small non-profit, the donor pool generally consists of your Board members, your volunteers and employees, and people in their respective social networks. A national or global non-profit draws donations from people the Board has never met.

Your donor pool may overlap the set of people who have benefited from your non-profit in the past, or who expect to do so in the future. If you represent a church, for example, your strongest and most reliable donor pool will be the congregation.

Your donor pool may contain people who have previously benefited from your non-profit, who have since come into money or resources, and who are turning around to give back to you so that you can continue your good work. That's how many medical charities or universities come by their donations.

The largest charities that operate at the national or international level, or that have a large presence within your state due to massive advertising and corporate penetration, have donor pools that contain people who have never had any direct contact with the charity except to donate. Consider, for example, the Salvation Army bell ringers at every store entrance throughout the Christmas holidays. Most of us have dropped money in the box at least a few times or perhaps browsed their rummage sales, but how many of us have ever received services from them?

Volunteers

Your *volunteer pool* is the set of people who work on your behalf, without pay. Not all of your volunteers participate in fundraising. Many people would rather work as part of the program, interacting directly with the baby trees or stocking shelves at a food bank. In fact, many people hate fundraising because they do not have a "sales" personality and are not comfortable asking other people for money or resources. There's more to fundraising than solicitation, of course: a well planned and executed labor based fundraiser can be very effective but requires almost no solicitation at all.

Whereas donors provide money or gifts in kind, volunteers provide labor. Some work to execute your program, some are administrators, and some are willing and able to raise money.

If you have volunteers who are willing to do fundraising, treat them as if they were made of gold, especially if they are effective at soliciting donations or sponsorship. These are the rainmakers upon whom your entire operation depends. Without the money they bring in, you have no program.

The great thing about a volunteer who's willing to do fundraising is that they ask nothing for themselves in exchange. Your return on investment, therefore, is infinite. Your non-profit needs as many of this kind of person as you can attract and keep.

The majority of your volunteers will be casual: These individuals show up once or twice, and then lose interest. They do not have an ongoing commitment to your organization.

Two dimensions of fundraising

Every fundraising technique in the world falls into one of four categories. The categories depend on two dimensions.

The first dimension deals with what you're monetizing: labor, or social capital. Exactly where is the labor or social capital coming from: the corporation itself, or the individuals connected to it?

If you're trading labor or social capital that belongs to the corporation, such as by selling things made by employee labor or using the company name to solicit donations through a telethon, you have a Type I or Type II fundraiser. If you are asking the volunteers and Board to provide their own labor or to solicit money or sales from people in their personal network so as to monetize *their own* social capital, you have a Type III or Type IV fundraiser.

Table 3: Four kinds of fundraising

	Labor	Social Capital
From The Corporation	Type I	Type II
From Your Volunteers and Board	Type III	Type IV

Examples of a Type I fundraiser include professional event ticket sales, merchandise sales, side business revenue, fees for services such as weddings, or public events. If you're a professional ballet company, selling tickets to the public for your annual production of the Nutcracker is a Type I activity.

Examples of a Type II fundraiser include solicitations such as mail or E-mail campaigns, telethons, social media campaigns, grant proposals, and solicitations of corporate donations.

Type III fundraisers require your volunteers and Board to perform labor in exchange for money. Public vending such as bake sales, amateur

159

ticket event sales, door to door vending, car washes, and stadium cleanup fall into this category.

Type IV fundraisers require the participants to draw social capital from their personal networks, for the charity's benefit. Examples include events I affectionately call "thing-a-thons" where people perform a repetitive act in exchange for money from their sponsors. Other examples are sales of somewhat overpriced products such as chocolate, wrapping paper, and other things to one's friends.

The sole factor that determines whether a fundraising venture is labor based or social capital based is whether or not the person or organization giving you money expects something of like value in return. If they do, the fundraiser is labor based.

Resource source

In the above table, Type I and Type II fundraisers rely heavily on assets that already belong to your non-profit, or that are already being budgeted for and paid for. While there may be a fair bit of volunteer labor related to a side business or professional event, most of the up-front costs have already been paid.

Type I and Type II fundraisers are usually only practical when your non-profit organization is already big enough to employ people full-time for purposes besides program activities. You must own or control real estate, have access to online donation utilities, and have the ability to plan and execute large-scale operations such as a professional performance or a public event like a fun run. The amount of dedicated attention required is beyond the scope of most small, regional charities. It requires multi-year commitment and a program impressive enough to attract the respect of complete strangers. The adage "it takes money to make money" applies to Type I and Type II fundraising.

Smaller charities are usually limited to the abilities and resources of the people directly involved with them. These are the Type III and Type IV fundraising activities. On a per-person-hour basis, they are less lucrative than Type I or Type II activities, however the work can often be done by children, teens, and less experienced people. The fundraisers that rely on social capital are far easier to organize, plan, and execute. They are suitable for casual volunteers.

Labor versus social capital based fundraising

In the above table, Type I and Type III fundraising strategies are labor based. They require that somebody's labor, or the result of someone's labor, is sold to the public. Type II and Type IV strategies

160

depend on social capital. The organization and/or its people are trading on their reputation in order to collect donations.

Classifying a fundraising activity

It's really easy to determine which quadrant a fundraising activity occupies. Simply ask yourself two questions.

Question #1: Does the majority of the income from this activity come from the Board members and their personal friends and family?

If the answer to this question is "no", then it is a Type I or Type II fundraiser. It relies on the charity's reputation and resources.

If the answer is "yes" then it is a Type III or Type IV fundraiser. It relies primarily on the reputation and resources of the individuals who support the charity.

Question #2: Does the person giving money get something of equal or greater value in exchange?

If the answer is "yes" then it is a Type I or Type III fundraiser. It relies on somebody's labor, either to produce or distribute product or to provide a service.

If the answer is "no" then it is a Type II or Type IV fundraiser. It relies on social capital of some kind, because people are donating or giving instead of engaging in a self-interested transaction.

Type I fundraising

Type I activities are not spur-of-the-moment. They either operate year-round, or they are complex events that require months or even years of planning. There is a heavy reliance on paid or professional labor, and the events draw money in from the general public.

Here are some detailed examples of Type I fundraising:

- A symphony orchestra sells tickets to a concert. The conductor and musicians are paid professionals, as are the sound and lighting technicians. Ushers and concessionaires might be paid or volunteer, and ticket sales are done chiefly online or through a contractor
- A homeless shelter uses part of a building it owns to run a consignment store for clothing and furniture. Three people are employed full-time and the rest of the staff is volunteer

- A zoo hosts an annual half-marathon to raise money for its operating activities. Each event takes about a year of planning but produces nearly a million dollars in profit
- A museum runs an onsite gift and souvenir shop
- The same museum charges a token admission fee
- A church has a building that contains classrooms, a small hall, and other facilities that are not in regular use except for once or twice a week. This space is rented out when not in use
- A church that owns a beautiful or historical chapel finds that non-parishioners want to get married there. Although they do not solemnize the marriage, for a fee they make the location available to others who bring their own minister

Type I activities are potentially lucrative because they attract the attention of people who don't see their activity as "giving" or contributing to the charity. They are getting something in exchange for their money that is worth more than what they are paying. Although this commercial exchange is not enough to fund the entire operation—even the most prominent opera and dance troupes rely on corporate and individual donors—it makes enough of a difference to make the operation viable.

When someone gives you money for a Type I activity, they expect good value for the dollar. If they are paying for a ballet or opera ticket, they expect a few hours of quality live entertainment. When they sign up for a charity marathon, they expect to compete in a high quality athletic event. If they go to the zoo or the museum, they expect to receive knowledge or entertainment in exchange for their entrance fee. At a secondhand store, people expect to buy used books, movies, or clothing for a fraction of what they are worth new.

Note that none of these activities can be set up on short notice. A consignment store requires a building. A charity marathon requires significant advertising and also the acquisition of permits. There are also big advertising expenses.

Type II fundraising

Type II fundraising relies on sophisticated knowledge, extremely good communication skills, and the ability to market the non-profit based on its track record. In Type II fundraising, you solicit the public, corporations, other charities, and sometimes even government. But you do it in a way that relies solely on the reputation of the organization. In other words, you don't make your volunteers hit up their friends or family in a personal capacity.

Here are some detailed examples of Type II fundraising:

- A medical research charity conducts an annual ad and solicitation campaign. This involves several weeks of billboard, radio, and TV advertising followed by two weeks of door to door solicitation
- A children's charity or public TV network conducts an annual telethon
- A charity's social media campaign goes viral and results in millions of dollars of donations
- A school makes use of a corporate grant to provide new sports equipment for its athletics department
- A community theatre conducts an annual mail campaign
- The regional United Way conducts an annual pledge drive in which thousands of corporate participants solicit pledges from their employees

Unlike Type I activities, Type II activities don't involve people or organizations getting anything in exchange for the money or resources they donate. Because donors are voluntarily accepting something of lesser value (or no value at all) in exchange for their money, Type II activities are classified as social capital based.

Like Type I activities, Type II activities require special skills and long-term effort from the people who engage in them. There is a relationship between the size of the program, the geographical area affected by the program, and the population and geographical area in which the charity has social capital.

Like all social capital fundraising initiatives, Type II activities are effective only in communities where the charity has actual social capital. A zoo in Topeka cannot effectively raise money in Chicago.

Type III fundraising

Type III fundraising is the most sustainable type of moneymaking activity available to small charities. When you get a group of volunteers together to wash cars, bake and sell cupcakes, or clean up a stadium, you're doing labor based fundraising. In exchange for a volunteer's labor, somebody who wants the results of that labor gives you money. It's good old-fashioned capitalism, except that the labor you're selling has been donated to you.

The only upper limit to the amount of labor based fundraising you can do is the number of qualified people available and the number of hours they can commit. If you have an extremely large group of people who want to work, you need not overwork anybody.

Although it's possible to saturate your local community with respect to a specific kind of labor—there's only so many times a park or stadium needs to be cleaned—there's no reason you can't have a field cleanup, a bake sale, a car wash, and a fun run open to the public if you're so inclined. You can re-use some of the same people if they'd like to try something different, and you will continue to get good results as long as you aren't asking anybody for more than they're comfortable giving. Indeed, a donation based car wash often nets more than a car wash with a listed price, because people give of their own initiative.

The only limiting factor associated with Type III fundraising is how much volunteer labor you have available. Work people too hard and too often, and they become tired and burned out. But a person with time available can do several Type III fundraisers every year and not feel overburdened.

Car washes and bake sales

A car wash fundraiser is simple and informal: you get some soap, some water, a friendly business owner who is willing to let you use the hose, and you converts the labor of a bunch of volunteers into a soapy, sudsy day. The best way to get money is to have a donation based car wash instead of posting a specific price. There's no active soliciting involved, because people who want to get their cars washed stop and respond to the signs. Everyone else drives right on by. It takes about a dozen people to do all the sign holding, money collecting, and washing. But if your location is good, it's possible to bring in up to three times the local minimum wage on a per-person, per-hour basis.

For a bake sale, volunteers bake confections and sell them to the public. The sales are usually single-serving and the profit margins are high for cupcakes that can be made with cheap ingredients like cake mix and store brand frosting. Avoid homemade items like banana bread or pumpkin loaf. There are fewer marketable slices per loaf, and because of all the expensive ingredients the profit margin is tiny. Most of the labor goes into the baking and cooking, but if three people bake two batches of cupcakes each and most of them sell, it's possible to bring in roughly one to two times the local minimum wage on a per-person, per-hour basis.

For car washes and bake sales, location is everything.

Cleanup and other contractor style fundraising

If your volunteers are willing to perform occasional physical labor or concession sales, consider contractor style fundraising.

University or commercial stadiums need to be cleaned after every home game, and frequently they need concession support, but the stadium can't afford to hire regular staff. Sometimes, instead of subcontracting to a cleaning company, they are willing to subcontract to one or more charities.

If you find a stadium, park, or commercial property that requires cleaning and that hires charities, you can often get the work. There's generally an application or negotiation process to go through, and you usually don't control the dates on which you're asked to clean.

Be creative. If you're able to mobilize a small group of people regularly and aren't afraid to use a Squeegee, you may be able to sell window washing services to businesses that have large storefronts. Since you're not worried about paying employees a fair wage (they're all volunteers), and since income tax and sales tax don't apply to you, it should be easy to price your services competitively. You most likely won't be able to serve a huge number of clients, but if you and a few friends are willing to spend one Saturday morning a month washing windows, it may be worthwhile.

Consider marketing your services to property owners. Call up some commercial property owners and offer to clean up the weeds in their light industrial park. Call up a local apartment complex and offer an apartment turning service for when someone moves out and leaves the place a mess. They can afford to pay you out of the departing tenant's damage deposit.

Unlike most concession work, which requires adults, cleanup work can be done by children or teens with minimal adult supervision. If your charity is a school booster club or any other organization that serves kids, you have an opportunity to involve the beneficiaries of the charity in part of the fundraising that helps them. It's also a great idea to expose kids and teenagers to the joys of manual labor.

Door to door service

Consider getting a group of people together and going door to door in a middle-class neighborhood, ringing bells and offering outdoor work to the homeowners. Raking leaves and trimming hedges are an option if you have a way to get rid of the waste. If you live in an area that gets winter snow, consider some opportunistic shoveling.

One of the best returns on your time and effort would be to buy some large stencils and a couple cans of reflective spray paint. Offer to stencil the house number on the curb in black and reflective silver paint, so that emergency responders and guests can more easily see the house number. It takes perhaps five minutes to close each sale and do the painting, and the service is usually worth at least $20 per house.

If you send people door-to-door, make sure you provide them with some kind of evidence that they're really there on behalf of your charity. Badges, credentials, letters, and other means of identification help reassure their customers that they aren't being scammed. That goes double if you are soliciting donations instead of offering services for pay.

Side businesses

Any side business in which your non-profit sells products or services is a labor based fundraising tool. A used book store or a volunteer with a knack for online sales are both capable of converting donated material into money. The same goes for bottle drives in parts of the country where deposits are collected on bottles or cans.

Successful side businesses have included tailoring and alteration services, craft sales, and even child care. Naturally, all businesses must be appropriately licensed depending on the kind of business being done.

Money earned through a side business is tax exempt as long as the side business does not compete with specific for-profit business (such as by selling commercial-type insurance). Also, the side business must never expand to the point where it becomes your primary focus and consumes the majority of your non-profit's time and resources. Specific activities that are never tax exempt, such as gambling, cannot be magically made tax exempt by being done in a charity's side business.

Sustainability of labor based fundraising

Labor based fundraising is the most sustainable way to use a volunteer pool. Unlike fundraising that relies on donations from people already connected to the charity or people in their social network, labor based fundraising allows you to sell products or services to people you have never met.

Revenue expectations

On a per-hour basis, the return on your volunteers' time investment will be bigger if you have a large annual event than if you have several tiny events. A large organization such as a zoo, a major animal shelter, or a symphony orchestra generally has only one major fundraiser per year, but the volunteers and employees who set it up spend months planning it and working toward it. It will generally be an athletic event such as a fun run or walk, it will require literally hundreds of volunteers, and the level of planning is big enough to require full-time employees.

Type IV fundraising

Every time you ask someone to give money to your charity without offering something of like value in exchange, you are monetizing social capital. This also applies to situations where you're selling something for far more than its market value.

You can generally solicit a group of people once per year. Any more, and you start to have diminishing returns.

Thing-a-thons

I've coined the term "thing-a-thon" to describe any fundraiser where the participants solicit pledges or per-unit donations while they jump rope, spell difficult words, run or skate laps, hit golf balls, or perform some other repetitive activity to raise money for a charitable venture. The idea is that their sponsors pay them only for the work they complete. So, prior to the day of the thing-a-thon, participants scurry around asking their friends, family members, and other people in their social network to sponsor them.

Thing-a-thons are the essence of social capital based fundraising. Sponsors receive nothing—not even advertising—in exchange for their donations. They donate simply because they care about the masochist who is offering to hit a thousand baseballs, skate a hundred laps, or perform some other painful but unnecessary activity to benefit the charity.

In the days of old, sponsorship promises used to be collected with pen and paper. This is still an option, but there are usually also electronic and online options that make it easier for people to participate even at a distance. The process and principles are the same as always: the people who care about the person doing the jumping, running, or other activity are rewarding him or her for devotion to the cause, and registering their approval financially.

Special events

A special event fund-raiser is any activity people pay to attend so that the school or charity can earn or keep a portion of the ticket price.

Smaller charities and non-profits host special event fundraisers at local restaurants, arcades, or other businesses that depend on a high volume of customers. A predetermined percentage of the sales that occur during that event are turned over to your school of charity.

This kind of fundraising event is only useful if you already need an excuse to get together in a restaurant, and if the vast majority of people involved with the charity are interested in doing so. Making a fund-raiser out of your annual banquet is a valid idea, as long as you don't get the idea that you're rewarding the volunteers somehow.

Non-profits with a high profile, such as political organizations or charities that already have lots of celebrities and wealthy donors, often host "gala" events. These are upscale evening celebrations resembling receptions. A catered meal is served, generally with alcoholic beverages because people are more generous when they're liquored up. Live entertainment is provided, and dress is semi-formal or even formal. Various honored guests and dignitaries are introduced, and there is sometimes dancing or a silent auction. There is also a discreet means by which the attendees may drop off a check or swipe a card.

For people who attend charity galas, the entire point of doing so is to make social and business contacts. People want to rub shoulders with folks who can advance their business or social interests. Nobody goes to this sort of thing to socialize with friends. They already get to hang out with their friends whenever they want to. Very few people think charity galas are fun, unless they are new money social strivers or people who enjoy fawning over politicians and other celebrities or unless they have an emotional attachment to the cause. Many people show up only out of a sense of duty. At any given charity gala, several of the guests will be in actual emotional pain from being around so many pretentious people.

People attend special events because they support the non-profit and want to be seen doing so. There is no other reason. Entertainment-wise, it is not an effective return on a guest's investment. However if you can afford to put on a grand event that is luxurious enough to attract attention, and if you happen to be located in a place such as Washington, DC., with a larger than average proportion of people with lots of money and a desire to spend it in public, you may be able to make money at a charity gala.

Product sales

Very few people truly believe that specialized cookies or popcorn sold by charitable organizations once a year offer a better dollar-for-dollar value than a comparable grocery store product. If they did, there's a good chance we'd see far more such products on grocery store shelves. People buy the cookies and the popcorn because they are being sold by someone they know, because they respect the charity the child is representing, because it only happens once a year, and because the product is good enough to be worth eating.

There are plenty of companies that specialize in helping schools, churches, and charities with fundraising sales. The idea is: they send you a stack of order forms, you distribute the order forms, and everyone goes around selling overpriced candles, magazines, wrapping paper, and cookie dough to everybody they know. The non-profit then mails in the completed order forms, pays for the product, receives and distributes the product, and keeps the rest of the revenue, which is generally less than half.

The problem with product sale fundraisers is that everyone who cares about getting value for the dollar (and by that, I mean the sort of people you want on your Board) hates them. People really, really dislike selling stuff or asking their friends for money. They are perfectly aware that the junk they are selling is overpriced, and the people doing the buying often do not actually need or want the overpriced magazines, cookie dough, or candles. These products aren't necessary to human survival, the edible ones are disgustingly unhealthy, and everything is available at a fraction of the price at a grocery store. Furthermore, at least half the purchase price goes to the fundraising company, not the charity. The frugal thing to do is to make a donation instead for half the asking price, and have 100% of it go to the charity instead. Both donor and charity come out ahead.

There are a very, very few situations where a product sale makes sense. If you don't have any money whatsoever and are a brand-new charity, your fundraising budget may in fact be zero. If that's the case, then a product sale may be the only way to go. Later after you can afford the gear for a car wash or a thing-a-thon you will get a far better return on your invested time.

Exhausting your social network

When you exchange social capital for money, the social capital you spent doesn't exist anymore. Each time you inflict your pledge sheet toting child on your neighbors or bring an order form for overpriced

169

wrapping paper or pizza dough into your office, you sacrifice a small amount of other people's respect or patience in exchange for a sale.

If the request you make is small and occasional, it is like asking for any other favor: your friend will most likely buy if he or she is able, simply because it's you who ask. Over time, if the rest of your friendship continues as before and you have a chance to reciprocate the favor, the social capital you used up for the transaction will grow back.

Generally speaking, a person's social network can handle no more than one to two social capital fundraisers per year, if the amount you request per person is reasonable. Keep in mind that most of your volunteers are helping more than one charity, if only because they have more than one kid. So you should not get them to request favors from their friends on your behalf more than once a year.

Reasonable versus unreasonable requests

How much money you can get out of a friend depends on that individual's resources and also how close you are to him or her. The closer your social tie, the more social capital you have, and the more of his or her resources you can request, and receive, without permanently damaging the social connection.

Generally speaking, you can safely ask for an hour's worth of take-home pay from a casual friend or trusted colleague whom you know well enough to be sure they're not going through a financial crisis. From a very close friend, a lover, or an immediate family member, you can typically ask for the equivalent of a day's worth of take-home pay.

Asking for a major gift creates a debt that must be repaid, especially if you are taking from somebody who loves you in order to give to someone else. The act takes a bite out of the social capital you have with the person who has given to you. It will not be replenished until you repay the debt by giving an equivalent gift. Such requests should be once-in-a-lifetime incidents.

Chapter 11: Fundraising Math

The last chapter focused on the qualitative aspects of fundraising: how to identify and classify different fundraising techniques based on what resource was being monetized, and the source of the resource. This chapter will focus on the quantitative aspects of fundraising.

This chapter introduces six measuring and estimating techniques. By the end of this chapter, you will be able to use simple arithmetic to determine how much money is coming in. You will be able to determine what your sustainable and maximum burst fundraising levels are based on your volunteer pool, and you will be able to perform tests to determine whether you are at risk of exhausting your volunteer and donor pool. Most importantly, you will be able to identify when you are in danger of exhausting your social capital.

Some of the techniques in this chapter focus on Type III and Type IV fundraisers, which are the ones most consistently used by small charities. They are also the highest risk techniques when it comes to exhaustion of the volunteer pool or of the social capital of the individuals doing the fundraising.

Calculating profit

Many of the techniques in this chapter require that you calculate the profit associated with a fundraiser. To do that, add up all the income the fundraiser brought in, and subtract the expenses associated with it.

Equation 5

$$Profit = Income - Expenses$$

You can calculate the profit from an individual fundraiser, from a category of fundraising, or even from an individual transaction. In cases where you have leftover inventory or materials, make sure the expense associated with buying them is not simply ignored.

The importance of accurate record keeping

All the techniques in this chapter rely on accurate record keeping. You simply can't evaluate what you don't measure.

Most charitable organizations are pretty good at counting their money, but fewer keep track of expenses. Fewer still keep track of volunteer hours. This is a serious mistake, and it's bad business management.

No for-profit business would survive if it failed to track its spending or its employee work hours. But for some reason, people new to non-profit management think it's acceptable to ignore labor that doesn't trigger wages or payroll taxes.

Act like a leader, not an amateur. Every time you have a fundraiser, write down who worked, and approximately how many hours each person put in. Know who your rainmakers are.

Know your volunteers

One of the best things you can do for your organization is to make sure your volunteers provide you with accurate information about themselves. This makes them easier to contact when you're putting together a fundraising activity. It also makes it easier for you to match people up with the kind of work they want to do.

If any of your volunteers have special talents or contacts due to the kind of work they already do for a living or have done for a living in the past, you might be able to capitalize. If, for example, you are running a charity athletic event that is open to the public, it's a good idea to have a paramedic team on hand. If you already have someone with the appropriate credentials, you might be able to cut your expenses.

Sometimes a volunteer is a good candidate for recruitment to your Board of Directors. An ideal Board for any non-profit should include at least one accountant, at least one lawyer, at least one computer professional, and for medical charities at least one doctor. Engineers or construction experts are valuable because of their knowledge of process. For education non-profits, teachers are vital. If the non-profit focuses on the fine arts, a performer is important.

Do not neglect the skilled trades, especially first responders. Nurses and mechanics have excellent problem solving skills, and first responders are trained to operate under pressure. Families that produce a lot of skilled laborers tend to have far healthier and more extensive social networks than families that produce professionals. Professionals frequently have to relocate not just once but several times throughout their careers. They frequently do not obtain their educations or their long-term jobs in the same cities they were born in, so they cannot expect to have the same level of family or community support as people who have lived in the same neighborhood for generations.

A professional commissioned salesperson such as a real estate or insurance agent is a great asset to any Board due to the size of their personal and professional contact list. Do not neglect car salespeople: they know how to solicit a sale, they're not afraid to do it, and they can be among the most proactive of your Type II closers.

Entrepreneurs not only have access to other entrepreneurs, but many are in a position to offer office or building space as an in-kind donation.

The people on your Board need not be practicing their professions full-time. If they are retirees, part-timers or homemakers, they may have more time available during normal business hours.

People under the age of 25 are often in demand for legwork or fundraising, but disregarded as potential administrators because of their perceived lack of "life experience". However, depending on the country and the socioeconomic class a person comes from, they may have a great deal of work experience. If a 24-year-old has been working for pay outside the home since age 13, put himself or herself through school, and is living independently, he or she most likely has a far better grasp of human nature than a 30-year-old who did not have to look for work until after finishing his or her master's degree at age 25. Which would you rather have on your Board of Directors?

Youth alone should not be a disqualifying attribute if you plan on keeping your volunteer or Board member for life. Indeed, having people from more than one generation on your Board helps smooth out leadership transitions and ensure organizational longevity because there are no major demographic shifts as one generation replaces another.

To get information about your volunteers, simply have each one fill out a sheet under the guise of "updating the contact spreadsheet". This information sheet should include:

- Name and address
- Phone numbers and E-mail addresses
- Month and year of birth
- Profession (former profession, for retirees)
- Type of volunteer work preferred (list options)
- Background in charity and non-profit work
- Number of hours per week available

173

- How they found out about your organization

At the beginning of the chapter, I promised six specific techniques to help you calculate exactly how much a group of volunteers "should" be able to raise sustainably.

Technique #1: Rat's butt count

The name of the technique comes from a colloquial phrase, "to give a rat's butt", meaning to care about something enough to give or contribute something trivial.

The Rat's Butt technique is versatile. It applies to charities of all sizes and types. It applies to money raised using all four different fundraising categories, and it works equally well on an exhausted aquifer as it does on a healthy one.

The goal is to quantitatively express how much your program is valued by the community it serves. It is based on a few key assumptions, specifically:

- You have a current program
- You have been doing fundraising in a way that isn't utterly incompetent, by communicating effectively with your volunteer pool and by engaging them in labor and social capital based fundraising
- There are people in your community who know about your program and care enough about it to give to you
- There are people in your community who know you and care enough to give to a charity that is important to you

This is an extremely simple test. Visualize it as going to all the people who have given a rat's butt over the last year, and collecting the hairy hindquarters, tail and all. Pile them up in the middle of the floor, count them, and you will have an accurate quantitative description of the community's opinion of you and investment in your organization (not just your program).

Step 1: For the most recent year, add up all your fundraising profits from all sources. Include both solicited and unsolicited donations.
- Include in-kind donations of space or materials (much like you would do when analyzing your program)

- Exclude money from asset sales such as real estate or capital equipment
- Exclude passive investment income such as real estate leases, intellectual property royalties, stock dividends, or savings account interest

Step 2: Understand that this dollar figure is your community's total investment in you, based on the program you've got, the credibility you have as individuals and as a charity, and the effectiveness of the fundraising activities you've been able to summon over the last year.

Step 3: The dollar figure from Step 2 is your maximum budget for next year. I say "maximum" because if the money was raised using unsustainable means, there's a good chance it is too high and you need to scale back your program.

If the number is distressingly low—the pile of rodent tush isn't as much as you need or want to execute your program—then it's time to start increasing your credibility, raising your profile, and checking to see whether you're making effective and sustainable use of your volunteers. Maybe people don't know about you, or maybe they know about you but don't care. You can solve the problem by delivering a phenomenal program *scaled to the resources you have available*. Then announce your success to the public and collect the love.

Technique #2: Quadrant test

This evaluation technique shows what kind of assets you have been monetizing, and how much you are relying on social capital compared to labor. Most charities have an unbalanced approach to fundraising. This isn't necessarily unhealthy, but you need to know where you stand. The test presupposes a few things. It assumes your budget is balanced and that you're not engaging in deficit spending, and it assumes you're not having debt problems or cash flow problems.

Step 1: For the most recent year, add up your fundraising profits from each separate initiative. (Note that "profit" means income minus expenses).

Step 2: Classify each income source by type, using the Type I through Type IV quadrant table in the previous chapter.

Step 3: Assign passive investment income such as stock dividends, bank account interest, and royalties to the Type I quadrant. Someone got value for the dollar and you did not have to mobilize any volunteers to make the income occur.

Step 4: Add up income obtained through sales or leases of real estate or capital equipment. Assign all of these to the Type I quadrant, but flag them as short-term gains. Each of these assets was created or provided through somebody's labor in the past, and whoever bought the assets should have obtained fair market value for the dollar. Add up this total and call it Q1A.

Step 5: Add up the totals in each quadrant (Q1 through Q4). Type I totals go to Q1, Type II totals to Q2, type III totals to Q3 and Type IV totals to Q4.

Step 6: Identify which Q1 or Type I income is not due to the sale of assets, and call it Q1B. So Q1B = Q1 – Q1A.

You now have Q1, Q1A, Q1B, Q2, Q3, and Q4. This means that you can compare the values in each of them and draw conclusions based on where your income comes from. Note that > means "greater than", < means "less than", and ≥ means "greater than or equal to".

If Q1 = 0 and Q2 = 0, your non-profit is in the infant stage: completely dependent on volunteers, most likely a regional charity with income under $100k per year. But if Q3 ≥ Q4 your charity is a healthy baby; if Q3 < Q4 your charity is not healthy and will bleed to death within two years unless changes are made

If (Q1 + Q2) > (Q3 + Q4) your charity is mature

If Q2 > (Q3 + Q4) and Q1A < Q1B, you have a sustainable fundraising operation. Congratulations!

If (Q1 + Q3) > (Q2 + Q4) your fundraising activities are most likely sustainable

If Q1A is greater than the totals in any other quadrant, your organization should have eliminated debt or acquired assets of greater value. If they did not, you have a cash flow problem.

If Q4 is greater than the combined total of all other quadrants, your organization is in serious trouble and is burning social capital. If your charity is more than two years old you are most likely seeing diminishing returns from your fundraising ventures. Your aquifer will be exhausted within a year. Treat this as an emergency.

Example

Suppose you have a program that teaches country line dancing to senior citizens. You have two key fundraising activities: dance recitals and performances where the public can buy tickets and make donations, and a thing-a-thon event once in a year.

If you receive no corporate support or grants from larger organizations even in the form of donated rehearsal or instruction space, Q1 and Q2 are both zero because you have no Type I or Type II money coming in. Chances are you're in your first year. By the time you've been around a first year, you should be able to negotiate at least some donated or low-priced rehearsal space, and that should be one of your priorities within the next year or two. Yet if you bring in more from your recitals and performances than you do from your thing-a-thons, Q3 is greater than Q4, and you are drawing more money from the greater community than you are drawing from family and friends, so assuming you don't have any cash flow problems and your bills are getting paid you've got a healthy little charity. Yet if the opposite is true, and you're relying more on thing-a-thons than labor based fundraising, you may be in trouble particularly since you get nothing from corporate or other donors.

Now, suppose your program has been around a few years. You've negotiated in-kind donation of rehearsal space from a local senior citizens' center, which makes for a sizable Type II income. You also have a side business in which you rent the use of a room from a local business and have one of your instructors teach line dancing to people from the community who are not senior citizens. This makes for a moderate Type I income. Indeed, if you add up the profit from your side instruction and also the value of the in-kind donation of space for your main program, you make more money that way than you do with thing-a-thons or ticket sales. Congratulations: Q1 + Q2 is bigger than Q3 + Q4, and your charity is now mature. But is it sustainable? If the value of your donated space is greater than what you're earning through thing-a-thons and ticket sales, then the answer is yes provided your budget is actually balanced, you have adequate cash reserves, and you're not losing money. Running the charity should be fairly comfortable.

Next, suppose circumstances have changed: the person you trusted to run your side business embezzled the money and ran off with it, and you had to refund some of the money to the customers. You pressed charges and found someone else to teach the classes, but in the middle of the year the senior citizens' center that gave you the free space went through a change of management and is now no longer able to offer you space at all. Do you see how this changes the stress level in your organization, when more of your money has to come from active fundraising?

Technique #3: Profit per person-hour test

This test measures the effectiveness of an individual fundraising initiative. It is particularly useful for Type III and Type IV fundraisers. The goal is to highlight areas in which you can make a given fundraising activity more efficient.

Evaluate each fundraiser separately. If you compare the ratios for each fundraiser, you will be able to see which efforts brought you the biggest return on invested effort. This doesn't necessarily mean one type of fundraising is necessarily "better" than another. You may have had a bad day, a bad location, or the wrong number of people.

Step 1: Add up the amount of money brought in by the fundraiser.

Step 2: Subtract the expenses associated with the fundraiser. What is left over is the profit associated with the fundraiser.

Step 3: List the people who participated in the fundraiser, and how many hours were worked by each. Some people will have put in more effort than others. Include people who were present but not actually working.

Step 4: Add up the total number of hours worked by all the people in Step 3. These are your person-hours.

Step 5: Divide the profit calculated in Step 2 with the person-hours calculated in step 4. This is the profit per person-hour associated with the fundraiser.

Comparing the profit per person hour of different fundraisers will show you areas in which an individual fundraising initiative might become more efficient.

Example

You have a concession stand that made $200 in profit over 5 hours at your high school whiffle ball tournament. One person staffed this stand and one person put in 5 hours of work getting the float, making the supply run, providing the vendor with a bathroom break, and doing setup and cleanup. Accordingly, your volunteers put in 10 person-hours. They made $200 over 10 person-hours or $20 per person-hour.

The next tournament, five people signed up to staff the concession, putting in a total of 5 person-hours apiece for a total of 25 person-hours. They made $250 in profit because a couple volunteers walked through the crowd selling drinks and popcorn. But even so, the profit per person-hour was only $10. This fundraiser brought in more money, but it was less efficient.

If you keep track of your efficiency, you learn pretty quickly to put only two people to work doing the concessions, and as they get better at predicting what the customers want and doing bargain shopping your efficiency rises to $25 per person-hour. But suppose you make a mistake: you don't rotate the staff and you don't pay attention when people are tired of the work. By the end of the season, your concession staff hates you. The same two people have been working every single event, and they want a break but for whatever reason you can't find a replacement. So the person in charge of stocking the concession doesn't go around finding you the best deals. Instead, she spends only two hours doing it, but pays more for the merchandise than necessary. This really eats into your profit margin, and to make matters worse the stocker starts leaving early and won't stick around to relieve the person doing the vending or help with the cleanup. So the person doing the vending has to duck out sometimes to go to the restroom, taking the cashbox but leaving the candy under the watchful but slightly corrupt eye of one of the kids. Some of the candy gets stolen and a sandwich fight breaks out so there are some damaged items. After just four hours, the disgusted vendor shuts down the stand, missing out on all the late-in-the-game water sales. You're stuck with a bunch of merchandise that can't be returned. When everything is totaled up, you've made only $60 for the six hours of work your volunteers put in. That's $10 per person-hour.

Identify overstaffed or inefficient fundraisers

Suppose you have an unusually high person-hour count at a particular fundraiser. For whatever reason, you had far more volunteers than you needed. This is a problem, because you've used up some of those people's available person-hours, and gotten nothing in exchange. If it is a labor based fundraiser, the solution is to have more events but to select fewer volunteers for each. Give everybody a turn, don't overload anyone, and make sure there's enough work for people to do.

Identify burnout

If your more recent fundraisers are less lucrative per person hour than earlier ones of the same type, and if the same people are involved, you have a burnout problem.

Over time, as a team gets better at putting on a fundraiser, they tend to become more efficient. But if the opposite is occurring and you're getting less return on invested time, start looking for reasons. If there's been a large staff turnover, the problem at first appears to be inexperience, but the root cause is volunteer burnout.

Technique #4: Combined market value calculation

This technique will show you how much money should have been raised by the volunteer fundraising team you've got, based on the amount of time spent fundraising last year. It relies on your fundraising statistics for the past year, and assumes you have made a full, concentrated effort to raise money.

The test relies on household income estimates for your volunteers. You will most likely not have access to this information, and it's a sensitive type of information so I don't recommend that you request or store it. However, if you've had your volunteers fill out forms as described at the start of this chapter, you can use online tools to make an educated guess about that person's earning power based on his or her profession and location. You will guess high for some people and low for others, but it doesn't matter since if you have a decent sized volunteer pool your guesses will balance out.

Step 1: Estimate the hourly wage for each volunteer. Do this by looking up the average pay for his or her profession in your area. If this is not expressed as an hourly wage, take the annual pay and divide it by 2,080. For a homemaker, use half the value of his or her spouse's estimated income. For a retiree, use half the value of his or her estimated work income. For the spouse of a retiree, use one quarter the value of the estimated work income.

Step 2: Add up the number of hours each volunteer spent on fundraising alone. Do not include hours spent painting walls in the office, editing your Web site, executing the program, attending Board meetings, or doing anything except planning and executing fundraisers. This number is the number of fundraising hours worked by the volunteer.

Step 3: For each volunteer, multiply the estimated hourly wage (from Step 1) by the number of hours that volunteer worked (from Step 2). The product represents the market value of the time that individual volunteer spent raising money for you.

Step 4: Add up all the individual market values calculated in Step 3. This is the combined market value of all the time spent fundraising.

Step 5: Understand that the number obtained in Step 4 represents the market value of the fundraising team you have. It is also the maximum best-case income you can expect from the volunteer fundraising team you've got, if you are limited to Type III and Type IV fundraising.

You may now draw conclusions based on your estimates and calculations. If the value from Step 5 is substantially less than the sum of your Q3 and Q4 values (from the Quadrant Test), your fundraising team is performing at peak capacity and is bringing in more money than expected. Check carefully to see whether you are starting to experience volunteer turnover.

If the success is due to having more fundraisers and they are producing diminishing returns, you are in danger of creating a burnout problem.

If the value from Step 5 is substantially higher than the sum of your Q3 and Q4 values, either you have a very new charity or your fundraising team is exhausted. The fundraising has been impressive, but is not sustainable unless you move the effort into the top two quadrants.

If you have had more than one Type IV fundraiser this year, and the same people were involved, your fundraising team is overdrawing their individual social capital.

The Individual Market Value calculation from Step 3 works for labor based fundraising because people are not willing to "waste" their time. Exactly what constitutes "waste" is a subjective decision. Some people are willing to work for less than minimum wage; others are not.

Example

DeShawn makes $50,000 per year. This works out to about $24 an hour assuming no overtime. He puts in 20 hours fundraising for you. The market value of his time is therefore $480. But the initiative yields only $200 per person. He will most likely be disappointed. But Sue, who lives off $700 per month in disability payments, gets $8,400 per year which would work out to a little more than $4 per hour if she were being paid for full-time work. She volunteers the same number of hours as DeShawn and brings in the same $200. But she's justifiably proud of her work.

People instinctively compare the amount of money made fundraising with the amount they earn in an hour. If the dollar figures aren't close, and if the fundraising activity yields substantially less than they're used to earning at work, the volunteer becomes frustrated and prefers to simply write a check instead of giving up his or her free time.

This calculation works for social capital based fundraising because people with similar income levels tend to cluster together socially. For a favor to a friend, once a year or so or more often if the gesture is reciprocated, people are willing to give up to an hour's worth of take-home pay (not to be confused with the hourly of gross income estimated in Step 1). This dollar figure will be higher for high income earners and lower for lower income earners.

Technique #5: Sustainable effort calculation

This technique is similar to the Combined Market Value Calculation presented as Technique #4. The only difference is that, instead of adding up the number of hours a volunteer *actually* spent, you add up the number of hours a volunteer *is willing to spend* on fundraising. This only affects Step #2 of the process. Use the same steps otherwise.

This technique is valuable in conjunction with the Combined Market Value Calculation, because it allows you compare the amount of fundraising your volunteers have been doing with the amount that they actually want to do. Whereas any individual might need to adjust his or her commitment due to family or work changes, if your entire volunteer base is doing more fundraising than they like or feel comfortable doing, you're asking too much of them.

Always make sure that you scale your program so that it requires fundraising effort from your team that is less than or equal to the Sustainable Effort value.

If for some reason your charity is in crisis, you can ask an extra 20% of time from the fundraising team for no more than one year, after which you must revert to normal fundraising. I call this a one year push because your fundraising group can sustain the extra effort for no more than one year.

One Year Push = 120% of the Sustainable Effort

After a one year push, you must fall back to normal fundraising activities for at least two full years.

You may also ask a team for the maximum burst effort, which requires an extra 30% time commitment for a period not to exceed two months. After this burst effort, the volunteers involved will be capable of zero fundraising for three full months.

Maximum burst = 130% of the Sustainable Effort

The maximum burst approach actually works well for organizations that have one or two gigantic fundraisers per year, and that do no fundraising otherwise. The important part is that the volunteer pool must be allowed to rest.

You don't sprint a marathon. If you aren't raising "enough" money, scale back your program to suit what's available or put more resources into getting and training new volunteers. If you don't let your volunteers rest, you cut open the goose that lays the golden eggs.

Technique #6: Donor pool health test

Up to this point, the chapter has focused on the volunteer aspects of fundraising. However, any major charity relies on significant Type II fundraising. These initiatives generally require a reliable corporate and individual donor pool.

What kind of donors exist?

In a healthy donor pool, you will have donors that are major or minor, regular or occasional. These are classified in Table 4.

Table 4: Donor classification

Frequency	Amount of Donation	
	Major	Minor
Regular (weekly, monthly, or annually)	Type A	Type B
Occasional (solicited or else on an impulse)	Type C	Type D

Type A donors are major backers. They donate based on personal ideology. The donation may come from an individual or from a corporation, but the individual or corporation making the gift often does not respond to solicitation. They tend to be sophisticated investors and philanthropists who are capable of assessing for themselves whether your charitable venture is healthy or whether their money is being used effectively.

Type B donors tend to tithe or to make donations through payroll deductions. These are generally middle-class people or professional workers. They respond to personal contact and personal solicitation but are generally hostile to cold callers. But they don't usually have the skills or experience to analyze your charitable venture the way a Type A donor will.

Type C donors are crisis donors who give based on emotional decision. They make unsolicited gifts in response to news stories, and may make bequests if they feel an ongoing emotional tie to your organization. However they do not respond to solicitation except in a genuine emergency.

Type D donors are holiday givers and spontaneous givers who respond to ads, to social media appeals, or to solicitation. For them, giving is a spur-of-the-moment emotional decision. This is the only group that responds positively to solicitation in any consistent way.

Exactly how many dollars constitute a "major" or "minor" donation depends on the size of your organization. For small charities, a "major" donation constitutes 5% or more of your annual operating budget. If you're a regional charity such as a high school booster club, small enough to file an E-postcard and have annual revenues of not quite $50,000 per year, then a "major" donor is one who contributes $2,500 or more.

For larger charities with annual budgets of several million dollars, a person or organization who contributes more than one percent of that budget is still shelling out more than a working-class person pays for a house. Contributions of $100,000 or more definitely qualify as "major".

Step 1: For the past three years, go through your donation lists and classify each donor as type A, B, C, or D depending on how much they give and when they give.

Step 2: For the past year, tally up the amount given by each kind of donor.

Step 3: Repeat Step 2 for last year, and the year before that.

Step 4: Look for significant changes in how donors give. See whether individual donors have changed quadrant, and see whether there have been changes in which quadrant has produced the most money.

You may now assess the behavior of donors over the lifetime of their involvement with your organization.

When Type A donors or Type B donors die, they frequently become Type C donors if they leave a bequest to your charity.

Type B donors frequently turn into Type A donors if they inherit wealth or start earning significant amounts of money.

Type C donors seldom turn into Type A or Type B donors, however they are worth keeping on a mailing list even if they have a reversal of fortune, because they continue as Type D donors.

Type D donors can become Type C donors if they leave a bequest, however they are more likely to leave their assets to family members or friends.

The proportion of money that comes from each quadrant will vary depending on what the charity is, but generally half will come from Type A and B donors and half will come from Type C and D donors. Type D donors are by far the most numerous: they're the ones who drop their change into a collection box without really thinking about it, or who routinely write out a few checks during the holiday season.

Analysis

What's "normal" for your type of non-profit will vary depending on the size and maturity of your organization.

All charities start off with the majority of their fundraising in the Type D quadrant. People donate when they are able, or when a fundraiser occurs, but they seldom get behind a charity in a big way unless they are founders. As the charity matures, some of the Type D donors will migrate into the B or C quadrants.

Type A donors are generally either founders, friends of the founders, or people who have been helped by the charity in a big way. If you're lucky enough to have them, leave them off your direct-mail list unless you have their explicit permission to solicit. They are not sensitive to significant changes in program, but they are very sensitive to management problems within your charity. If you are losing Type A donors due to reasons besides their death, it's because you alienated them.

Type A donors understand their worth and are vulnerable to changes in their personal relationships with people on your administrative team. It is vital to manage the social capital relationship with all Type A donors and to understand what it is that ties them to the group. If they are close friends with your Executive Director and you have to fire that person, understand that unless you can replace that personal connection to the Type A donors, you will lose the donors also.

Type B donors are the most interesting of all the groups. They seldom exist outside of organized religion or organized payroll deduction programs that allow them to direct their donations to a favored charity. But they form the backbones of most churches, scouting programs, and youth sports organizations. Invariably, they (or family members of theirs) are heavy consumers of your program and also volunteers. This puts them in ongoing contact with each other, and the result is that the program, fundraising, and volunteer pools overlap informally. This can create a wonderful sense of community when things are going well, but it is also susceptible to clique behavior.

Tithing is more common in some religious traditions than in others. If your sect is not one that emphasizes tithing and you have somebody who does, or if you are a secular organization who is receiving a regular payroll deduction or monthly donation from someone, this is a person with a major emotional and spiritual commitment to your organization. He or she may be open to a more formal leadership role.

If you have Type B donors who don't know each other, discreetly find a way to introduce them to each other. Find ways to socialize with them once in a while, because they are your information network. They are far more attuned to problems with the program than any employee or administrator could possibly be.

As your Type B donors go, so goes your church (or other organization... as I mentioned tithing is mostly a church thing). Type B donors are extremely sensitive to problems with your program, especially if they are due to personnel. If you are losing Type B donors for reasons besides death, out of town moves, or their own financial hardship, take a hard look at whether you've made any changes to your program lately.

Type B donors are frequently more loyal to each other, and to shared ideology, than they are to your organization specifically. Abuse one, and you risk losing many. This is because they are pillars of your community, and so they have social capital with one another as well as with you. If your organization changes its direction or its rules in a way that offends the sensibilities of a Type B donor, that donor will leave. When this happens, they take others with them.

Never solicit a Type A or B donor by mail or phone unless you know him or her personally. If you do, you will most likely lose that donor. However, a direct personal appeal will often result in a donation. Just make sure you don't do it through a mass mailing or robo-call effort.

Type C donors are crisis donors. They willingly open their pocketbooks in an emergency, but they seldom think of supporting your charity when times are good. They are seldom steady volunteers, but will help out with one-shot activities such as filling sand bags or rolling bandages. You can only effectively solicit donations from them in an actual emergency where they have some kind of emotional contact with the people or animals who are in danger. But the good news is that they come out of the woodwork if you advertise.

It makes no sense to track whether you are retaining or losing Type C donors, but if you have a genuine emergency where people are in danger and your program is in a position to help, simply advertise what you've got. Do not try to add Type C donors to a mailing list unless you're in the business of crisis response, and don't try to convert a Type C donor into anything else. Save your donor development time and resources for Type A and Type B donors.

Don't confuse the donor type with the donation amount. Type C donors can be extremely generous especially if they have just won a lottery or received an inheritance. You may receive more from a single

Type C donation than a long-term Type A or Type B donor gives in a lifetime. These donations are generally unsolicited.

Type D donors are the people to hit up with your annual pledge drives or annual mailing campaigns. They don't mind being solicited by mail or E-mail as long as it's not constant. They will give a small amount, when prompted, but they respond to prompts and not to crisis.

You can predict the maximum productivity of your Type D donor pool by adding up each person's total donation per year. It is simply impossible to get more. So, sophisticated charities limit themselves to just one or two mail or direct campaigns per year.

Chapter 12: Why People Give

In order to build a donor and volunteer base, it is first necessary to understand why people give. This is the last of three chapters devoted to fundraising, and it emphasizes the emotional aspect of giving.

The last two chapters were primarily intellectual and clinical, and it's always useful to be able to determine how much can, or should, be raised under normal circumstances. But ultimately people give because they want to. Unless you can understand why people want things, and unless you can appeal to that want, you can never expect to convince people to support your venture with money or labor.

I am lumping volunteer labor in with donations because the dynamics that inspire people to open their calendar are the same as the ones that inspire them to open their checkbook. Volunteers are just as important as donors, because if you had to pay all the people who perform the fundraising and other thankless activities your charity needs to run, you might not be able to afford to stay in business.

The volunteer base and the donor base aren't always the same, but they generally overlap if only because most charities use volunteers to help raise money. Your administrators, such as your Board of Directors, typically serve on a volunteer basis, and are frequently major donors as well.

Converting a volunteer into a donor isn't always possible, nor is it cost effective if it means the donor is no longer providing labor.

Although it's the donor base that gets most of the attention, your volunteer base is the backbone of your organization. Whether they're conducting the program by providing services to the greater community, or raising money for the program to be put on, or performing administrative services to allow your charity to operate, they are your biggest source of labor. For a small non-profit company, they will often be your only source of labor, money, or resources.

Three ways to give support

Human beings can provide support to one another in only three ways, each of which has a corollary in the physical world.

Aid: they can reach down and pull a struggling person up

Community support: they can allow a peer—someone on the same level as themselves—to lean against them for support, or

Boosting: they can stand beneath someone and boost him or her to a higher level

There are no other ways for one human being to help another.

If your program exists to meet the physical, spiritual, educational, or emotional needs of human beings, you are asking your donors to perform at least one of these three types of giving. Activities that benefit animals or the environment are different: people give simply because they want the results they believe you can produce.

In what way are you asking people to give? Are you asking for them to reach down and pull up, to give temporary support for a peer, or to boost?

How does your program give support?

Consider each of your program activities. When you think of the relationship between the people doing the work or giving the money, and the people receiving the benefit, are you asking your donors and volunteers to aid, to support, or to boost by pushing somebody else up from beneath? If the majority of your program activities are of the aid, community support, or booster variety, you can actually think of yourself as being that kind of organization.

If you're an aid type organization, you're most likely asking people to provide emergency or recovery assistance, or to help people or animals less fortunate than themselves. Medical and environmental charities are generally aid type. Medical research organizations are also generally viewed (and marketed) as an indirect form of aid. So are educational or scholarship institutions providing, as Andrew Carnegie famously quipped, "a ladder for those who wish to climb." Even if you're providing permanent relief from poverty in the form of housing or education, your program ultimately pulls people up.

If you're a community support type of organization, you provide something of value to a group of people who know each other. The givers and the recipients come from the same general pool of people, who are uniting to work toward the greater good. Indeed, many who are givers today may be recipients tomorrow. They continue to give, and to participate, because they believe they are helping to build a necessary institution that will be around for a long time. Nearly all churches fall into this category, as do community centers, private schools, fraternal orders, trade unions, homeowner's associations, and credit unions.

If your organization provides something that can only be used or enjoyed in person, such as a zoo or a fine arts performance, its impact is only really felt among people who can easily drive there and it can be regarded as a community charity. Some hospitals fit this definition, if they do not provide specialized services of the type that would justify patients flying in from out of state.

If you're a booster organization, you provide a select group of people with an opportunity to enjoy a recreational activity they would otherwise not get to experience. The products and services you provide fall into the "nice-to-have" category, not the "need" or "want" category. This doesn't necessarily affect your tax exempt status, because promoting athletic competition or fine arts performance are tax exempt activities according to the IRS.

If you have a large organization you may have many program activities. Take a moment to sort them by type, because how you market your program (and the people to whom you market it) will depend on whether you're asking your prospective givers to aid, to support, or to boost.

Marketing strategies for "aid" programs

Human beings are altruistic by nature, and even toddlers like to help another person in trouble. So most of us are willing to reach down and pull up in order to benefit a stranger, if they believe the stranger's problems are not of his or her own doing, and if they believe that help from them will bring lasting relief. This is why disaster relief initiatives collect so many Type D donations: people instinctively want to help.

If you want to attract Type D donors, present your charitable activities as something that helps people in distress. Identify the people (or animals, or environment) in distress, specify the way in which you are providing assistance, and provide some reasonable evidence that your kind of aid is producing results. It also helps to be able to convince donors that they're participating in a spontaneous uprising of support.

Do something different

Make sure to differentiate your program from all the other organizations currently vying for your donor's attention, and make sure you aren't re-plowing the same ground somebody else just harvested. In other words, use a fresh approach.

One of the reasons the 1985 "We Are the World" recording produced tens of millions of dollars in famine aid to Ethiopia (along with "Tears Are Not Enough" in Canada and "Do They Know It's Christmas" in Britain) is because it coincided with extensive news media coverage: people were seeing footage of actual starving children inside their own living rooms. In those days, mass celebrity endorsement was new, and people also weren't being hammered incessantly by the give-give-give-give drumbeat they now face every time they buy groceries or go to work.

The "We Are the World" initiative was so heartfelt, spontaneous, and financially successful that it was repeated in 2010 for earthquake relief in Haiti... but with far less commercial success. Critics pointed to the lower caliber of star talent, the mediocrity of some aspects of the production, and the greater accessibility of music overall. These factors should not be ignored but they are not the root cause of the failure. The social context has changed since 1985. By 2010, people had become saturated by charitable solicitation, celebrity endorsement, and disaster relief advertising. They recognized manipulation when they saw it. Nobody believed the aid effort was spontaneous. Indeed, it came across as just one more celebrity cash grab.

The 2014 "ice bucket challenge" for amyotrophic lateral sclerosis (ALS) research raised millions of dollars for disease research and provided enough funding to not only fund ongoing research but to conduct entirely new experiments, one of which led to a discovery that advanced ALS research by several years. It was marketed almost exclusively online. People would douse themselves in ice water and/or write a check, upload the video, and publicly "call out" or identify three friends who had not yet taken the challenge, inviting them to do the same. It was fun, it was fresh, and it was effective. The ice bucket challenge was not limited by geographical distance or within a small group of people: participants called out future donors from among their online friends, who did not necessarily belong to the same social circle as the person who challenged them. This allowed the fundraising initiative to jump across geographical regions and to move between radically different groups of people.

Three factors allowed the ice bucket challenge to go viral. First, the charity conducting it was a disease research charity, which was in a position to create a feeling of affinity with the donors being challenged, because their program benefits everyone who suffers from the disease or who might contract it in the future. Had the same challenge been attempted by a regional charity like a city symphony orchestra, it could not have gone viral.

Two other two important factors that allowed the ice bucket challenge to go viral were the use of social media and the pyramid-style structure of the challenge which encouraged people to make use of their own social networks. The amount of money at stake wasn't big enough to put a major strain on the pocketbook of the person being challenged, the sight of people being doused by cold water was mildly entertaining, and overall it was a fun, creative activity.

The final aspect of "We Are the World" and the Ice Bucket Challenge is the underdog appeal. The organizers definitely found a need and proposed a means to satisfy it, but they also appealed to a slightly countercultural, underdog trend in society. People want to be involved, but if you offer them a way to be involved that flies in the face of what they see as traditional or conventional, it becomes even more appealing.

The impermanence of interest

As with all viral trends, the Ice Bucket Challenge eventually exhausted the pool of available donors. Donations tapered back to a more sustainable level, and other online giving initiatives stepped in.

The important thing to remember about Type C and Type D donors is that they give based on an emotional impulse. You can generally only get a knee-jerk reaction out of somebody once.

If you want to attract something besides a Type D donor, you need to do more than harness an emotional impulse. To commit to ongoing giving the way a type B donor does, or to set aside a major portion of one's wealth as a bequest the way a type C donor does, a human being needs to feel an ongoing commitment to the cause. He or she needs to be more than an altruist: he or she needs to be connected in some way to the community being served.

How to sell ongoing aid programs

Disaster relief initiatives raise a lot of money because people feel a sense of urgency. They just can't summon up as much of a sense of criticality over their community library or the local addiction recovery center, unless they're about to close for lack of funding. Then people feel a sense of urgency. So, for some charities, there's an incentive to manufacture emergencies.

Operating right on the ragged edge is irresponsible, and manipulating people into believing the charity is about to close is dishonest. Since the need of an ongoing aid program is constant (as opposed to a disaster relief program that requires burst donations to deal with disasters as they occur), it's unreasonable to rely solely on Type D donors.

Ongoing programs need ongoing donors. That means Type A or Type B donors.

To attract Type A philanthropists or Type B tithers to an ongoing aid activity, your organization must establish itself as a permanent institution to help lift people up on an ongoing basis. This is one of the situations in which it helps to have a brick-and-mortar facility: you can't name a building, a laboratory, or a conference room after somebody if you don't own one.

You must also direct the aid to people that belong to the community with which the donor identifies. If you collect money for scholarships, you'll have more luck if the recipients belong to the same ethnic group, or the same neighborhood, or the same school as the people you're hitting up.

If you're a medical research charity, you will be very attractive to people who have lost a loved one to that disease. Some of them may become Type A or Type B donors over time. The Type A donors will help you simply because you advance their interests. The Type B donors will help you because of a need to support a community to which they belong.

Identifying "community support" programs

A community support program provides ongoing services of some kind, either to the members of your organization alone or to the surrounding neighborhood.

The most obvious community support programs are the service clubs explicitly granted tax exempt status, such as Rotary, Civitan, Lions, and Kiwanis. These exist for the sole purpose of providing volunteers and organizers to other charitable ventures in the community. But any charitable venture that benefits the immediate geographical area qualifies. Zoos, museums, and libraries qualify. So do credit unions, trade unions, and even private clubs.

There are five factors that distinguish a community support program from an aid program.

First, with community support programs people expect reciprocity. Even if the donors don't benefit directly from the program, people give in the belief that they're supporting an organization that will be there for them or their children should they ever need it. With aid programs, people don't usually expect to need disaster relief or medical research themselves.

Second, the money and resources raised from the community stay in the community they were raised, and are used to execute the program on-site. Whereas aid programs often act like a wealth transfer between a rich community and a poor one, community support organizations keep most of the money local.

Third, people are willing to give to the point of personal inconvenience or discomfort when they believe they're providing a permanent benefit to the neighborhood they live in. Tithes, large gifts, and major bequests are not unusual in community support programs, although they are unheard-of in aid programs *unless the donor feels a personal connection to the people being helped.* Indeed, aid programs that have a community support component are far more successful in recruiting long-term donors and volunteers.

Fourth, support from donors tends to be long-term when it comes to community support organizations. People join not just for a day or week, but with the intention of making a long-term or lifetime commitment to your organization and its goals. The contributions are part of a planned giving process rather than a spontaneous decision to give.

Finally, a community support program requires ongoing direct contact between members in order to accomplish its goal. The contact need not be face to face (since telephones and online communication now exist) but members simply have to spend time with each other and know each other socially in order for the giving or service model to work.

Kicking it old school

For an illustration as to how community support programs work, simply consider the kind of service or charitable organization that existed in Western Europe during the mid to late 1300's. The Middle Ages predated government welfare programs and public schools. The Crusades were over, but the Renaissance hadn't started yet. Medical science was in its infancy, and Europe was still recovering from the Black Plague. Famine and war still happened from time to time, but although there was vast economic inequality between the richest and poorest people, peasants generally worked hard but ate fairly well. The mass migration into the cities triggered by the Industrial Revolution hadn't occurred yet.

195

Neither had the Enlightenment. Most people even in the noble classes were illiterate, relying on clerks to write letters and documents.

During this time, the wealthiest families paid for such medical care, elder care, food, and education as they required. Everyone else made use of the services provided by various abbeys, convents, and religious orders. If you were old or sick, or an orphan, or in need of work, there was help available. You might have had to go to the next village or town to get it, but someone was always available to provide the medieval equivalent of medicine or counseling.

Church facilities had among the largest collections of books, maps, and information. The first primitive hospitals and retirement homes were run by religious orders. Similarly, the first museums were churches or abbeys that held items purported to be sacred relics. People who had money and spare time frequently made pilgrimages to visit these relics, and to see the magnificent cathedrals built at the expense of some wealthy patron or another. Indeed, this is how tourism got its start.

Generally speaking, the Church got many big donations and bequests. Tithing, or giving ten percent of one's income to the Church, was mandatory in most places. Few people minded, because most people made use of at least some Church-run services at some point in their lives. Everyone who lives long enough eventually needs medical help or care.

The vast majority of the money raised by donations, tithes, or Church-run farms was used locally. Some was given directly to people in need, and people could see their donations at work.

The Church generally improved land that it owned, employing builders and tradesmen to construct abbeys that were designed to last for hundreds of years. A medical retreat built one year continued to be used for decades, so that each generation benefited from at least some of the work done by its predecessors.

Since medicine was in its infancy, there was no such thing as organized medical research. Scientific research was usually done independently and was self-funded. But monastic schools and universities existed for a long time. These were generally created and funded either by the Church or by a local city government or monarch.

Medieval Europe also had trade guilds, which were the early equivalent of modern trade unions and who routinely helped their own members. There were associations and societies of merchants who exchanged loans and financing (somewhat like a modern credit union), and although private member social clubs didn't appear until the 1600's, there have been closed secret societies and fraternal orders since at least the 1300's.

Now, suppose you could put your charity in a time machine and travel back to the Middle Ages. Setting aside any religious or technological features unique to the modern era, would you have fit in somewhere? Might services like yours have been performed through the medieval Church, or through one of the trade guilds?

If your program provides ministry of any sort, housing, education, or necessities for the poor, or even a museum or hospital, and if you provide services chiefly to the geographic region that supports you, congratulations: you could have "kicked it old school". You also have a community support program.

Aid charities don't fit the old school model

Most modern aid charities could not have existed during the Middle Ages. Because of limits to technology and infrastructure, it was nearly impossible to help people who lived far away. It took days for a message to get from one city to another, so people injured in an earthquake or flood would generally die before help arrived. In times of famine, it made more sense for people to simply migrate to areas where food and work were available. Not only would they eat sooner, but they would be in a place where they stood a chance of feeding themselves long-term instead of stuck out in the boonies waiting for the next relief shipment.

During the Middle Ages, there was also no such thing as organized international missionary activity. Individuals often wandered about as itinerant preachers or ministers preaching either official Church doctrine or their own personal insights. But they lived off the land or from the charity of people who lived in the places they went. The colonial effort didn't really begin until the early 1500's, and even then the primary purpose was to acquire wealth for investors or colonists, frequently at the expense of local populations who were enslaved or slaughtered depending on circumstance. The modern missionary model, in which people in a wealthy country raise money to support a medical or education initiative elsewhere, simply didn't exist.

Marketing strategies for "support" programs

Community support programs can be divided into two categories: the ones that exist primarily for the benefit of their members, and the ones that provide necessary services to the community, neighborhood, or city. Either way, your fundraising strategies necessarily revolve around *causing your community to raise money to support something that benefits it.*

Regardless of what people would like to believe about the limitless abundance available in the universe, a human being's resources are finite and limited. Also, unlike stranger aid, aid to a peer can turn into a habit when the person being helped keeps coming back for more and more aid. So, people considering a peer support program generally need to believe in three things: representation, results and reciprocity.

Representation

People seldom find it worthwhile to contribute significant, ongoing effort or resources to benefit a community they aren't part of. Do not expect to be able to get much out of people you intentionally exclude.

If your organization has requirements for membership that make it impossible for a specific person to join, don't expect that person to write a check, paint a wall, staff a table or sell tickets for you. "We don't want you, but we want your money" will earn you no respect. So if you restrict membership, the appropriate amount of time and money to spend marketing your fundraisers to people outside your potential member pool is zero, unless the donor receives something in exchange for his or her money such as a calendar or circus tickets. You are better off marketing your program to existing members, prospective members, or people who could be members if they wished. If this pool of donors and volunteers isn't big enough, find a way to expand (and market) membership and influence within your group. If you run a trade union and most people who are eligible aren't signing up, have a membership drive.

One example of expanded membership is the introduction of women's auxiliaries for all-male fraternal societies and clubs. Much of the work involved in fundraising is thankless, repetitive drudgery. Looking around them, it became obvious to male club members that recruiting their female family members to do the legwork was a great idea, particularly since for a brief period in the 1950's they were unlikely to be employed outside the home. So most service clubs invented some version of a Ladies' Auxiliary was born, and many clubs started accepting women as full members.

Marketing representation works because human beings love to believe that they, personally, are making a difference. They also like to feel as though they have some say in the decision making process. One reason why credit unions are so successful is because they play to their members' desire for ownership. Instead of being bank customers, they are their own customers. So they are generally willing to pay slightly higher interest rates and to get by with a narrower range of available services compared to a conventional bank.

Results

You can frequently sell a program by playing up the results of a charitable activity. Publishing a human interest story and showing how people get long-term benefit from your program can draw support even from donors who disagree with your ideology. When faith based groups can show lines of people being fed in their soup kitchen or count how many people are served by their homeless shelters, they get donations even from atheists because it's obvious they're doing good and necessary work in the community.

People need to see not just progress toward a distant goal, but actual success. If they do not see it, they become disillusioned quickly. Once resentment sets in, you lose the volunteer or donor. The solution is to break major projects down into short-term ones. If a donor is helping to pay for a wheelchair access ramp at the community church, it will be easy to see when the work is complete. But if you're raising money for a new building five years in the future, don't expect people to stay focused. You will be better off setting a one-year goal to raise a portion of the money, and presenting that accomplishment to your group as a sign of success. That will allow you to use the bandwagon marketing technique: everybody likes to join a winning team.

Even ongoing expenses can be tied to something that can be tangibly measured. Instead of trying to raise money for a general building or maintenance fund, present key projects that have a beginning, a middle, and an end. Collect qualitative and quantitative evidence that your program is making a difference for people in the community, and always have a few talking points showing how your organization is becoming more solidly established over time. Permanency sells.

Reciprocity

In community support organizations, the people who do the work and contribute the resources generally also expect to partake of the results. People who help build a church or school expect for their children to be able to attend it. But the expectation of reciprocity is most evident in organizations that exist solely for the benefit of their members, such as trade unions or private social clubs.

Reciprocity is something you can advertise when soliciting donations. If you're able to present your program as something that appeals to the donor's self-interest, you're far more likely to get the donation.

Selective peer support

If your organization provides ongoing support to members of the community, people who help peers on more than an occasional basis need to believe certain things:

- The help being given is actually needed
- The help being given is actually effective, and
- The help being given is not making the problem worse, such as by keeping the recipient from developing necessary skills

If you're having trouble attracting Type B donors despite being a church or religious-themed organization wherein tithing is common, there's a good chance your donors don't see their donations as strengthening the community they live in. Before you do anything else, find out whether this belief has a basis in fact.

Peer assistance and tithing

Tithing, or giving a sizable portion of one's gross income (a full ten percent in some religious traditions) is a classic example of giving more than is comfortable. It is an ongoing commitment, and it leaves a household with substantially less than it might otherwise have. But money that is tithed does not vanish: it stays, for the most part, in the community that raises it. Sometimes it is spent on facilities or materials to provide spiritual benefit to the congregation. Other times it is distributed to poorer members of the community. Either way, the community is strengthened.

Most people who tithe do it as part of a religious practice, but there are atheists and agnostics who recognize the community, emotional, and money management benefits of planned giving. They may not necessarily call it "tithing", and the percentage of income might not be precisely ten percent, but atheists and agnostics value community just as much as theists do. They seek out charitable ventures that benefit their community but that do not have a religious focus. These tend to be educational, fine arts, medical, or animal related charities.

You will also find disporportionate atheist and agnostic participation in charities that are unpopular with fundamentalist religious groups. So if your charity focuses on reproductive health care for women, women's rights, or rights for transsexual, lesbian, gay, and other non-"straight" people, it is reasonable to expect more support from the unchurched. This goes back to alignment of interests: groups of people who perceive themselves (accurately or inaccurately) as being threatened by a common enemy are willing to band together to achieve completely unrelated goals.

Minimal degrees of separation

Community support programs are uniquely limited. Aside from a very few grants that might be available, it's extremely difficult to attract interest from outside the set of people who benefit from them. The only people who care about your senior citizens' center are the people who use it and the people who care about them.

Most support charities fixate on the people who use their services, and completely ignore those people's friends, families, and business associates. This is a mistake, because the Internet and social media now allow people to share ideas (and money) across long distances. If you maintain an online presence, you may be able to find people who care despite living far away.

Marketing strategies for "booster" charities

Most human beings are emotionally and psychologically incapable of voluntarily subsidizing someone they believe is luckier, wealthier, or more talented than themselves, unless they envision that person as somehow being a representative or extension of themselves. Perhaps the person being boosted is working toward a shared goal, such as by running a marathon to raise money on behalf of a charity. Or perhaps there's a strong emotional tie between the person doing the boosting and the person being boosted.

There's a reason why high school "booster" clubs are composed almost exclusively of parents of students who are participating in the activities, and why the booster volunteers generally move on after their children graduate or lose interest in the extracurricular activity. Once the person the booster cares about moves out of the set of beneficiaries, the desire to boost goes away.

Booster clubs often suffer from an internal focus on fundraising: all, or nearly all, of the labor and donations come from a few people on the administrative team. The group is never successful in drawing attention or resources in from the surrounding community. Private schools and charter schools are especially susceptible to this. Sometimes it's because they haven't been around long enough to have lots of financially successful alumni. Other times, their alumni don't stay local and attribute their success in life to other things. There's a perception that people wealthy enough to afford private schools don't need help from the rest of the community, and frequently students from private or charter schools are insulated from the community and appear to do absolutely nothing to improve it. If you want to raise your profile, attack these public perceptions by providing examples to the contrary.

If you want to market a booster program, the only way to do it is to either identify the people who benefit as being worthy of financial support from the greater community, or to play up the connection between the donors and the people who benefit. People, especially small business owners, love to support children's sports leagues and school athletics. Not only does it allow them to "give back" to the community that supports them, but it provides a way for them to advertise and maintain a presence in the community.

Chapter 13: How to Run A Successful Event

This is another chapter about logistics. It introduces event based fundraising and provides a general description of what you need in order to make the activity successful. "It takes money to make money" is not always true. As this chapter will show, it's possible to put together a very successful fundraiser without spending large amounts of money if you have sufficient social capital and if you know your target market.

This chapter will focus on social capital based fundraising. Labor based activities such as car washes and bake sales have already been discussed, and the chapter on booster clubs includes detailed instruction about how to run a concession stand.

Thing-a-thons

Earlier in this book, I introduced thing-a-thons as an example of social capital based fundraising. In order to make a thing-a-thon work, you need a pool of volunteers who are willing to solicit and collect pledges. You need a venue of some sort that is appropriate to the activity. Finally, you need a few things to make the event at least a little bit fun for the participants and to raise the profile of your charity a little bit.

Identify who your designated masochists will be

Figure out who's going to be soliciting pledges, doing an activity, and then collecting the money. For charities that do not benefit humans, such as animal shelters or environmental protection organizations, you should already have a pool of volunteers. Use these, and also use the members of the Board and their families. In all other cases, the primary source of volunteer effort should come from the people who benefit directly from the charity.

If your charity benefits children under twelve years of age, or if you are a booster club of some kind, understand that the children for the most part will not be soliciting donations themselves. All the work will be done by the parents.

Some categories of people are more successful than others in soliciting sponsors. Children are more successful than adults, especially if the activity looks or sounds painful.

Choose an appropriate activity

Consider who will be doing the repetitive activity, and pick an activity relevant to the people who are doing it. If you have a sports charity, your beneficiaries will be the obvious source of labor. So pick something related to their sports activity. Hockey or figure skaters can have a skate-a-thon where they skate a hundred laps around an arena. If basketball is the sport, have each participant shoot a hundred hoops. I've seen schools make money by having their students jump rope, run laps, or spell words.

The more masochistic the activity is, the easier it is to raise money. I once participated in a judo throw-a-thon where we threw each other a hundred times onto the mat from waist or shoulder height. So I can say from personal experience that it's easy for a kid or teenager to raise money if he or she can look someone in the eye and say: "I want this so badly I'm willing to hit the ground a hundred times for it."

For charities with an adult focus where most of the people raising money are Board members and their families, you can incorporate sports that are not related to your program but that have something to do with the preferred recreational activities of your Board members. Consider a golf marathon, curl-a-thon, or tennis point-a-thon. This will provide a bit of exercise and recreational activity.

Find a way to make the participation quantitative. Multiples of 100 are effective for marketing, but they should represent a significant effort. 100 laps around a track an eighth of a mile long is still twelve and a half miles. That's a reasonable distance for seasoned adult walkers or runners and a few well conditioned teens, but not for children or senior citizens.

When to not use a thing-a-thon

If your charity has a youth focus but emphasizes at-risk youth or foster children, it's generally a bad idea to ask them to try to raise money from their families. Most of them do not have functional families that are capable of contributing, and that's why the kid is at risk in the first place. Foster kids are seldom in contact with family members at all. Even when a family network is available, it can be too dysfunctional to support fundraising. Too many kids do all the work of selling the chocolates or collecting the pledges only for the money to be stolen by an addicted or self-absorbed relative.

Six to eight weeks in advance

Pick a date for the thing-a-thon that is at least two months in advance. If it is an outdoor activity that may be postponed due to bad weather, identify the rainout day.

Secure the venue as quickly as possible. Do not announce the fundraiser date before the venue is booked unless you are completely confident that you will have a backup location. Ideally, you will be able to get the use of the venue for free. If you're raising money for a community center expansion but you already own the location and there's a basketball court already present, you can set up a dunk-a-thon or a basket-a-thon anytime you like provided you aren't interfering with any of your existing programs. Likewise, if you're already leasing space for your gymnastics program or dance program, just work the thing-a-thon in during or after a normal lesson.

Start soliciting donations for refreshments, decorations, and incentives for the participants.

Four to six weeks in advance

Start socializing the idea of your thing-a-thon with parents, staff, students, and the general public. Put up posters. Talk about it. Get people excited about it, and sign up volunteers who are willing to collect pledges. Make sure that everyone knows when and where the thing-a-thon will be.

If you run a booster club, consider making participation mandatory for the students who benefit from your work. The participation need not be at the event: a student might help by organizing and distributing pledge sheets, counting money, or handing out refreshments at the event.

See to it that the people who volunteer will receive something special that the other people don't, to acknowledge their effort and contribution. A special bracelet, or hair ribbon, or gold star on the wall with a student's name on it is worth more than the dollar value of the item. The feeling of pride a student has when earning such a thing is the motivation to do it.

Make up the pledge sheets. You may be able to find a template online. If not, a word processor will do the trick if you create a table. Each sheet should have the name of the person collecting the pledges, the purpose of the pledge, the name of the charity, and the date.

The first column of the table should be for the donor's name. The second column is for the donor's phone number so you can collect the pledge later. The third column is for the donor's address so you can mail or deliver the appropriate receipt for donations $20 and up.

The fourth column is the per-unit pledge. If you're doing a swim-a-thon, this is the pledge per lap. Every time someone makes a pledge, the student or volunteer fills in the first four columns. The rest of the columns do not get filled in until the thing-a-thon is complete and the pledges have been collected.

The fifth column is for the total due, which will be the per-unit pledge from the fourth column multiplied by the number of units the volunteer completes. Do not complete this column until the thing-a-thon is complete and the volunteer knows how many units of work he or she did.

You may also include a check-mark column to indicate that you have received the full amount from the donor. Do not fill it in until you receive the check or the payment. In some cases, a donor won't care how many units your volunteer completes and will simply write out a check or give cash. This simplifies life for your volunteer, who no longer has to hunt down the person who made the pledge.

For donations of twenty dollars or more, you must provide a receipt. You may do this on the spot, or after the fact. The receipt includes the donor's name and address, the date, the amount given, and the name of your charity complete with your EIN.

Three weeks in advance

Distribute the pledge sheets to all your volunteers. Allow no less than two weeks, but no more than three weeks, for people to go around collecting pledges and donations.

Figure out who your logistics people are going to be. You'll need someone to supervise the safety aspect of the activity, and some means to keep track of who's done their laps or units.

If the person doing the counting doesn't recognize each athlete by sight, you're going to have to have people counting and keeping track of multiple athletes. In a swim lane, there might be three or four athletes at a time, and one volunteer standing at the end of the lane can count laps for everyone in it. If people are going around a track, you may use parents or some other person based on the honor system, or you may have one volunteer count laps for up to half a dozen people provided they are somehow identified with numbers or some similar means.

You may have participants wear identifying colored swim caps, streamers, or ribbons if you wish. Just make sure to have some means of counting people quickly. For the most part, you'll have an easier time of it if you buy the materials in advance and have them ready. For runners going around a track or skaters going around a rink, I prefer to get several different colors of construction paper and make armbands or badges with a name or number on each. Then I assign all the orange tags to one counter, all the yellow tags to another, and so on. I find each counter can easily keep track of half a dozen kids at a time so long as the badge or tag is on the outside arm.

Don't try to make unique badges or numbering systems up the night before the event.

Three days before

Collect all the pledge sheets and any money donated so far. Make copies of the pledge sheets and keep one. This accounts for money already donated and also allows you to see how much each volunteer solicited. If you've decided to send out receipts centrally, you can get started on receipt mailing for the donations you already received.

If you are giving out prizes or incentives for the people who raise the most money, this is your chance to calculate who the winners are. Do not reveal the winners before the event. Keep people in suspense.

The day before the event

Make sure any necessary setup has been done. If you have access to the venue in advance, go in and set up refreshment stations, equipment, and other things necessary for whatever you're doing. If it's a gymnastics vault-a-thon, make sure there's a seat for the counter who will mark off each athlete's vault attempts.

See to it there's a sheet of paper with each athlete's name on it, and make sure there's some posted, written order in which the athletes will be going. The counter at each swim lane or each vaulting horse should know who should be credited with what, at all times.

Make sure you know who your counters, referees, timers, and other volunteers are. Make sure you know who is staffing the refreshment stand.

The refreshments, incidentally, should be free. Offer at least water and cup servings of some kind of sweetened but uncarbonated sports drink. Depending on how early in the morning it is and how cold it is outside, you may also offer coffee. Cookies or homemade cupcakes are also excellent refreshments, but this is your opportunity to share out and give away some of the donated food given by your sponsors.

If it's at all possible, set up a microphone with an amplifier so that someone can read off the names of athletes as they finish.

The day of the event

Mention your sponsors as often as you can. Use the microphone to direct people to the refreshment stand and to identify athletes as they complete their required number of thing-a-thon units. Also announce and acknowledge people who brought in significant numbers of pledges. Make sure the free goodies are on hand so that each volunteer receives the appropriate reward.

As the volunteer leaves, give him or her a copy of the pledge sheet, but fill in the number of units completed so that the last two columns can be filled in.

The week after the event

Allow at least a full week for people to contact the donors who supported them with pledges, and get the pledged money. As the money comes in, mark off what each volunteer brought.

Send out receipts as needed. It's also classy and appropriate to send thank-you notes or letters to the individuals and businesses that provided you with material or financial support.

Special note: crashing somebody else's thing-a-thon

One of the most brilliant fundraising strategies I've seen in a long time is when a charity leverages off of another charity's public event such as a marathon or half-marathon. This strategy costs very little and can produce impressive results especially if you're able to get plane tickets or hotel rooms donated or at a deep discount.

Identify one or more runners to participate as designated representatives of your charity. This runner does extensive fundraising online and in person. Should he or she meet the necessary threshold (or even if the threshold is not met), fly that runner to the particular marathon. Put him or her up in a hotel, provide special gear with your logo emblazoned on it, and take lots of photos to enhance your social media presence.

Some airlines and hotel chains have charitable giving programs. As a 501(c)(3) charity, you may well qualify for help. You may be able to set up a system whereby people donate their unused or unwanted travel points. Or, you might even be able to solicit donations of plane tickets. The value of plane tickets or hotel rooms given to you by donors may indeed be tax deductible if they itemize their deductions. If you know anybody whose air miles or hotel points are about to expire, consider soliciting a donation for one of your runners.

The money an individual runner raises for you may not be equal to the full market value of the plane ticket, the hotel room, and the runner's registration fee. However, if you've been intelligent about how you get the plane tickets and hotel rooms, you will still come out ahead financially while seeing to it that you're numbered among the biggest charitable organizations around.

Gala or party events

Everyone has a mental image of a charity gala: a bunch of expensively dressed people standing around sipping expensive drinks while music plays in the background. From time to time, rich people remark on how nice it is to see each other, exchange recommendations for plastic surgeons, and use the words "summer" or "brunch" as verbs. At some point, people either drop off a check or make a bid on an auction item they don't really need or want. Supposedly everybody there is having a good time being seen supporting the charity.

That's a nice mental image, I suppose. It just isn't accurate.

Charity galas can indeed involve donations, silent auctions, and raffles but the absolute last thing people care about is dressing up for the privilege of eating rubbery catered chicken and listening to a kind of music they don't actually like while hobnobbing with friends they already see on a daily basis.

A very upscale gala is an exercise in power brokering. The guests are attending to network, not just to be seen. That's what they're paying for with the high-priced ticket: access to power they wouldn't otherwise get. If you're setting up a gala to raise money for somebody's political campaign, for example, you're selling access to the candidate and to other powerful people who support him or her. If you're setting up a gala to raise money for your museum, you're selling access to people who have power in different domains, and who at least nominally care about the museum.

Not one of your guests considers the ticket price as payment for the food or the entertainment. The music may not be to their taste, the catered meal is far lower quality than they could get at home or in a comparably priced restaurant, and they aren't there to hang out with friends because they already hang out with friends whenever they wish. Your guests consider the ticket price as something that provides them access to people they want to be seen with, *whose attention they cannot otherwise get.*

A less upscale gala can be held in someone's living room or a church basement, but you're going to have to provide decent food, some background music, and perhaps a raffle or entertainment of some kind.

Your ticket price

Take your estimated expenses and divide them by the number of guests. That will be your nominal ticket price, but keep in mind that you will be giving some tickets away for free.

Catering and your venue will be your two biggest expenses, but you also need to budget for live entertainment. You should also have an open bar, unless you're a conservative charity from a religious tradition that bans alcohol.

For live entertainment, before dinner you should have acoustic music of some kind. A pianist is the cheapest kind available and you may be able to get the services on a volunteer basis. Classically trained pianists and keyboardists are easily available if you simply advertise or take referrals. A solo flautist, harpist, violinist, or classical guitarist could also be a good choice. Small ensembles such as string quartets may be an option. But avoid anything with vocals. If acoustic music isn't available, use recorded music, but keep track of the volume.

Stick to the kind of music your audience actually likes. There's absolutely nothing wrong with playing blues, show tunes, or even heavy metal if that's how your audience likes to roll. If you're inviting people to a motorcycle gala, have everybody show up in their riding leathers (instead of black tie), have some thrash music or Southern rock playing in the background, tap open a keg, serve some barbecue, and raffle off motorcycle gear.

After dinner, you may combine dance music with a silent auction if your sensibilities permit dancing. Otherwise, stick with background music that has no vocals.

If you care about whether or not you're displaying good taste, set up a gaudily yet expensively decorated donation box put somewhere discreet enough to require people to look for it but obvious enough that every single human in the hall will see it. Include some pens and envelopes to collect addresses so you can send the appropriate tax deductible receipt. This box should not be easily accessible from the door. No doubt you trust your guests, but since your gathering is not secret and at least a few of your guests will donate cash, have the presence of mind to pay someone to keep an eye on your cash box, and don't make it easy to steal.

If you do not provide a donation box, have your master of ceremonies explicitly ask for the diners or guests to stop what they're doing and write out a check. This should occur after the meal has been served and the plates have been cleared away. Provide access to pens, but please do not put them on the table like decorations.

Whom to invite

If you can't offer your attendees a networking opportunity, don't bother to throw a gala. If you're going for an upscale crowd, you need to pull in at least one local politician, at least one judge, at least one reporter (you have to give that pair of tickets away for free) and at least two successful local entrepreneurs. Besides that you need a handful of professionals, and some color. For color you want local celebrities: athletes and entertainers will do. If you've got a conservative angle, you need some military guests ranked at or above major and representatives from at least two corporate employers that favor what you do.

Get a token representative from the local United Way and a couple other main charities (because you trade... they attend your gala and you attend theirs). Most importantly get someone from each of the local old families.

An old family is one that is extremely well established in the local social scene. They aren't necessarily wealthy, but their power generally comes from having owned land in the area for generations. In medieval Europe, these would be members of the nobility. In practice, these are the families whose names you may see on social registers, on the sides of hospital and university buildings, and occasionally in small print on a "donated by" plaque. These are notoriously hard people to solicit if you don't already know them, and for the most part you don't want their money. You want their presence, although in most cases they prefer that you don't advertise it. Most of their major donations are made anonymously. If you want to raise money through a gala, you need at least one old family backing your charity, because old families are the repositories and arbiters of a region's social capital. This is the name you allow your Board members to drop when they're talking about who else is coming to dinner.

If you've been in town a full year and don't know the names of at least some of the local old families, you are not an effective power broker. Go to the library or some other place public records are kept, and find out who has been involved in founding key charities, founding political parties, and establishing centers of learning or healing. Those are the surnames you want to type into a search engine.

The rest of the guests can be social stuffing: Realtors, insurance agents, car dealership owners and such. They show up hoping to troll for new customers and hoping to be seen.

Guest-wise, you pull in powerful people by offering them the opportunity to network with somebody with more power still, but in a different domain. The trick is to pull in influential people from multiple domains by using your Board of Directors and their personal contacts. Each member of your Board ought to be able to get at least two or three guests either from their own family contacts or their own business or leisure activities.

If you've got a theme (such as the motorcycle gala I suggested earlier), invite everyone you can find who is active in the industry. Sell tickets to, and solicit silent auction or raffle items from, everyone in sight who wants access to bikers who spend money.

Why it works

The judge doesn't care about the lawyers who will be kissing up all night, but would love to kick it with the reporter, the politician, and the head of the local United Way. The politician will be sucking up to the car dealers, entrepreneurs, and insurance agents. The military guests will be playing "who's got the retirement strategy" with the corporate representatives, who will be playing "who gets the no-bid contract" right back with them. The athletes and local celebrities will be playing "sponsor me please" with the local entrepreneurs, while the reporter discreetly snaps pictures of everyone involved. So everyone will have someone who covets association with them, and everyone will see someone they'd like to meet and get to know.

Remember that gaudily decorated box I mentioned? Sometime before the end of the evening, everyone will drop off a check for an amount proportionate to the size of the big, wet, sloppy power-gasm you gave them that evening. The dollar value will be amplified of course by alcohol from your open bar. Booze is a well known loosener of tongues and purse strings. They don't call it a social lubricant for nothing.

To gratify your biggest donors, seat them next to your most prestigious guests based on the particular domain in which they have less power than they'd like. Have a few of them speak for a few minutes before bringing in your main speaker of the evening. Basically, what you're doing is throwing a power brokering theme party, with your charity as the theme.

The most important aspect of your gala evening is talk. If you provide dance music, make sure there aren't any vocals, and make sure that even an elderly person with a hearing aid can have an enjoyable conversation. Most of the old family representatives will be, well, old. So are a fair number of the local philanthropists. Retired people, or people who make their income from businesses or investments they own, may make up close to a quarter of the people you invite.

Silent auctions

A silent auction is an event where you put a bunch of donated items on a table and people write down their bids. At the end of the evening, the highest bidder gets each item. The goal is to raise money for the charity, so people often bid more than the item is worth.

Silent auctions are best combined with gala or benefit events where the tickets have already been bought in advance. If the attendees have already taken their wallets out several times by the time the bidding begins, they will not be in a mood to give. Therefore, you may combine a silent auction with a celebratory dinner, a benefit performance, or any other activity where people buy tickets in advance or else pay at the door. Do not combine it with a restaurant based or club based fundraiser where people are already paying for food, drinks, tips, parking, and everything else.

Other kinds of parties

Suppose you, and the members of your Board, read the description of the charity gala and would gladly pay money to avoid having to experience it. Maybe you and your spouse don't own any formal wear, you find jazz music puts you to sleep, and you have never been able to stand classical music but would enjoy some nice Texas two-step.

Maybe you don't live in a big city where there's a symphony orchestra or a big museum. But for whatever reason, you've got a cause a lot of people believe in. Maybe the school needs a new roof, or you'd like to build a community center with a swimming pool for the kids. Perhaps you're a branch or a larger environmental or service charity that has relevance to the local community.

Compared to urban charities, rural and small town charities are far more likely to focus on hunting, fishing, and other outdoor activities. They tend to have more of an emphasis on wilderness conservation and on public facilities that are simply provided by larger towns or cities through tax dollars. Churches, lodges, and other societies and circles are legitimate, ongoing sources of social activity. A lot of the time, they represent one of the only sources of family-friendly evening or weekend entertainment.

In a place like this, a power-brokering party like the charity gala I described earlier wouldn't make sense. What makes sense is to throw the kind of party people would love to attend. Are there a lot of farmers in the area? Then make it a barn dance. Is it a mining town? Host it in the local union hall.

Provide the kind of food people like to eat and the kind of music people want to hear. Don't be afraid to roast an entire pig or prepare a gigantic amount of beef brisket. Hire musicians from the immediate area and give those struggling artists a bit of a financial boost.

You definitely want to attract people with a high income, or a high net worth, or both. The key is to have the kind of entertainment they like. Start first by talking to some of the people on your donor list. They may appreciate hearing from you to be asked for advice instead of being asked for money.

If you get everything right in terms of your guest list, it's possible to host a small but profitable fundraiser right in your home particularly if you have good snacks and an interesting raffle.

Raffles

There are two kinds of law that apply to raffles: federal law and state law. Depending on the laws of the state you live in, raffles may be considered a form of gambling and may be either prohibited or subjected to taxation or oversight. Sometimes if contestants must answer a skill testing question in order to obtain the prize the raffle can be considered a means of selecting a person who performs work in exchange for reward. Look up the laws of your state before announcing or conducting a charity raffle.

Federal law is simple. If the value of the item being raffled off is higher than the ticket price by more than the threshold for having to declare income ($600 as of 2016), and if the payout is more than 300 times the value of the raffle ticket, the person who wins it must declare it as income and you must also file Form W-2G. The obvious way to avoid paperwork, therefore, is to keep the value of the prizes under $600 and the value of the tickets above $2.

Any item you raffle off has to be legal for the winner to possess. If you're conducting a firearm raffle, for example, it's up to you to make sure that the person who receives the prize is not a felon. You can control this process by making sure each person who sells tickets knows the buyer.

Raffle items are almost always donated. But the most successful raffles are the ones with a specific theme. Guns, electronics, jewelry, and vehicles are always popular but so are handmade quilts, power tools, and original pieces of art. Provided there's some way to establish the market value of the item, you must issue the donor a tax deductible receipt.

A successful raffle brings in more than the retail value of the prizes. Suppose, for example, that you are raffling off five new computers worth $400 apiece. You should expect to bring in at least two thousand dollars. Obviously, you could sell a thousand tickets for two bucks apiece and advertise a 1 in 200 chance of winning, which is reasonably attractive. That's fine if you're going door to door, selling tickets to friends, or setting up a stall at your state fair. But what if not all of your tickets sell? Every ticket sold is an extra transaction, and if you pick your ticket buyers well you can get a better return on invested time by printing fewer tickets and charging more for them.

Mass ticket sales are not the answer. It costs effort to sell each ticket no matter what the tickets cost. Selling a $1 raffle ticket takes the same amount of time as selling a $100 ticket. To bring in the same amount of revenue therefore takes a hundred times more asking, writing, and change-making if you're selling the $1 tickets. Your sales force has a finite amount of time to do the selling, and a fixed number of times they're willing to hit people up.

Sophisticated raffle organizers optimize the volunteer resources by limiting the number of tickets sold, by targeting the tickets to specific items a buyer might want to win, and by charging a higher price for the tickets.

Consider the computer raffle I mentioned earlier. Suppose you raffled off the five $400 computers, but instead of selling a thousand tickets you only sell a hundred and charge $20 per ticket. People would therefore have at least a 1 in 20 chance of winning a computer. This is the kind of raffle financially sophisticated people prefer. They will receive no tax deductible receipt for their effort, but their odds of winning are higher than they would be if they bought twenty tickets out of an unlimited number. If you find perhaps a hundred people who care about your charity and combine a raffle like this with the sort of party they like to attend, you could have an extremely successful fundraising "gala" without the champagne and power brokering.

When not all the raffled items are equally valuable or attractive, if you only have two or three major items it's best to have a "First Prize", "Second Prize", and so on. This works if you've got a mixed bag of prizes where one or two are noticeably more expensive. But the technique can backfire. I once sold tickets for a raffle where the first prize was a big-screen television and the second prize was a pair of tickets to a professional hockey game. Although the dollar value of the tickets was worth much less than the television, hockey was so popular that most games were sold out. The tickets were therefore the most attractive prize.

When you have a bunch of raffle items of various prices and values, and when they are of diverse enough types for ticket buyers to be very interested in one but not another, it sometimes makes sense to sell tickets and let buyers apply the tickets to items of their choice. This will improve the odds for people who are interested in the less popular items but stimulate ticket sales overall.

Section III: The Administration Domain

This section contains seven chapters and most of the technical information in this book. Administering a charity so that it runs smoothly and sustainably requires more knowledge and insight than simply raising money or executing a program. It requires a great deal of thought and foresight, with constant attention to changes in the economic and social conditions affecting both donors and beneficiaries.

Ironically, administration is the domain where most people who run small charities brag about spending little or nothing. In cases where there's not much money to begin with, donors like it best when their contributions are directed toward program activities instead of fundraising or management. I often tell people that small charities have no business paying for administration, and that it's a kind of activity you should be able to get done for free. This, of course, means that YOU are going to be the one providing the skills and the know-how. So naturally it makes sense for me to give you the tools you need to do the job.

Maxims and Equations In This Section

Maxim #8: Your organization's social capital exists only where your supporters and recipients are.

Maxim #9: A charity's volunteer turnover rate should never exceed its beneficiary turnover rate.

Maxim #10: If you exceed the limits of your social capital, work won't get done unless you pay for it.

Maxim #11: Charity must flow downhill.

Maxim #12: Nobody ever voluntarily subsidizes someone with a higher standard of living.

Maxim #13: Never try to expand beyond the minimum size you have to be to accomplish your program.

Maxim #14: A charity with less than $150,000 (2016 dollars) in annual revenue should never pay for administration.

Maxim #15: The bigger your charity becomes, the less you can use labor as a substitute for money.

Maxim #16: No charity with an annual cash budget of less than $150,000 (2016 dollars) should ever buy real estate.

Maxim #17: When you receive or spend money is just as important as how much of it you receive or spend.

Maxim #18: D&O insurance is like a raincoat, not a condom. It will keep you from getting soaked in a random downpour, but it offers no protection if you're actively screwing someone.

Equation 6:   Spending Limit = Total Operating Budget − Contingency

Chapter 14: Budgeting

Administration is the third of the charitable domains, along with program and fundraising. Although it tends to receive the least attention, and it tends to be the most overlooked kind of work, the administration domain is the easiest one to mess up. I therefore devote seven full chapters to it.

This chapter focuses on *budgeting*: the process of making a financial spending and business plan for your organization. This is something you should do before the start of every fiscal year. If you have a multi-year program (such as a film production) you should make a budget for the entire program, and then break it down into year-by-year and month-by-month budgets.

Why you need a budget and spending plan

When you have a budget, you have a good idea what you can afford, and what you can't afford. You need not plan down to the last dollar, either: the best budgets allow enough flexibility to let you take advantage of opportunities when they arise.

There are individuals who run their households and small businesses without a formal budget, because they have a good intuitive feel for how much money they have to work with, and how much they can reasonably spend without overdrawing their checking accounts or missing a bill. That strategy, however, doesn't work for a non-profit because you are accountable to the Board of Directors.

Having an annual budget allows you to communicate with the rest of the administration team and show exactly how you plan to implement the long-range plans of the Board. It provides a starting point for discussion about cash flow, and it also ties nicely into the annual report.

How to make up your budget

Budgeting is the process of figuring out what you can do with the resources you've got. You've probably got a long list of things you'd like to do, but your resources are finite. So the obvious first step is to figure out what you've got.

Your money available might consist of:

- Savings collected in prior years for the purpose of being spent this year
- Expected fundraising income
- Pledged donations from reliable donors
- Expected money from side businesses
- Investment returns, such as interest
- Less liquid assets that are to be sold off, and
- Grant income or other payments that have already been earned or promised, but that have not yet been received

How to find out how much you have available

Your available money consists of the unspent money from previous years, which we call the *balance forward* from last year, plus any money that can be sustainably raised, plus pledged donations. side income, planned asset sales, investment income, and other sources of money.

Step 1: Check your bank account to see whether it contains money that has been raised over previous years for the express purpose of being spent this year. This is a very conservative way of estimating the budget, but it's very easy to understand and explain.

If you do not limit your annual budget to prior years' fundraising, simply check to see whether you've raised *any* money in past years that's earmarked for expenses this year. Do not include your cash reserves or long-term investments in this calculation. Do not include money that has been specifically earmarked and contractually committed to a task.

The results from this step gives you the *balance forward* from last year.

Many parent-teacher associations rely solely on prior-year fundraising to fund their current programs. It's not necessarily a sustainable way of operating, because it's still possible to exhaust a volunteer pool with over-ambitious fundraising, but it has the virtue of presenting you with an instant dollar figure: your budget for this year is your balance forward from last year. So you can stop right here. Otherwise, continue to the next step.

Step 2: Estimate your sustainable fundraising income for the coming year. Do this by performing the Sustainable Effort calculation from Chapter 11.

Do not give in to the urge to simply copy your fundraising figures from last year, unless you are operating under identical conditions. It's reasonable to expect turnover and changes in the economic climate. If you made a big push last year, chances are that your labor pool is overworked and need to rest. Even if you get fresh labor, inexperienced workers are less efficient than experienced ones.

The results of this step will give you your estimated fundraising income.

Step 3: Calculate your *advance pledged income* by adding up any pledged money from your Type B donors or other sources of pledged income. People who give through tithes or payroll deductions are usually very predictable in their giving. You might see a small amount of change or turnover through the year, but not much. Note that these should be unrestricted donations, not things that are set aside for a specific activity or program purpose.

Step 4: Calculate your *estimated side business profit*. Here it's acceptable to use your net gain from last year, as long as your side business hasn't had any major windfalls or new long-term commitments.

Step 5: Calculate your *estimated investment returns*. For savings accounts, the annual percentage rate or APR is generally a good source of information, but if you haven't gained or sold investments the past year it's reasonable to use the average of the last five years' rate of return. Apply this percentage rate to the amount of money you're planning to keep invested throughout the rest of the year. It's true that short-term investments can earn interest or profits too, but treat that income as a bonus.

Step 6: If you are planning to sell any significant assets this year, list the estimated profit as *estimated asset sale profit*.

Step 7: If you have been awarded a grant that has not been received, or if you've collected money that you've agreed to apply to some specific purpose (and which was therefore excluded in Step 1). Add it all up and call it *restricted money*. This money has limitations on how it can be used.

Step 8: Add the totals from Step 1 through Step 7 together. This is your *total operating budget.*

Step 9: Subtract your *contingency* percentage from your total operating budget and set it aside. For a new venture your contingency should be 10% or even higher. If you've been in business a while and you have a few years of expenses to help you estimate with, you can get by with just a 5% contingency.

Contingency money is the money you will spend, but you don't know what you're going to spend it on. When you have an emergency of some kind, you dip into your cash reserves to pay for it, and you replenish your cash reserves with your contingency money. Having contingency money gives you a little bit of extra financial stability.

Step 10: Your *spending limit* is the amount left over after Step 9. It's the total operating budget minus the contingency.

Equation 6

Spending Limit = Total Operating Budget − Contingency

The goal is certainty

The idea, when you make a budget, is to use money you're sure of. Do not count any chickens before they are hatched. Don't count grants that you "might" get, or factor in any income from new, untried, unproven forms of Pied Piper fundraising.

If by chance you get some windfalls through the year, or if fundraising goes better than you expect it to go, good for you. Save the money as a balance forward for next year, or pay off some debt, or get a money market account and stuff your cash cushion. *You are forbidden to plan your budget with the expectation of getting windfalls or grants that have not yet been formally awarded to you.*

There are charities that use the previous year's budget as a starting point, and begin with the goal of raising the same amount of money, or more. That's backwards. It leads to not being able to sleep at night. Follow steps 1 through 8, and you're guaranteed to have a budget that's realistic and sustainable. Your next step will be to plan your spending to fit within that budget.

How to make a spending plan

Now you have a spending limit, which is the amount of money you have available this year. Notice that some of this may be restricted income. The dollar figure you calculated in Step 7 must be applied to the specific purpose for which it was raised. You do this by adding up your expected and planned expenses.

Step 1: Write down every possible expense you can realistically expect to have in the coming year. Include insurance, utilities, salaries, and everything else. Write down a dollar estimate next to each expense. If you guess slightly high or slightly low, it doesn't matter, because low guesses on some items will be offset by higher guesses on others.

Step 2: From your list of expenses, make a list of existing commitments. Include every single payment you're contractually obligated to make. These include lease payments, debt service, payment for goods and services you have ordered or received, and taxes if you happen to not be exempt from them. If your lease expires part of the way through the year, include only the remaining months. This is because your organization reserves the right to move at the end of the lease term.

If you have employees, include two weeks' worth of salary or wages, or whatever notice period there would be if for some reason you had to lay them off immediately. If you signed an employment agreement promising a month's worth of notice, write down that payment for each employee. If you'd be buying out a contract of some kind and there's a penalty for early termination, figure out which one would cost you less and write down that cost.

This, by the way, isn't a plot to lay people off. This is a way to quantify what you would still have to pay if you did.

Put these existing commitments on your spending plan and check them off of your list of possible expenses.

Quick crystal ball test: Are your existing commitments (from Step 2) are greater than your total operating budget (from Step 8 of the budget instructions)? If so, your organization is about to go insolvent and will face extreme cash flow problems later in the year, if they have not already hit. Consider shutting the venture down completely, or else plan some asset sales.

Step 3: Make a second list of *mission critical* expenses. These are not the expenses necessary to run the program. They are only the ones necessary to keep you in business. Insurance, filing fees, audit fees, and such belong here. So does antivirus software and anything else that is standing between you and total disaster. There should not be any program spending here.

Step 4: Add your mission critical expenses from Step 3 to the existing commitments from Step 2. If the sum is less than your spending limit, you can have the mission critical items too. Add them to your spending plan, and congratulate yourself: you get to stay in business for another year. The "needs" are covered.

Step 5: Now, add your restricted income to the total from Step 4, along with any other necessary expenses related to doing the activities tied to the restricted income. If the total is still less than your spending limit, give yourself permission to perform the specific activities paid for by the restricted income. Add these activities and the associated expenses to your spending plan.

Step 6: Now that your organization's needs are taken care of and your restricted income is accounted for, go back to your list of remaining expenses and classify them into two lists: "wants" and "nice-to-haves".

Continuing to rent a building after the lease expires, for example, is either a "want" or a "nice-to-have" because you reserve the right to move somewhere else. The same goes for the remaining wages or salary of each employee after the minimum notice period. If your organization saves some of its annual income, setting money aside for savings and investment is most likely a "want". It's definitely a good practice, but it's possible for your business to stay open without it. Bagels on Friday, however, are definitely a "nice to have".

During this step, identify any items you could arrange to have donated or done on a volunteer basis. If you've been having cash flow problems, taking those expenses out of your spending plan and getting the resources some other way will help you save your liquid assets for things that require money.

Step 7: Rank the items on your "wants" list in order of importance. Utilities, for example, will most likely come before new curtains. Then, one by one, add the "wants" to the spending plan. As long as you're below your spending limit, you can keep adding employees and expenses to your spending plan. These are the people and the operations you get to keep.

Step 8: If you've gotten through all the "wants" and still haven't reached your total operating budget, congratulations: you're running a venture that's basically stable and sustainable. You may now begin with your list of "nice to haves". Add them to your spending plan one by one, until your spending plan equals your spending limit, or until you have no more nice-to-have expenses. (Running out of nice-to-have items has never occurred once in human history, but you might be the first.)

Step 9: When reach your spending limit, stop adding any more expenses. You've reached the limit of what you can afford with the resources you've got. Even if there are items on your remaining list that are very important to you, you cannot afford them at present. Postpone the purchases until next year, or until you receive a windfall, or until you attract enough volunteers and donations to be able to afford more.

This year, you can't have anything except what's on your spending plan. If there are employees who haven't made it into your spending plan by the time you reach your total operating budget, you have to be honest with them and let them go as soon as possible. The same goes for if you have to cut people's hours or cancel a contract with a vendor.

It's sometimes possible to rearrange priorities so as to keep a key employee by postponing a major purchase, refinancing a loan, or getting creative about different kinds of expenses. But sometimes it's just not possible to hold onto everything. At that point, you have to be prepared to make tough decisions. This is where the expensive mammals—white elephants and sacred cows—will drag you down.

Budget time is when you, and possibly the Board, may have to change the scope of your program, agree to lay off a loyal employee who depends on your charity for his or her living, or wrap up a longstanding lease or business agreement that's become too expensive to keep. For organizations that do not stick to their initial spending plans, budget time is painful. But it's also the time when you see opportunities to renegotiate leases, refinance loans, and get key items donated.

How to make a spending schedule

Your budget tells you how much you have available to spend. Your spending plan tells you what purchases you are able to make. Now, all you need to do is to get the timing right. You need to figure out *when* you're going to make your purchases, so as to make sure the money is available when you need it. You also need to coordinate your spending activities with your fundraising.

For this section, let's pretend you manage a tiny private operating charity: a memorial fund that gives out scholarships. Your goal is to give out three $5,000 scholarships per year.

You have an endowment fund that produces $500 per month after management expenses and reinvestment. You're also receiving a $2,000 grant in March and a $3,000 one in April. In October, you get $1,000 from a former recipient of the scholarship. In December, you get about $5,000 from holiday donors in your extended family.

Suppose you start with a balance forward of $1,000 that is left over from the last program cycle. Your program year starts in September. To award three scholarships by the following August, you spend $300 per month in March and April advertising and promoting the scholarship. In May, you spend $200 on postage and expenses related to accepting the applications. In June, you announce the recipients and pay $500 in advertising and correspondence. Three $5,000 scholarships go out in August. Aside from this, you have no major expenses because you operate out of your best friend's law office. You don't set aside a contingency fund because your expenses are so predictable, and you have no need for insurance.

Step 1: Make a simple chart with four columns: the month, earnings in that month, expenses for that month, and the cash on hand at the end of the month. In the example case, you start with a $1,000 balance forward, and every month you get $500 from the endowment fund.

Table 5: Scholarship Foundation Spending Plan

End of month	Income	Expense	On hand
Sep	$500	$0	$1,500
Oct	$1,500	$0	$3,000
Nov	$500	$0	$3,500
Dec	$5,500	$0	$9,000
Jan	$500	$0	$9,500
Feb	$500	$0	$10,000
Mar	$2,500	$300	$12,200
Apr	$3,500	$300	$15,400
May	$500	$200	$15,700
Jun	$500	$500	$15,700
Jul	$500	$0	$16,200
Aug	$500	$15,000	$1,700
Sep	$500	$0	$2,200

This program cycle starts in September, when you start raising money for the next scholarship the following August. Table 5 contains a full year of program, plus one extra month to show the next year's starting point.

You're earning money steadily over the course of the year, and spending very little of it except for one big chunk when you pay out the scholarships in August. But by the time you write the check, there's money in the bank to cover it: the "On hand" column never has a negative number in it.

Step 2: Make a line graph with the months of the year along the bottom and a separate line for each of the dollar figures.

Figure 5: Spending plan, scholarship fund

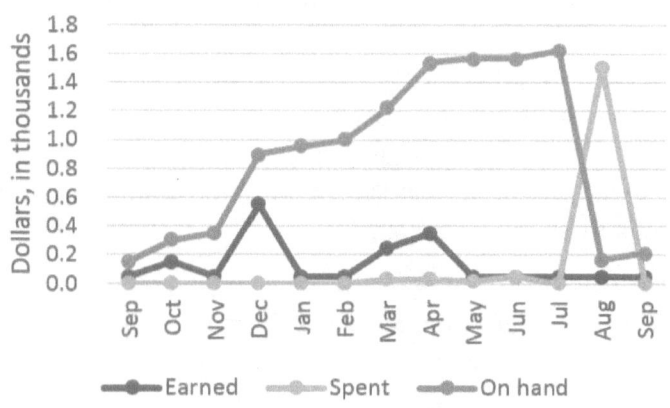

This a healthy organization: look at those curves.

Notice how the cash on hand builds up before the spending hits. The "On hand" column never goes negative. This means the organization doesn't have to borrow, and no money is being spent on debt service.

Step 3: Calculate whether you have a budget surplus or a budget deficit. Add up the totals for a full year of income (September through August, in our example case). Then add up all the expenses through the same time frame. In our example case, the scholarship charity gains a total of $17,000 and spends a total of $16,300. The income is greater than the expense, so there is a budget *surplus*. If the expenses were greater, there would be a budget *deficit*.

Step 4: Calculate your net cash flow. Do this by subtracting what you started with from what you ended with. In our example case, we calculate the program year as having started at the beginning of September, with $1,000 balance forward. On the last day of August, the ending balance is $1,700. This means you gained $700 over the course of the year, and have positive cash flow.

$$\$1,700 - \$1,000 = \$700 \ net \ cash \ flow$$

Congratulations: your charity is making money. The balance forward from this year, if everything goes well, will be $1,700 instead of $1,000. You could continue like this year after year and still conduct your program.

You can use this same technique to plan your fundraising and spending next year. Just make sure you schedule your fundraisers to make sure your cash on hand peaks before you need to spend the money.

Executing the plan

The success of your spending plan depends on the team's willingness to stick with it. If you've got an employee or officer who for some reason insists on spending money on things that aren't on the spending plan, that person needs to be put in check.

Don't procrastinate

If you've got cuts to make, make them quickly. Nobody likes cutting back a program or laying people off, but if you procrastinate you will end up spending money you can't afford to spend. Every day you do this, you go through money and social capital you can't get back.

Don't engage in deficit spending

Many businesspeople are risk takers. They're willing to gamble by going into debt and taking risks by committing money they don't have. That might work sometimes in the for-profit business world, but in the not-for-profit world you're not here to gamble.

During the year, opportunities will come up to snap up a nice asset or to get a good deal. Some unexpected setbacks will also occur. That's what the contingency money is for.

Don't let yourself be seduced by the notion that you will magically develop the ability to earn more money to cover your budget shortfalls. If you ask your fundraising team for more than they can sustainably produce, the well will eventually run dry, and then you'll start to lose your volunteers. It's a very bad idea.

Don't reallocate money during the year

Once you've allocated money for something, you have to be disciplined about your spending. If your utility bill is a bit higher than you expected, it's OK to pay it, but if it's lower than you expected, you don't have the automatic right to assign the extra to some new expense that isn't on the spending plan. For all you know, next month's utility bill might be higher than you expect. *Draw what you need from contingency instead.* If you need to reallocate more money than this, you have a bona fide emergency and should call an emergency Board meeting to address it.

Manage contingency money intelligently

If your spending is pretty steady throughout the year, it's reasonable to expect to spend roughly 1/12 of your contingency money every month. If you go over this amount slightly, reduce your next month's contingency allowance. If, in any particular month, you don't use your contingency money, simply roll it forward into the next month in case there's an emergency.

Don't be afraid to spend your contingency money: it's not your cash reserves or your savings. Contingency is an "above the line" expense: it is money you will spend on something or other, but exactly how or when you'll spend it is not known at the time you draw up the spending plan.

Important things to remember

You should expect to have more than one round of discussion and brainstorming every time you create your budget. The Board of Directors may have some ideas as to whether the program activities you're funding are in alignment with their long-term goals for the organization. Whoever is in charge of the fundraising may have some information about new opportunities or new volunteers.

The more people you involve in the budget process, the more likely you are to find out about game-changing shifts in the social and economic environment where you're operating. Also, the more people look at your numbers and estimates, the more likely they are to correct bad cost estimates or to point out ways you could get labor or materials for free.

The down side to involving other people involved in the budget process is that you frequently have to defend some of your decisions as to what is "in" and what is "out".

Needs, wants, and nice-to-haves

Some of your program expenses are mission critical, meaning that it's impossible to execute your program without them. These expenses can be thought of as needs. It is impossible to substitute anything else, and it is impossible to get by with a donated equivalent.

One example of a mission-critical expense is the medicines distributed by a vaccine clinic. Although you may be able to negotiate a lower cost per unit by buying in bulk and by dealing directly with the drug or vaccine manufacturers, ultimately money is going to have to change hands. Cutting out the vaccines is not a viable option, because you can't get rid of them and still have a vaccine clinic.

Another example of a mission critical expense is the heating bill for a battered women's shelter in a northern state. The building is mission critical because you have to house people 24 hours a day, 7 days a week, and placing them in the homes of volunteers (like some animal rescue organizations do) is not practical for safety reasons.

Not heating the building during the winter isn't an option, because people are living there. In fact, even if the building were vacant, it would have to be kept above freezing to ensure the pipes do not burst. It might be possible to negotiate a lower rate from the utility company, but once again money must change hands.

Wants are different from needs, because they represent things your non-profit *should* have, versus things it *must* have in order to exist. In a pinch, you can get by without them for a short period of time by substituting a similar item or service.

Suppose, for example, that you run a gymnastics club. Clearly the athletic practices must happen somewhere, and clearly athletes must be able to use the mats, bars, vaulting horses, and beams necessary to practice technique. But, is it vitally necessary that your organization own the gear it uses? Perhaps not. If you're just starting out, it may be practical to borrow or rent someone else's. So, whereas a balance beam is definitely a need, exclusive access to a balance beam is a want, or perhaps even a nice-to-have.

Brainstorming alternate ways to satisfy wants

Let's reconsider our imaginary animal shelter from Chapter 8. Through luck or expert management, it was fortunate enough to have space donated to house the animals. But suppose something changed: suppose the building was sold, and the new owners were not willing to provide space for free.

If the animal shelter was yours, how would you go about finding ways to house, feed, and provide medical care for all those animals? Well… charities in the past have successfully provided housing through animal foster programs where they are housed with volunteers. Similarly, it might be possible for your veterinarian to join an existing practice that already has a surgery, and negotiate a reduced rate for services. Or, you could simply rent space for the vet office, hang out a shingle, and offer your vet's services to the public on a part-time basis so as to subsidize medical care for your animals. The remaining staff could then focus on pet food collection and distribution to the homes of volunteers, or else on outreach programs to recruit new pet foster homes.

So, in the case of the animal charity from Chapter 8, the specific building was not actually a "need". Nor was the vet, nor were most of the staff. Once you free yourself from the idea that there's only one way to solve a problem or achieve a goal, you realize that there's more than one path up your mountain.

Earlier in this book I introduced my Maxim #1, which says that *human "need" as expressed by demand for your program, will expand to consume and then exceed all available resources.* This insight is drawn from decades of study of human nature, and I list it first among my maxims for a reason. It is vital that you, as an administrator, manage people's expectations both within and outside your organization. You must set limits on your program, because the people who need it and use it won't.

Hedonic adaptation is a phenomenon where human beings adapt to whatever life hands them. Rude shocks like a bad injury or illness devastate people, but a year or two after they get accustomed to their new limitations, they tend to have the same overall level of happiness as they did before they got hurt or sick. Similarly, winning large amounts of money or getting married doesn't actually make people happier in the long run. There's an initial boost, but it wears off, and after a couple of years people are at the same level of happiness as they had before. People just adapt to whatever the new "normal" might be.

So, what does hedonic adaptation mean to your charity? It means that there will never truly be "enough" to do everything you want to do. There will always be nice-to-haves that you simply can't afford.

As an administrator, you have the unpleasant duty of ranking the different expenses and opportunities before you, and figuring out which things to buy first. The very first step is to separate the needs from the wants and the nice-to-haves. Set aside money for the needs first, and never borrow money to satisfy a want or a nice-to-have.

Never get so attached to a key individual that you start sacrificing program activities in order to pay his or her salary. For a very small charity, paid employees are a nice-to-have. Paid administrators are even deeper in the nice-to-have zone.

How to fail at budgeting

People get in trouble when they forget what budgeting is. Instead of figuring out what they can do with the resources they've got, they do something else.

These are some of the ways charitable ventures goof up the very basic process of creating a budget and spending plan.

Doing it backwards

Non-profit management isn't the *Kama Sutra*. You can squirm, wiggle, and contort yourself into all kinds of financial positions, but if you don't scale your spending to suit the available funds, you'll have a painful and unsatisfying experience.

Instead of designing a program that suits the money they can raise, some charity administrators do the opposite. They set a spending goal and then try to raise enough money to cover it. Inevitably, they overestimate either their stamina or their expertise. Either they exhaust themselves

232

before the climax, or they try what they think is a sophisticated technique only to realize they are over-leveraged, overexposed, and about to lose their assets. Yes, it's extremely naughty of them.

To avoid screwing yourself, ensure you plan your spending based on the available money. Not the other way around.

Fantasy Football

The second you start making business decisions based on what you'd *like to have*, what you *wish you had*, or what you *hope to get someday*, you're not budgeting. You're fantasizing.

There's nothing wrong with a good fantasy once in a while. I enjoy my share of bull sessions with my friends, where we talk about things we'd like to make happen. But I don't confuse that activity with business management.

The evidence suggests that people can tell the difference between fantasy football and NFL play: nobody's showing up on the 50-yard line at the Super Bowl armed with only a tablet and a cutesy team name. If only people could apply the same distinction to the budgeting process, and not base their fundraising estimates on wishful thinking! The problem with like-to-haves, wish-you-hads, and hope-to-haves is that *none of them actually exist.* They're all figments of our imaginations.

When you see an annual budget and spending plan, find out how the management team got their fundraising and spending goals. If they pulled them from the same place James Bond keeps his dinner jacket, run for your life before they also produce the Highlander's sword.

We don't make budgets based on imaginary money. If we wanted to do that, we'd abandon charitable ventures and run for elected office instead.

Trying to spend your way out of a cash flow problem

It's mathematically impossible to solve a cash flow problem by making it bigger. That would be like noticing that the train you're on has a slight wobble, and trying to fix it by speeding up and shaking more vigorously from side to side.

It's the same in the not-for-profit world as it is in your personal life: you have far more control over your expenses than you have over your income.

You bring your cash flow under control by watching your spending, not by trying to increase your income.

Keep your regular expenses low. If it's possible to get something done by paying for it in a way that's reducible at need, do that instead of

233

signing up for monthly instalments. This means that you save up for the things you want instead of buying them on credit.

Suppose you're saving for new flooring by setting aside a little bit of money every month. If you get an unexpected expense one month, you can always decide to not set the flooring money aside after all, and to buy the flooring later. If you buy the flooring instead with credit payable in monthly payments, you end up paying more because of the interest on the loan. You also don't have the flexibility of being able to defer a payment. Sure, you get to enjoy the purchase "now" instead of later, but it's at the expense of your future flexibility.

When times are tough and an organization is losing money, some good expense control strategies are:

Reduce the expenses that can be reduced. You do this by scaling back your consumption. Use less electricity and heat. Forego unnecessary spending, and find cheaper alternatives. Consider scaling back your program.

Delay the expenses that can sensibly be delayed. Make do with the resources you've got instead of spending on new equipment. Repair things instead of replacing them.

Eliminate unnecessary expenses.

Piling on debt

Debt has more of an impact on your organization's cash flow than any other type of business commitment.

Unlike the interest a bank might pay for the cash reserves you keep in your savings account, the interest you pay on a loan is outbound cash flow.

Interest for an unsecured loan (such as if you've borrowed money to repair your church roof) is almost always higher than for a secured loan (such as the mortgage for your church building). This is because a secured loan is backed by an asset of some kind, and the asset represents a way for the bank to potentially get its money back if things go wrong. Unsecured debt is a lot harder to recover.

Relying on grant money

This is the section that gets me in major trouble with professional grant writers, but it contains things that have to be said. First of all, grants are NOT for normal operating expenses, nor are they emergency aid. There's an entire chapter on grants later in this book, so I'm going to defer discussion as to how to go about getting them, and focus on how they should be *used*.

When you receive a grant, the organization that gave it to you intends for it to be used to accomplish a specific goal that provides permanent benefit to the community you serve. They might want for you to produce a film documentary or conduct a scientific experiment, and publish the results. Or, they might want you to expand your program by making it available to a new community.

Grants are restricted income. Many grants specify that a minimum percentage has to go toward the purchase of equipment, and they restrict how much can be spent on administration, rent, or debt. If you decide not to do the thing you got the grant for, you're obligated to return the money.

Organizations that hand out grants for program expansion frequently try to make sure you can afford to continue running the program without their ongoing support. In addition to asking for your financial information and annual reports, grant-giving organizations often make sure that you can afford your proposed program expansion *by making you pay for at least part of it, or by making you put up the money and reimbursing you afterwards.*

That's right: when you apply for a grant, you're making a business proposal, and it will most likely cost you money to hold up your end of the deal. If you can't show the grantor that you're serious enough about a special project or program expansion to raise or set aside money for it yourself, don't expect sympathy from the grantor.

One of the worst things a charity can do when it's hard up for cash is to go after a grant. If you're short on operating capital, the absolute last thing you should be considering is something that expands your program. You are far more likely to need to scale your program back. Chasing grant money puts you in the hole, because even before you get a yes or no decision from the grantor, the money you commit to the proposal is tied up and you cannot use it to fund other existing activities.

Real estate fixation

One of the biggest dangers facing small charities in general, and churches in particular, is real estate.

For reasons unexplained, having and maintaining a dedicated meeting or worship space is one of the primary goals of most churches in the United States. Culturally speaking, it is not considered good enough to imitate the practices of the early Pilgrims, where small congregations of one or two dozen people often met in the home of one of the congregants. Nor is it deemed acceptable to simply get together in fields, public parks, or outdoor locations as many shamanic traditions still do. Only dedicated real estate that is not used for any other purpose appears to satisfy both the requirements of the organized religious bureaucracies and the egos of the people who minister or worship there.

To earn legitimacy in the eyes of the general population, and to earn favor within their own religious hierarchy if they have one, small churches and small congregations routinely stretch beyond their means in order to rent or buy worship space. Once they have it, they also have to pay to heat it, light it, clean it, decorate it, and maintain it.

Given that religious organizations are supposedly set up to promote worship and ministry, and also to provide service to the poor, sick, and helpless, I personally expect to see the majority of every church's program spending directed toward those tasks. When I see a church that is spending more on its worship space than it is on the rest of its entire program, I generally say that the church in question is not in the business of saving souls, serving the poor, or engaging in charitable activities. It's in the business of owning or controlling real estate.

For some reason, people who administer small religious organizations and who fixate on real estate do not seem to have a problem with actually being in the business of owning or controlling real estate to the point where it leaves them very little in terms of resources to do other things. But they get extremely upset when I point the fact out, or when I draw attention to the fact that most of their money goes toward supporting their building as opposed to what is in their program statement. Yet I find that if I can just get them to add *providing a dedicated venue for worship* to their program statement, they suddenly develop the ability to make intelligent business and budgeting decisions about real estate, and they are no longer emotionally attached to reducing their consumption. They become able to find other sources of money or resources that have previously eluded them. When they defeat the hypocrisy, they receive insight. From what source the insight comes, it is beyond the scope of this book for me to say.

Real estate creates expenses that go well beyond the mortgage. Depending on where you are and what the real estate space is for, you may have to pay property tax. The space must be heated, cooled, lit, and supplied with water and sewer service. It must be cleaned and kept free of mold and insects.

You're responsible for what occurs on the property you own. As I mentioned back in Section I, if somebody has an accident on your property, you must pay to fix whatever damage is done. This sometimes goes well beyond medical expenses, especially if the damage was caused by your failure to maintain or repair the property. Allowing an unsafe condition to persist isn't OK, and your liability won't be reduced simply because you can't afford to pay. Most companies (non-profit and otherwise) buy insurance to protect themselves from suits related to accidents on their property. But the insurance won't help if you, or whoever else has access to the space, have been negligent.

If you've got a non-profit business—church or otherwise—and more than half or your money is being spent on real estate, your building should be a key part of your program activities. This means, your program must either require a very specialized space (such as a medical clinic) or 24-hour access to space (such as for a hospice or a youth hostel).

Leasing property is often easier than raising the money for a down payment so that you can own it. But most of the expenses related to ongoing ownership still apply. The space still has to be cleaned, and you—not your landlord—are usually obligated to repair and maintain the space. If you're renting out part of a light industrial or retail facility, you may benefit from landscaping and exterior maintenance provided by the property owner or manager. But this isn't free either. It might be billed to you on a monthly or quarterly schedule, or it might be built into your rent.

Getting out of a multi-year lease is often harder than selling a property. Whereas you can often find a buyer for your building if the price is right, and the mortgage payments stop once it's paid off, commercial leases have teeth. If you decide to cancel the lease, often your only real option is to declare bankruptcy and to go out of business. It's just as bad as being underwater on a mortgage.

One of the subtler dangers of having dedicated space is that your employees and customers get used to it. If you're used to having a dedicated worship space and have to give it up for some reason, going back to a bargain-basement facility will be harder on the congregation than if they had started out in a bargain-basement location and never left.

If your program could be run out of your basement, a public library, a school, or donated space, then it should be, until such time as you can afford all the expenses related to the space it on less than 50% of your budget.

Chapter 15: Classify By Logistics

When it comes to not-for-profit ventures, size matters. The strategies that work well for national charities are poorly suited to regional or small ones, and vice versa. Part of your duty as an administrator is to make sure your organization selects the fundraising, advertising, and volunteer development techniques that are appropriate to the size of business you've got.

By the end of this chapter, you will be able to describe the size and complexity of your charitable organization in a variety of different ways. This will help you when it's time to promote your not-for-profit company, and it will also help you evaluate different promotional and fundraising initiatives that may be proposed to you. The next chapter will focus on selecting fundraising and recruitment strategies based on your size and geographical classification.

You have probably already noticed that there's an entire consulting industry that sells management, investment, and fundraising advice and services. Many of these consultants focus on churches and charities although there's an entire industry that caters to election campaigns. The industry, overall, has made a sincere attempt at self-regulation however as of 2016 there is no government-backed licensure system such as the kind that exists for lawyers, doctors, real estate agents, hairdressers, or massage therapists.

Professional grant writers who subscribe to a national association also submit to a measure of oversight and enforcement from them in terms of ethics and standards. However most people who write grant applications are volunteers or employees representing educational institutions or small to mid-sized charities. There's a bit of mystique associated with the grant-writing profession, and because there's no government-imposed standard or registry for grant writers and membership in national associations is voluntary it's possible for any random idiot to hang out a shingle. Even if the services they offer are competent, a freelance grant writer for hire often doesn't operate with appropriate ethical standards.

Not all of the products or services consultants provide are appropriate to all organizations. Some options simply don't scale well, and others make sense only for a very large venture. So, pick what's right for your not-for-profit corporation, and leave the rest.

Criterion #1: Size

The scale at which a charity operates will influence the type of management, and the type of fundraising, that is appropriate. Although a high school sports booster club, a megachurch, and a performing arts center may serve the same geographical area and have the same type of tax exempt status, they have radically different kinds of resources and donors.

Small charities, such as a high school booster club, typically have (and require) no real estate and no paid employees. Their expansion potential is generally limited by volunteer turnover and the fact the volunteer and beneficiary pools overlap.

Larger charities are more likely to actually need dedicated real estate and paid employees, however they also tend to attract more long-term donors. The bigger the charity becomes, the more administration and oversight is required. Administration expenses increase simply because bigger businesses are more complex. They generate paperwork and accounting that requires more time and commitment from key individuals than can generally be obtained on a volunteer basis.

Here is how I classify a not-for-profit company based on the size of its program and the budget required to run it.

Table 6: Size Classification

	Small	Medium	Large
Annual Budget (including in-kind donations)	Less than $200,000	Less than 2 Million	Greater than 2 Million
Non-income-producing assets	Less than $100,000	Usually about $1 million	Millions of dollars' worth
Income producing assets	Savings or money market account	Stocks or securities	Real estate, stock, securities, intellectual property
Individuals served annually by program	Tens	Hundreds	Thousands
Regular donors	Tens	Hundreds	Thousands
Program volunteer pool	Tens	Tens to hundreds	Hundreds
Fundraising volunteer pool	Tens	Tens to hundreds	Hundreds to thousands
Paid program employees	One to five, part-time	Two to ten, part or full-time	Tens to hundreds, full-time
Paid administrators	None if run properly	One to two, part or full-time	Several, full-time

Depending on the kind of charity you have, it may have attributes that put it in more than one column. A small art museum, for example, might have several million dollars' worth of paintings and sculpture, but rely chiefly on volunteer docents and have only two or three paid employees. A large private operating foundation might have hundreds of millions of dollars in assets, give away a million or two every year, but have no volunteers, regular donors, or fundraising pool at all. In between, an animal shelter might have several paid employees and hundreds of dedicated volunteers, but the number of human beings actually served by the charity is zero, since the accommodations and medical services are provided to animals.

The geographic size of the region served by the charity, or the average size of donations made, do not necessarily predict a charity's size. Two churches might serve the same neighborhood, but one may have a few dozen members while the other has several thousand. A zoo or local museum may serve just a small municipal area, but rake in millions through small but highly advertised fundraising events focusing on the community that benefits from the facility being there. But a special interest lobbying group might receive a handful of big donations each year from people sprinkled thinly all over the nation.

The only real defining characteristic that dictates whether a charity is small, medium, or large, is its average annual budget. A charity with an annual budget less than $200,000 from all sources, including in-kind donations, must be treated as a "small" charity regardless of how many other assets it holds or how many people it serves or employs. A charity that has a variety of sophisticated, high value income producing assets and a sizable donor pool should generally be considered "large" regardless of the size of program it fields every year.

Criterion #2: Geographical Region

One way to describe the community you serve is in terms of geography. You can also use geography to describe your volunteer and donor pool.

Map exercise

Suppose you want a large graphical presentation of some kind to display at a conference, a charity ball, or a donor recognition project. You're creating a map to show off the number of people and organizations that support you, and also the impact of your organization in the immediate area.

Step 1: Get a map, enough poster board or Styrofoam to cover the back to reinforce it, and a bunch of long pins with round balls on the end.

Step 2: Set aside pins of four colors:
Red pins represent individual or family donors (you may ignore corporate or grant-type donors).
Yellow pins represent volunteers.
Green pins represent recipients of the charitable benefit.
Blue pins represent places where you have done fundraising.

Step 3: Go through a year's worth of records, and collect the addresses of the people, stores, or locations for each of the five groups. Obviously not all museum attendees will sign the guest book, but if you pay out scholarship money you will obviously know the recipient's address. You will also know the addresses of any drop boxes, car wash fundraisers, stadium cleanups, or other activities.

Step 4: Affix the map to the backing, and push a pin of the appropriate color into each approximate address. Not all of the pins necessarily need to fit: you can choose a pin with a larger head to represent multiple people or places, and an occasional donor or recipient from an area not on the map can be represented by putting the pin into a separate square or circle indicating that the location is not shown.

When you're done, you'll have a nice graphical representation showing where your labor base is (yellow), where your donors are (red), where your fundraising operations are (blue), and where your recipients are (green).

Now, what kind of map did you instinctively pick for this exercise?

If it's a neighborhood map showing just part of a city or county and nearly everyone fits inside, you have a neighborhood charity.

If it's a city map, you have a municipal charity.

If it's a state map, you have a state charity even if the vast majority of the blue and yellow pins are clustered in and around a particular city, especially if there are clusters of both blue and yellow in more than one city.

If it's a map of the United States, you have a regional charity if you have blue and yellow pins in more than one state. You cannot raise money in any given state without being registered with that state's Attorney General. Also, if your blue and yellow pins appear in more than five states, what you have is a national charity.

If it's a map of the world and you have blue and red dots predominately in the USA but green dots in other countries, you have an international charity. A global charity is one with each color of dot in at least one other country besides the USA. If money is also being raised in England and Italy to benefit recipients in Argentina, for example, the corporation you registered with your state and with the IRS is very likely to be an affiliate of a larger charity or church.

Community overlap and optimal range

In the map exercise, you actually created four sub-maps representing your donors (red), volunteers (yellow), fundraising activities (blue), and recipients (green). If you were to take a piece of string or an elastic band and stretch it around the outermost red dots, you'd have a blob showing where the donors come from. You could do the same for each color of dots and graph the locations of the recipients, the fundraising activities, and the volunteers separately.

Depending on the kind of not-for-profit you run, your donors may not live in the same community as the people who benefit from the charitable work. Missionary work or disaster cleanup generally occurs far away from the area where the money is being raised. NGOs, or non-government organizations, often raise money in wealthier nations and spend it in poorer nations.

The *optimal* range of your venture depends on the purpose for which your organization exists.

Some programs really do require a fixed location and a building—zoos, schools, hospitals, museums, shelters, food banks, and libraries come to mind. In order to benefit from the charitable work, a recipient must either live locally or be willing and able to travel. If the people who benefit from your work are chiefly local, most of the people who care about the work that you do will be local too, and there's nothing you can do to change that without opening a new location.

Maxim #8: Your organization's social capital exists only where your supporters and recipients are.

As you learned earlier in this book, all fundraising requires you to monetize either labor or social capital. You can't sell labor in an area your volunteers can't physically get to, because they've got no way to show up and do the work. You can't monetize social capital in a region where you don't have any.

Time or money spent marketing in a region that cannot possibly ever benefit from your charitable work is a waste of resources unless the people to whom you're marketing have a special affinity for the people being helped. So, if the kind of marketing you're considering involves billboards, posters, radio or TV ads, you'd better make sure the community you're targeting has people who already support charities similar to yours.

244

You get more reliable donors, and bigger donations, from cooperating with charities that operate in markets where you'd like to expand. So, identify the socioeconomic group that values the program you wish to deliver. Then find a charitable venture they also support, and join that community by supporting that charity too. Purchase advertising space in their printed ballet programs, cooperate in a labor based fundraiser, or exchange ministers for a weekend.

This might seem counterintuitive to anybody from a conventional business mindset, because advertising is supposed to produce a return on investment. Simply supporting or giving to a community is antithetical to many conventional business models, however it's about time not-for-profit ventures recognize what Nike and Reebok have known for a long time: you really can't expect to get support from those who never see you give it.

Criterion #3: Affinity clustering

I've coined the phrase "affinity clustering" to describe the way a charity's supporters relate to one another socially. Your supporters will have low, medium, or high levels of affinity clustering based on how much they hang out together when they're not getting together for their primary purpose. The more people hang out together, the faster they build social capital with each other.

Low affinity clustering

A group of people with low affinity clustering has people who seldom know each other at all, and whose paths do not cross except when they get together to do something in support of their group purpose. An example might be students at an adult education class. They sit in the same room, but seldom exchange E-mail addresses or phone numbers and don't get together outside class unless they are working on a group assignment. When the term finishes, each student goes his or her own way. There is no sense of community or long-term commitment.

If your charity has low affinity clustering, turnover in the volunteer pool is extremely high. Individuals are not expected to have long-term commitment to the group, although they can be very dedicated in the short term. The Board can be expected to turn over completely every five years or so, and volunteers help mostly on a casual basis. You have no Class B donors. This is not necessarily bad.

High affinity clustering

A group with high affinity clustering is composed of people who have strong emotional and social bonds with each other. They hang out together all the time even if they aren't related to each other or located in the same place. They're friends on social media if they use it, their children play together, they get together for meals or recreation, they celebrate each other's important life milestones, older adults frequently develop business ties with each other, and young adults frequently date or select marriage partners from within the group. An example might be a rural Mennonite church. There might be thirty or forty different families, and even though not all individuals necessarily get along with one another, they cooperate to provide schooling for their children and emergency aid should one family have a fire or other disaster.

Group members tend to be highly committed over the long term, and turnover is low except among newcomers, who are sometimes unable to integrate. At least part of the low turnover rate is due to the fact that members see membership in the group as part of their personal identity, or even as a key defining characteristic. Indeed, within a given family or social circle, membership in the group is not considered optional.

A group with high affinity clustering tends to have subtle inner circles of leaders and organizers with similar interests, levels of education, social views, and wealth levels. If the group has been around for more than a couple decades, sometimes the leadership ossifies to the point where newer or younger members feel left out.

If you run a charity with high affinity clustering, you have a lot of type B donors. You have entire families as members or volunteers, and within each family multiple generations contribute. You don't have to worry about getting your volunteers to stick around, but you have to watch out for clique behavior.

Medium affinity clustering

A group with medium affinity clustering has characteristics of both the extremes, simultaneously. There is a lot of variety in the commitment level of members. Some of them come and go, but others come and stay for life. One of the chief characteristics of medium affinity clustering is that people stick around out of love for the other people in their group. Their primary allegiance, in fact, is often not to the organization but to their peers. Many form lifelong bonds based on shared experiences, and seek out each other's company even when they're not participating in organized group activities.

A group with medium affinity clustering has a strong social community that is not contiguous. There are several subsets of people who feel a close emotional bond with one another, and who socialize outside the group's primary activity. There's enough variety within the group to ensure that most people can find others of the same ethnic or socioeconomic background. The group tends to be large. Membership in it is voluntary, stereotypes about it have a basis in fact, and it's possible for people to retain a sense of identity even if their active participation is over.

If you run a charity with medium affinity clustering, you tend to have both casual volunteers and long-term ones. There are varying levels of commitment and involvement, but people seldom compete to see who can do the most.

Identify the affinity clustering in your organization

Unless your organization is very small, you're unlikely to know much about your donors or volunteers when it comes to age, ethnicity, or any other demographic information that looks good on a spreadsheet. In fact, the only way to get reliable information is to look at the fundraising records. If for some reason you haven't kept good records about who worked and who didn't, you'll have to get down into the trenches yourself and interview some people.

- How long do your volunteers last?
- Do your Board and your volunteers hang out socially, travel together, or frequent the same Web sites?
- What is your Board turnover like?
- How long do people continue to benefit from your program?
- Do people in the volunteer and donor pool have social capital with each other?

If more than 90% of the Board turns over within five years, and if Board members no longer see each other after quitting or finishing their terms, you have low affinity clustering.

If the spouses and children of Board members regularly socialize with each other, if you've had more than one person from the same family on your Board (not necessarily at the same time), if a past Board member returns for another term after having spent some time off the Board, or if Board members hang out socially with volunteers and former

247

Board members even after finishing their terms (they will seldom quit), you have high affinity clustering.

With medium affinity clustering, small subgroups bond to one another. If the majority (but not all) of your original Board is still part of the community five years after your charity was founded, if your volunteer pool contains people who socialize with each other online and in person, but if you also have people occasionally quit the Board, you have medium affinity clustering. There are people who have social capital with each other, but people don't automatically accord each other significant social capital just because of shared membership in the group.

Churn, turnover, and affinity clustering

A high turnover rate is normal when there's a connection between volunteers and recipients of the charitable benefit, and when recipients of the benefit age out of the program. Many youth programs such as school booster clubs or parent-teacher associations retain their volunteers only as long as those volunteers have children in the program. Unless there's a way for people to stay involved at a later date, each beneficiary goes his or her own way when he or she no longer fits the very narrow focus of the program.

A high turnover rate among volunteers and administrators is only organizationally dangerous when it exceeds the turnover rate of the recipients of the charity.

Maxim #9: A charity's volunteer turnover rate should never exceed its beneficiary turnover rate.

If you have human beings or individual animals as recipients of your charitable venture, their involvement might be short-term or long-term depending on the goods and services you provide and on the kind of need that exists in the community you serve. But the volunteers who provide the services or who raise money to buy the goods should generally not burn out or turn over before the individual recipients move on.

The level of affinity clustering in your group is not necessarily related to its size or geographical distribution, because not all communities are physically co-located. University alumni, for example, are often scattered around the globe but many of them continue to have an interest in their former school's athletic program.

Simply serving a particular age and demographic group doesn't necessarily reduce a charity's affinity clustering. Consider the Boy

Scouts, who go out of their way to encourage long-term loyalty to their organization. They have programs for boys in many age groups and draw their leaders from the pool of former program recipients. Some Scouts continue to support the program through donations, volunteer work, or introducing their sons to the program. In the process, they get to know other Scouts and their families. Family activities increasingly revolve around scouting related trips or outings, and the higher level of affinity clustering will indirectly produce organizational stability not found in a parent-teacher association. Yet, the Boy Scouts cannot be considered as having a *high* level of affinity clustering. Membership isn't socially mandatory within families or social groups, and not all of the boys who join develop lifelong bonds with other Scouts. Indeed, not everyone becomes an Eagle Scout.

Optimal size and region based on affinity clustering

Your affinity clustering will affect your charitable venture's optimal size and geographical range. This is because charities take more work to run when they cover a bigger geographical area. They require more communication, more record keeping, and more work just to exist. You can get the work done by paying for it, or by cashing in social capital. Most charities do some of both.

Maxim #10: If you exceed the limits of your social capital, work won't get done unless you pay for it.

Your organizational memory and continuity can come from your community, or it can come from paid employees who have an incentive to stick around for the long term. Of course, employees require payment, and payment requires money. There's therefore an indirect relationship between the geographical area you cover and your budget.

Low affinity clustering

If you have a low level of affinity clustering and are a **small** charity, *never try to grow behind the neighborhood region.* You need strong community identification in order to keep up communications over a large distance. If you try to operate your program in more than one location, as a municipal charity does, then unless the same group of people run the program in all locations, your group will split up.

If you have a **medium** budget, you can afford to hire an administrator in addition to someone to conduct your program. This will allow you to expand to the municipal region and conduct your program in more than one location throughout the city. Paid administrators must have an intelligent approach to volunteer recruitment to compensate for natural turnover, but they can also provide organizational memory and continuity. If you expand to the state level, you will need at least one local representative to conduct your program. Do not rely on social capital. *You must pay this person.*

You will most likely not be able to expand beyond one state. It will cost too much to set up parallel operations in another state and still maintain the kind of communication and control you need from your primary site. Without strong bonds of loyalty between you and whoever is operating your out-of-state office, there's no incentive for the second state's team to stay affiliated with you. Indeed, they may save money by going it alone. You may be better advised to recruit an out-of-state team and have them form an independent but similar organization.

If you have a **large** budget, you can hire whomever you need and operate beyond the state level, at the national and international level. The loyalty you need will come from paid employees. You'll have a few long-term donors and volunteers who feel an emotional connection to your group, and you'll be able to afford some kind of payroll department and legal team to make sure you operate within the law. However, without some significant ideological or emotional tie to one another, your people will find it very difficult to run a global charity that has bases of operation in different countries.

Medium affinity clustering

If you have medium affinity clustering, you can begin to use social capital to get labor and long-term organization, instead of money. When you've got a strong community that exists outside of your charitable venture, it provides continuity that you don't have to purchase. People in your community have social capital with one another, and you're in a position to draw on that sense of connectivity.

With a **small** budget, you can sustainably operate at the municipal or state level without too much trouble as long as you don't require a lot of real estate. Two or even three local offices are practical if you can run out of somebody's home. If, for example, you have an animal rescue and fostering program or a charity that collects and distributes lap quilts to veterans, you can get by with a small budget simply because you don't need a brick-and-mortar storefront.

Whereas an organization with low affinity clustering has to start paying for administration early, a charity with medium affinity clustering doesn't have to start hiring people until they expand into another state. At that point, you're going to need to pay those people, and that requires a bigger budget.

With a **medium** budget, you can operate beyond the limit of your state and possibly at the national level provided your real estate needs are not significant. Disease relief and research charities, scholarship organizations, and some churches can function at a national level even with a budget of less than a million dollars, provided they focus their effort on their program and don't waste a lot on internal communication. A limited international program, such as a very small-scale missionary operation or an initiative to provide school supplies to children in a poor nation, can succeed long-term with a medium budget.

With a **large** budget, you can easily operate at the national or international level, and can consider having a global program. A medium level of affinity clustering provides the minimum level of social continuity and structure that can allow you to operate globally. More is better.

High affinity clustering

If you have a solid, sustained community behind you, one that consists of multiple generations and groups of like-minded individuals, you can get an astounding amount of work done without a lot of money. You can also command a very high level of integrity and loyalty from your people, and expect fewer problems with fraud and other shenanigans.

If you have a **small** budget, you can operate beyond the state level so long as you rent out no real estate. You can do small-scale, labor-intensive fundraising and not have to worry about turnover due to the enormous community loyalty. But you will very seldom be successful if you try to split fundraising up between states. However, it's possible to conduct a successful international operation.

If you raise money exclusively in one state, town, or neighborhood but spend it in a needy state or country, you can stay under $200k per year and still operate a tiny micro-loan operation, religious mission, or medical supply transfer program. The key is to have reliable people at both ends of your supply chain. If you are sending latex gloves, first aid supplies, or even money to a hospital in a poverty stricken nation, you have to make sure the money is being spent the way you intend it to be.

251

Otherwise your international charity will deteriorate into what my father described as "the poorest people in a rich country giving to the richest people in a poor country."

If you have a **medium** budget, you can operate effectively in up to three states at the same time. But when you expand into each new state, you have to essentially create a copy of the organizational infrastructure you've got back home. Phone lines, post office boxes, and real estate cost money. So unless it's your intention to expand into a national charity, you may want to consider splitting off your operations in new states, so that they become independent organizations with their own reporting requirements and assets. This will eliminate an entire layer of administrative expense.

If you have a **large** budget, the world is your oyster. This is the level of commitment and finance that would allow you to create a global charitable conglomerate such as an international church or a global relief charity. You might have people that care deeply and passionately about your mission, but you're still going to need their full-time attention, and since those individuals still need to eat and to earn an income, if you want them on a full-time basis you're going to have to pay.

Chapter 16: Size Matters

The last chapter provided a way to classify and describe your charity based on size, geographical region, and the kind of affinity clustering that exists (or does not exist) in the community that supports you. It also made some suggestions about the optimal size and geographical distribution for your organization. This chapter identifies appropriate marketing and fundraising strategies for the kind of organization you've got.

In this chapter, I'm assuming that you've already paid attention to the material I introduced earlier. If you don't have a budget and spending plan, if you're trying to meet unreasonable fundraising goals, or if you've got a cash flow problem, *you need to fix that basic structural problem first*. Nothing in this chapter can help you if your organization is basically unhealthy.

The simple fact is that there's no such thing as a one-size-fits-all approach to fundraising or marketing. You must select the techniques that suit the charity you've got, and set the others aside until and unless the technique suits your resources.

I'm reminded of the Cinderella story: not the modern Disney one, but the original story by the Brothers Grimm. In that story, the evil stepsisters who mutilated their feet so as to fit into Cinderella's tiny slipper came to a bad end. Don't do that to yourself. You have to go with the shoe that fits, even if you miss out on the heir to the throne. Really.

Ways to exploit high affinity clustering

Regardless of your budget and geographical distribution, if you benefit from having groups that hang out with each other when they aren't busy working toward your charitable purpose, great news: you also have a means of spreading the word about your organization. People, it turns out, often participate in more than one social group.

As Malcom Gladwell pointed out in *The Tipping Point*, not everybody works, plays, and lives within the same community. Some people intersect multiple communities. Identify and cultivate these people, and get them to each bring three friends to one of your public events… friends from communities that aren't already represented well.

Marketing within an affinity cluster

If your organization contains a lot of people from, say, an online gaming community, it may make sense to buy advertising or links from forums where they hang out, or from related forums. This is because the same community that produced the handful of volunteers you've got may contain more that you simply haven't met yet.

Human beings often have multiple interests and participate in more than one community. Most people belong to at least one workplace, at least one extended family, at least one church or spiritual community, and at least one school or athletic community. These might not be brick-and-mortar communities, but the more variety you have, the more communities you can mine for potential volunteers and Board members.

The greater variety you have on your Board and in your volunteer pool, the more communities allow you to sink a well.

Class as an affinity cluster

There's also a lot of socioeconomic stratification in our society. Within the same city or town, people of similar education and work backgrounds hang out and socialize with each other. There's also vertical stratification, where people split apart based on ethnicity, education, language, and interests. It's not accurate to assign people a social class based solely on income, because whereas a person's income may vary over his or her lifetime, his or her social circle seldom changes much.

Maxim #11: Charity must flow downhill.

Your program will receive more support from some groups than from others, but make sure you never ask someone to raise money for, or to give to, people from whom they should rightly be expecting support. If you've got a sports charity, for example, it's reasonable to ask adults to raise money for children's competition expenses, but it's less reasonable to ask children to raise money for the adults unless the adults in question have some situation that makes the children more capable.

Compared to children, adults are not a charitable class unless they are sick or injured. Parents are often willing to let their kids raise money to benefit other kids, but they are not willing to let their kids be exploited by somebody who is more capable of doing the work. So they aren't likely to raise money for a group of local 25-year-olds to travel to play basketball... unless it's in the Special Olympics or the Paralympic Games.

Charity is a much easier sell when money and resources flow downward from the more affluent to the less affluent, from the able-bodied to the less capable, from the adult to the child (or elderly person), or from the healthy to the sick. Never violate this principle by asking less wealthy people to subsidize more affluent families.

Maxim #12: Nobody ever voluntarily subsidizes someone with a higher standard of living.

If your program features something often considered a luxury, such as the fine arts or advanced education, never solicit donations from people who couldn't afford it for themselves if they wanted to. People take care of their own families first. While they are often willing to share what they've got, they are seldom willing to pay for other people to enjoy a luxury they can't provide to their own families.

Suppose you run a ballet company. You're not going to be able to raise money from college students, minimum wage earners, or pensioners unless you also provide a clear benefit to someone they personally know or perceive as needy. But socioeconomic class in the United States can be fluid. Today's college student is frequently tomorrow's dot-com mogul or patent attorney, and nearly all multimillionaire fast food franchise owners started out flipping burgers or working the front counter.

If you want to raise future volunteers and donors from this group— and you definitely should—the only way to earn social capital is to start performing a useful service.

Pick a dress rehearsal date close to the performance, where you've already booked the venue and you're already paying the performers. Then, find every Title I elementary school nearby and provide matinee tickets to all the fifth grade children so that they can enjoy a field trip during the day. If the venue is big enough, invite more kids. Give leftover dress rehearsal tickets to college and university students, and take advantage of the opportunity to talk about your new volunteer initiative. Some of them may be willing to staff a concession booth or provide usher service for you. The very least you can expect from an initiative like this is to attract some new volunteers. You will also plant the seeds for a new generation of potential donors.

Class mobility is part of the economy in all industrialized nations, particularly the United States. Just because a child is being raised by poor parents in a have-not neighborhood doesn't mean he or she won't grow up to be an adult with a strong income and charitable habits one day. That adult will be far more disposed to give to your charity, or to a charity like yours, if he or she remembers it having made a positive difference.

Selecting an optimal region

Depending on what your program is and what kind of community you have to work with, your charity will have an optimal geographical range at which it is most efficient and sustainable. You may also wish to consider whether the affinity clustering you've got is helping or hindering your fundraising and program activities.

Maxim #13: Never try to expand beyond the minimum size you have to be to accomplish your program.

Expansion for expansion's sake is a bad idea, because the bigger your charity becomes, the more money and resources are needed for administration as opposed to program expenses. A multinational medical charity like the Muscular Dystrophy Association, for example, spends almost a quarter of its donations on administration and advertising. In 2015, 77% of its revenue was spent on program expenses. This works for the MDA because of the sheer number of people it helps: it funds disease research, provides support for disease sufferers, and is actually a very efficient charity for its size. But if your school's parent-teacher association or your local youth sports organization spent one dollar out of every four on its own administrative expenses instead of on the kids, you'd be rightfully upset.

Neighborhood charities

If your program serves a co-located community, such as the students of one school or the senior citizens in one neighborhood, do not try to expand your program beyond the neighborhood it serves. You can increase your budget or expand your program by offering more services, but you won't be successful if you market in an area where people can't benefit from your work. High school A cannot easily sell chocolate bars to benefit its marching band if it's trying to sell in a rival school's district.

You can increase the budget of a neighborhood charity by appealing to more people and businesses in the area. By building affinity and strengthening community connections you will be better able to collect money. By offering more services you can make sure you stay relevant and catch the public eye.

If you have low affinity clustering or a very narrow age range for the recipients of your charity, your volunteers will tend to turn over rapidly, and will very seldom be with you for more than five years. One year, or one season, will be your average commitment level. But this means they expect to work hard and to do a lot of short-term social capital fundraising. Since your pool of volunteers refreshes itself every couple of years, you can draw more resources without exhausting your community.

If you have a neighborhood charity, it's reasonable to have two to three fundraisers per year, and two of them can rely on social capital. One can be a sale, one can be a thing-a-thon, and another can be a labor based activity like a car wash or a stadium cleanup.

Municipal charities

This size is ideal for programs that require the use of real estate, such that the program recipients must be present to benefit. Most churches operate at the municipal level, as do dance programs, theaters, private schools, museums, or groups devoted to an obscure hobby or interest such as gold prospecting.

Sports clubs can only attract participants from within easy driving distance. A sport such as racquetball or golf will generally attract people from the immediate area, and there may be several such clubs in the city, so a popular sport often ends up being practical at the neighborhood level. For more obscure sports like luge, wheelchair rugby, or dodgeball, people are willing to travel farther to practice or compete. This means that, although a medium-sized city will have many swimming pools and baseball diamonds, there is generally only one place to learn Sumo wrestling, fencing, or birling.

Reliance on real estate or expensive, specialized equipment is a key factor that will keep you from expanding into other cities, because there's a sizable cost to expanding into another location.

You will generally have a lower volunteer turnover rate than a neighborhood charity, so you can't afford to go hot and heavy with the fundraising. It behooves you to pay attention to the health of your volunteer pool. But you can still afford to involve everyone in at least two fundraising activities per year although you are better advised to seek out Type B donors. If you're a church, consider introducing planned giving as a normal concept. It need not be a full ten-percent tithe.

Planned giving isn't just for churches. It's for any organization where people have a long-term commitment to an organization. Anyone who has a lifelong relationship with your charity may appreciate a chance to give a little bit every month. You may also have access to employer-based directed donation program through your local United Way. Failing that, you can often set up a Web site or service that can make automatic monthly deductions from a donor's bank account or credit card. Just make sure your tax receipts go out on time. Credibility is everything, so you will have to put significant effort into bookkeeping and record keeping.

If by chance your program has a high turnover rate, and volunteers or recipients are with your organization less than five years, it is extremely unwise to try to expand beyond one city and its immediate area. You cannot operate for long in more than one city at a time when the volunteer turnover rate makes it impossible to build long-term relationships with local representatives in other cities, and they will find it easier to operate separately instead of relying on you to manage the money or coordinate things at a long distance. You will not be able to add enough value to justify their cooperation.

Consider this: if the average commitment to your organization is four years, and you have five people on your Executive Committee (President, Secretary, Vice President, Treasurer and Executive Director), you would expect to lose one of these every year. That's survivable, but when the same thing is happening in your branch offices those offices will eventually grow apart.

There's such a thing as a "vanity" charity that is run chiefly by one person. I really don't like the term because it suggests that the charity in question is badly run or that it doesn't do good work. These are generally small charities that are limited to what the key donor can afford to give. There's absolutely nothing wrong with that: most animal rescues and no-kill pet shelters are run this way. They are lean, efficient operations that do a lot of good in the short term, but they have a weakness: they cannot survive the loss of the key founder or donor unless the people involved with the venture develop a massive sense of loyalty to one another and a sense of community that transcends the immediate purpose of the charity. If by chance you have a vanity charity, do not try to expand beyond the municipal level.

State charities

If there's a way to run your organization without relying on real estate, and if people typically stay involved with your organization longer than five years, you can often expand beyond one city and operate at the state level. Not-for-profit private schools often do this, as do scholarship foundations and charities that specialize in advocacy, lobbying, or raising money for other kinds of charity. But the most effective kind of state charity is the one that can be administered centrally while providing services in a distributed fashion so that people can operate independently while seldom having to travel to the central location.

Animal fostering, where dogs or cats are housed in individual people's homes and brought out for public viewings or adoption initiatives, is a perfect example of centralized administration and distributed execution. So are major arts or sports programs that occur only a few times a year, but that are interesting or compelling enough to convince people to make an overnight trip. A world-class opera program, a film festival, or a music festival can easily justify advertising in more than one city, or even out of state. But there's a difference between advertising your program and soliciting donations. You might advertise globally to attract concertgoers from Europe or Asia. But that doesn't mean you run a volunteer program there.

Sport traditions with strong, cohesive communities of practitioners are good candidates for expansion and can operate sustainably at the state level. Each local office sets itself up and runs independently, but uses your central location for banking, payroll, Web hosting, and other business operations.

The state or region is the biggest you should attempt to grow if you have a small budget of less than $100,000 per year.

Multi-state regional charities

Expansion beyond the state level is viable ONLY if you have high affinity clustering, a ton of money, or both. It is extremely difficult to do this with a small budget because of the expenses associated with maintaining a point of contact in each state.

The more money you have, the less affinity clustering you can get away with. Churches, for example, do better than sports leagues do when expanding into multiple states.

This can be an optimal size, if the execution of your program does not require special skills, training, or licensure. If you have a medical support charity that provides groceries to disease victims, for example, you could easily open up multiple satellite offices in several states, have each state governed by its own central office, and maintain one "home" office overall. Or, if you have a foundation for the arts or are in the business of granting scholarships or bursaries, such that the amount of administrative hours required is quite small, it may make sense to operate in several states.

National charities

This is the optimal size if you have a medical research program, or if you can take advantage of an existing network. If, for example, you are focused on lobbying you may be able to take advantage of existing political, social activist, and similar organizations that network with one another.

At this level, it is reasonable to pay for administration because keeping the different branches of the charity in contact with each other becomes a full-time job. It also requires the sort of long-term, single-minded dedication that cannot often be found on a volunteer basis. It's also necessary to have a brick-and-mortar office of some kind, simply to house the full-time employees.

It's an extremely bad idea to try to run a regional or national charity on a shoestring budget.

International charities

This is an optimal size for aid charities that raise money in the United States to be spent in a needy nation elsewhere. The annual budget may be small, medium, or large depending on the kind of donation or services being solicited. A small missionary or education initiative, for example, can be run on less than $100,000 per year provided the individuals doing the actual travel to the developing country have the appropriate language and technical skills.

If you run an international charity, it's important to make sure you operate within the law of every country where you execute a program. Make sure you understand the culture and history of the area and its people, because there are often weather, economic, religious, or cultural influences that have helped make the situation into what it is. The stereotype of the Great White Savior who swoops into a village intending to right all the wrongs and help the villagers live happily ever after, but who ends up doing more harm than good, has a solid basis in fact. Too many "relief" initiatives, in which free food is provided to drought-stricken regions, have driven local farmers out of business or have strengthened local warlords instead. Too many "building" initiatives, where well-meaning foreigners build wells, schools, and other infrastructure in an area that lacks such amenities, turn the villages into targets of attack later. Too many "aid" programs create economic dependencies that eventually leave the local people worse off than they were before.

In order to make sure you know what you're doing, it's reasonable to hire local help in the form of drivers, translators, lawyers, and—when practical—technical help such as doctors, nurses, and engineers. This takes money. It also requires a lot of legal oversight to make sure you're operating within the rules. All this expertise, of course, has to be paid for.

Global charities

This is not an optimal size for very many charitable ventures. Operating at the global level and registering, collecting, and performing program activities in multiple countries simultaneously requires an incredible amount of money and resources. If you are a religious organization, a global emergency relief operation like the Red Cross or Doctors Without Borders, or a global wildlife advocacy program, then you need to be able to put people in place on short notice throughout the world. You therefore have a good reason to operate globally while coordinating your operations out of a central location. But before trying to operate at a global level, first consider whether you may be able to better meet your goals by focusing on just one country or region and cooperating with like-minded, similar operations to serve other nations. *You don't have to do it all yourself.* It's acceptable to share the work with others through some form of confederacy or agreement. If you can accomplish your goal by working with someone else, consider that.

Optimal size

Financially speaking, bigger is not always better. Raising more money, applying for more grants, and collecting more assets only makes sense to the extent to which those assets can be used to execute your program. Spending money simply because you have it is a sign that you've collected too much. So is continuing to raise more money than is needed to fully accomplish your goal. For example, if you run a service to provide low-income people with tax advice, and if you're serving every single person in the area who wants the help, then your program has thoroughly saturated the market.

One of the first signs that you've collected and accumulated too much money is that people start pressuring you to give it to them for things not related to your program.

Maxim #14: A charity with less than $150,000 (2016 dollars) in annual revenue should never pay for administration.

If the kind of program you run is going to be limited to the municipal level or less, and it doesn't require the exclusive use of real estate or special equipment, consider staying small and scaling your program to fit the available resources. You will keep your volunteers longer, burn out fewer people, and run more sustainably in the long term.

Optimally small charities

Examples of charities that are most sustainable at the small level include:

- School booster clubs
- Local recreational sports leagues
- Churches with less than 100 members
- Private operating foundations
- Extremely refined special interest groups based on unusual hobbies or sports

If you want to expand your program and serve more people, consider branching out into different age groups. If you want to recruit more donors, work to increase your representation in different age, ethnic, and socioeconomic groups within your city. This makes it possible to grow bigger financially so as to expand your program, without the logistics battle that will come from expanding beyond the municipal level without a medium to high level of affinity clustering.

For extracurricular sports or activities that focus on individual participation, it's possible for a child or adult to stay interested in fencing, archery, gymnastics or martial arts for years. In these cases, it's possible to create and promote affinity clusters in your group simply by providing continuity in administration and instruction. However, you accomplish this goal by hiring instructors, not by hiring administrators.

There are some kinds of charitable venture that can conduct business in several states, or even run an overseas program, without bringing in or spending much money. Examples include private operating foundations, scholarship charities, small scale religious missions, family charitable trusts, and grassroots political action committees. They get by on very little money because the people who provide the program do it on a volunteer basis. There is very little turnover from year to year.

If there's something about your program that causes people to age out after just a few years, and if there's also a strong connection between your volunteers and your beneficiaries such that people only contribute when their own friends or family members benefit, it's an extremely bad idea to try to grow beyond the small level. If the majority of your volunteers are casual or short term, and the volunteer turnover rate is above 30% per year, when you try to expand beyond the small level the overwhelming majority of your attention will shift. Instead of focusing on your program, you will spend most of your time herding cats.

Small size suits charities that don't rely on real estate, or where most of the consumable resources needed for the program can be donated. It doesn't mean that you never hire help when you need it, but most of the help you hire will be part-time. Youth sports coaches, pro bono lawyers, and other people who expect to put in only a few hours per week do expect to be paid, but they don't expect to rely on you for most of their household income.

If you have a small charity, never consider paying an outside expert to write grants for you or to perform fundraising. Also, do not buy real estate (even to conduct your program) if it's feasible to rent it instead. The extra credibility you think you'll get from owning the resources isn't worth the loss of flexibility.

Optimally medium charities

You should strive to achieve, and maintain, a medium size if you need more than one person who has special skills, whose attention needs to be focused on your charity on a full-time basis. A wildlife refuge needs a custodian of some kind, forest replanting requires a central point of contact to manage the volunteer training and tree supply, and the clinic requires a nurse to administer the shots. A food bank needs somebody to coordinate volunteers to sort and distribute food hampers and to match completed food hampers to applicants. That doesn't mean there isn't room for volunteers. In fact, volunteers can almost always provide most, or all, of your unskilled labor.

If you absolutely require dedicated land, real estate space, vehicles, or expensive equipment in order to execute your program, you're not going to get away with being a small charity and should do the fundraising necessary to become medium sized or even bigger. If you run a community theater, an art gallery, a museum, or a homeless shelter, this could be your best and most sustainable size.

Running as a medium charity instead of a large one often requires compromise in terms of quality or geographical range. Instead of hiring world-class Flamenco dancers or touring jazz musicians, for example, you might provide exposure and experience to local talent and accept that you're never going to be able to attract the star power necessary to draw viewers in from out of state. Instead, your strategy will be to build a pool of long-term supporters who come back year after year to see what you're doing next. You will have to cultivate local philanthropists instead of hitting up national endowment funds.

You may have to accept that some kind of delegation or cooperation is necessary in order to accomplish your goals. If you have a medical or science focus, you will most likely not be able to operate your own research facility or cultivate your own research talent in-house. This doesn't mean you can't endow a chair at a local research hospital or university, or that you can't give out a medical research grant. If your focus is on film, you may not be able to operate your own production studio, but that doesn't mean you can't hand out grants to help independent production companies film a documentary about something that interests you.

Internally, there is a very good chance that you will require enough employees to be subject to minimum wage, anti-discrimination, and benefits laws. You are unlikely to get by with just listing everyone as a 1099 contractor unless they are entertainers hired short-term for a particular show or production. Your year-round work will be done by people who receive a steady paycheck. So you will need accounting software and a payroll system, although you can most likely get by without a formal human resources or legal department.

You will almost certainly have to pay for at least some administration in the form of executive officers. You need not have a CEO or CFO, but an Executive Director or other full-time employee will be necessary. You will need someone to concentrate on donor management and fundraising.

With this charity size, you're going to have to do more than rely on the Board and their immediate social networks to raise money. You'll have to have a plan and a unified approach, and it may be practical to seek out grants for specific programs or initiatives.

For medium charities, having some kind of office space, post office address, and dedicated phone line and Web site enhances your credibility.

Such things are not necessary for small charities (and in fact can be a waste of resources), but if you would like to take advantage of local volunteer-producing resources such as a Civitan club, a university, a large company that lends out executives, AmeriCorps, or some similar source of free or low-cost labor, you need an actual office and a place for these individuals to work. This need not be in a building you own.

As with a smaller charity, it will most likely make better sense to lease the space you need, instead of buying or building your own.

This is the smallest size charity where it is reasonable to consider paying somebody to raise money or to write grants. This could be an employee, a contractor, or even an outside service. Feel free to hire a consultant to improve your process or to teach you how to run a more efficient thing-a-thon.

You will notice that, at this size, it becomes irresponsible to brag about how 100% of all donated money goes toward your program. It's acceptable to start setting aside 10% or more of your revenue for administrative necessities. In fact, if you don't do this, you will damage your organization long-term. Unlike a small charity that relies on a core group of dedicated people, your charity's institutional memory and culture will come chiefly from the people you hire. Not paying at least some attention to developing, educating, and providing a career path for the people who work for you will cost you those employees long-term.

Optimally large charities

A large charity has the luxury of operating in whatever geographical region best suits its program. It can run a private university, a major museum, or a national professional sports league. But like a for-profit corporation of similar size, it requires internal structure. A human resources department, legal department, accounting department, and advertising team are all vital to success, as is some kind of brick-and-mortar location.

A large charity cannot be credibly run out of somebody's home. You don't need a fancy building or lavish furniture unless they've been given to you by a generous donor whom you wish to publicly acknowledge. But you do need a street address of some kind. A post office box simply won't do.

Like a for-profit company of the same size, your charity needs intelligent, reasonably well educated managers and executives. You will need administrative assistants, janitorial services, and of course the people who actually run the program. Yet it's not unusual to spend a quarter of your income on this kind of administrator. If you have to do a lot of logistics work to coordinate emergency response activities, you might even need training facilities or a fleet of vehicles.

This is the size of charity that can effectively conduct a global operation. Disaster relief, ongoing international ministry, or education services can be provided this way.

Any venture that requires major up-front costs, such as building or starting a hospital or university, requires vast amounts of capital. The need for money also doesn't stop when you're finished building your zoo or museum. So your fundraising and volunteer pool should optimally be large as well.

Maxim #15: The bigger your charity becomes, the less you can use labor as a substitute for money.

Small charities, like small companies, are flexible. The bigger you get, the harder it is to change direction quickly or gracefully. However, large or even gigantic charities run on social capital whenever they interact with the public.

So long as the volunteer base isn't exhausted or drained of social capital, a local youth soccer league can raise money for uniforms by conducting bake sales and thing-a-thons. Having an extra one is no big deal, because the budget shortages (if there are any) are on the order of a few hundred or a couple thousand dollars. The athletics department of a major university, however, might have a budget shortfall of half a million dollars or more. There's no such thing as a bake sale big enough to bring that kind of money in.

A large charity has to advertise both its services and its fundraising activities. It takes planning, concentration, and a P.T. Barnum style buildup to attract the media attention necessary for a major cancer pledge drive or a telethon for a public television station.

A large charity's donors tend to be geographically distributed. Medical research and disaster relief charities are supported by people in every state or sometimes all over the world. There's seldom a way to physically get them all together to clean the building or do a thing-a-thon, even assuming you'd want to. So the bigger you get, the more you need to focus on cultivating donors.

As your charity expands, you will use volunteers in different ways. They will perform fewer administrative tasks and operate entirely in the fundraising or program capacity. So they will do more of your canvassing and telethon solicitations, and they will man the phones at your crisis hotline or spend time mentoring at-risk kids or feeding disabled veterans. They may still serve on the Board of Directors in an unpaid capacity. But they will seldom continue to make hiring decisions, prepare the annual report, or organize the next pledge drive.

The bigger your charity becomes, the more it functions like a large business, and the more it resembles a big corporation. Grow enough, and you'll need an accounting department to handle payroll and expenses. You'll need a human resources and legal department to handle things like finding new employees to replace the ones who retire or quit. You'll need janitors, computer professionals, Web site designers, and more. In an extremely large charity, therefore, the act of managing becomes similar to that of managing a business conglomerate.

How to deal with an overgrown charity

If you ever reach the point where your organization has become too unwieldy, you have options. You can embrace the growth by investing in administrative infrastructure to make the extra scale manageable. You can do the opposite and scale back your program. You can split up your organization geographically or by function by "spinning off" smaller groups so that each group can focus directly on the parts of the progam that are relevant.

When your charity grows, expect it to become less efficient. Adding an accounting department, for example, doesn't contribute directly to the bottom line by bringing in more donations or revenue. But the salaries paid to the people you employ and the expense associated with providing office space must come from somewhere. Nobody would seriously suggest that a large business operate *without* payroll or human resources services, however during a growth stage it's sometimes possible to outsource general business operations by hiring contractors.

Dividing up operations by creating an entirely separate charity is another option. The United Way, for example, is divided by geographic region. Each state, or portion of a state, has its own administrative structure, bylaws, and executive team. The money raised in that region therefore stays in it. Large churches often divide by geography, opening new houses of worship as the congregation gets big enough to support them.

Division by operation is a situation in which a program gets too big and complex for the administrative team to handle it. Earlier in this book I introduced an imaginary adult day care facility that was originally a church program. This is one of the most difficult ways to spin off a new charity. Unlike division by geography, where you start with the same business model and divide up revenue sources based on where the donors live, division by operation requires you to choose administrative structures based on what's best for the new program.

The most touchy subject, when splitting or creating a new charity, is how to divide the debt and the revenue. It can be a little bit like a divorce. You obviously don't control what individual donors do, however it's irresponsible to start a new venture without a clear idea about how to fund it. Frequently the parent charity or church will agree to provide a specific amount of funding for a specific amount of time. But this kind of sponsorship often has an end date, so whoever in charge of the new charity does eventually have to secure replacement income.

Chapter 17: Volunteer Management

In the last chapter, I showed how the way you use volunteers changes depending on the size and geographical distribution of your charity. In this chapter, I'm going to introduce a few tips on volunteer management.

Scale the program to fit what you have available

It's the same with volunteer hours as it is with dollars: there's labor involved in putting on a program. It's possible to convert labor into operating capital by doing labor based fundraising, but it's also possible to convert operating capital into labor by hiring people to do the work. The smaller your charity is, the more you can effectively monetize volunteer labor by using people for fundraising instead of, say, program execution.

That being said, most of the time the volunteer hours you have available are the only ones you're going to be able to get. You therefore have to balance or optimize so as to use them in the most effective way.

Manage volunteer hours as though they were money

Remember the exercises where you broke down your program into needs, wants, and nice-to-haves, and examined each in terms of what it cost? You can do the same exercise with volunteer hours. In fact, if you know how many hours were put in over the course of the year, you can determine exactly how much each budget item cost you. You can even present the figures to your Board.

Wouldn't it be nice to say: "this activity cost us nine hundred person hours, but that one cost us only forty-five"? It's possible, but only if you keep track of how you "spend" your human labor resources as efficiently as you keep track of how you spend your money.

Things that are measured tend to improve. If people know they have to state how many hours they spent writing each grant proposal, some people feel competitive enough to focus their attention better and work harder so as to be more efficient on a per-hour basis. Others feel a desire to put in more hours.

Do not allow overt competition

Announcing who worked the most hours or who brought in the most money is penny-wise and pound-foolish, except as an incentive for a short-term fundraising effort such as a thing-a-thon. Pitting people together to compete based on annual performance is unwise because it creates an unfair distinction between different kinds of volunteer.

People with good writing skills and a "sales" personality may be able to raise more money in less time by engaging in fundraising activities, but the person who answers the phones at a crisis line or spends hundreds of hours training a service dog is bringing in nothing. Yet the work still needs to be done.

Have a budget and work within it

Budget your volunteers' time, allocate specific amounts of time and effort to the tasks, perform the most critical tasks first, and use the leftover resources to go after "want" or "nice-to-have" items.

Everyone must participate in fundraising, but nobody should be forced to sell or solicit

Consider adjusting your policy so that every single volunteer must perform a small amount of fundraising. This need not be direct solicitation or sale of overpriced catalog items, and it's best not to ask people to do cold calling unless they're psychologically comfortable with it. Instead, provide some labor based volunteer work opportunities such as cleanup, window washing, car washes, street address painting, or bake sales. In exchange for never having to sell anything to anyone, people are often very willing to give their time.

Consider involving beneficiaries

Donors love a peek behind the scenes, and many volunteers are more emotionally satisfied when they get to interact directly with the kids, animals, or other beneficiaries of the program. It therefore makes sense to find at least one recipient who is willing or able to act as a spokesperson when interacting with the public.

If the beneficiaries of your work are able-bodied, capable, and old enough to help out, they should not be immune from having to work a little, if only to understand what other people have to do in order to get the money to pay for their basketball tournaments.

Too many adolescents and teens, especially the ones involved in school sports programs, develop an excessive sense of entitlement when other people work so that they can play. Government and charitable initiatives to provide education, food, and entertainment are pervasive enough for some people to develop a very distorted view of what they "should" be getting from other people in a community under normal circumstances, and they develop a distorted view of the level of effort and amount of resources it actually takes to provide adult mentors from the community or the use of a supervised gym for an evening dance instruction program. Involving the beneficiaries of the fundraising in the work helps deter that sense of entitlement.

Don't encourage people to believe their talent pays their way

Allowing people, especially young and able-bodied people, to avoid contributing labor to finance their own activities creates a very distorted view of what it takes to "earn" an opportunity. Many young people truly believe that they earn opportunities just by showing up, simply because nobody has ever taken the time to show them otherwise. Others truly believe that their skills on the ball court or on the football field more than justify their place on the team, and that they "pay" their way by practicing more and competing more. By investing in their own excellence, they believe that helping their team win more raises their public profile and draws in more donations from the community at large. It's very seldom true. Oh, if your kid is the next Michael Phelps, Mariel Zagunis, or Simone Biles, they may get a lot of public attention for their wins. Depending on their sport, they might eventually be able to make some money out of it through a college scholarship or perhaps even professional play or celebrity endorsements. However, for the most part, sport is a money sink especially when it comes to children.

To groom a young athlete to earn a full-ride scholarship requires years of investment in gear, lessons, and competition travel. Millions of families set out with this goal, and invest both time and money to help their child become an elite athlete and makes enough money from the sport to justify the investment. When it works according to plan, the result is a made-for-TV movie. Too often, the kid gets injured or simply burns out long before college scouts come sniffing around. A die-hard sports parent is most likely not going to be willing to sit down, add up all the money they spent on special training and competition teams, calculate how much that money would have grown if it had been invested in a tax deferred education account, and compared the results to the price of tuition and books at the local state school.

Most sports families would be better off financially if they let their kids play recreationally through the school or through a cheap local

271

league and put money into a tax deferred education fund instead of paying for expensive private lessons and traveling competition teams. The stress load on the family would be lower and the family would also have more opportunity to develop friendships and extended family ties instead of constantly being "too busy" to participate in their own communities or develop social capital in their own churches or neighborhoods.

You, as a charity administrator, do not have to drink the bathwater. Because most of the people you're helping through your charitable work are *not* your kids, you don't have to pretend they're the next Marcus Dupree.

Instead of jumping on the talent-worship bandwagon and treating star athletes as being exempt from the rules that apply to ordinary mortals, start early and instill an understanding of what it takes to raise money for competition. An athlete who has to personally wash cars or clean a stadium in order to receive new uniforms or a chance to compete is far less likely to develop ego problems.

Avoid inurement based on fundraising

Never tie people's benefits to the amount of fundraising they do. That will cost you your tax exempt status. The Capital Gymnastics case illustrated that raising money for your kid's athletic club is not charity when participation is mandatory and the money raised is earmarked for the families of the individuals who raised the money.

In the Capital Gymnastics case, parents set up a booster club to raise money to cover the cost of their children's sports activities. The money was never paid out directly to students or their families, but was spent on competition related expenses for the entire team. However, benefit was tied to participation. Families that did not do fundraising had to pay a sizable fee instead in order to compete, and there was no way for a needier family to receive financial help. Each family's fundraising was credited to that particular child. This constituted a private benefit transaction even though the money was not given directly to the athlete.

Inurement and private benefit, by themselves, are not the Bogeyman. The entire purpose behind charity is to create a benefit for someone who needs help. There's such thing as a charity set up solely to benefit people of a charitable class, such as cancer victims. Money cannot be set aside for a specific person determined in advance (as in, the John Doe Cancer Fund cannot collect money solely for John Doe and Mary Roe), but it can be given out to people who go through some kind of application or vetting process. Most medical and disaster relief charities do this as a matter of course. The IRS sees no problem with identifying specific people to receive aid, provided of course there's a consistent and fair process to determine who gets the help. There should be no easy way to abuse the process so that it's a glorified way to funnel money to charity insiders and their families.

The easiest way to avoid inurement or private benefit is to find a way to make sure everyone benefits equally from the fundraising. Buy uniforms for the whole school band, or pay the transportation expenses for the whole karate team including the coach.

If you are dividing the benefit equally by buying things that benefit the whole team, such as uniforms or transportation expenses to an out of state competition, no person benefits more than the next. If you don't set aside money for individuals in particular, you're not committing inurement.

Never restrict benefits based on fundraising

Raising money for yourself, or for your own kid, is not charity. It never has been, and it never will be. If you are collecting money for a group activity, fundraising cannot be a condition of participation for the beneficiaries.

Public schools can get away with requiring members of the softball team or the wrestling team to perform fundraising work, but when you try to take the same approach to a children's baseball league or competition soccer team you will run into trouble because some families simply aren't going to do fundraising. Either they can't, or they simply won't. Nobody, especially not a child, is likely to come to you and say: "hey, one of my parents is a drug addict, and last time I collected money for pledges they stole it all and got high. So is there any other way I can raise money?" A lot of the time you simply have to provide a path for participation to people who aren't pulling their own weight.

It's reasonable to keep a list of who has done work and who has not. It's OK to use social pressure to help get people and families to participate in raising money. But limit the pressure to phone calls and peer pressure. *Under no circumstances may you withhold benefits to any person simply because he or she did not perform fundraising.* You may not kick a kid off the soccer team because his parents could not drive him to the stadium cleanup, and you may not use money raised by a family's fundraising to offset participation fees or expenses that would otherwise be mandatory. There must always be a way to help the neediest (or, in a few cases, the laziest) families to share the benefit.

If you allocate money to specific people based on fundraising, what you have is a private benefit transaction. That's not a tax exempt activity. Neither is inurement (a situation in which a portion of the income *inures* or accrues to a particular person or family such that it is set aside for their exclusive use). The only time you should be allowing people to raise money for their own individual benefit is if it's part of your process for helping needier people cover a bigger share of the expenses related to participation. Even then, it should be only a small part of your operations and it should also contain a means test of some kind.

Disproportionate benefit should be needs based

The IRS does allow small amounts of inurement and private benefit if the person receiving extra aid belongs to a member of a charitable class. Setting aside a portion of your school's cheer team budget to pay for the uniforms of kids whose families cannot pay the participation fees or cannot participate in the fundraising is a charitable and acceptable thing to do.

It's OK for disproportionate benefit to occur, provided it's to someone in a charitable class and provided you've got some kind of impartial process in place to make sure the money isn't being funneled to an insider. It's OK to give out scholarships or bursaries that benefit individuals. Handing out meals to homeless people in a soup kitchen is also a way of serving people directly. It's even OK to sign up patients at a local cancer clinic and write them all checks to cover grocery and utility expenses for the times chemotherapy makes them too weak to work. But look at what all of these initiatives have in common: they're set up to benefit people who are sick, or homeless, or in school. They have nothing whatsoever to do with whether the person getting the benefit logged enough hours at a bake sale.

Disproportionate benefit should be at arm's length

An arm's length transaction is a situation in which the seller does not choose the buyer, and the donor does not directly choose the recipient. The IRS likes it best when you have a process in place to determine who gets a scholarship, who gets their sports competition expenses paid, and who gets their medical expenses covered. They also like to see evidence that people who stand to benefit from a transaction are recused from making decisions about it. If the person doing most of the work is, or is related to, the person receiving most of the benefit, then what you most likely have is a corrupt and illegal insider transaction. Do not allow your volunteers to dip their beaks. The easiest way to do this is by having and enforcing conflict of interest policies.

Volunteers are not fungible

Something is fungible when it's interchangeable with another of its own type. A five-dollar bill works equally well if you want to buy a bottle of water or a small amount of gasoline. Also, if you have two five-dollar bills in your wallet, either one will do for either purpose.

People aren't quite the same way. They have unique skills and personalities that make them better suited for some kinds of work than others. A quiet, introverted person is less likely to be effective at sales or solicitation than a gregarious person, unless the introvert takes special steps to learn how to sell. People who work low-pay, "burger-flipping" jobs are your most valuable volunteers if you are a small charity that relies a lot on labor. This is because they are among the fastest and most efficient cash counters and will be adept at setting up a concession area to maximize product sales.

It's possible to train anybody to sell tickets, to bake cupcakes, or to solicit contributions door to door. That doesn't mean that people have the slightest interest in learning how to get good at the work. People who hate selling, hate it with a passion. There's absolutely nothing you can say or do to change this basic reality.

Ins and outs of mandatory fundraising

It's very tempting to just decide that all volunteers must participate in fundraising. If the sole purpose of your charity is to raise money for a good cause, it's a no-brainer. Booster clubs, charities that raise money for scientific research, arts funding, or disaster relief, and any not-for-profit corporation that raises money for lobbying or election purposes obviously exist for no purpose but to raise money. For anybody to get involved in, say, a parent-teacher association and expect to not help raise money is, frankly, silly. However if you run a program that is not solely dedicated to raising money for other purposes or organizations, there are a few cases where you should consider letting people off the hook.

Specialists

You will also get at least a few highly qualified people who are very good at what they do, but who refuse to do fundraising. Accept the deal if and only if they have unique skills and can provide a service you would

275

otherwise have to pay for. For example, if you run an avian rescue center and an avian vet is volunteering a few hours a week to help splint wings and imp in feathers, don't be stupid. Take the high value labor and use the specialist for things only he or she can do. If that person wants to be off the hook from a fundraising perspective, consider allowing it.

People who provide coaching or instruction in sports or the fine arts are generally also providing a specialized service. A sports coach usually has to train for years to be qualified to instruct, and has generally received some kind of ranking within his or her community. Many sports, such as swimming, require coaches to be certified, to pass an emergency medicine course, and to pass a background check. Dance instructors require years of training and are generally retired performers. So, you cannot generally tap a random volunteer on the shoulder and say: "You! You're going to be the ballet teacher today."

A person who is performing a task that does not require special training or expertise, such that the task could be performed by anybody, is not a "specialist". Your executive team should not receive specialist exemption. Nor should the person who "only" wants to do the bookkeeping or write grant applications. Any adult with reasonable math and writing skills can be taught to do those things.

In-kind volunteering

If you have someone who is providing a service, such as your annual audit, on a volunteer basis instead of for pay, this is another example of a person who should be exempt from any policy you might have that says every volunteer must help with fundraising at least some of the time. You have already had a significant benefit you would otherwise have had to pay for.

Don't demotivate people

You will have a few "workhorse" volunteers who are willing to do the difficult tasks such as talking to people who are applying for food bank benefits and sometimes redirecting them to other forms of help if they do not qualify. Managing the front desk of the museum might involve dealing with customer complaints. There will always be jobs that are, frankly, drudgery. People who do them without complaint are actually a rare breed.

You don't have to "motivate" your workhorses. As my father once pointed out, people who volunteer to do a task are already motivated. You don't need to fire them up or make them participate in cutesy song and dance sessions as though they were about to go sell vacuum cleaners. What you can do, and what you must do, is keep these people from becoming *demotivated*.

There are plenty of ways to knock the motivation out of your workforce. Anything you do that makes it more difficult or costly to volunteer nibbles away at that person's motivation. At different times, I've seen charities restrict access to parking for volunteers, requiring them to stay out of the spaces close to the facility which were reserved for paid employees. I've seen volunteers put to work alongside people who were paid for their time, performing the same tasks at the same time (which is a violation of the Fair Labor Standards Act). I've seen volunteers be forced to pay for access to school games or sports competition in order to be allowed to run the concession stand, and I've seen volunteers be forced to buy special uniforms, special credentials, or special licenses for the dubious privilege of representing their charity.

You're well within your rights to insist on minimum standards of professional dress, but when you force people to buy your overpriced and ill-fitting T-shirts in order to do unpaid work for you, it chips away at your social capital with your volunteer base.

Your volunteer team, like your donor base, runs on social capital. It's possible to run the well dry. My father noticed that, once people lose their motivation it's extremely difficult for them to get it back. Should something excite them, it's likely to be something from outside your organization. They will then become motivated to leave and go do something else. Accordingly, as a manager, my father found it far better to seek out motivated people, refrain from *demotivating* them, give them what they need to do their work, and then stand aside and let them perform.

Make it easy to serve

The more barriers to participation you can remove, the fewer will remain for your volunteers. If you can make volunteering a natural, smooth process that is convenient and simple, people will do it for longer.

Don't nickel and dime people.

If you absolutely must have team T-shirts, if it is vital or necessary for your workers to be able to recognize each other from a distance or to be recognized by members of the public, do not make your volunteers pay for them. Provide them. You don't need to give them away permanently, and it's acceptable to wash and reuse them if you're a small charity that's permanently broke. If you plan to do this, don't buy T-shirts. Spend a few extra dollars and buy polo shirts that continue to look like new even after they have been through the laundry a few times.

If you have a sports team or dance troupe that is traveling, have the decency to cover the travel expenses of the coach, instructor, or other person who's coordinating the effort. This person should receive, at the very minimum, a safe place to sleep, food, and some form of transportation he or she does not have to pay for. Coaching and teaching are labors of love, and most people aren't in it for the money, but at the same time it's not reasonable to expect to keep a coach if he or she has to pay for the privilege.

When possible, invest in your volunteers

I once got an extremely good turnout for a special kind of concession volunteer work that required alcohol service. It was a professional sports stadium that routinely lent out its concession stands to tax exempt charities. A few of the booths sold beer and wine. So in order for the charity to have the opportunity to earn money by staffing the booth, the volunteers had to conform to state law and have valid alcohol server's licenses.

A few of my volunteers already had alcohol server's licenses because they had recently worked in places that required licensure. But I didn't have enough people who were already trained. So, as an incentive to get more people to participate, I offered to have the charity cover the cost of the server's licensing course for the volunteers. This was a legitimate business expense since we wouldn't have been able to get the concession work otherwise.

The licenses created an economic opportunity to the young adults who earned them. Long after their volunteer commitment was over, they were left with a credential that was valid for the next few years. At least one of them used the license to apply for restaurant jobs that were previously out of reach. This constituted a private benefit, however since the credential was necessary in order to perform the fundraising, and since the training was available to any volunteer of legal age, it did not violate the IRS's rules.

If the volunteer work being done requires special certification such as CPR training, consider paying for it. Also, if you have coaches or teachers providing valuable program services, consider covering at least some of the cost of the certification or background check process. If they must belong to some national accreditation organization in order to be qualified to provide the services they give you, consider paying their annual dues.

Spread the fun stuff around

You will always have some work that is more interesting, higher profile, and more "fun" than other tasks. Do not allow these activities to be monopolized by people simply based on seniority. There's nothing that disappoints eager volunteers more than the moment a new theater volunteer realizes she will never be able to help with the costumes or set design because the people who have been around for years have called dibs on all the interesting work.

Isolate and eliminate toxic people

If you've got a bully, a drama queen, a control freak, or a person with the business ethics of a rattlesnake, you probably already know it. Bite the bullet and get that person to leave. But before doing it, examine carefully whether you're confusing disagreement with disloyalty. Getting rid of people simply because they're willing to be the bearer of bad news is never wise. The person who's willing tell you when they think your head is stuck somewhere it doesn't belong is quite possibly your most valuable resource.

Before you decide some individual is "toxic", take a look at whether they're a bad fit. Also consider whether they know what they're talking about and whether they're trying to warn you about the very predictable consequences of bad decision making. If you're taking on a lot of debt and piling up the risk, or if you're breaking the law, or if you've let the organization become a life support system for a clique of insiders or for an expensive mammal, the person's complaints probably have a basis in fact.

Find a place for those who disagree with you

Over the years, I've met people who governed nations, founded political parties, led successful businesses, and even commanded armies. Only a few of these interactions came solely from family connections: I've gone out of my way to cross paths with people I think I can learn from. The contacts don't necessarily result in long-term correspondence or personal friendships, and I'd venture to say some of the people I've interacted with may not remember me in particular. But one of the things I've noticed is that every single one of the most successful leaders has had a way to make sure he or she listens to opposing points of view and is not surrounded only by people who have also drank the bathwater.

Find a place in your organization so that the person who thinks you're spending money unwisely has a way to contribute without being dunned for donations or pressured to spend an inordinate amount of time doing fundraising. If you are actually running sustainably, your fundraising demands should not be excessive and the volunteer in question may simply be very frugal. Just because that person disagrees with you doesn't mean he or she is wrong, but it doesn't mean he or she is right either. There's probably still room in your organization for both of you.

Finding a place for people who disagree with you allows them to continue to contribute in a positive fashion without being constantly in conflict with everybody. This prevents a lot of misunderstanding and allows you to occasionally benefit from being told you're wrong *before* you make a devastating mistake.

Identify and deal with burnout early

Don't let a burned out person continue in a role that puts him or her in contact with other people. When people are overloaded and stressed out, which can happen for reasons that have nothing to do with your charity, give them a break. This should not be done as punishment. It should be done as a proactive, intelligent way to limit organizational stress.

Instead of making demands on exhausted people, allow them to rest and give them light duties that have very clear start and finish points. The tasks should also produce a reasonable return on invested time, and be the sort of activity where it's possible to see progress. It should also involve very little interpersonal interaction and very little conflict resolution. Burned out people should not be representing your organization, training new people, or interacting with people.

Burnout prevention

The best way to deal with burnout is to prevent it. Never take on so much of an organizational workload that you can't afford to give somebody a break to deal with a sick spouse or a new baby. If you're operating so close to the bleeding edge that people are scaling back or ending their involvement, you are trying to do too much with too few people and too few available hours.

Remember the Rat's Butt exercise from the fundraising section of this book? The goal was to establish exactly how much money could be reasonably and sustainably drawn out of a community. It applies to volunteer hours as well. If you're asking people to put forth their maximum burst effort for an extended period of time, then be aware that you will have to provide an equivalent amount of time off after the burst effort is over.

One strategy to prevent burnout can be called load spreading. The idea is to make sure there's a small amount of ongoing effort that is well within the capability of your volunteer pool. If your program is seasonal, you have the option of using the off season to raise money so that you can focus on using your volunteers for the "fun" program activities when they are in season. This spreads out the workload.

Load spreading works well if your organization relies on small-scale, labor-based fundraising. Stadium cleanup, concessions, and similar events must be run in a way that does not sap the energy or effort of the people doing it.

The advantage of load spreading is that it doesn't create a high level of stress for anyone who is otherwise in control of his or her time. The disadvantage is that it doesn't mesh well with people whose lifestyles are seasonal. Anyone who has children in school knows that some times of the year people are likely to be out of town and therefore unavailable. People also like to spend holidays and free time with their families. There is also a risk of the majority of the work falling consistently on the same people.

A second burnout reduction strategy is what I call "burst and rest". For this strategy, you have a few key times of the year when volunteers must be available, and where people will work very hard. But the periods of hard work are followed by weeks or months when the volunteers or workers do nothing.

The burst and rest strategy works well for programs that are seasonal or that require large amounts of volunteer effort for a short period of time. It also works well with high-profile activities like a fun run or a major gala and silent auction. If your program is seasonal, your fundraising can be seasonal too if it coincides with, or slightly precedes, the program.

You have to let people rest. There's a reason that many religions emphasize the need for a regular day of rest, fasting, reflection, and meditation. People and animals are not physiologically capable of operating at their maximum potential for long. If you read manuals about software development or other kinds of business where team leaders are encouraged to ask for and get routine overtime work and extended work weeks from their workers, you will probably also notice that the authors recommend an extended vacation after the burst effort is over. That part of the strategy is seldom followed.

Maximum fundraising effort is like rapid software development, Keynesian economics or Communism: people readily follow the parts of the strategy that are easy to do or that produce an immediate benefit to them, but after the initial idealism wears off they're not as willing to continue with the bits of the strategy that require things that are inconvenient or unpopular. Heavy taxation during economic booms, or paying for employees to take an extended vacation after months of mandatory unpaid overtime, is something the people in charge tend to just skip. They don't realize that the part they're skipping is the portion of the strategy that allows the aquifer to replenish. So they come to the conclusion that the strategy as a whole "does not work". That conclusion is actually supportable, because in order for the strategy to work sustainably the people engaging in it have to be much more mature and committed than the average human being.

The "rest" part of the burst-and-rest strategy seldom happens in for-profit businesses, because workers and employees are viewed as expendable. But if you want to have a hundred-year charity, you cannot afford to lose or replace a substantial part of your workforce every year. Your institutional memory is in your long-term employees and your volunteers. Also note that, unlike software developers who depend on their employer for their income, your volunteers can pay their bills without you. Ask too much of them for too long, and you will lose them. Some will stay longer than others if they are emotionally committed to your organization, but that's when burnout culture and the resulting toxicity start to develop.

Chapter 18: Selecting A Strategy

This chapter discusses the best and most appropriate donor and volunteer management strategies based on the size and geography of your venture.

Neighborhood and municipal strategies

These strategies apply to small, medium, and large charities wherein the program is confined to one city or less. Look at your map and ask yourself the following questions about how you're treating the region that supports you:

- Are we effectively building and maintaining our social capital across many socioeconomic and ethnic groups, so that we see a diverse Board membership?
- Do we recruit volunteers and administrators from within the geographical region we serve?
- Do the people who give to us do it because of affinity, or out of a desire for reciprocity?
- Do we publicly take credit for the positive results we get?
- Are we often seen supporting other charitable ventures in a way that does not interfere with our program?
- Is our balance of Type A, Type B, and Type C donors in proportion with the kind of work we do?
- Do we perform a unique service, such that if we disappeared tomorrow the gap would not be easily filled?

If the answer to any of these questions is no, then there's a very good chance your organization is short on social capital. Solve that problem first.

Constantly expand your donor and volunteer pools

Donor and volunteer pools turn over constantly. People die, move away, or shift into a life stage that requires time and resources formerly given to charity. Unless you replace these people with fresh blood, and find a way to allow newcomers to feel welcome and valued, your charity will strangle.

One of the worst things that can happen in a small charity is for the management team to consist solely of veterans to the point where newcomers feel excluded. This problem is not necessarily due to clique behavior among the veterans, although it can be a contributing factor.

There are two things that every small, localized charity must do to stay vital. They must maintain community awareness, and they must find ways for newcomers to have a satisfying volunteer or donor experience. Maintaining a donor and volunteer pool isn't enough. You have to constantly act as though you're recruiting.

Maintain community awareness by cultivating the local press. Newspapers and TV channels are always looking for positive human interest stories, but don't limit yourself to mainstream news. Find and cultivate competent bloggers as well. They love being taken seriously as journalists, and some of them have legitimate journalistic skills and experience. Focus particularly on sites that cater to demographics that aren't well represented in your volunteer or donor pools already. If you're a sports or athletic charity, learn the name of each sports journalist in town and arrange occasional interviews for your athletes.

Don't expect advertising or media presence to generate donors or volunteers overnight. Your goal is to put your logo and name in front of people hundreds or even thousands of times so that it becomes familiar, before asking for the proverbial sale. Build brand recognition, but don't spend a large amount of money doing it.

Consider using your Board to network. Participate in online forums and make your presence felt at other charities' public events. Become a person with access to multiple social groups. If your town or city has a Civitan, Rotary, or Kiwanis club, join it. Start attending the meetings, and volunteer for other groups besides your own.

When you start to get volunteers from outside the social circles of the veterans, make sure to give them at least some of the juicy, interesting work. Make use of younger, tech-savvy volunteers to build and update Web sites, and to promote your group on social media. This will help them to enhance their professional experience, build their résumés, and increase their status among their peers. It also promotes your organization within a peer group to which you might not otherwise have access. It can take a year or two before you build enough social capital within that peer group to generate an unsolicited donation, but that's the milestone you're looking for.

Embrace labor based fundraising

For a charity your size, labor based fundraising is a fantastic idea. It promotes group cohesion, it provides visibility to the greater community, and it doesn't have to scale beyond your immediate area. It also gives the opportunity to tell prospective volunteers that they will never have to solicit or sell. A surprising number of hardworking people deeply dislike asking other people for money. You're never going to be able to overcome what may be the result of a lifetime of cultural influence. So you might as well use it to your advantage. Seek out volunteers who hate to sell, and ask them to introduce you to all of their friends.

Every time you clean up a local park or stadium, or sell cupcakes outside a friendly grocery store, someone outside your organization sees you and notices that you are making a positive impact in a way that affects him or her. That person might not be part of a community that sees you executing your program and helping people, but he or she may be inspired to get involved.

Limit social capital based fundraising

Have, at most, one fundraiser per year that relies on sales or exploitation of people's personal networks. The size of the organization you have means that your donor pool, your volunteer pool, and possibly your recipient pool overlap a lot. I'm not telling you to never have another candle sale or thing-a-thon, but your focus needs to be on bringing money and labor in from outside your existing sphere of influence.

Effective use of mailing lists

Mailing newsletters out to your mailing list is a good way to keep your existing donors and volunteers in the loop, but it doesn't create any new exposure. A dollar spent on printing or postage will generally produce donations from your existing opt-in mailing list, but it won't expand your donor pool by getting you even one donor you don't already have.

There will always be turnover in your donor pool, simply because people die, move away, or lose interest in your organization. If you have events that are open to the public, such as musical performances or museum exhibits, a mailing list can actually be a good way to contact

285

ongoing supporters, but only if you are constantly inviting people to join it.

Review your mailing lists regularly to remove addresses that return your mail. There's no sense wasting postage or alienating a recipient. Also, don't insult people's intelligence by buying someone else's mailing list or phone list and pretending they're a long-time donor. People know exactly who they have or haven't written out checks to.

If you use E-mail lists, use only opt-in lists. Make sure you cull the list regularly and remove bounced or out of date addresses. Provide some means whereby people can be immediately taken off of your mailing list. Be mindful of anti-spam laws and never purchase an E-mail list from someone else. If you are composing the E-mail yourself, make use of the "bcc" or blind copy feature so that nobody who receives the E-mail can see anybody else's E-mail address. This is a basic courtesy to people who trust you with their contact information.

Use social media intelligently

It is vital to *have* an online and social media presence, because there's an entire age demographic to which an online presence is necessary in order for an organization to be credible. It makes sense to use social media to coordinate volunteers or to spread the word about fundraising opportunities especially if you want to attract and keep volunteers from the younger generation. Having one or two volunteers whose sole job is to design and maintain a Web page or to promote your organization on social media is a great way to attract aspiring journalists or marketing specialists, who can later use their volunteer experience in the work world.

Use social media to supplement paper, poster, or mailed announcements. If you're selling products that have to be ordered in advance, such as cookie dough or candles, make use of your social media page to promote the effort.

Don't invest too much effort in trying to put together a viral donation campaign like the ALS Ice Bucket Challenge. Viral campaigns work by triggering an impulse to give from Type D donors. That impulse only occurs when the prospective giver feels at least a tiny bit of potential affinity to the group receiving the money, and when there's a possibility the "good cause" being supported could eventually help the donor or someone in his or her community. Disaster relief, medical research, and similar charities are the kind of organizations that stand a chance of making their fundraising campaigns go viral, but high school booster clubs or city symphonies just don't have the ability to help people at a distance.

Have and enforce a social media policy

Many businesses create and enforce social media policies to make sure that their employees use social media responsibly and do not attract negative attention to the business. Since your charity is a business (see Chapter 1), you should consider doing the same for your employees and volunteers especially if you issue people E-mail addresses or social media accounts as part of their work.

Your policies should forbid people to publish other people's personally identifying information. If you are a medical charity, publishing information about somebody's medical condition is a violation of the law. If you run a counseling clinic and an A-list Hollywood celebrity is making use of your services, you'd better not allow your staff or volunteers to mention it. All it takes is a careless "wow, I just met Joe Schmoe at the office today!" to do serious damage to your reputation.

There are predatory "reporters" out there (and I'm putting the word in quotation marks to distinguish these people from legitimate reporters) who make their living by digging up and publishing sensitive, private, or potentially embarrassing things about public figures. Don't cooperate with them. Even if Joe Schmoe really does have a problem with his kidneys, if he chooses to not share this fact with the supermarket tabloids, respect his decision.

Have some idea in mind about how to enforce the policy once you have it. Employees can be fired, and volunteers can be terminated.

Stay away from debt until you have the cash flow to feed it

At this level, you have to imitate Napoleon who said: "I will either pay cash, or I will pay nothing." Raise the money, then spend the money. Don't commit to spending money you haven't got, and definitely don't get into long-term debt that requires regular payment unless you're a regional charity with a very large budget and income, like a museum or hospital.

Strategies for one-state charities

Suppose your organization is registered with the Attorney General of one state, and executes a program that benefits people from multiple cities or towns within that state. It's possible that most of your supporters and charitable recipients are concentrated within one county or city, but your program operates in multiple areas that are not necessarily adjacent to each other. Not all the people who contribute or benefit from your operations are within easy driving distance of each other. This makes it difficult to coordinate fundraising or media relations, so compared to a neighborhood charity you're going to have to be more organized.

Local representatives

In every area you conduct fundraising or program operations, you need at least one person to coordinate activities and serve as a single point of reference. He or she need not be a Board member, but should have access to decision makers so as to voice concerns that may only affect that area. This local representative need not set up fundraising events independently of the main venture, but has to be able to summon volunteers from his or her community to conduct fundraising activities.

It's important that the President or Vice President (not just any Board member) regularly communicate with all the local representatives. He or she should meet in person with them at least once or twice a year.

Limit labor based fundraising in favor of social capital based initiatives

Expanding from the municipal or neighborhood level to the state level is the most critical part of a charitable venture's development, because the kind of fundraising that makes you successful at the neighborhood level just doesn't scale well when your volunteer pool is scattered geographically. To successfully raise money at the state level, you have to consciously reduce your reliance on volunteer labor based fundraising and increase your emphasis on other ways to get money. However, most charities don't understand that they need to replace labor based fundraising. This means the same number of volunteer hours are required as if your labor pool were concentrated in one neighborhood.

Every year, select at least one sales or solicitation based social capital fundraiser in which everyone can participate. It can be a thing-a-thon, provided it doesn't require all the participants to drive to a different city. Or, it can be a sales based fundraiser.

Keep central control of the money

Ensure that money raised within each region gets collected, deposited, and controlled by your central office. You do not want your local representatives to conduct independent fundraising and distribution unless you have some insight into what is going on. Too many state charities suffer unnecessarily when a local representative starts making hiring or fundraising decisions without involving the rest of the charity. It leads to perception of conflict of interest, and it makes your organization vulnerable to corrupt or inexperienced local representatives.

Spend more liberally in areas where you rely on a local representative

You will keep your local representative, and his or her collection of volunteers, only as long as they understand that it's in their area's financial interests to stick with you instead of setting up their own charity. They need to see that the amount of money you spend on their church, or athletes, or homeless pets, is greater than the money they raise on your behalf. They need to feel as though they have a slightly disproportionate amount of influence with your parent organization.

If at any point you begin to exploit your more distant regions, you will lose them within two years. That's the amount of time it will take for them to notice that they're not getting a fair return on their investment, and to do something about it.

Use technology to empower distant supporters

If the local representatives don't feel as though they have a voice in your organization, and if they don't feel as though their region is benefiting more from association with you than they would if they set up independently, you're eventually going to lose them. They require your attention, and they require a feeling of equal membership in the group.

Offering Board membership to local representatives is wise, but only if they can attend the meetings. They might not have to travel in person, if you can find a way to provide a telephone or video conference during Board meetings so that they can attend remotely.

More sophisticated media approach

You will need at least one volunteer to manage media relations. Unlike a small local charity, you can't afford to focus solely on bloggers and conventional news media within just one region, even if the majority of your supporters or recipients are concentrated in one place.

If you have someone from a more distant region who for some reason is unable to coordinate volunteers for fundraising purposes, he or she may be valuable as a media coordinator for your entire state. Put him or her in charge of things like press releases.

Use volunteer administrators when possible

No small charity should ever have to pay for administrators or leadership, because it shouldn't be a full-time job. This is just as true if you're geographically dispersed as if you're all in the same neighborhood. If there's actual demand for your program and your budget is less than a quarter million dollars per year, you should be able to raise that without hiring anybody.

Maxim #16: No charity with an annual cash budget of less than $150,000 (2016 dollars) should ever buy real estate.

If your budget is less than $150,000 in 2016 dollars, you should be able to get what you need out of the community you serve, including program space, without exhausting your volunteer pool and without having to hire anybody to raise money or manage the charity. If for some reason this isn't happening, then you need to take a look at your volunteer pool and your labor distribution within it.

Most small charities that hire administrators turn into life support systems for that administrator. Most small churches or other charities that buy a building turn into a life support system for the mortgage on that building.

If you need volunteers, recruit them. If you need space, rent it or better yet solicit it as an in-kind donation. But if your budget is low and you find that you can't get the volunteers or space you need without paying for it, this is a sign that you don't have as much community support as you think you do. So scale your program back, or else start drumming up support by building your volunteer pool, until you're back in balance.

Strategies for larger charities

If you operate at the national level, you need to pay attention to communications infrastructure and long term asset management. This means you'll start paying significant amounts of money for people who do this kind of work. This is a level at which it makes sense to hire professional marketers and fundraising specialists.

Larger charities, particularly those with the name "foundation" in the title, are frequently endowed with large amounts money or income producing assets that are donated or willed to the charity by wealthy people. These endowment funds are so large that the interest and profit from them are enough to cover most of the expenses of running the charitable program. Hospitals, libraries, and museums are often set up based on this kind of donation. But a stock portfolio has to be managed, and so does income producing real estate. So it's not unusual for a charity with a big endowment fund to have to pay somebody to manage it.

Just ask for money

It's not unusual for a very large charity to have an organized pledge drive or fundraising event on the national scale. A national charity dedicated to funding research on heart disease cannot rely on small clusters of people to independently host a bunch of car washes or bake sales: they have highly organized pledge drives. Many of them do make use of local volunteers or teams, but there's a centralized approach. In addition, large charities are more likely to command the attention of at least a few extremely wealthy or famous people. Celebrity fundraisers or gala events designed to draw large amounts of money from well-heeled donors are a very cost effective option, because they bring in substantially more money than they cost to run.

You can "just ask" if you're already a household name. If you're a public broadcasting station or a nationally recognized medical research or relief organization, your organization has social capital of its own. People know it and recognize it like an old acquaintance or even a friend. It's permissible, and even necessary, to allow people to give to you and to provide them with easy opportunities to do so. Allowing people the opportunity to give of their own accord, without being directly solicited by you, actually builds your social capital with them because it allows the donor an opportunity to identify with you and to feel kinship and strength. So, advertise. Have a public fundraiser where a bunch of your corporate partners sell pieces of paper cut to resemble shamrocks, Easter eggs, or anything you like provided it catches the eye.

A large charity can generally afford to hire people to manage its assets, its fundraising, and the organization of its volunteer pool. It can also afford to have specific, targeted goals that can be best met by obtaining grants from corporations or charities that specialize in raising money. In fact, it can afford to pay people whose sole job is to raise or administer the charity's money. It therefore makes sense for the charity to have a brick-and-mortar location that is not necessarily the same as the place where the charity does business or provides its services.

Look three years ahead for cash flow management

When a large charity runs into cash flow problems, it might not be due to theft or irresponsible spending. Perhaps an income producing asset drops in value or vanishes overnight, such as when a patent or intellectual property copyright expires. But many of these changes are predictable. If you put all your eggs in one basket, for goodness' sake make sure you watch the basket.

Maintain sizable cash reserves

Sometimes you can't predict bad luck. Suppose the stock market takes a dive, and there's no longer enough money to provide this year's scheduled college scholarships or funding for independent documentary filmmakers. This is not necessarily the fault of anyone associated with the charity, but it does happen sometimes, which is why large charities typically keep six months to one year's operating expenses in cash reserves.

For a large company of any kind, liquidity means flexibility and resiliency. So resist the temptation to spend every available dollar.

Use debt intelligently

Your debt should obviously never exceed your assets. Pay attention to the kind of debt you've got. But unlike small or regional charities, you shouldn't be avoiding debt.

Secured debt is the kind that is backed by an asset of some kind. A mortgage on some real estate owned by your charity is secured by that real estate. If you sell that asset, the money received goes first to the mortgage holder, and then to you.

I prefer to never use secured debt for anything but program activities. Administrative and fundraising activities should never require your organization to borrow money. If they do, your organization is in serious trouble and has a liquidity problem. Cut spending, sell off assets, delay expansions, or engage in fundraising to correct the liquidity problem before you do anything else.

Large charities can and should also make use of unsecured debt. Corporate purchasing cards, buying office furniture or other supplies using manufacturer credit makes sense, but make sure someone is watching the spending because purchases can easily get out of control if there's no effort to budget.

I do not recommend expense accounts for executives. Instead of having a company credit card for travel or executive expenses, negotiate with a bank to provide credit cards directly to each person who needs one. This credit card is in the name of the individual and is tied to his or her own credit rating. He or she is solely responsible for paying any charges that are put on it. Every time somebody travels or makes a travel related purchase on the card, have that person submit an expense voucher and process the application immediately, so that your employee is repaid before the credit card bill is due. He or she can then settle up independently. This gives you, and your organization, the opportunity to reject excessive or unacceptable expenses.

Maintain an Internet presence

You can't afford to ignore mainstream media, and at this point, the Internet is mainstream whereas television and radio are... well, not exactly obsolete, but less dominant than they've been before. Print media is not the powerhouse it used to be.

Make sure you have access to at least one tech-savvy person who can manage your social media feeds. Publish often, but keep the information short and to the point. Consider more than one form of media, because people who do not like to read may still be moved by a video clip or a song.

As a national or international charity, you have best access to people who grow up hearing about you as a household name. Your next generation of supporters are the ones who are still in school.

Make strategic alliances with other national or international ventures

I'm not suggesting that you team up with your competition, but there may be some ways to get access to significant assets by teaming up with a large company. You can borrow executives from established large corporations, and you can trade advertising with organizations that have donor bases that don't (yet) overlap with yours. For a medical research charity to partner with a university or hospital is almost a no-brainer, but other kinds of ventures can exchange or share resources.

If you're a wildlife refuge or a zoo, would it be out of the question to hit up a local scouting or mentoring organization to propose a field trip or a supervised overnight camp-out in exchange for some help stuffing envelopes or cleaning up? If you did, you'd be exposing your program to both the existing adult volunteers and the up-and-coming kids. Or, if you're a professional organization or union of some kind, why not team up with a local school club where the activities relate to what you do for a living? In exchange for an opportunity from you that doesn't necessarily cost you money, you may get a small amount of free labor and perhaps a future contributor.

Collaboration can open up grant opportunities that were previous out of reach for a smaller or mid-sized organization. An excellent example of collaboration is in the medical research field. Individual researchers working for a university or a private company rely heavily on doctors and hospitals to find patients and to administer clinical trials. They in turn work with disease-specific fundraising and assistance charities to provide logistics support for the patients. No one charity provides all the care and support for the patients, and no one charity raises all the money to do it. But there's division of labor: the researchers don't have to waste their extremely valuable time cleaning stadiums and the people who are good at raising money focus exclusively on doing that.

Chapter 19: Solving Cash Flow Problems

The concept of cash flow was introduced in Chapter 6, so you now have a basic vocabulary. You also have some techniques to predict and control the movement of money into and out of your organization. This chapter will show you how to recognize when cash flow is going wrong, and teach you how to correct the problem.

More notes on negative cash flow

While it's always safer and more sustainable to make money instead of spending it, just because you've got negative cash flow for one month, or even one year, doesn't mean you're operating irresponsibly. You might be investing in an asset that is about to produce a lot of money, or you might be expanding your program by preparing a new building. Either way, as long as you've got the cash on hand to pay your bills, you can keep operating. The problems arise when you no longer have enough cash on hand to do that.

Deficit spending is not sustainable

In Chapter 6, we looked at an imaginary scholarship foundation that raised money all year so that they could write some big checks at the end of their program cycle. The month they wrote those checks, they spent far more than they made and temporarily ran at a deficit for that month. But since they had the money on hand to cover the big expense, the planned deficit spending didn't hurt the organization. In fact, saving up for a big expense is a normal and legitimate way to do business.

Obviously, if the same organization spent more than it made every month, it wouldn't be able to write those checks every August because pretty soon the bank account would be empty. They'd have to start borrowing money to cover expenses, or sell off part of their endowment fund. That's always bad news for reasons that will be clear later in this chapter.

One thing is certain. If you spend more than you make, it will eventually catch up to you until you have nothing left.

Out of cash doesn't mean poor

Your organization can be wealthy but cash-poor. If all of your money is tied up in real estate or capital equipment, you can run into cash flow problems despite having a lot of assets and no debt. If a major grant doesn't arrive in time, or if an asset takes longer to sell than you expect, it's easy to end up short of cash at payroll time.

Cash flow and timing

When you spend and receive money is just as important as how much of it comes in or goes out.

Suppose you have a charity with spending goals similar to the scholarship endowment fund earlier in the book, but without the investment account. In order to spend, you must earn. Your spending plan looks like this:

Figure 6: Spending schedule, scholarship fund

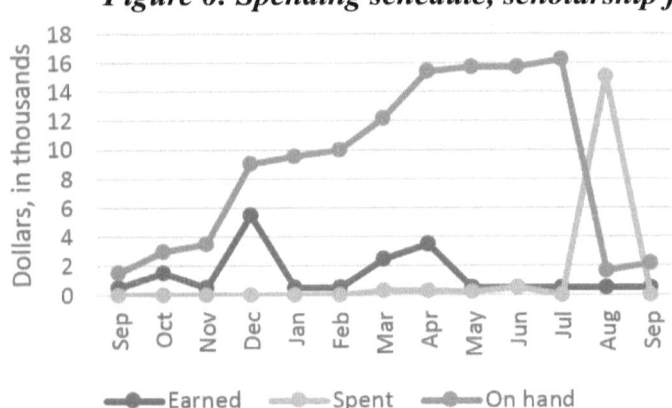

The above graph shows how you plan to spend your money. You plan to have a holiday pledge drive and a fundraiser in the spring, and expect a $3,000 grant in April. You will send out the checks in August. Aside from that there are few expenses.

But suppose things don't quite go right. You buy your office supplies and advertising early, in November, and save $100. But due to a family tragedy, only $1,000 is raised in December instead of the expected $5,000. The $3,000 grant arrives in July instead of April, and because of a miscommunication, the scholarship checks goes out in June instead of August. You have to borrow money to pay interest and penalties, but dig deep and raise money over the summer. You end up with this:

296

Figure 7: Actual spending, scholarship fund

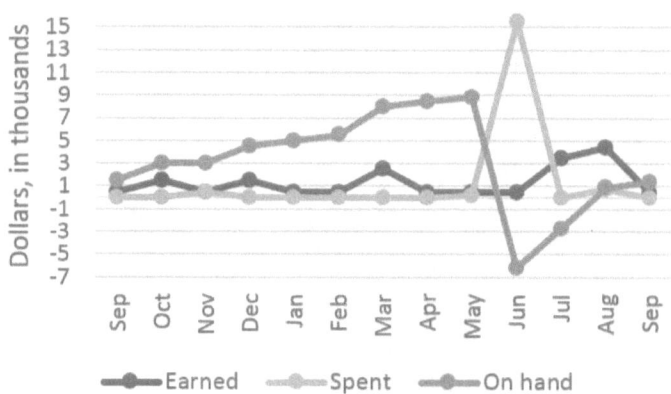

This isn't such a pretty picture, because of the way the cash on hand goes negative. Borrowing costs money.

Maxim #17: When you receive or spend money is just as important as how much of it you receive or spend.

The difference between the two spending curves is due entirely to timing. Suppose you make the timing worse: spend nearly all of your $16,300 budget up front. You borrow, so interest and penalties cost you about 1% each month. It doesn't seem like much at first, but for whatever reason your organization isn't able to replace the money quickly. Perhaps you lose a key donor or maybe your investments aren't generating the return you'd like because of changes in market conditions.

At the end of the year, despite spending $700 less and raising $1,100 more, you finish with barely more than what you began with, at the cost of serious damage to your volunteer pool. The difference comes from having to pay for debt service on money you borrow to cover the spending. Also, the problem that triggered the budget shortfall wasn't necessarily due to anyone's ignorance or incompetence. It was just bad luck. But, for whatever reason, the bad luck this time was bigger than your cash reserves.

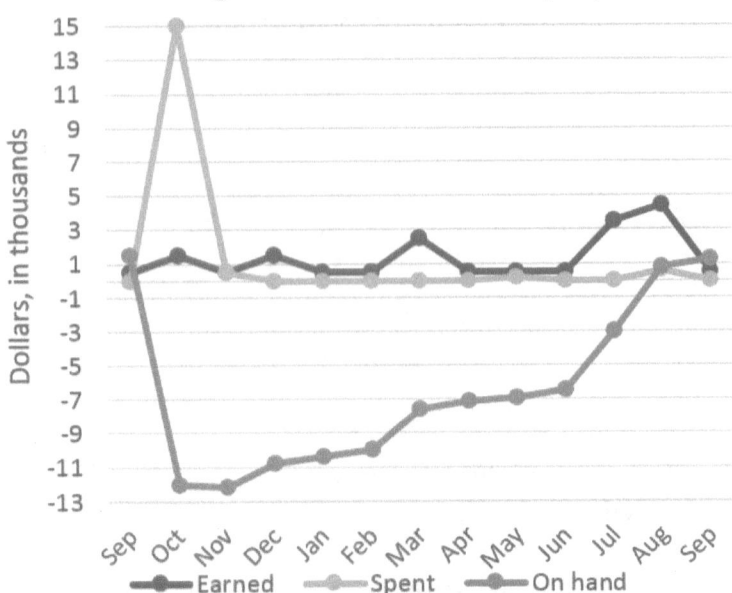
Figure 8: Cost curve, stressful year

Earned ● Spent ● On hand

Here is the cost curve of an organization that was able to recover from a major expense in the month of October. Suppose it's your charity. For whatever reason, you had a big expense in the month of October and had to borrow money to cover it. This behavior, *deficit spending*, is common in government as well as in business. It's a dangerous habit to get into. So, if you can avoid it, you don't start. Instead, you tighten your belt and manage your outbound cash flow.

To avoid deficit spending, you begin *before* the crisis occurs. You make whatever decisions are necessary to kill off any sacred cows or white elephants. When a crisis hits, all expansion and acquisitions are put on hold until the debt is paid off. No employees are hired or paid. Although you have access to credit (you must have had it, in order to rack up a $15,000 debt), you don't use it.

Notice how the lines converge at the end of the fiscal year? This convergence means your charity was able to earn enough money to repay the debt and end the year with a positive balance. In the above graph, your fundraising team is up to the task of raising enough money to pull the charity out of its bind. See how the earnings peak higher and higher as the year goes on? This reflects a growing volunteer pool, a healthy administration, and a group of people who are committed to working with each other. Instead of becoming less productive as the year goes on, they become more effective and are able to bring more money in. By the end of the year, the cash on hand is greater than zero.

One way to see how healthy your spending plan is would be to plot out the money you plan to earn, spend, and have on hand throughout your program cycle. See if any of the lines go negative, and if they do, look at whether your cash on hand converges again. If it does, the hit you're planning to take will be survivable. If the cash on hand doesn't climb back up above zero, your charity is going to go into a tailspin from which it may not recover.

Here's an example of a charity that's out of control. It starts out with the same circumstance as the one in the previous example: the decision to borrow money to cover a big expense in October. The charity is unable to recover, and in late August, it dies.

Figure 9: Cost curve, dying charity

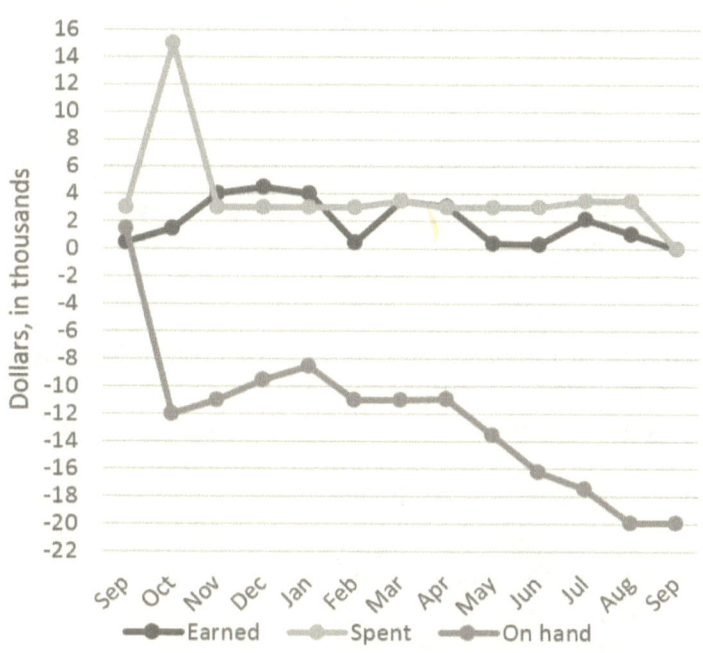

This charity starts out in a reasonably good position, but it's got an expensive mammal of some kind. Each month it pays $3,000 for salary, rent, or some expense a scholarship charity probably doesn't really need. The expense may be unavoidable due to a contractual agreement, or it may reflect something that has enough support from the administrative team to be exempt from cuts. Either way, if you add up all those $3,000 hits you end up with far more than the big single expense in October.

In October, the charity makes made a big purchase of some kind without having the money to pay for it. The volunteer base rallies heroically, digging deep and making some headway, but unfortunately each month the expensive mammal eats up almost all that they bring in. Try as they might, they manage to reduce the debt but the moment they try to rest, their expenses continue so they end up farther underwater. Twice more they try to raise money, but the well is running dry. People start burning out by the summer and give up in August.

Strategy #1: Prioritize

When a tree isn't getting enough water, it scales back its energy expenditure to suit its available resources. First it drops its fruit, then its leaves, then its outermost twigs go dry. Everything is sacrificed to keep the central trunk and root alive as long as possible, in the hope that it will rain again. That's what you've got to do as a leader if you want to turn Figure 9 into Figure 8 and claw your way out of debt.

Unlike trees, we humans are capable of making changes and proactively going after what we need, but it's important to allocate time and resources intelligently. When a tree is dying for lack of water, it doesn't waste its resources making fruit. When a charity is bleeding money, it needs to scale back its expenditures in every single area, including program.

It's like when you're in an airplane and the oxygen masks drop: you must put your own on before helping the person in the seat next to you. If you don't, there's a good chance both of you will pass out. Some kinds of first responder training are also set up so that it's impossible to rescue all the victims without dying. One of the roughest parts of this kind of training comes when an aspiring firefighter (for example) has to choose between trying to save a fire victim and exiting the simulated building before his or her air runs out. The purpose of the training is to teach people to take risks, but to save their own lives if necessary. Those who cannot disengage and make the tough decisions fail this kind of test and wash out of training.

Division by criticality

If you're solving a cash flow problem, there's a good chance you've got to throw somebody out of the lifeboat. You're going to have to take away something that people depend on by cutting a program, laying off staff, or selling off assets. *Before you do, make sure the amputation you're about to make will actually guarantee the survival of the organism.*

The "most critical" expenses are the ones without which you cannot have an organization of any kind. Note that I didn't say a *program* of any kind. In the most extreme cases, charities have been known to scale back, delay, or even suspend parts or even all of their program activities.

Program suspension

If your charity is a tree, your program is the fruit. It is the result of some people's generosity and other people's labor, produced organically and offered as a gift to others. Generally there's a seed inside, and the seed consists of your ideals and values which may—or may not—be taken along with the rest of the fruit, and passed along.

Trees drop their fruit first during a drought. So should you. Nothing gets a community's attention better than losing access to a valuable program. People couldn't care less whether you lay off a bean counter or a functionary. If they lose access to something they need, such as their regular Sunday sermon or their homeless shelter, they pay attention.

You don't have to cut your program completely. You might be able to mothball it and postpone some activities until later.

Strategy #2: Scale down

Depending on the kind of charity you have, you might be able to just do a little less of everything.

Division by domain

One way to scale back a program is to cut all budgets by a specific percentage, and then see what you can do with what's left.

Each type of expense can be broken down in terms of whether it's a program, fundraising, or administrative cost. Some, such as heat or lighting, may apply to all three groups if they share the same space, so the practical thing to do is to divide based on the fraction of the total space used by each domain. For labor, such as an Executive Director who performs multiple tasks, divide by the portion of time spent pursuing each task.

Do not succumb to the temptation of declaring all of your Executive Director's salary as a "program" expense if the majority of his or her time is spent writing grant proposals, soliciting donations, or setting up fundraising activities. The only activities that are "program" deal with delivering the goods and services listed in your program description to your target market.

The vast majority of an Executive Director's duties are not program related. Pretending that they are, in order to get a better rating by national or international grading organizations, is actually a sign of a sacred cow.

In any case, erroneously labeling an Executive Director's activities as "program" simply guarantees that staff member will the first to be cut if you select a program suspension strategy.

Resist the temptation to cut fundraising expenses to zero. If your organization relies on more than thing-a-thons and low expense fundraising, this will guarantee money stops coming in. Make sure you don't have any sacred cows in the fundraising department, and be willing to make cuts, but don't zero out any domain entirely.

Cutting administrative expenses to zero is only rational if it's a voluntary move on the part of the paid administrators. If it's not, the people whose positions you are eliminating to replace them with volunteers have a legitimate employment complaint and grounds for a lawsuit.

Scaling back by domain is a relatively fair way to cut, except the cuts may have disproportionate impact.

Strategy #3: Liquidate

Selling off assets is roughly on par with amputating a limb or firing good people: you're lightening your load in one way but depriving yourself of a long-term benefit.

Liquidating assets to pay down debt obviously only works if you have something of value to sell. It's a one-shot measure intended to free up some money temporarily while you get your organization into a better and more sustainable position. It's like throwing some (or all) of a ship's cargo overboard in a storm.

You should consider liquidating only if there's something to save. If you're selling off every available asset to the point where you've got no way to run a program or raise money to run one in the future, you're better off shutting down and starting again from scratch. Volunteers and donors like to see results in exchange for what they give, and they are generally unwilling to make sacrifices solely to pay off someone else's debt.

Liquidation *must* be accompanied by some other cost cutting strategy or else the sacrifice is for nothing.

Liquidate only after you've run a cost and spending analysis and graphed out your cash flow for the next program cycle and the next year. If the liquidation doesn't result in the two lines converging (barring any pie-in-the-sky estimates based on hope or hype), don't postpone the inevitable. Go directly to Strategy #5 and shut down the charity in a controlled fashion that will harm people the least.

Strategy #4: Cash infusion

You can sometimes ask your administrators to dig deep, write a big check, and make personal financial sacrifices in order to get you through a rough time. Sometimes you can make a big fundraising push. But this will be effective only if the conditions that created the cash flow problem no longer exist. If you're still feeding an expensive mammal or digging yourself further into debt, no self-respecting donor will put even one cent into your operation. A codependent idiot might, if they're not busy enabling an alcoholic or a problem gambler at home or at work. Yet codependents seldom have much in the way of time and resources, because what they have is leeched away by enabling moocher friends and relatives.

Before you pursue the cash infusion strategy, make sure you're not asking people to double down on a bad bet.

Strategy #5: Shut down cleanly

This is where you give up on the idea of saving your charity and focus on saving the people and resources you can, so that you can create a hundred-year charity out of what remains.

At times, you will inherit mistakes so serious they can't be corrected with the resources you've got. Or, you will make a mistake so serious that you or your company cannot recover. Maybe, no matter what you do, you can't get the lines on your cash flow graph to come together. Maybe you've lost a major lawsuit or have a debt so crippling you can't ever hope to function and run a program while burdened by it. Or perhaps the economic conditions in your area have changed to the point where your program is no longer needed or where the greater community can no longer afford to support it. Shutting your charity down while you still have social capital is the only way you can expect to start cleanly with a program that serves the community sustainably.

Encourage your employees to find other jobs. Write letters of reference. Call in favors from people you know. Try your best to make sure that the people who have relied on you for income have the best possible chance at landing another job.

Return any grant money you may have taken but not spent. If you are insolvent, or if you have outstanding debt that cannot be paid off even after your assets are liquidated, declare bankruptcy and shut down the charity. Any remaining assets not claimed by creditors should be forwarded to a successor charity as per the procedures outlined in your Bylaws.

It's always disappointing to shut down, but if you do it cleanly you and the rest of the administration team will retain your health, your sanity, and your credibility. This is vital, because those are the things that will be needed if you decide to try again with a new charity or a new administrative team. People who found charities seldom lose their interest in improving the world, unless they have been ground up so badly that they are cynical and disillusioned.

Strategy #6: Exit the burning building

Just as there are alcoholics who won't accept that they have a problem and career criminals who refuse to change their ways, there's such a thing as a charity that doesn't want to fix its cash flow problem. When enough Board members are committed to a fiscally irresponsible or illegal course of action, regardless of the reason, then unless you want to be held legally and financially accountable for the results yourself, you must resign.

Resignation should never be an idle threat, and you shouldn't threaten to resign simply because a vote doesn't go your way. But if you've made a good faith effort to correct a cash flow problem, there is no relief in sight, and you cannot get the executive team or the Board of Directors on board with any of the above five strategies, you have to leave before the damage is irreparable and before the organization makes a legal commitment to a course of action that results in financial disaster.

If you want to run a sustainable charity, the most important thing you can do is to team up with other people who have the same goal. If you are surrounded by people who prefer to fly by the seat of their collective pants, who refuse to stay within a budget, who refuse to follow the laws that apply to them, and who insist on making long-term commitments without any idea how to keep them, these are not people who want to be involved with a hundred-year charity. They might make all the right mouth noises, but if there's ever a difference between a person's words and his or her actions, believe the actions.

One of the hardest things I've every had to do was to resign from the Board of Directors of a charity that was committed to self-destruction. I didn't resign until I'd tried everything I could think of to save the organization, which included some knock-down, drag-out arguments with the executive team and the other Board members. Oddly enough, years later I ran into the former President in a parking lot, and the first thing he did was to apologize. He related a story of how the charity collapsed, devoured by its own debts and lack of social capital less than two years after I quit. It turned out that, by resigning instead of being present when the charity signed a contract without having the resources to uphold its end, I saved myself from being a party to a lawsuit when the charity (predictably) breached the contract and the other party went after the Board and Executive team in a personal capacity. The D&O insurance the charity had would not cover anybody who had breached their fiduciary duty by voting to sign the contract and then voting to break it.

As you have perhaps realized, I've got a big ego. I like it when I'm right about something, and that's one thing that motivates me to learn from my experiences and to become a better decision maker. So on the subjects where I develop experience, I tend to be right a lot more often than average. So I've learned to graciously accept apologies from other people when my predictions come to pass.

Accepting the former President's apology was a big ego boost but it was bittersweet. The good feelings that came from being right were tainted by the bad feelings that came from seeing how much the struggle had aged my friend. The stress had worn down a person who was rightly known for integrity and good character while creating no benefit for the community at large.

For a moment, I felt a little bit guilty for having escaped and spent the same years enjoying service on the Boards and volunteer pools of healthy organizations. Then I realized that my effort and donations during those years had produced lasting value to the community through service to a fraternal order, a homeowner's association, and a handful of craft and skilled trade based service charities. During the same time frame, my friend tried his best to save his doomed charity. He put in at least as many hours and at least as many dollars to his venture as I did to mine, and most likely more. But he had nothing to show for it except worse health and a lower net worth.

If you walk out of the burning building by leaving a charity before its leaders get into serious legal trouble, try to take as many people with you as are willing to come. I don't mean that you need to raid the clerical pool

305

or scare off the janitor. But other people on the Board of Directors who are at risk of being implicated or involved in, say, illegal activity deserve to be informed of the risk they are taking. Do so. If people would still rather stay, leave them. You can't save them, and these are adults who have the right to burn themselves out if they so wish.

Chapter 20: Planning For the Worst

Charitable ventures attract optimistic people who are accustomed to working toward something they believe will improve the world around them. In a positive environment, it's easy to forget that unexpected things happen sometimes. You live in a world where accidents, natural disasters, and human malice still exist. That's no doubt one of the reasons you founded or joined a charitable venture in the first place.

Make every decision mindfully, and ask yourself what the results would look like a hundred years down the road. In a hundred-year charity, long-term planning is not reserved solely for the Board of Directors. Everyone involved with the charity in a decision making capacity needs to consider the long-term impact of what they do.

While we all hope for the best, it is prudent to run a non-profit in a way that mitigates some of the most obvious risks. This chapter will discuss risk in general, and then address four of the biggest and most common risks facing non-profit businesses that are not related to bad management decisions. It will also provide specific mitigation strategies that help limit the damage associated with those risks.

Your relationship with risk in general

Since your goal is to create and run an institution that will last a hundred years or more, you cannot afford to gamble as readily as people who don't care whether or not their institution survives them. A hundred years from now, your successors will be affected by some of the stupid mistakes you make today.

Before making a major decision to expand a program, sell off a major asset, change direction, hire an employee, or acquire real estate or other potentially expensive belongings, make sure you consider the worst case scenario. I know of one small charity that hired an Executive Director who happened to be extremely sick. About a month after the ink was dry on the contract, the new administrator was diagnosed with a major and incurable illness and became unable to work. So the little charity was saddled with a person who was unable to attend meetings, unable to perform effective work on the charity's behalf, and in fact unable to do anything but make use of the health benefits package.

I'm not suggesting a zero-risk approach, but anytime you hire, buy something on credit, or do something that requires insurance, you're taking a risk. Consider the worst case scenario and what your organization would have to do to survive it. The risk-balancing, upside/downside approach recommended by stock analysts and MBAs trained to run publicly traded corporations are mathematically sound but far too aggressive for a hundred-year charity.

Risk #1: Loss of a major asset

In a perfect world, there would be no such thing as destructive fires, earthquakes, or other natural disasters that wipe out buildings, vehicles, and other things your non-profit uses to conduct its business. It's impossible to accurately predict where disaster will strike far enough in advance to guarantee you'll never take a loss due to natural disasters. In fact, if you have buildings or vehicles at all it's very reasonable to predict that you'll eventually have hail, wind, or flood damage. Similarly, if you have computers it's very reasonable to predict that you'll eventually have a hard disk failure or pick up a major virus.

In a perfect world, people wouldn't desecrate churches, steal the copper wire out of an animal shelter, or break into a charity's offices and wreck all the computers. But the world we live in is not perfect. Vandalism happens. So does theft. Sometimes even the friendliest non-profit company is the victim of human ugliness.

Because charitable ventures attract optimists, and because you are engaged in making the world a better place, you may not be used to thinking of yourself, or your non-profit company, as a target of attack. Newer, less experienced Board members or volunteers are often surprised by the need to prepare for such an incident, and many who are interested in cost cutting will point to insurance or data backup as one possible way to save money. Such an approach is penny-wise but pound-foolish.

One very useful exercise is to go through a list of your non-profit's belongings, and ask: "if this item disappeared right now, could we still run our program?" If the answer is no, you may have to come up with a mitigation strategy to limit the damage done should you lose that asset.

Mitigation #1: Data Backup

Backing up your charity's computer systems regularly to a separate drive, scanning digital copies of all paperwork, and storing it in a different location from your offices, is the single best thing you could possibly do to ensure you can keep running in case of a fire. Depending on the amount of data you generate and the level of security you need, it may be prudent to pay for a regular backup service.

Even if your non-profit uses no computer resources at all, it makes sense to regularly copy your address books, bank account statements, phone lists and mailing lists. Similarly, make sure at least two people have access to banking information or the authority to access the bank account at the same time. This way, if a key employee or volunteer dies or quits, the charity itself is not paralyzed and someone else can pick up the work.

Mitigation #2: Firewalls and Anti-Virus Protection

A *firewall* is a computer, or software that runs on a computer, to act as an electronic traffic cop for data flowing into or out of a computer network. It can be used to limit network traffic between different parts of a network, such as to protect personal information in the computers that handle payroll or donations while allowing other people doing unrelated work to use the same network. It can also be used to help protect the entire network from outside access, while still allowing employees to receive E-mail or access the Internet. No firewall is a perfect defense against a determined hacker, but having firewalls will protect your system from casual browsing and make it much harder for automated botnets to harvest data from you or to plant malware on your system.

Anti-virus software checks periodically to determine whether harmful code has been introduced to a computer. Since new computer viruses and malware are constantly being created, manufacturers of anti-virus software regularly send out updates for their code. This is not free, and there are generally licensing costs that go along with having anti-virus software.

Everybody deserves to learn how to spot suspicious E-mail messages and attachments, and how to identify callers who solicit personal information. Providing this kind of training for your staff reduces the chance of a successful phishing attack that can compromise a computer on your network.

Mitigation #3: Property and umbrella insurance

If your non-profit is open long enough, and if it has physical assets such as vehicles or buildings, eventually there will be a natural disaster of some kind. Also, if it maintains any kind of noticeable presence in the community, the odds are high that it will be the victim of vandalism, theft, or some other human attack.

It's impossible to predict exactly when or how theft or vandalism will occur, or exactly how it will happen. Locking up unattended buildings or vehicles at night is a good business practice for everybody, but it does not prevent a fire. Nor does it prevent insider theft.

Property insurance will pay for repair or replacement of property, particularly real estate, in case of fire or other damage. Comprehensive coverage for automobiles, and casualty insurance for smaller items such as furniture, are also types of property insurance. The goal of property insurance is to provide money to replace key items if they are stolen or destroyed.

All of your real estate and vehicles should be insured for their full replacement value, even if there is no mortgage against the property or item. It is also wise to purchase fire, flood, and earthquake coverage to cover repairs for partial damage.

When buying property insurance, consider also whether your charity has furniture, computers, or anything else that it could not afford to replace immediately out of cash reserves. A church that uses sound equipment in its religious services or commercial kitchen equipment as part of its community services program would be wise to list those assets and make sure there is coverage in case of a fire or theft.

Umbrella insurance is a type of catch-all insurance that kicks in when another policy is exhausted, or that covers things not addressed by the specific policy. Examples may include extended loss of use coverage, for when a building is damaged by fire, or loss of income coverage.

A small service-oriented charity that does not own the building it occupies, and that is proactive about backing up its data and maintaining property and liability insurance, generally does not require umbrella insurance. But any charity that has a net worth of more than $250,000, or that owns real estate, should consider it.

Risk #2: Liability

Your business is liable, that is to say financially and legally accountable, for what it does. There are two types of liability: criminal liability (where the person who does it goes to jail) and civil liability (where the person who is in the wrong is sued and made to pay a settlement). Both kinds of liability apply to non-profit companies and the people who run them.

One of the biggest disasters that can befall a charity is if somebody gets hurt so badly that the charity cannot afford to pay the settlement. All it takes is one very bad accident, and a charity's savings and assets can be completely wiped out, leaving the charity with a debt it cannot afford to repay. This generally causes the charity to file for bankruptcy or else shut down completely.

Under some circumstances, if you are on the Board of Directors or an officer or executive of the company, you may be held personally liable for the results of the decisions you make, and for what you use the business's resources to do. The fact you're a non-profit company in no way protects you.

A long time ago, the laws of the United States acknowledged a concept called *charitable immunity*. According to the concept of charitable immunity, a charity (not necessarily every non-profit company) was exempt from all forms of tort prosecution, simply because it was a charity. So if someone slipped on the ice outside a homeless shelter and broke an ankle, they couldn't sue the shelter for the costs related to caring for their broken ankle, if the shelter happened to be a charity.

Charitable immunity was a noble idea while it lasted, but is no longer the law in any US state. These days, if someone slips and falls outside a homeless shelter, they have every right to sue and collect damages. Similarly, if a contractor is hired to fix that homeless shelter's roof, completes the work, and is not paid for their work, they have the right to sue. When suing a not-for-profit company, many tort lawyers routinely name the executive officers or Board members in a personal capacity also.

Mitigation #1: Liability and CGL Insurance

Liability insurance is purchased to cover claims made when your non-profit is at fault for an accident of some kind. Most automobile insurance contains some driver liability coverage. In fact, it is not legal to operate a motor vehicle without some proof of financial responsibility, such as a card showing evidence of a liability insurance policy. The law does not require people to carry insurance to cover damages to their own vehicle in case of an accident, but liability insurance for vehicles is mandatory.

If your non-profit has a vehicle, every driver who operates it should be licensed and insured in a personal capacity (for non-owned vehicle coverage), however since you own the vehicle you must also purchase liability insurance to cover accidents that occur while the driver is operating on behalf of your company.

If your charity owns real estate, your property insurance policy most likely includes coverage for personal injury or accidents that occur there. This will protect you if a storm brings down a large tree and it lands on somebody's car, or if someone trips on a crack in your sidewalk or slips on ice in front of your building. It makes sense to check your policy and be aware of the kind or amount of coverage you have. If you rent your space, you do not necessarily have personal injury or onsite accident coverage. It may make sense to buy some.

Commercial general liability or *CGL insurance* is not related to property or vehicles. It protects your company from claims related to misconduct by an employee or volunteer.

CGL insurance does not necessarily include sexual misconduct coverage. But, for churches and youth service groups that require regular contact with human beings, sexual misconduct coverage is available to help cover the legal expenses should someone ever file a suit based on false allegations. The extra sexual misconduct coverage helps protect the charity against the rare but horrible cases where a sexual predator or con artist gets through the rigorous screening process and uses his or her position of trust to prey on others. In those cases, CGL insurance will help to settle the suit and provide some help and comfort to the victim. CGL with sexual misconduct coverage will generally not protect a person who is actually found guilty of a sexual offense.

CGL insurance, even with sexual misconduct coverage, is not a substitute for screening volunteers or employees. In fact, most CGL policies explicitly require that the business that buys it have a reasonable policy in place to screen out predators.

Liability coverage, including CGL, protects only the party that purchases it. If a claim were to be filed against somebody connected to your non-profit in a personal capacity, CGL will not necessarily provide the right coverage. Ultimately, CGL protects the company that buys it, not the individuals who work there.

Mitigation #2: Malpractice, E&O, and D&O Insurance

There are three special kinds of insurance designed to protect your volunteers or employees from financial consequences due to accidents, mistakes, and other things that can go wrong during the work they do for your charity. Unlike your company's CGL or automobile insurance policy, these types of insurance protect them in an individual capacity.

Malpractice insurance is a type of insurance for doctors, lawyers, social workers, and other professionals. It protects against claims related to incorrect performance of professional duties. Depending on the company offering the insurance, it can be marketed as *professional liability insurance* or *Errors and Omissions (E&O) insurance.*

If your non-profit company provides dental, legal, or medical services to anybody, every person who performs these services on your behalf should be covered by this type of insurance.

Although some medical and legal professionals already have malpractice insurance, especially if they work full-time in their disciplines and only perform part-time volunteer work for you, it makes sense to buy this type of insurance to cover nurses, social workers, and other people who perform services on your charity's behalf. If you are a larger charity such as a hospital or clinic, and if you employ people full-time to perform medical or legal services to the public, you cannot omit this type of insurance since no sensible professional will work for you without it.

Errors and Omissions (E&O) insurance is a type of liability insurance that protects a company's employees and volunteers from claims related to mistakes made during the regular exercise of their duties. Tax preparation, accounting, engineering, and investment firms routinely buy E&O insurance to protect their employees. If your non-profit business provides financial services, counseling, or other kinds of service where there could be legal consequences to giving bad advice, you need to provide the same level of protection that those employees would reasonably expect if they were employed in the private domain.

A non-profit company that provides medical care, legal advice, or financial advice to the public, but that does not also carry E&O insurance, is unlikely to attract experienced employees or volunteers.

Directors and Officers (D&O) insurance is a type of liability insurance to protect the directors, executives, and officers of a company from claims related to the performance of their administrative duties. It protects them from suits or settlements related to decisions they made while running the charity.

D&O insurance differs from E&O or malpractice insurance. E&O or malpractice insurance is generally intended for people who, due to their profession, are regulated or licensed by a state or national association. Every state has a bar association for lawyers, a licensing program for professional engineers, and a medical association for doctors and nurses. To be accepted into these professional associations requires specific education and demonstration of sufficient skill in some kind of testing process. There is no corresponding licensing system for directors, executives, or officers of a non-profit company. Anybody can hang out a shingle.

D&O insurance comes into play when someone files suit against a company and names the administrative team in a personal capacity. It protects the administrative team.

D&O insurance has limits. If a director or officer has breached his or her fiduciary duty and has an undisclosed conflict of interest, or has engaged in actual fraud, embezzlement, bribery, or other abuses of his or her office, he or she can be sued by the company for failure to act in the company's best interests, and D&O will cover nothing.

Maxim #18: D&O insurance is like a raincoat, not a condom. It will keep you from getting soaked in a random downpour, but it offers no protection if you're actively screwing someone.

Risk #3: Critical loss of social capital

Charities cannot draw donations or labor from groups they have alienated, because the well has run dry. Whether the loss of favor is temporary or permanent depends on how severe the incident was and whether it is survivable.

The kind of scandals or incidents that aren't survivable are the ones that involve outright predatory behavior.

Mitigation #1: Avoid ideological temptations to enable predatory behavior

This sounds like a no-brainer, but it isn't, because charities keep making this mistake. Churches, unfortunately, are more likely to enable predatory behavior than to actively root it out and punish it. It's due to an logical blunder people sometimes make when they confuse their ideology with reality.

I've coined a phrase, "cafeteria justice", to refer to the notion that, once a person has "paid" for his or her crimes by suffering legal consequences, he or she should be offered the same opportunities and trust as a person who has not offended, even if the high-trust environment has already contributed to more than one cycle of offending and "paying". At a cafeteria, you can take whatever you want provided you pay for it. Once you've paid, you can come back and get more. It's a valid business model but it fails horribly as a penal strategy. It is also not a sustainable non-profit behavior because it destroys the community to which the offenders are given repeated access.

Cafeteria justice is a problem in the non-profit and religious community. It is based on the flawed assumption that the needs of the offender (to move on and live a life that is not dominated by the offense and its consequences) are more important than the need of the community (to not be the victim of future offenses).

While there are cases in which even violent offenders have reformed and become productive members of society, those individuals earn the trust a little bit at a time and understand that they are not automatically entitled to it. Such trust as they receive is a result of consistent reliable, mature behavior. They have to prove themselves, not just once, but over and over again.

An offender with the cafeteria justice mentality believes that "I'm sorry" should turn back the clock to a time before the first offense was committed. He or she always has an excuse as to why the offense was someone else's fault, and believes he or she is entitled to a second, fifth, or umpteenth chance simply because he or she wants one.

There's also a problem in many religious communities that emphasize forgiveness by asserting that it's morally desirable or even necessary for victims to not only "forgive" people who have done horrific things, but to trust them and permit them the opportunity to reoffend without first seeing evidence that the offense won't recur. Victims who are unable or unwilling to do this are punished or even expelled from the community, because they do not have the moral right to protect themselves from future abuse. Offenders, having supposedly been forgiven by some higher authority, are treated as spiritually cleansed and morally worthy, whereas victims are unclean and morally unworthy unless they go along with the charade and allow further abuse to occur.

Forced forgiveness is one of the most disgusting ideological perversions I've ever seen. It takes a concept—forgiveness—which is intended to allow a victim to not obsess over the past and to allow a community to recover from an offense, and twists it into an institution designed to provide repeat offenders access to victims.

There has also been a recent trend in which religious organizations or charities have knowingly hired people into roles where they have unsupervised access to the public, despite the fact that the employee has previously been accused of, or convicted of, sexual misconduct. This is a classic example of putting one person's needs (the pervert's) ahead of the community the charity is supposed to serve. It's also an example of magical thinking: this individual will change if and only if he or she is trusted, therefore we should trust him or her first and look for evidence afterwards.

It's not possible to get much more stupid and still be able to breathe.

People in non-profit administration enable predatory behavior because they are confused about what community they are supposed to be serving. They get the idea that a predator's need for trust and for respect within a community is more important than a prospective victim's need to not be abused.

The law does not agree. Charities have lost enormous lawsuits after "protecting" predatory people by moving them to other communities or other jobs where they end up re-offending. Don't be the next example.

If you really want to provide former offenders with a chance to prove their worth in an environment where their previous behavior is not held against them, risk yourself in a personal capacity. Invite an embezzler to manage your 401(k) investments. Hire a thief to house-sit while you're out of town. You have the Constitutional right to the pursuit of happiness, and if your pursuit of happiness requires that you allow other people opportunities to hurt you, rape you, steal from you, or even kill you in order to prove how rehabilitated they are, go for it and knock yourself out.

What you do not have the right to do, no matter what your ideology might tell you, is to set an innocent person up to be victimized.

The people who rely on your non-profit for counseling, medical help, safe shelter, religious ministry, or any other service you care to provide, are generally already in need. You do not have the right to make their problems worse. Nor do you have the right to damage an innocent person's faith in humanity, or—worse still—in the religion or God you purport to serve. Protecting a predator does that. If you're going to protect someone, protect the victims. Protect the innocent children and the people who don't know they're in danger.

Mitigation #2: Due diligence

Due diligence is a process of making sure the people you're dealing with are who they say they are. A background check is part of this activity, if you want to employ someone in a paid or volunteer capacity. But it also applies to people who perform work on your behalf. You are accountable for the things done by the people you employ, and also for the services you contract out.

There are plenty of get-rich-quick artists who will tell you they have a foolproof way to earn large amounts of money. The fact they need or want money in exchange for this knowledge should raise a huge red flag.

Do not buy contact lists. There is no such thing as a list of people who have signed up to be cold-called in their homes or businesses, by charities "just like yours". Anyone who claims to be able to sell or rent you such a list is lying. The list in question has most likely been stolen.

Do not make use of solicitation services that claim to have a base of known donors who have a history of donating to charities "just like yours". These are cold callers who have managed to get their grubby little fingers on somebody's donor contact list. Everyone on that list is willing to pay money to be taken off of it, but they're not going to be very anxious to help you.

I once offered a cold-calling charity a substantial donation in exchange for the name and address of whoever sold them my contact information. It didn't result in me getting that information, and in fact the cold caller became verbally abusive. Luckily I already had that particular charity's contact information and was able to follow up aggressively enough to get off their call list.

Remember that any philanthropist wealthy and powerful enough to be worth cultivating as an ally is also wealthy and powerful enough to make a very bad enemy.

Mitigation #3: Do not protect wrongdoers

Provide appropriate liability insurance to protect your administrators and volunteers in the case of false accusations or accidents, but do not allow anyone to abuse his or her role in your charity in order to offend.

In the past, large charities, schools, or religious organizations have responded to allegations of sexual abuse by moving the alleged perpetrator around so as to enable him or her to avoid the very predictable consequences of being a predatory pervert. All that happens is that the charity takes the hit for the individual's actions.

There's no such thing as an individual person who's more important than your charity. No matter how big a pillar of the community might be, he or she is not worth the sacrifice of the people your program serves.

You may, if you wish, correct and retain a volunteer or employee who is caught stealing or embezzling. But you cannot keep someone who preys on the community you serve.

Mitigation #4: Keep incompatible program activities separate

If you want to set up a non-profit to provide job or accommodation opportunities to people whose past predatory behavior has made them unemployable, go for it. It would be a very noble and charitable venture and it would provide lasting benefit to society. Felons are a legitimate charitable class, and they often lack education, employment opportunities, and places to live. If you want to help people turn their lives around and become productive citizens after they are released from prison, make that be the focus of your charity. Don't dress the charity up as something else.

If you want to serve felons, focus your resources on helping them live healthy lives within the law. But understand that they may have impulses or pressures that make it difficult to avoid re-offending if put in an unstructured environment where it is easy to do so. Therefore, make sure you never combine a felon employment initiative with a youth ministry, a school, a credit union (for financial predators), a daycare, or a homeless shelter.

Mitigation #5: Document and address conflicts of interest

Many charitable non-profit companies have ongoing problems due to conflicts between key power players within the organization. Although some of them are in fact personality conflicts, the vast majority of them are due to misalignment of interests or out of control egos. These in turn are almost always the result of bad decision making or indecisive leadership by the Board of Directors or the various officers or executives of the company.

Conflict of interest occurs every time someone who is in a decision making capacity with the charity stands to benefit in a personal or family capacity from the outcome of his or her decision. This can include any of the following actions:

- Self-dealing, in which charity resources are used to buy or rent goods or services from insiders
- Situations in which insiders and their families receive preferential treatment including services or resources from the charity
- Decisions related to employee pay or compensation, when made by that individual

Any time an individual with decision making authority has the potential to benefit financially from a transaction, there has to be a means in place to identify a conflict and recuse him or her from that decision.

Risk #4: Incompetent successors

We build our charities, clubs, churches and other beloved institutions hoping to enjoy them throughout our lives, but sooner or later we do have to hand over control to others. We all get old. We all have other things that happen in our lives that take attention away from our philanthropic activities. Illness and family emergencies are not solely for the families served by our programs. Ultimately, we all die.

It's the same in a not-for-profit business as it is in a bakery or construction company: the founders generally like to stay active, but if everything is built around one dynamic individual, then the loss of that individual generally leads to the collapse of the company. Wise leaders therefore plan to eventually turn over the active management to somebody else.

Mitigation #1: Have an intelligent succession plan

Accidents happen and so does sudden illness. When you've been hit by a truck and are in critical condition in the hospital, it's too late to start training your Vice President as the President-Elect. It's far better to cross train more than one person in the different executive duties, and to rotate between leaders.

You may not simply do as a leader in a for-profit business might do, and name one of your heirs as a successor in the Bylaws or Articles of Incorporation. Once you incorporate a not-for-profit company, it belongs to the community, not to you... especially if it's a public charity. But this doesn't mean you can't identify people who have the right mentality and approach, and train them to take over and run the show when you are no longer able to do so.

Consider some form of job shadowing. Many relatively inexperienced people accept the Presidency of a not-for-profit company with a six-figure annual budget without realizing how much work it is or how many hours a week it requires. It's very easy to swan around at a celebratory luncheon, but it's not so easy to plan and execute three fundraisers per year, write ten grant applications, solicit a hundred possible new corporate donors, and stay up to date with your tax filing. They call it volunteer "work" for a very good reason. It's not play, and some of the duties are time-critical.

319

Many not-for-profit corporations use the Vice President position as a way to train a President-elect or a successor. If you're able to have past Presidents or executive team members on the Board of Directors it will create valuable depth of experience.

Mitigation #2: Educate your Board and your employees

Human beings don't read minds. If you want people to understand what you're doing and why, make sure you stack the Board of Directors with people who want to build and operate a hundred-year charity, and who know what it takes to get there. Pay special attention to people who don't understand why cash reserves are necessary or who are so growth-obsessed that they don't realize when they are taking risks.

I'm not saying to never take risks. I'm saying you have a fiduciary duty to the organization you're running. That means you're legally obligated to put its interests first financially and also in other respects. This means you need to be intelligent about risks and you need to plan for the worst case scenario. You also need to educate your fellow leaders in how to do the same.

People make mistakes all the time, but if they have the tools to recognize when they're off track and how to recover, the charity you build will be resilient enough to survive after you're gone.

Always make sure you have competent people on the Board. They should have enough experience and enough business skill to be able to tell whether the organization is running the way it should. Many successful charities trade Board members, such that one person sits on more than one Board of Directors. It's very good to have one or more Board members that have experience running other successful charitable ventures.

Avoid the temptation to load up the Board of Directors with inexperienced people. You can and should have a few of them—they provide useful energy and initiative—but your Board should also have people who have years of experience in not-for-profit administration.

Many charities use the Board of Directors as a kind of a bullpen that can, if necessary, produce replacements when the current executive team members retire or leave. This is a great strategy provided the replacements have the skills and the time to devote to charity management.

Mitigation #3: Have a hundred-year plan. Communicate it constantly.

If your current trends continue, what will your charitable venture look like a hundred years from now?

Consider real estate, if you require the use of it for your program. Mortgages are available for thirty years, but some of the modern construction techniques for steel and concrete buildings result in a structure so flimsy that it will begin to collapse before the mortgage is paid off. So, twenty-five years from now, you may be left with a collapsing or barely-usable building plus an ongoing mortgage payment. Your organization will be exactly where it is today, but with the ongoing burden of a mortgage payment that hampers its cash flow. Is that what you intend? No? Then you'll have to be more selective about your building construction.

Most American buildings are not actually designed to last a hundred years. The fashion is to create fifty to sixty-year buildings, to demolish them as they reach the end of their expected life, and to build something different. If you propose to follow this trend, then plan to pay for an entire new building every few decades, and be advised that the building you plan to buy or build is not a one-time purchase.

If you would like for your hundred-year charity to occupy an important landmark known for its historical significance, then set aside the money necessary to maintain such a building. The costs may be higher than you think. Also, pay attention to construction and materials. Meanwhile, don't do stupid things with money or contracts, and constantly weigh the prestige of occupying an important building against the costs of the building maintenance.

Many hundred-year charities elect to lease office space, light industrial space, or other accommodations so as to avoid excessive maintenance costs, and the decision to save money by doing so is one of the key factors in maintaining the hundred-year charity's sustainability. If the building you occupy is a factor in what makes your charity unique and that brings in operating capital through tourist dollars, you'd better take care of that building. If you run a museum located in an old church that is also a historical landmark or that has some unusual feature such as a great work of art or an event of historical importance, then do what it takes to maintain that resource.

It's wise to talk about what your venture should look like a hundred years down the road, but this shouldn't be a pie-in-the-sky baloney session where everyone fantasizes about "what if". Having read this far, you know the difference and you can tell whether or not your organization is taking steps that will plausibly result in the things being discussed by raising the necessary money, providing the necessary program, and choosing resilient flexibility over risk.

Mitigation #4: Delegate authority

One of the most important things you can do when running a hundred-year charity is to give other people the chance to lead. They will make mistakes sometimes. They will sometimes be overcome by circumstance. But they will always learn from the experience. Give them an opportunity to do this in a controlled, low-stakes environment.

Before you make somebody into the new Vice President, let them plan and execute at least one major fundraising initiative. Before you make somebody into the new Treasurer, make sure they are capable of doing bookkeeping. If you want to replace yourself as President or as a member of the executive team, start by grooming several possible successors and giving each of them authority and a chance to lead.

One of the worst things charity administrators do—and founders are exceptionally bad for this—is to hog all the actual administrative authority and to insist on overseeing everything. This is a very useful behavior in the early stages of a charity, but if you don't have experienced people five years down the road, you're doing something wrong.

Section IV: Special Topics

This section contains some important topics that require special attention. None of them can be shoehorned neatly into the program, fundraising, or administration domain. Grants, for example, cannot be thoroughly discussed as an aspect of fundraising, although raising money for program expansion by soliciting grants is a perfectly normal activity. In order to understand grants well enough to write an acceptable proposal, you must understand how to use grant money once you've got it. When you begin with the end in mind, you will find it much easier to communicate your goal and discuss ways to use a grant to achieve it.

Some specific not-for-profit structures, such as booster clubs and non-501(c)(3) organizations such as unions also deserve their own chapters because they have some unique issues and challenges. Accordingly, I have set space aside for them in this section of the book.

Maxims and Equations In This Section

Maxim #19: You will receive a grant only if you prove that giving you money will advance the donor's agenda.

Maxim #20: Raising money for yourself or your family is not charity.

Maxim #21: Don't lie about your money or resources.

Maxim #22: Pursue grants only for things that are in alignment with your mission and program, and that you've already planned to spend money on..

Maxim #23: Well-run charities can respond to minor emergencies without disrupting program operations, because they have an emergency fund.

Maxim #24: Not paying your bills because you gave away the money is not an example of morality or good stewardship.

Maxim #25: If fundraising competes with something similar in the private sector, it's business activity.

Maxim #26: The Board of Directors is the dog, and the executive team and employees are the tail. Never let the tail wag the dog.

Chapter 21: Grants

A grant is a gift of money from the government, a business, or some other charity. It doesn't just fall from the sky. You have to apply for it, with a coherent and well thought out proposal showing how the money will be used. You have to convince the organization that hands out the grants that you will use the money in a way they approve of, and that your organization is stable enough to execute the program described in your proposal. The money also comes with strings attached that restrict how it can be used.

In a hundred-year charity, the Board of Directors must vigorously supervise the grant strategy of its executive team. How the executive team applies for and uses grants can influence the program growth in ways that may not be consistent with the Board's vision. Small, regional charities are particularly vulnerable to overreach: when they receive a large grant, it can change the direction of their entire program. The temptation to misuse grant money is intense, but despite popular belief human integrity generally prevails. I once had the honor of watching the Board of a charity that was shutting down hand back grant money to an organization that had issued it.

Organizations that hand out grants aren't doing it simply to be nice. *They have an agenda.* Some of them want to create a lasting contribution to science or the arts. Others want to ensure a bigger pool of recipients have access to the specific services you provide. They aren't necessarily able to perform the work themselves, but they recognize that your organization has the skills and opportunity, so by giving you a grant they are trying to do charitable work through you, using your organization as their hands. They also expect to have access to resources and money you have already set aside. They're willing to boost you, but only if you're climbing in that direction already.

Maxim #19: You will receive a grant only if you prove that giving you money will advance the donor's agenda.

The organization giving the grant is hoping to permanently improve the world in some way. This might be by helping you create a lasting contribution to science or to the arts, or by increasing the number of injured tortoises you can rescue. Perhaps they want to make sure the children in your city have access to a low-cost after-school dance program. But their goal is not to fund your work on an ongoing basis. Their goal is to give you the push you need to pay the initial costs associated with your expansion so that you can start running sustainably again on a larger scale. This is why major projects with clear start and end dates tend to attract grants. Ongoing program operations do not.

Part of the grant proposal process requires you to provide the grantor with information that will allow them to weed out weak or badly run charities, or charities that do not have the resources to take on the kind of project they want to fund. This isn't because they're being mean to you. They're simply looking for the right alignment of interests so as to accomplish their goal. They really aren't interested in taking you on as a business partner of sorts if you can't hold up your end of the bargain.

Grantors expect to see progress. They want to see the film they're paying to help produce, and they want to read the lab reports and the publications from the medical research they funded. You will never be paid simply to play or have fun: grantors expect to see quantitative results. Indeed, regular status reports are generally part of the grant proposal.

Grants aren't regular income

Suppose you run a charity that provides music instruction to children from needy families. It's reasonable to ask for, receive, and use money to provide sheet music and instruments. But it's not reasonable to ask for a grant to make next month's regular payroll. Why? I've said it before several times: grants aren't for regular operating expenses.

No charity should ever rely on grant money as a way to keep its doors open. A grant is intended as a way to expand or improve your program by providing expensive equipment, or to fund a short-term project of some kind such as a film, a scientific experiment, or an oil spill cleanup. If you're having trouble making payroll or if your charity is deeply in debt, the last thing you should be thinking about is how to expand. You've got to fix your existing debt or cash flow problems first.

Time criticality

There's often significant turnaround time between when the grant application is written and when the money is received. Depending on the amount of money you're requesting and the kind of organization that gives it out, you may not see a cent for several months. Accordingly, when you apply for grants do not spend or commit the money before you know whether or not you're getting the grant. You may not add the grant money to your budget until you have written confirmation that the money is yours. You may not spend a cent of the money tied up in the grant proposal until you have confirmation that your proposal was declined.

Paying for grant writing services

Writing grant proposals is something most university researchers learn to do. Paleontologists, microbiologists, and computer scientists make use of graduate students for free labor, but eventually they have to buy equipment or pay overhead expenses for the use of lab or computer resources. Fine arts productions are especially expensive since most universities rely on money from concert and lecture hall rentals as a source of revenue. A professor's skill in finding and bringing in sizable grants is one of many factors that determine who gets tenure and who doesn't. But aside from athletics departments that are known for having enormous budgets, very few colleges and universities can afford to pay people to write grant applications full-time.

Many professional grant writers, particularly those who do not affiliate with a governing organization, work on commission. The size of the commission is negotiable but ten percent of the value of the grant is the general asking fee. You owe the grant writer nothing if he or she fails to bring in money for you. But if he or she pulls in a million-dollar grant, you owe a hundred thousand dollars. Check the fine print on the contract, and see whether the commission is due upon confirmation that the grant has been awarded, or on the arrival of the grant money (which may be several months in the future). Can you afford to cover that ten percent out of your regular cash flow without serious impact to other aspects of your program? If so, go for it. If not, your charity is too small to consider hiring a grant writer. Go after the proposal yourself.

If you'd like someone with sophisticated grant proposal writing skills to hunt up money for your parent-teacher association or youth charity, the best thing to do is to find a volunteer who's an adjunct professor at the local university. Graduate students and young professors rely in part on their proposal writing skills to feed themselves and to advance their educations.

If you're going to hire a professional, first find out whether your state requires professional donation solicitors to register with the state. Then check to make sure the consultant you're hiring is in fact registered.

Most professional grant writers do not work on a straight commission because it creates a conflict of interest. In fact, the Association of Fundraising Professionals (AFP) has a list of ethical guidelines for professional fundraising consultants that forbids them from entering into any contract where their compensation involves finder's fees or a percentage of what they bring in. Beware the "professional grant writer" willing to work for a share of what he or she brings in for you.

It's very rare that a grant will be awarded with full knowledge that a percentage of the money will be paid off the top to the person who wrote it. Grantors are sometimes willing to consider a proposal that contains administrative expenses related to a program expansion, but they almost never pay for fundraising. If you clearly show that a tenth of what they give will be skimmed off the top, you will not get the grant. Also, if they have reason to believe you will find a way to chisel away a tenth of the budget from other things such as the equipment or program expenses, your grant proposal will be declined. Automatically allocating a percentage of a grant to a specific individual is called inurement, and it's not a tax exempt activity.

Potential for conflict of interest

Because it's customary and normal to pay grant writers on commission, some small and medium-sized charities use commissions as a way to pay their staff. Be very, very careful when you do this.

You may pay bonuses to an employee, such as an Executive Director, for writing a successful grant application. You may scale the compensation to the size of the grant. However, you may not earmark a percentage of all grant or donated income to accrue to any individual. That breaks the law in two ways. First, it's a private benefit transaction because money is allocated to an insider for something besides reimbursement of expenses or market value payment for services rendered. Second, it's a form of inurement because money is being allocated to an individual.

You must always provide donors some means of donating that bypasses inurement related to compensating people for successful solicitation. In fact, that path to donation should be the default. If someone spontaneously decides to write you a check or to sign up for a monthly directed deposit, nobody should be entitled to skim off ten percent.

You may occasionally allow people to take credit for the money they raise by soliciting friends, acquaintances, or family members, and to have a say in how it is spent. However people should not ordinarily be raising money for themselves. It's both inurement and private benefit.

Maxim #20: Raising money for yourself or your family is not charity.

The law allows a small amount of inurement if it's a trivial portion of the program budget, and if it's to benefit people of a charitable class. A member of your staff with sufficient skill to write a successful grant proposal is almost certainly not.

Potential for abuse of commission policy

Allowing an employee or contractor to take a percentage of all the grants he or she helps solicit tends to open up a gray area. Does the same commission apply to solicited donations from corporations? From individuals? What if the donation comes from one of the people who volunteers with the charity, or who is a member of the Board? Does the commission apply to those donations too?

If a donor makes a directed donation to pay down debt or to help make payroll, it is completely and totally unacceptable to skim ten percent off the top and hand it to anybody. Directed donation money must be used for the purpose for which it is donated. Also, directed donation money cannot be directed to a specific charitable recipient: that would be another example of private benefit.

Overall, I don't approve of allowing staff or employees to augment their pay by soliciting donations or grants except to the extent that the donation or grant money allows you to expand your program and provide more paid employment hours for that person. Allowing people regularly associated with your charity to dip their beaks for a percentage creates a gigantic conflict of interest and also open your charity up to accusations of inurement and private benefit transactions, either of which can cost you your tax exempt status.

If you simply must hire a grant writer on commission, pick someone who is not presently a member of your volunteer or donor pool, and who is not related to anybody in a decision making capacity at your charity.

Pick someone out of the proverbial phone book instead, and vet that person to ensure he or she does business in an ethical and legal way.

Grant money is not fungible

When you receive a grant, it's like a dedicated donation. Money given to an art museum to purchase sculptures must be used for that purpose, not to repaint the walls or to pay staff. If you redirect the grant money toward another purpose and the organization that gave it to you finds out, they have a duty to make a reasonable effort to get the money back. That won't necessarily involve a suit, but it might. Also, if the misuse becomes public knowledge, you may not be able to get grants from other organizations.

If you misuse or redirect a government grant, any top administrator who knew about the abuse but failed to report it can face criminal charges.

When to use restricted donations in grant proposals

Money received from fundraising directed to a specific task must be used on that task, however it's perfectly legal to write a grant proposal to obtain the rest of what you need. In fact, this is what grantors expect you to do. When you raise money specifically for the same task for which you're soliciting the grant, it shows you're serious about the activity.

Allocated resources committed in the proposal are also locked up

When you apply for a major grant, you're writing a business proposal. Granting organizations want to know what other resources you have available to commit to the proposed activity. This lets them determine whether you have skin in the game already, and it lets them assess whether moving forward with your proposed activity will disrupt the rest of your operations.

If you've committed a resource to a grant activity, you may not spend it on another task even if it's not money from a restricted donation. Until you have a yes or no decision from the grantor, you must consider that money frozen or locked up, just as if it were a directed donation.

If your budget is so tight that spending the money in your grant proposal on a different activity means that you won't be able to move forward on the activity the grant is supposed to fund, then you must either cut or delay that other activity, find some other way to pay for it, or simply not apply for the grant. If the reply to your grant proposal is "no", then you may consider the money unlocked for the purpose of the grant.

Restrictions on how you use money that occur because you commit that money in a grant proposal are in addition to other kinds of restrictions. Money that is restricted because it was raised for a specific activity can still be committed in a grant, if the grant is for the same activity. For example, if you've raised money or accepted donations to buy equipment for your fencing club or to produce a film promoting your church and its religious values, you can definitely mention that money in a grant proposal in order to get help from others. If the grant proposal is not successful, you may still not reallocate the money to, say, staff salaries or roof repairs. The money is still restricted to the purpose for which it is raised.

Identify one or more appropriate goal

Begin with the end in mind, and have a specific goal you'd like to achieve through a grant. What do you want the grant for? What do you want to accomplish that requires a gift of money? What evidence do you have that the goal will be accomplished?

Remember the "needs, wants, and nice-to-haves" exercise from the budgeting chapter? For a grant, you should already have met all your needs and a substantial number of your wants. Take a goal out of the wants or nice-to-have column.

Planned projects and program expansions are good ideas for grants because you have already figured out what you need and how much it will cost. You will have already set aside at least some of the resources needed. This is vital for a reviewer to see because they represent commitment to the goal from your charity and the community that supports it. You're putting your money where your mouth is. The resources need not be in the bank, but if they are based on fundraising estimates, last year's profit and loss statement will show whether they're realistic.

You can pick out a goal that was not selected for the current budget, if and only if your organization has enough cash reserves and savings to free up at least a quarter of the resources needed for the first year of execution, without threatening the rest of the program.

Keep in mind that, if you get a grant toward a planned activity and end up with more than you need, you may not be able to reallocate money without the permission of the people who gave it to you.

Write down the goal

You must present your goal in a way that is SMART: specific, measurable, achievable, realistic, and timely. It must also be in alignment with your overall mission and goals for your program.

Specific

A specific goal can be explained in terms of *who, what, where, when,* and frequently *how* and *how much.* "Fund our archaeological dig" is not a specific goal. "The grant will provide $50,000 to cover transportation, living and equipment expenses for two archeologists for six months at Utah Site #6 from November to February of next year." is a specific goal.

Suppose your proposal for funding for an archaeological dig also includes the statement "Mary Doe and Richard Roe will serve as principal investigators" and a brief biographical description that shows why they are qualified to do so. Now, the "who" is clear. Money is being solicited from a grant organization and the principal investigators are identified by name. The "what" is also explicit. The money, in an amount clearly specified, will be used to cover transportation, living, and equipment expenses. The "where" and "when" are clearly spelled out, along with the how much. The "how" in this case is the grant. That's where the money is coming from.

Measurable

A goal is measurable if you can tell whether it's been achieved or not. Examples of measurable goals might be: "Distribute 10,000 copies of our religious texts in our community in time for the holidays" or "pay for 100 children from the high school band and choir to attend an out of state competition".

Achievable

If you're a fan of pie-in-the-sky bull sessions about what you'd like to do if you had enough money, you will have to work hard to limit your ambitions in front of the sponsor.

Consider the time and resources required to execute the plan. If there's a deadline imposed by circumstances beyond your control, throwing money at a problem won't create a solution. If you want to take a team of university students to a solar car competition where the vehicle they build will race against other vehicles, and you don't have a vehicle or even support from the school faculty or administration, you're missing key resources that the grant sponsor can't provide. You'll be much more successful if you can show that you already have all the other ingredients in place and only need a bit of cash to make everything work.

Realistic

Some motivational speakers recommend setting a totally unreasonable, unrealistic goal for yourself, complete with consequences if you fail, just to find out what your limits are. That's fine if you have no life experience or have never actually pushed your own limits. But for most adults the advice is manipulative bunk. It's also a terrible way to approach a grant application or to write a proposal.

Your grant applications are more likely to succeed if your organization has experience in the type of program activity you describe. "Conduct a state level dance competition to provide young adults with performance and feedback experience" is achievable if you've already got some experience setting up local competitions. If you've never set up a dance competition before, and if you're not a dance related charity but, say, a food bank, then you stand a very good probability of failing. No grant issuing organization likes throwing its money away.

Consider the scale of what you're asking for, relative to what you've got. "Send our judo team to an international championship" is a realistic goal for a school that has athletes who have recently placed well at state or national championships. It is completely unrealistic for a school that has never sent athletes to competitions out of state or that does not host or attend the existing local competitions.

It's easier to get people to give you money if the goal you're setting is one step or level beyond your current capability. If your judo team currently competes only in local tournaments, consider raising money for an out-of-town tournament before an out-of-state one.

Your track record is relevant. At some part of your grant application, you should discuss similar work your organization has undertaken successfully. You stand a much better chance of finding funding for a full-length documentary film if you can show that you've successfully produced a short 30 to 45-minute one.

The last important aspect to realism is funding. Most grants are cooperative and they require you to put up some of the money yourself. This means it's unwise to present a "plan" to build a new roof when you haven't set anything aside for it yourself. Funders want to see that you've got skin in the game. Show that you're serious about the proposed project by providing evidence you've set aside enough money to cover your portion of the expenses.

Time-Bounded

A goal has to have an end date, a deadline, or some specific time frame. Saying you'll finish that stage production "eventually" or distribute those religious tracts "later" will not satisfy any serious donor or grant authority.

Identify necessary resources

Once you have fleshed out your goal, write it down and admire it for a while. Then start looking for what it will take to get there. It's reasonable to have five or six different goals. If you're a research institution, you probably have several teams of scientists with good ideas they'd like to test. If you're a high school booster club, you've probably got more than one big competition or performance you'd like to attend.

At least some of your potential goals will conflict with each other. No person can be in more than one place at a time, and if key personnel are committed to one project they will most likely be unavailable for another. But don't worry about conflicting goals for now. Just write down all the goals and put each one in its own column, or on its own page.

For each goal, write down what you need to attain it. Include people, space, funding, and other expenses such as transportation or entry fees. Break everything down to a dollar value. The more detailed you can be, the better. For example, to take the high school choir to an out of town competition might require twelve hotel rooms for one night plus gas, food expenses. But if new uniforms are also something you need, write those up as a separate goal. You may luck out and find a grant big enough to allow you to meet more than one goal if they don't conflict.

Identify available resources

Look at your existing budget and find out what you've already raised and set aside for the activity or purchase in question. If you have enough to pay that expense in full and plan to do so anyway, highlight it anyway. The new finch aviary for your zoo or the upgrade to your clinic waiting room is the sort of thing a grant might cover.

List any resources you have *that have already been allocated to this goal*. If you've already raised money for a new X-ray machine for your clinic, then if any of that money was given as a directed donation explicitly for that task, it cannot actually be reallocated without the donor's permission. So list it as money that has already been raised for the project.

If you have a specific amount in your budget for projects like the one for which you're soliciting the grant, do not claim that the entire amount is available "if you get the grant". Many small charities make the mistake of soliciting every grant in sight and allocating the same resources to each. Then, if they receive more than one grant, they do not actually have money available to hold up their end of the agreement. Asserting that a pool of money is available "for grant related activities, including this proposal", and respectfully declining any grant that would require you to commit scarce resources twice, is a reasonable compromise.

Maxim #21: Don't lie about your money or resources.

Never claim money is available for grant related goal activities if you would have to take it out of another existing program. The granting organization's goal is not to hurt your charity or to put a crimp in your cash flow. They truly want to do something beneficial, not harmful. Putting you on the hook for a bunch of spending when you don't actually have the money to do it is a grave disservice.

There is one exception to the above maxim. If you have scheduled fundraising or donor solicitation planned and intend to direct it to the project for which you are soliciting the grant, you may make a reasonable estimate as to how much money will be available. Using the techniques in the fundraising chapters, it's possible to calculate how much you can reasonably expect to make at a thing-a-thon or similar event. Simply pulling out your notes from the previous similar event should give you all the information you need.

Identify the shortfall

Grants are given where they are actually needed. If you already have more than enough money available to fund a program improvement or expansion, no donor will see a reason to expect more. There should be a sizable difference, generally less than 50%, between the amount of money it takes to execute a project and the resources you have available for it. This amount, adjusted as necessary for administrative expenses, is the dollar figure you should ask for.

Finding grants

As soon as you know what you're looking for, you can go hunting for the right flavor of money. Here are a few ideas for you.

Internet search engine

Write down phrases that relate to your charity and your goal. Then type these phrases into a search engine one at a time and see what turns up. "High school math club grant" or "Philadelphia PTA grant" may turn up options.

Don't rule out phrases that can lead to names or even addresses. "Endowment for the Arts" or "Music Education Foundation" may lead you to an article or credit which mentions a name.

Find a known giver

Some grant organizations prefer to develop long-term relationships with a charity. If they've helped you before, perhaps they will help you again. Also consider organizations that have funded similar kinds of work for other people. If the John Doe Endowment for the Arts helped provide money for a history documentary, and you want money for a documentary about a different era, then by all means hit up that donor.

It's definitely worth your while to check out the major sponsor list for other charities in your line of work. Private operating foundations keep a low profile, and they seldom advertise, but the ones set up to support the arts tend to be open to several recipients of the same sort. Get a program from someone else's recent production, and look at the back. If you produce documentaries, buy or rent somebody else's and look for a "funding provided by" or "with help from". This credit will not contain contact information.

Special interests of grantors can be very narrow. If the Molly Roe Memorial Trust bought a telescope for another high school's astronomy program, they might buy one for the high school where you serve on the PTA. But you might not have much luck hitting them up for a new wheelchair ramp at your church.

Trade journals and periodicals

Every once in a while a big corporation decides to give something back to the community, so they solicit grant proposals. There are still trade journals and periodicals (some print and some online) especially in the performing arts. Why not subscribe to a few publications that make sense for your program? Then, when they arrive, read them.

Don't just browse the headlines looking for ads. Check out other articles about other programs similar to yours, and look for phrases such as "sponsored by" or "with a grant from". This can give you more names to look up. They most likely won't be online or in the phone book:

private operating foundations and family trusts value the privacy of the people who run them.

The IRS Web site

Remember how I mentioned that contact information for private operating foundations will seldom be published? There's one place you can look them up electronically, if you have the name. Go to the IRS Web site, and find the page containing the "Exempt Organizations Select Check".

The IRS Web page will tell you whether the Susan Doe-Smith Memorial Foundation still exists and has tax exempt status. You can see where it's located, and by that I mean the city and state where they are incorporated. You can also check the EIN, which is the unique ID given to the charity or the foundation.

State Attorney General Web site

Once you have the charity's official name, city, and state, go to the state Web site where the Attorney General lists all the corporations, and look up the not-for-profit corporation bearing the name or "Doing Business As" (DBA) you found on the IRS Web site. Each not-for-profit corporation must register with its state, and provide an address or agent for people to contact.

Write down the contact information, then pick up the phone and call the registered agent. Deliver your 1-minute "elevator speech" into the voice mail (or in conversation with the human being who answers, if you're so lucky). Introduce yourself, explain the program you've got, explain the project you have in mind, and ask whether they are accepting grant proposals.

Troll for vendors

Take a look at your budget, and write down the companies that are providing goods and services you use, or that are used by the people who benefit from your program. Obviously if you're a wildlife rescue facility this won't be a great strategy, but if you're a dance school or an elder care facility there will definitely be manufacturers who make products your community uses every day. For sports charities there are sometimes outright sponsorships available, although if you're a children's sport charity you must be careful to not mess up children's NCAA eligibility.

Many times, you can get in-kind donations more readily than money. This is also a legitimate thing to solicit. Why buy what you can get for free? But keep track of donations and be prepared to issue a receipt.

Corporations like tax deductions too, and they thrive on positive publicity. So at some point during the proposal process, make sure to talk about your social media presence, your Web site, and all the other ways you plan to publicize the donation.

Government

Local, state, and federal government programs sometimes distribute money to help fund public service initiatives. Requests for proposals may be found on local school board Web sites and on various government Web sites.

If there's a government agency that relates to what you do, check them out. National laboratories and scientific research or technology companies often fund school robotics clubs or science fairs. If you're a food bank, the Department of Agriculture may have something for you. Disaster relief organizations should hit up the Environmental Protection Agency or the Federal Emergency Management Association.

Selecting grants

Do not go out and apply for every grant you see that has something to do with your program. Opportunistic grant seeking is a big problem for small charities because they often lack the resources needed to do their part or to execute the plan if the grant is not approved. Going after a grant simply because it's big can change your program focus and create a mismatch between your mission and your program.

Maxim #22: Pursue grants only for things that are in alignment with your mission and program, and that you've already planned to spend money on.

Never go after a grant for something you don't need, don't want, or can't use. Chasing money just to bring it in is a mistake for three reasons. First, it takes up time and other resources you could be using to get other money that can be used in a more beneficial way. Second, if you get the grant, the money must be set aside for the specific purpose tied to the grant, and it cannot be used to pay down debt or for other expenses. Finally, if you get the grant it will tie up money and resources you already have, that could otherwise have been allocated to critical expenses.

Applying for a grant

To apply for a grant, you need a proposal and some background information.

Your proposal should start with a short paragraph explaining how much money you need and a brief description of what the project is. Tell why the project is necessary and how adding it will create lasting benefit to the community your program serves. If you're filming a documentary or conducting scientific research you should be able to show how you're advancing your field by contributing to the body of knowledge. If you're buying sports equipment, talk about creating opportunities for athletes to participate. Show how what you propose to do will benefit the charitable class you serve.

Next, discuss your goal in terms of "who", "what", "where", "when", "how" and "how much". You can reorder paragraphs to tailor your proposal based on what you're asking for. Include an itemized budget and spending plan. Discuss the timing of the different expenditures. Explain when you expect the project to be finished.

Next, show why you are a stable organization. Include a copy of your Bylaws, Articles of Incorporation (so the person reading your application can see that your proposal matches your mission and program), and your last annual report. The annual report should include your balance sheet (where any assets and debts will appear) and your profit and loss statement. Also include a budget for next year. Most grantors have a list of documents they require that include what I have listed here. They may want to see two or more years' worth of annual reports and they will of course want to see evidence that you have money set aside to pay for your share of the new development.

Next, show why your organization produces results. List some of your notable accomplishments over the past year, and include some photos of people or animals that have benefited from your work.

Finally, write up your conclusion: Because of your track record, your stable performance based on your annual report, and the merits of the important work you propose, you believe your proposal qualifies for the grant. Thank them for their time and consideration.

Before sending in your application, make sure you have included every piece of information requested. Fill out any relevant forms, dot the I's, cross the T's, and *make a copy of the application for your records*. Keeping an electronic copy is also wise. You will be able to reuse entire sections on different grant proposals in the future.

The approval process

When you submit a grant application, you will most likely get an acknowledgement that it was received. That notification usually will tell you when the review committee will reach a decision, and when you can expect an answer.

Grant proposals are frequently reviewed by a group of people, with different members of the committee looking at different aspects of your proposal. It's not easy: they are seldom comparing apples with apples. They do what they can to be impartial when they review applications. They make their decisions, and then communicate directly with each applicant.

Sometimes, the reviewer or review committee will contact you requesting clarification or changes. This is an extremely good sign, because it means they're looking at your application. Give them the information they need, and try to be helpful.

There's a relationship between the size of the grant and the complexity of the application and approval process.

If you get the grant

The very first thing you should do, upon receiving a grant, is thank the giver. This should always be done by phone and in writing. Use your best letterhead, and take the time to write a proper thank-you letter by hand. If you can do it in person, better still.

Not all private operating foundations want publicity, so if you've received a grant from a discreet family trust or foundation, ask permission before announcing it. Businesses and government agencies, however, thrive on publicity provided it's positive. Yet their logos and service marks are copyrighted, so make sure to get written approval before using them. This approval is seldom hard to obtain and an E-mail notification is fine.

When the actual money arrives, send a receipt promptly and include all the appropriate tax information including your EIN. How the entity that gave you the gift does its accounting is not your business, but make sure you give them what they need to account appropriately for the gift.

Execute the plan

Once the money is in your hands, you have an obligation to the grantor to make sure the work gets done. Much of the time, you'll have to free up money or raise money to match some or all of what the grant covered. Begin the work on schedule, and keep careful records as to what was spent.

All donors appreciate regular progress reports, especially if there's a way to include pictures. Corporations use the information for advertising, and churches or fundraising charities stimulate their donors by providing examples of their effort in action.

Penalties exist for misappropriation

Misappropriation is a type of theft. It occurs when you raid money set aside for task A and use it to accomplish task B. Examples include using directed donations and grant money for purposes other than what they were intended to do. The money isn't actually being stolen—usually—but it's being spent in an unauthorized way. It's a rather subtle type of fraud. Frequently it's related to granted or earmarked money that has been given for a specific operation.

The priorities of donors or grantors don't always quite match up with your organization's needs. Having a pool of money set aside for, say, a wheelchair ramp or a program expansion can look pretty attractive if a storm rips up your roof and you need to pay the insurance deductible. But it's very important to make sure the executive team doesn't dip into grant or directed donation money *without first getting the permission of whoever raised or supplied that money.*

Grants come with strings attached. You do not have the option of spending grant money on anything but what it was given for. Misappropriating grant money is a type of fraud, even if you're using it for a good cause or to help the charity out of an emergency.

As an officer or administrator of a charity, you have a fiduciary duty to your organization. That means you're legally obligated to act in its best interests, and to make money decisions that put the charity first.

The US General Accounting Office (GAO) investigates allegations of waste, fraud, and abuse. If you've received federal funds and are using them for any purpose besides what they were issued for, the GAO reserves the right to audit you. Keep in mind that, when it comes to criminal charges, you're personally accountable for what you do with the charity's money. Your insurance won't protect you or cover your expenses if you're tried for embezzlement, which can easily happen if an Executive Director decides to use grant money to pay his or her overdue salary.

Watch out for private benefit transactions, which are sometimes closely related to misappropriations. Misappropriation happens when the entire charity has had a big reversal of fortune—such as the loss of a major donor—or has an agenda that doesn't quite match up with what they told the grantor. When that occurs, there are frequently other ethical shortcuts being taken.

I want to take the opportunity to point out that emergencies happen, and your donors understand that. If you really have an emergency, put together a plan to replace the money and then take the issue to the donors or grantors. They will often give you permission to reallocate the funds. If you have permission, particularly in writing, then reallocating the money is not misappropriation at all and is completely legal.

Chapter 22: Booster Clubs

A booster club is a charity formed for the sole purpose of raising funds to support athletic, arts, or other activities. This chapter discusses special concerns and issues related to booster clubs.

Turnover

Most booster clubs are attached to a public or private school or university. They are generally formed of parents or alumni whose children benefit from the booster club activities. So, unlike a hospital or environmental charity where the Board of Directors and administrative team can expect to serve for more than five years apiece, a booster club experiences constant turnover. This is normal because parents only participate in the charity to the extent it benefits their children. Once a student graduates, the parent loses interest and moves on to other activities.

Parents do not leap instantly into booster club activities, so it is rare to find a high school booster club parent who serves longer than three years unless you are lucky enough to have a family where multiple children attend the same high school and are involved in the same activity.

Earlier in this book I introduced Maxim #9: your volunteer turnover rate should never exceed your beneficiary turnover rate. Booster clubs are more prone to high volunteer turnover than any other kind of charity. They are notoriously unstable when it comes to volunteers and administrators. When you consider that children generally stick with activities for at least two years through high school, even a well-run booster club is in danger of losing its institutional memory because parent volunteers seldom last longer than their own children's involvement.

You will have to mitigate against volunteer turnover. The most important thing is to make sure you aren't burning people out. The booster club experience shouldn't be a constant quest for money. Make sure to manage the expectations of the school departments that rely on you for funding. The athletic director, fine arts teachers, and other heads of teams or clubs need to understand that your goal is to supplement their programs, not to fund them exclusively or remove the need for student or community fundraising.

Scope creep

I recently advised a Board member of a school PTA that had been stretched beyond its limit for years. The Board member described a very sound philosophy of raising money each year in order to fund the following year's activities. Unfortunately, the school administration had at some point decided that they were responsible for drawing up a list of "must-have" items that exceeded the PTA's ability to raise money. Not just by a dollar or two, either: they were being asked to exceed their maximum burst effort year after year.

The school in question was a Title I school in a poor district where parents struggled to make ends meet and where the majority of the children qualified for free or subsidized lunch. Most of the parents were blue-collar workers and many worked in the service industry. They in turn were connected to friends, neighbors, and family members who were much like themselves: struggling to get by. There just wasn't much money to be scraped together out of the community.

Recall that, in the fundraising chapters of this book, I gave you a way to estimate the maximum fundraising power of each volunteer: the dollar value of his or her per-hour take-home pay (or, in the case of a couple, half the net income of the pair). This is based on the observation that people mostly hang out in family or peer circles where everyone earns about the same amount of money. In a school where most of the parents are lawyers or optometrists, the fundraising power of ten randomly selected PTA volunteers will be far higher than in a Title I school. The school administration either hadn't noticed this fact, or they chose to overlook it.

Over the past several years, the school had responded to ongoing funding cuts and increased student numbers by asking the PTA to step in and provide the necessary money. This eventually included the salary for the computer professional who kept the school network going. This kind of infrastructure expense is generally borne by the school, not by the parents or the students.

You should never be raising money to pay staff or teacher salaries.

One of the things I recommended to the Board of the struggling PTA was that they calculate the safe, sustainable fundraising limit of the volunteer pool they had, based on the average family take-home pay in

344

their district and the number of volunteer hours available to them. I recommended that they scale the following year's budget to fit within that number, instead of breaking their backs to reach a fundraising goal.

Inurement

Inurement is a state of affairs in which money raised by a specific individual or family is earmarked for the use of a particular individual or family. Raising money for yourself, or your own kid, is not charity. Raising money for someone else's kid often is, especially if there are student athletes whose families cannot afford uniforms or other participation related expenses. This is why booster clubs generally raise money for an entire athletic or fine arts program, and spend money on coaching or other things that benefit the students as a group.

Booster clubs are susceptible to inurement because people figure out very quickly who is doing the work and who is not. Most athletic or music clubs have minimum participation requirements for stadium cleanups, thing-a-thon participation, and when one student isn't pulling his or her weight, the others notice. Parents, too, are capable of realizing when other families are quick to sign their children up for benefits but slow to participate in fundraising. Many parents who have the means to simply pay for their children's participation prefer to do so instead of selling overpriced holiday wrapping paper to their friends and co-workers. But they seldom want to subsidize other families who put in less time or effort.

A small amount of inurement is permissible by the IRS, but the IRS has never published a specific percentage beyond which inurement becomes unreasonable. Organizations where the money committed to individuals is less than 20% of the annual budget tend to not be harassed or threatened with tax court, however the rules are enforced sporadically and I personally prefer to err on the side of caution. I keep inurement below 10% in any organization I run, just to be on the safe side.

Advertisement

You have to be visible if you want to succeed as a booster club. The people who benefit from your work—your own children—need to know who's putting forth the effort so that they can go to the state spelling bee or a chess tournament. You also need to recruit the kids as labor whenever it's practical. This doesn't necessarily mean that you must draft them into a thing-a-thon or a network based sales fundraiser. Induce them to work a concession or book sale instead.

Make sure the school staff knows you're there. Get your booster club mentioned in announcements, and take up space in the school newspaper. This will help get the attention not just of students but of the other parents.

It makes sense to have a social media site for your PTA. That way, you can use it to comment on news stories and communicate with your pool of prospective volunteers.

An E-mail tree or call tree, while somewhat obsolete among students, is a very good way to get parents and grandparents involved.

Concessions

The single best way to raise money is to exchange something of equal value to a willing customer. Concession sales are one good way to do so. But to run a profitable concession, you must find an appropriate venue, select items to sell that suit the tastes of the people who are buying, obtain enough of a sales margin to earn a profit even if you don't sell out of everything, and have adequate storage space between events. Let's consider each of those aspects, in order.

The venue

School sports and arts events are tailor-made for a booster club concession because they take place in the school gymnasium. There's a captive audience, people have been socialized to eat and drink at sporting or arts events, and students and parents are generally hungry because the activities overlap with mealtimes. Meanwhile, the school cafeteria and other ordinary sources of nourishment are closed. It's even possible to restrict whether the audience brings food or beverages into the venue.

You don't need a commercial kitchen, and if you have access to one you don't need to cook. All you really need is a table, a cash box, and a way to keep beverages cool. If you have access to an electrical outlet and a drip coffee maker, you will find that coffee provides one of the best profit margins available.

Your sales merchandise

Concession sales are a type of retail business. Your goal is to raise money. Therefore, when selecting items to sell, you must consider not whether the item will be popular, but whether it will be profitable. Ask yourself the following questions:

- What is my minimum cost to offer the item at all?
- How many of the item must I sell to break even and recoup my initial purchase price?
- How many of the item am I likely to sell?
- Have I a way to store the item, or must I sell it immediately?

Most concession items are not bought by the unit. They are bought by the package, the carton, or the case. Sometimes you can buy the item in a ready-to-sell condition, such as with a bottled drink or a candy bar. Other times you can buy components and, with very little labor, produce a cup of coffee or a sandwich that can sell for much more than the price of its components.

Items that must be sold immediately include perishable foods, time-sensitive coupons with an expiry date, and tickets to entertainment or sporting events. Anything that will lose some or all of its utility over time, but that is not immediately perishable, should be considered semi-perishable even if you have a safe and secure way to store it.

If you're going to be storing food or drinks, make sure that they're being stored at room temperature or close to it. Chocolate bars don't do well in a hot garage during summer. Canned beverages will explode if they freeze, and anything in a plastic bottle can become contaminated by the bottle material if the bottle overheats by being stored in a hot car, van, or shed.

Be mindful of your profit margin and volume

Your biggest money-makers are going to be donated items, bottled water, and coffee. On donated items, your profit margin is infinite provided the goods actually sell. People expect to pay at least a dollar for bottled water or coffee, because that's the going rate for a similarly-sized item at a convenience stores. But the amount for which you can sell an item tells only half the story. In retail, you make your money when you buy and not when you sell. Pay too much for an item, and even if it sells you have to work far harder for your money.

Consider the following exercise. Suppose a case of two dozen bottles of water costs five dollars, and fixings for at least a hundred cups of coffee costs twenty. Suppose energy drinks are available in packages of four, at ten dollars per package, but the drinks can be sold for three dollars each. Here's what happens.

Table 7: Earning $80 In Beverage Profits

	Coffee	Bottled Water	Energy Drinks
Units Bought	Fixings	5 cases of 24	40 packs of 4
Cost Per Unit	n/a	$5	$10
Purchase Price	$20	$25	$400
Drink Sold	100	105	160
Drink Sale Price	$1.00	$1.00	$3.00
Gross Sales	$100	$105	$480
Leftovers	Some	15 bottles	None

When the sale ends, you will have to have done almost five hundred dollars' worth of business selling energy drinks in order to make the same money as you could have made selling about a hundred bottles of water or cups of coffee. Your cash outlay for the energy drinks will be twenty times higher than it would for the coffee.

High-ticket items will not sell in large numbers unless the cost is low relative to overall attendance. A price point that works at a professional baseball game will not work at your high school baseball tournament, and although people are willing to drop a hundred dollars on merchandise at a NBA game they will not have the money available if they're cheering on their kids at your middle school game. In general, they won't be willing to spend more on souvenirs, refreshments, or fundraising items than they spent on their individual admisisons.

Your customers are going to be on a budget. A customer with three dollars in his or her pocket can afford to buy an energy drink, but nothing else. The same three dollars, however, could easily pay for a candy bar and a small bag of chips if he or she decides to drink water or coffee instead.

Shop intelligently

As the above exercise shows, it pays to buy low. The more you pay for an item, the less of a profit margin you have if you wish to sell it at a fair price. Therefore, do not wait until the last minute to buy your sales merchandise. When you have identified a non-perishable item you wish to offer, pay attention to which of the grocery stores or warehouse stores have sales in progress, and buy cheap. This maximizes your profit margin.

Warehouse stores such as Costco or Sam's Club may seem like an ideal place to do your concession shopping, but consider how many units of a food or beverage you must buy. Whereas you can easily get a package of six or eight sports drinks at a grocery store, at a warehouse store you must commit to twenty-four or even thirty bottles of different flavors. Even if the price per unit is attractive, consider whether all the flavors will be equally popular. I find that red sports drinks sell better than yellow ones, and that there's always one kind of drink that nobody really wants.

Try to avoid having items left over unless they can be returned or bought by you or somebody else. Storing service items, condiments, or napkins is reasonable but beware of spoilage. Be especially careful with the mayonnaise because the raw egg in it is a perfect element for the kind of bacteria that cause food poisoning.

Beware excess variety and avoid leftovers

Try to provide no more than six drink options, three sandwich options, four salty snack options, and five candy options including granola bars. Three fruit options and one vegetable option will usually suffice.

If you buy "variety packs" of different snacks or drinks, you will notice that although there will be roughly the same number of each kind of item in the box, the items will not be equally popular when offered for sale. To break even on the box or package, you will generally have to sell at least half of the items in it. But there's always one item that hardly anyone wants. Exactly which it will be will be hard to predict except from experience selling to the same customer set.

Leftover commercial food that comes in cans, bags, or packets can be kept for months—or years—depending on the expiry date. But it cannot be kept forever, and it usually has to be stored at room temperature. Unsold merchandise from one event can be sold at the next concession, if there is one, but you will still have to purchase the most popular items. You definitely do not want the unpopular items piling up in your storage space, because nearly all your profit is in those unsold items. If you must have profit tied up in merchandise, at least make sure it's merchandise you have a chance of selling.

I believe that buying unpopular items simply because they have a low per-unit price is false economy. I would rather pay more for items more likely to sell than have unpopular leftovers. What can you do with them, really, except sell them for a lower price? If you drop the price enough, eventually you are selling those items at a lost and it eats into your profit margin. Holding onto them makes no money, and trying to sell them over and over again takes up valuable counter space and storage space that could be used for items that will sell.

It's always better to get rid of an unpopular item than it is to store it. If that means selling it at a loss, so be it. The money you make selling the unpopular merchandise can still be used to buy goods that can be sold for a profit. When the money is tied up in the merchandise and the merchandise won't sell, you get nothing for your time and effort.

I try not to get into the habit of buying unpopular merchandise to begin with.

Don't make a habit of putting merchandise on sale

A concession is not a retail store where you can have a "loss leader" item that's offered for sale at a lower price than you paid for it. Retail stores have loss leaders because they need to get people to go out of their way and come into the building. Once they have arrived, they are likely to buy other items before leaving. That rationale doesn't apply to you: your customers are already in the building, so they don't have to be led in, and they don't have to be cajoled into doing business with you. If they want the food you have to offer, and if it is reasonably priced, they will buy it. If you mark an item down, people will buy it *instead* of a full-priced item.

I once worked a donut concession for a charitable venture that had secured a booth at a state fair. All the donuts were prepared offsite and brought in by truck. But they had to be sold within a specific time limit. At the end of the day, leftover food had to be either thrown out, given away, or sold. The man in charge of the concession decided to give the donuts away so they would not be wasted. That worked the first day. But the fair ran for nine more days. After the second day, the people in the booths nearby realized they could get a far better deal by refusing to buy during the normal business hours and "waiting until the donuts are free". Word spread quickly and soon there was a horde of people waiting for free donuts at the end of the day, but our sales during the day were cut in half.

Everyone likes a good deal, but if people reject your regularly (and fairly) priced merchandise because they think you'll drop the price later, you're not going to have much of a profit margin. If you find it impossible to sell a particular item at a profit, stop selling it completely and never offer it again. You are not a retail store that relies on a "loss leader" to get people in the door so that they buy more on the way out.

Complimentary items

As an incentive for your volunteers, offer complimentary bottled water, but do not feed them unless they are working more than four hours and the items you're offering them are donated. Giving away high-priced, low-margin items such as energy drinks or candy bars is a bad idea, because when you have to sell an entire package in order to make a profit, losing one item from that package due to theft, complimentary items, or damage wipes out your entire profit on that package.

You can give bottled water away generously to every volunteer who works three or four hours for you, receive the full benefit of having provided that incentive, and not put a dent in your profit margin.

Pricing

A concession is not a silent auction. You cannot get away with marking your prices up to an exorbitant rate because the proceeds go to charity. When people buy utilitarian items such as food or clothing, they expect to get reasonable value for the dollar. They will therefore not be willing to pay several times the going rate for a bottle of water or a bag of chips. Rather than pay your inflated prices, they will smuggle their own snacks into the venue.

Although most Americans have been conditioned to believe they will be physically harmed if they go more than an hour without eating or "hydrating" (apparently a more expensive and scientific process than simply having a drink of water), the only people who truly need food or water immediately are athletes engaged in an endurance activity. You mostly won't be selling to them. You'll be selling to the spectators. These are completely sedentary and don't actually need to eat or drink over the course of a normal high school football game.

When someone chooses to buy a food item from you, they aren't actually satisfying hunger or thirst so much as treating themselves or their children. Americans are willing to spend money on treats, and to buy items even if they are not the most cheaply priced versions available, but they are not willing to pay exorbitant amounts. They prefer to make a cash donation.

People expect to pay more than the average retail price for fundraising activities, however they also show up with the express intent of supporting your charity. Not so at a concession. Every single one of your customers is in the building to see the game or the performance. They didn't come to support you, and the only reason they're doing business is to treat themselves to something that enhances their experience. You're providing the treat, and you're also providing convenience in the form of onsite sales that do not require them to leave the venue.

For treat food, customers will generally pay the same price for concession items that they would pay at the nearest gas station or convenience store, where food and drink items are priced and sold individually. You need not compete with grocery store prices. But you cannot get away with selling at movie theater prices: when people go to the movies or a professional sports game, eating overpriced popcorn is part of the experience they expect and are paying for. When people attend a high school basketball game, they're parenting.

It is customary and reasonable to round up the prices on each item to the nearest quarter. You do not have to add tax if you are tax exempt. If you are not tax exempt, price each item so that when you add the tax on it the result ends up being a round number or the nearest quarter.

Payment

Most concessions still operate chiefly in cash. People like to pay by card, and if you or your organization has access to a Smart phone or tablet with an Internet connection, it may make sense to add an online payment account especially if you have a mobile operation that must function at a cross-country meet or other outdoor location. Do this only if the money you make from the sales will offset the fees associated with having the account.

If you must buy a cellular phone and pay for bandwidth along with the fees for the card payment mechanism, you will find it almost impossible to make the money back from your cash flow. Your concession will turn into a life support system for that cellular account. Result: a sacred cow that does not advance your booster club's primary purpose one bit.

If you have a permanent location for your concession, such as in a church kitchen attached to a regularly used facility, adding a cash register may be useful. This makes no sense if you support outdoor events.

Float

Since cash is king, make sure you can make change. The float is a sum of money that you start with. It will be chiefly in one and five dollar bills, unless you have items costing a multiple of twenty-five cents in which case you will need a roll or two of quarters.

Generally speaking, you will see almost all your large bills in the first half-hour of being open. This is because people make a point of having enough cash to make a purchase. So they get cash back on a debit card transaction or make a stop at an automated teller before coming to the event. The fact many people no longer routinely carry cash means that fewer people these days have one or five dollar bills in their pockets or wallets. This means they will arrive with twenty-dollar bills only. Earlier wisdom about how much of a float to have did not take this reality into account.

It's reasonable to have a float worth about a third of the business you expect to do. Never start with a float of less than two hundred dollars: that's just ten transactions' worth of business when a customer buys a bottle of water and pays with a twenty-dollar bill.

Onsite food preparation

I have one piece of advice about onsite preparation of food. *Don't.*

If you run a booster club concession, never sell perishable food that has to be prepared onsite. It's fine to offer a few pieces of fruit, many of which can be saved and offered again the following week. It's also OK to sell grab-and-go sandwiches, cupcakes and such. But don't waste labor on food preparation unless you're hiring your group out to an existing organization that allows charities to temporarily form part of its labor force.

It's often tempting to bring your own grill and set up a burger stand or a miniature sandwich shop. But there are a lot of hidden costs such as propane for the grill and condiments for the burgers.

When you cook, some of what you prepare will be wasted. Somebody will drop a freshly made sandwich on the floor or burn the burger patties. It's far better to put together some grab-and-go sandwiches the night before or the morning of the event. The sandwiches need not be commercially made, but you must follow the local health code for food preparation. If you sell prewrapped grab-and-go food, you have fewer opportunities to accidentally contaminate it. Unlike hot food that stops being appetizing after an hour or two, a wrapped sandwich kept at the right temperature is still fresh at the end of the day.

When you sell perishable food, there will always be excess product at the end of the day. It cannot be re-frozen and there is a maximum amount of time it can be refrigerated. This is fine for a large operation because the kiosk will generally open again in a day or two so the unsold merchandise is not a loss. Even at the end of the season, some opened condiment containers, an opened package of seven remaining hot dog buns, and a package of wieners with six remaining is trivial. For a small operation like yours where the next opportunity to sell is a week away, having leftovers like that will be a total loss. It could represent your entire profit margin on hot dogs. The up-front cost associated with getting everything necessary for hamburgers, including meat, buns, cheese, plates, napkins, condiments, and garnish, could easily put you in the red.

Finally, the more you offer cooked food the more your customers will behave as though they're in a restaurant where their food will be made to order. Making each hamburger or order of fries exactly the way the customer wants will take triple the labor force compared to selling the same customers a grab-and-go sandwich and a bag of potato chips. This is because you will need one person to handle the money, one person to cook, and one person to clean up. As soon as people decide they're in a restaurant, they instinctively expect other people to clean up after them. Also, cooked food is sloppy. It has to be served on plates or in wrappers, condiments get spilled everywhere especially if there are children around, and you will go through far more napkins than you would if you sold granola bars.

The conclusion I want you to draw from all of this is that cooked food only makes sense if you can operate on a very large scale. Otherwise, it's going to be very difficult to make money on cooked food and still operate within your local health code. Most of the materials for cooked food have a large up-front cost and you must sell several items before turning a profit. That's fine if you're running a restaurant or a large operation such as a university stadium concession, but risky for a far smaller operation.

You may, if you wish, sell food that is frozen or refrigerated, and provide access to a microwave. This provides all the advantages of serving cooked food with none of the liabilities or oversight.

Donation cup

Do not allow your volunteers to accept tips, but provide a donation jar so that people who want to support your charity can do so. People are seldom more than willing to pay the going rate for a quotidian item such as snack food, but some of them will gladly give you money. Human psychology is weird that way.

A donation jar, where people can see that others have already dropped in their spare change, is more successful than an opaque box or jar because human beings are herd animals. Salt the donation jar by putting in some coins and bills.

Labor based fundraising tips

Your labor pool consists of the students and their families. Most of them won't have the slightest interest in contributing money, time, or resources. In fact, expect the vast majority of the work to come from 5% of your parents or fewer. That doesn't mean people won't volunteer to help. They'll make all the mouth noises about wanting to volunteer, they'll put their names on a sheet, and they'll give you their phone numbers and E-mail addresses. This doesn't mean they'll show up.

Over-subscribe

Until you find out which of your volunteers are reliable, sign up at least twice as many as you need for each event. If you're considering setting up an ongoing event, understand that not every family will be available to work each time. This is especially important if you're doing work during normal business hours. Most people are simply not willing to use vacation days or to take time off work to help raise money for their children's activities. Some believe it's a waste of their time because their children benefit from the fundraising done by other families. Others believe that the kind of work available is beneath them. A lawyer who bills two hundred dollars an hour would generally rather write a check than give up four or five hours on an afternoon to raise fifty to a hundred bucks for the PTA. It's wise to provide a means for doing so, but recognize that by doing so you aren't going to guarantee the individual in question will be willing to actually write the check.

Long-term commitments require at least twice as many people as one-shot commitments. If you've got a task that requires, say, twenty volunteers on an ongoing basis for things like stadium cleanup or large-scale concessions, you should have a pool of at least eighty to a hundred people who start out saying that, yes, they want to come help every time.

Over-communicate

Have at least five ways to contact everybody. This should include an E-mail list, telephone numbers, paper messages given to the students, instructor announcements in class, and group text or social media contact. More than half the parents and kids will still be told that they "didn't hear about" the fundraiser. The vast majority of them simply do not wish to be contacted. They simply wish to appear willing and available to work. That's why they won't tell you if their phone number changes, they won't add your E-mail address to their approved senders' list or even open and read their E-mail, and they take great pride in not using social media.

355

No matter what system you have in place to contact people, expect some of them to deliberately sabotage it so as to blame you for not contacting them. However, the same parents who dodge the work will be the first to criticize the job you're doing with the volunteers who bother to show up.

Have a bypass option

For the people who can afford to write a check in order to avoid fundraising, offer just such an opportunity. For some respectable amount of money, allow them to get off the hook for one fundraiser per year. For a little bit more, let them slack off of all of it and be exempt from solicitation. Then cash that check, and allow that family to spend more time enjoying their free time and activities.

Allowing people to buy their way out of fundraising is extremely unfair in some people's opinion, because it allows wealthier families to get the benefit of the fundraising without participating in it. There's a school of thought that says it's beneficial for student athletes to have some participation in the fundraising process to keep them from developing a sense of over-entitlement. At the same time, a check from a wealthier family at the start of the season is extremely effective because it can provide seed money for concessions or other ventures.

Overall, I believe that allowing people to buy their way out of fundraising is a practice that has more advantages than disadvantages. It's not up to us to make life fair, and it's not up to us to correct widespread economic inequality. But whatever option you provide shouldn't create an obvious clique of students who don't have to participate. Buying the right to not have to fundraise doesn't mean the student doesn't have to participate in team activities, particularly those that occur during practice time. Offsite activities like stadium cleanup, which occur over the weekends, typically don't involve the entire team at the same time. If there are two to three sets of kids whose duties rotate, the fact one or two kids are missing isn't obvious.

On the day of the thing-a-thon, the concession, or whatever else you choose as a fundraiser, if some of the students are involved then *all* of the students should be involved. Not having to do fundraising shouldn't mean that the students whose parents wrote a check should sit on the sidelines while their teammates run around a track or jump rope. That has very serious social consequences and is poisonous to team dynamics especially if fundraising occurs during the school day or during normal practice hours. Non-participating students can still count laps.

Chapter 23: Unions, Clubs, and Homeowner Associations

This chapter contains information relevant to organizations that exist primarily for the benefit of their members.

Trade unions, private clubs, fraternal organizations, and similar not-for-profit corporations are not regarded as serving a charitable purpose, but they have partial tax exempt status. Donations to them are not tax deductible for people who itemize their tax returns, but they do not pay federal income tax on those donations or on most business activities they undertake for money.

Income sources

Unlike a public charity, which might solicit contributions door to door or rely on an advertising campaign, your organization is typically limited to three sources of income: the dues collected from members as a condition of membership, investment income from assets owned by your organization, and on rare occasions fundraising performed by the members and their immediate families.

You also have the option of voting to impose an "assessment", which is an extra one-time fee collected from all members to offset some large but irregular cost that is too large to be paid out of the regular cash flow. Examples might include the replacement of the clubhouse roof or the resurfacing of the tennis courts.

For the most part, fundraising will not be successful if your members are performing it for themselves. If you're fortunate enough to be a member of a union or a private club, you're already ahead of the vast majority of people from whom you wish to draw support. If you want to get money or resources from outside your immediate circle, you must overcome the insider/outsider conflict. You do this by making sure you do not benefit, either individually or as a group, from the fundraising.

Your public profile

I'm not recommending that anyone use a positive public image to cover up bad behavior. However, there are times when the goodwill of the community is indispensable. If your labor union needs to go on strike, your employer will come to terms much faster if it customers stay away.

Labor unions in particular have lost much of the social capital they built up in the 19th and early 20th century. Having accomplished most of the goals for which they were created—safe working environments, reasonable hours, and an end to child labor—unions have gradually become less relevant as a force for social change as the emphasis shifted to collective bargaining for the benefit of their members. Also, every once in a while a union is used for corrupt purposes.

A union that pickets an employer that breaks a collective agreement by firing someone unfairly will get popular support, but only if the same union hasn't recently been seen doing something dirty. Getting caught in a pay-to-play scandal or an embezzlement scandal is bad, but using the threat of a strike to extort unreasonable concessions from an employer during a routine contract renewal negotiation is worse. It's possible to treat an employer so poorly that nobody wants to do business with you. You might gouge a few extra dollars out of the employer for a while, but if you kill the goose that lays the golden egg your members will be the ones unemployed in the long run.

Do not engage in illegal activity

This sounds like a no-brainer, except that the Tammany Hall scandals didn't happen all that long ago, and they didn't occur in a vacuum. To many people, labor unions are already disreputable simply because of shenanigans that occurred in the past.

One of the great things about labor unions is that you have access to young, idealistic, high-energy people who are looking for a place to belong and a way to shape their self-identities in positive ways. Such people can make great representatives, but they don't always know the history or laws related to labor unions.

"Shaming" a business that decides to not renew your contract when it expires, or that chooses a non-union subcontractor that submitted a bid lower than yours, is an example of killing the goose. Sure, people get to picket and attract attention, and it interferes with the business you want to punish, but do you really believe the people against whom you're retaliating will break a contract with someone else in order to do business with someone who's screaming and draping banners on their property? Nobody thinks those antics are funny and it doesn't impress the customers either.

Pretending to be the victim of a labor dispute when your contract has expired or when you have never had members of your union employed by a business is dishonest. Interfering with business activities, hanging banners accusing the owners of illegal activity, and publishing false reports in order to retaliate for not being chosen due to the customer's desire for a lower bidder, is actually illegal. If it can be proven to cost the business money, your union can and will be charged with slander and libel based on the way you presented the false information.

Control your members

Sometimes bad employees hide behind union protection despite doing some pretty disgusting things. When you allow or encourage your members to engage in street harassment of people who are simply passing by, it's not reasonable to expect the people who are being verbally abused, catcalled, groped, or threatened to support you later. Some of the people your union members are attacking are people in a position to decide whether their company gets the next construction bid. If the members of your union feel so over-empowered and over-entitled as to abuse a stranger in public, call a meeting and explain the facts of life.

Charitable ventures

Many unions donate money to charitable ventures focusing on education, medical research, or some other thing selected by its members. This is a wise and time-honored way to turn money into social capital. The smartest union leaders solicit input from the rank and file members as to which charities to help. This increases everyone's emotional investment even if the vote goes against them.

Private Clubs

A private club differs from a service club because a private club is organized solely for the benefit of its members, even though it might perform a great deal of charitable activity. Whereas dues to a service club are tax deductible, dues to a private club, such as a golf and country club, are not.

The purpose behind a private club is to have somewhere to go during the day or at mealtimes to socialize with people with whom you have something in common. Clubs therefore have facilities that are of interest to their members. One seaside town might have a yacht club, a tennis club, and a golf and country club, and a person might be a member of one but not another. Another similar town might have two golf clubs but no yacht club because it is too far inland.

The advantage of a private club is twofold: it controls access to some pleasant resource that is available for member use only, and it controls access to a select group of people who have too many demands on their attention. Depending on the resources your club has, you might employ groundskeepers, tennis pros, janitors, wait staff, and more. Employment by the club does not constitute license to use the facilities, except under limited circumstances such as an employee golf tournament.

Money management

The costs of maintaining a golf course or marina can be enormous. New members typically pay a sizable initiation fee and also monthly or annual dues for continued access. The initiation fee is the new member's share of an equal slice of what it cost to start up the club. The original founders, after all, paid to buy the land and cover the set-up expenses. Even if the founders are dead, there is no reason for new members to not contribute their fair share financially.

Membership is a private club is not automatic, because in many ways a member is a part owner in the club, and nobody can be forced to accept another person as a business partner. Although the liabilities of the corporation are limited to its assets, you will find it best to choose members who can be reliably expected to represent the club well and to pay their dues. So no member can be added without the approval of the existing members, and he or she must be invited to join.

Member screening

Considering the education, moral character, employment, and means of a new member is vital. Removing an unsuitable person from the club is a lot more difficult than admitting somebody is. Therefore, most private clubs have some formal screening or vetting process.

A club that has enough members to keep everything running smoothly does not need new members. You do not have to accept everyone who expresses an interest. Indeed, if you have too many members, your existing members will find the club overcrowded and will not be able to benefit from your facilities. Nobody wants to pay club dues but be unable to get a tee time. Accordingly, you need not admit anybody to your club that does not bring something useful and worthwhile.

Many private clubs consider the business or social connections of an applicant as well as other more quantitative screening criteria. This is particularly true of "pure" social clubs that do not have tennis or other sports facilities, and that gather together solely for social and business networking purposes.

Limits of the law

For the most part, the government does not interfere in club member selection. You can be as bigoted, sexist, racist, ageist, classist, or whatever-ist as you want to be, right up to the point where membership in the club becomes a factor in somebody's employment, hiring, or promotion. At that point, the company that refuses to hire or promote based on non-membership in a particular social club may well be guilty of illegal discrimination if that person is ineligible for club membership based on gender, race, or some other federally protected attribute. Your club won't get in trouble (usually) although they may get some bad press. Your members, however, may be on the hot seat along with the companies they own or manage.

It is generally wise to communicate this fact to new members, who might otherwise be tempted to get carried away by flaunting their newfound exclusivity.

Homeowner's Associations

A homeowner's association, or HOA, is a collection of people who own real estate in the same building or subdivision. Condominium complexes are governed by the HOA, which collects dues and assessments from all the members, makes the rules, and generally hires a property manager for day-to-day repairs and maintenance of the common areas.

The goal of a HOA is to provide a uniform standard of living to everybody in it. It maintains the common areas and also enforces such appearance, pet, and occupation bylaws as its members vote to pass. It is run by an executive team that generally consists of a President, Vice President, Secretary, and Treasurer. The Board of Directors is either the entire body of membership or a subset of those members who volunteer for the duty.

Avoid favoritism and pettiness

People generally volunteer to serve on a HOA because they want to make their neighbors miserable. Selectively enforcing policies against people you don't like, winking and nodding when your friends break the same rule, and harassing some of your neighbors for doing things that are not actually against the rules, are things for which HOAs are famous.

Many experienced homeowners refuse to buy in a HOA controlled property simply because they do not like to be abused or fined for things they did not do or that are beyond their control.

Enforcing policies

Every once in a while, somebody is unwilling or unable to pay dues or an assessment, or disputes one of the fines you decide to levy against them. Besides harassing phone calls, nasty letters, and the occasional act of sanctioned vandalism, you really only have one tool to legally enforce your bylaws: the lien.

Liens

A lien is a little bit like a court judgement, except it constitutes a legally binding burden on the title. You cannot sell your real estate if there is a lien against it. Whatever money you receive will first go to pay the lienholder(s), which might include the HOA, before your mortgage holder gets paid.

Chapter 24: Private Operating Foundations

Whereas most charities are "public", meaning that they get their money from a variety of different sources, the law allows for the creation of "private operating" charities, particularly charitable foundations and trusts where the purpose is to distribute (and occasionally raise) money for other charities. Such foundations seldom solicit the public for money or resources, and are usually a way to organize and direct the charitable ventures of a wealthy family or individual.

As I mentioned in an earlier chapter, a "foundation" is generally based on a large pool of money that is invested in a way that produces income. Real estate produces rent, intellectual property produces royalties, and stocks produce—in a good year—gains and dividends. However all of these means of getting money have something in common: they must be managed.

If you are operating a family foundation, your Board of Directors will generally be family members. So long as the relationship is known and disclosed, the fact you are related to another Board member does not constitute conflict of interest. However you must make sure to keep the personal and business interests of each "insider" separate from the charity's interests. This chapter will discuss how to do that.

The three domains of not-for-profit business (program, fund raising, and administration) will look a little bit different for your kind of charity. There are some specific issues almost completely unique to private operating foundations.

Program

Your program will generally not involve a lot of direct contact with the public, although your activities must benefit the public. The private operating foundation is for individuals and companies who either can't have, or don't want, extensive contact with the public in a charitable capacity. If you are fond of discreet giving and do not wish to waste money rebuffing solicitors, a private operating foundation will give you the ability to "just write checks".

Depending on your charitable goals, the private operating foundation designation may not be right for you. If you want any significant interaction with the public, such as by founding a youth sports league or operating a battered women's shelter or an addiction recovery center, you are likely to attract attention and donations from the public, and those who donate and who use your services tend to eventually want to have a say in how the money is used or administered. Also, if your effort is focused in a specific location on a specific task that involves human labor, in order to accomplish that task it makes sense to actually set up the church or charity *as* a church or charity. But if your goal is to not actually *do* these tasks but to support other people who do, and if you plan to fund your charitable activities personally through your business or family resources, a private operating foundation will be perfect.

As a private operating foundation, you will chiefly be reviewing grant applications, scholarship applications, and other means by which you transfer money to other charities or to individuals. At times you may identify a charity in need and make an unsolicited gift. But you still need the kind of focus that comes from having a program statement and a shared goal or vision. Accordingly, take the time to figure out exactly what you want your charity to do, write it down, and periodically check to make sure that you're still on track. You will be more vulnerable to program drift than a public charity especially if the rest of the administration team is composed of your friends and family.

You will generally be giving money to other charitable ventures such as churches, educational institutions, museums, or hospitals. If you are creating an endowment for the arts, you may give away grants that help fund a new film or a ballet production. Many independent filmmakers rely heavily on grants like these, however if you're funding an independent film created by a private company or an individual instead of the fine arts department of a local university, you need some means of vetting the recipients to prove to the IRS that you're not simply using the charity to funnel money to yourself or to your friends and relatives without paying tax.

Self-dealing and how to avoid it

Any time you give money to an individual, such as through a scholarship or a grant, you need a process and review mechanism to make sure the process isn't being abused. Also, any situation in which somebody connected to you stands to gain financially from a business transaction needs to be scrutinized. *Self-dealing*, or using the charity to help your own company, your family, or yourself, is a violation of the law governing your tax exempt status.

Because private operating foundations tend to be run chiefly by family members, and because some of the assets they own or control are unusual or illiquid, they are far more vulnerable to self-dealing than other kinds of charity. For example, if you need to sell an asset such as a painting or a piece of land, you may be more successful in finding a buyer through your personal network than through an agent or an auction house. But if the sale ends up being for less than the fair market value, you just made a gift of some of the charity's assets to an insider, which is both a private benefit transaction and self-dealing.

It's easy to get into a self-dealing transaction by accident. Suppose your private operating foundation is giving away scholarships, and you plan to pay a group of people to collect the applications, go through them, discard any disqualified applicants, and present the winners for your review. This requires some office space and a conference room. Luckily, your company happens to own a building nearby that has the necessary space. It may make sense for your foundation to rent or lease the necessary space from your company, possibly at a discount. But this is a self-dealing transaction *even if your business is losing money on it.*

Accepting less than market value as payment for your work, space, or other assets is *not* an effective way of making a donation to your foundation. It will cause nothing but trouble. If you would like to make an in-kind donation and charge zero, go for it. Otherwise, don't.

It may seem odd that transactions on which the private interest loses money in favor of the foundation should be punished as severely as deliberate attempts to funnel the charity's assets to others. But it takes time and money for the IRS to investigate even the benign cases. Administratively it was easier to simply ban all self-dealing, in the interests of the taxpayers who fund IRS investigations.

To avoid self-dealing your private operating foundation should never make any payment or transfer any assets to a *disqualified person* who is either a member of your administrative team, a family member of someone else who is, or a business owned by someone who meets that definition. This is true regardless of whether something of equal value is being given in exchange. If you have made a self-dealing transaction, you should keep a record of it so you can justify the transaction and ensure that the sale of an asset or the payment for services rendered was in fact done at market value.

You don't have to receive money or property to receive benefit. Every time your charity spends money on something that benefits you, a member of your family, or a business in which you're an owner or partner, it's potentially a self-dealing transaction. This includes products or services for your use. This might include travel or living expenses not related to charity business, or even payment of fees or fines on your behalf. Such transactions are also not tax exempt activities, and they can cost you your tax exempt status.

You can use your charity to buy things such as sports memorabilia provided that what you buy is put to charitable use. Suppose you buy the ball from the home run that clinched the World Series, or suppose you're at a silent auction for another charity that is auctioning off autographed NBA jerseys. You can use your charity's money to buy such things *if* you put them to charitable use such as by donating or lending them to sports museums or by auctioning them off again to fund your charity's own program activities. But if you buy the home run ball or Super Bowl ring just to display it in your study, you'd better use your own money to do it.

You are legally permitted to reimburse yourself, your family members, or other members of your Board for legitimate business expenses undertaken for your charity. This might include travel expenses related to your program. For example, if you are funding medical research, construction, or anything else that requires a sizable grant it is reasonable to make a site visit to see your funding in action provided it does not excessively disrupt program operations. However, if you are doing other business while on the trip or if the majority of your time is spent vacationing, do not expect to be able to pad your expense list and do not expect to be able to stay in luxury hotels. The IRS permits reimbursement of reasonable travel expenses but relies on the General Services Administration (GSA) to establish the per diem and accommodation rates for business travel to a given area. In general, if a reimbursement wouldn't be a tax deductible expense for a comparably sized for-profit business it won't be deemed a legitimate business expense for you either.

When you reimburse yourself, or an executive team member, for travel or business expenses undertaken on behalf of the charity, the same kind of reimbursement must be available for an employee or volunteer doing similar work at his or her own expense. If all the spending and reimbursement goes to one or two people who coincidentally happen to be members of the executive, it's a red flag. That doesn't mean something bad is happening—the person being reimbursed may also be the coach who travels with the chess team—but it's something you should scrutinize closely. The individual doing the travel or receiving the reimbursement *must* be recused from the decision to pay that particular expense, and must have nothing to do with the writing of the checks. It looks particularly good if the individual in question is not even a signatory on the charity's checking account.

There is one final argument against self-dealing that has nothing to do with the law. It comes down to basic dignity and taste. If you're wealthy enough to have your own charity, be it a private operating foundation or something else, then in my opinion (and the opinion of everyone else whose opinion matters) you can also afford a plane ticket. Just because the IRS allows you to be reimbursed for some of those expenses doesn't mean it's a good idea to act as though you don't have enough money to pay for something you've decided to do.

If you're having a cash flow problem in your household or your private business, find some other less public way to fix it. You may have to temporarily withdraw from charitable activities until your finances recover. Do this discreetly by taking time to focus on family or medical concerns. Failing that, make use of the stereotype of wealthy people as being slightly eccentric, and lose interest in the charity by allowing yourself to be distracted by something else. But treat a personal cash flow problem like an unzipped fly: fix it immediately and in private. Do not take money or resources from you charity to maintain a personal image. It doesn't work: self-dealing is a very obvious symptom of a money problem to anyone sophisticated enough to know what a private operating foundation is.

Although I benefited, as a child, from the effort my parents put into sports charities and school charities, I never received any sponsorship or reimbursement not available to other athletes who went to the same process. As an adult, I decided to never expense reimbursement from charities for which I volunteer. I will accept a complimentary bottle of water or snack, if the same is available to all the volunteers, but when it comes to paying for a hotel room or a plane ticket, my role is not to accept help from others. My role, as a charity founder and administrator, is to *provide* help and support to others through sponsorship and donation. While I understand and acknowledge that there are people who want to help run a charity but who cannot afford to pay all the expenses related to their participation, and while I have no problem reimbursing them for the costs, it is simply not my role to dip my cup in that particular punch bowl.

If you own a business that provides products or services that would be useful to your charity or a family member's charity, then the best way to stay on the right side of the law and public opinion is to donate them outright as an in-kind donation. Selling the services to the charity, at any price, constitutes self-dealing. It's legal if you do it at fair market value, however you also need some means of determining what fair market value is. If you're providing the use of your company jet or a vehicle from your fleet, calculate what the cost would be if the charity were to hire a similar service as a charter, and use that number.

Resist the temptation to think of your private operating foundation as an extension of yourself or your business interests. The entire purpose of creating a separate legal entity is that the money you give to it *is no longer yours*.

Recusing a stakeholder

To *recuse* yourself, or someone else, is to take that person out of the decision making process. Whenever a decision stands to benefit somebody financially, as a private benefit transaction, a self-dealing transaction, or even a decision about whether to change a person's salary or bonus structure, the person who stands to benefit needs to not be involved in the decision. He or she does not get a vote in the proceedings, and should ideally not be present when the topic is discussed in a Board meeting or an executive meeting. That doesn't mean the conversation has to be secret. It shouldn't be. But being able to prove that a person who received a check from your organization didn't do anything inappropriate is always wise.

If you have to recuse one or more people from a vote or decision, the remaining people present should still be enough to make up a *quorum*, which is the minimum number of Board members or executive team members to make a decision or vote valid. Exactly what percentage of your Board or executive constitutes a quorum will depend on your Articles of Incorporation.

Recipient charities

The kind of charity you elect to fund will influence the tax exempt category of your foundation. It may even influence whether your foundation can remain tax exempt at all.

You should avoid the 501(c)(3) designation if you spend a lot on lobbying through your foundation or if you give extensively to other lobbying charities. Likewise, if you propose to give money to politicians or to election campaigns, you cannot expect to get or keep 501(c)(3) designation for yourself. Giving money to such organizations is a non-exempt activity and it opens you up to scrutiny.

Be advised that if you give money to a charity identified as a domestic or foreign terrorist organization, you risk having all your US assets frozen or even confiscated. By that, I mean more than just your foundation's assets. I'm talking about your company's assets and also your personal checking account. Your private operating foundation is connected to *you*, and if money flows out from it to a group involved in random terrorist nonsense, the obvious conclusion is that you're fully aware of it.

It's annoying to have your assets frozen. Trying to run a charitable venture without a bank account is difficult and time consuming, convincing the authorities to release money so you can pay your electric bill is no easy process, and there's nothing the media likes quite as much as a juicy story about how this blue-blood family or that tycoon or businessperson is supporting white supremacy or similar stupidity.

Vet all of your recipients, even if they are applicants for a grant that you've advertised. The FBI maintains a list of domestic terrorist groups. Before you give, verify that the organization to which you're giving money isn't on it. Check that the EIN number you've been given matches the address and name of the charity you think you're supporting. Make sure there's nothing wrong with them, because anything that's wrong with them will end up sticking to you.

Fundraising

Organizationally, a private operating foundation is much like a vanity charity, but it gets more respect because of the real or perceived wealth of the people involved. The difference is that a vanity charity operating as a public charity relies on cash flow that incorporates the public, whereas your charity's cash flow and investment capital will come chiefly from your personal assets, your family's donations, or your privately held company.

People do occasionally make gifts to their friends' private operating foundations as part of an estate management strategy or to repay a social or business favor. Also, people who have personally benefited from the foundation or who have heard about its work sometimes make type C or type D donations or bequests. But these are rare, irregular events. The vast majority of your private operating foundation's inbound cash flow should come from you, from people and businesses connected to you, or from income producing assets the foundation already owns.

Overt advertising for the purpose of raising money is inappropriate for a private operating foundation. It is legal and appropriate to accept donations from outsiders, provided they are appropriately receipted, but solicitation of such donations really shouldn't be part of your business strategy. If a friend slips you a check at a cocktail party and tells you they'd like to help out, or if you receive a random donation from somebody who heard about you, or if you get a phone call from somebody's executor saying you've received a bequest, that's a nice windfall but you shouldn't plan on receiving them. It is enough to allow your organization to be mentioned in the program of the opera you supported, or in a short clip at the beginning or end of the documentary for which you provided funding. People who want to team up with an organization that does the kind of work you do will come looking for you based solely on evidence you have supported similar programs in the past. Of course, the same can be said for organizations that want to hit you up for a grant.

In general, it's best to make sure that the people and charities that *need* to know about your foundation can get in touch with you easily, but that the information is limited to those with a genuine need to know. The more you expose your foundation to the public for fundraising purposes the more you will expose it to solicitation. How much time or effort you want to put into rebuffing unwanted attention from grant seekers is up to you. There are charitable foundations where a paid administrator serves as a central point of contact. You may, if you wish, maintain a Web site that automates the donation process donations or provide online directory access. Whether you want your foundation to be easily visible to search engines or to people browsing the online Yellow Pages depends on how much you want to answer the phone or reply to E-mail.

If you want your foundation to be a hundred-year organization, you must stabilize its cash flow. This means you must wean it off of cash transfusions from you and your friends. You do this by endowing it with enough income producing assets to not only conduct its program year after year but to pay for administration.

Administration

There are two kinds of administration that require your attention if you have a private operating foundation. You must manage the day-to-day operations of the organization, *and* you must manage the assets and investments that provide your foundation with its income. How much of the work you do personally depends on the size and complexity of your foundation.

If you want your private operating foundation to become a hundred-year charity, you must make it financially independent of your support by setting up an endowment fund that will cover program expenses out of the interest or return on invested assets. Second, you must budget for *and pay for* an administrator besides yourself in order to provide continuity. Finally, you must have an intelligent succession plan.

There's going to be a minimum size below which your charity isn't going to be indefinitely sustainable. My rule of not paying for administration for any budget of less than $150,000 (in 2016 dollars) applies just as much to private operating foundations as it does to children's sport charities. Unless your foundation's invested capital is generating at least $150,000 independently from growth and dividends, it will not be cost effective to hire someone to manage the organization and to provide continuity in case you die, go broke, lose interest, or have to bow out for other reasons.

So, how do you get your foundation's invested capital to throw off $150,000 per year safely and sustainably? Well, your nest egg has to be big enough. How big of a nest egg do you need? That depends on the kind of invested capital you expect to have, and how much you're willing to spend to maintain it.

To get $150,000 out of an index fund using the 4% safe withdrawal rate, the fund should have invested assets of at least $3.75 million. If the income is coming from some less liquid asset such as land or patent royalties, the 4% safe withdrawal rate may be too high or too low depending on what the asset is, the kind of income it generates, and whether its earning power will one day be reduced.

For example, in a strong market where the cap rate on a specific kind of building is 10%, the rent on a $1.5 million dollar building might generate the $150,000 you need. However there are other expenses that go along with such a building such as repairs, utilities, taxes, and the occasional upgrade. These expenses may or may not be covered by the tenant, and if you've got a commercial lease and lose that tenant the income on the property goes to zero and stays there until you can find a replacement tenant. So, to provide reliable income of $150,000 you might need $2 million to $3 million in real estate depending on what the market does. Furthermore, to get the money you have to have somebody cashing the rent checks and hunting for a new tenant when each lease expires. Even on commercial real estate or leased land, where management expenses are relatively low, human effort is required to manage it. The same goes for other kinds of asset. Patents and copyrights expire, loans eventually get repaid and bonds mature and have to be replaced by different investments. The effort required in seeking out new loans or bonds is generally the sort of thing you have to pay for.

I don't recommend that smaller private operating foundations (with assets worth less than about $4 million) rely on the kind of income producing asset that requires ongoing attention from an expert. Even if you're accustomed to doing this work yourself, when you die or have to turn the organization over to a successor, will she or he be willing to put forth the same amount of uncompensated effort? If not, it may be time to either start paying for management (and experiencing the impact on your program while you still have time to make adjustments) or to switch to a low-effort form of investment.

Low-effort investments include bonds, money market accounts, bank accounts, and no-load or low-load mutual funds with small management fees. I like index funds best because nearly all the investment related work is taken away. Is it possible to earn a higher rate of return? Of course—but the advantage of a well managed index fund is that it takes much of the expertise and nearly all the labor out of managing the investment side of your foundation.

The upshot of all of this is that, when it comes to private operating foundations, size matters. If you can't put three or four million dollars into a core endowment or nest egg, consider scaling down a few years and directing your foundation's investments more internally... or else consider the public charity approach. If your cash flow depends on revenue from your business or your personal or family donations, that's great while you're alive, but your foundation won't survive you for long if you don't leave it a sizable bequest. Even if you do, if the team running your foundation after your demise isn't experienced in handling and investing that amount of money, they are unlikely to become overnight experts.

Chapter 25: Final Thoughts

This chapter contains a few last insights I've collected over more than thirty years' worth of volunteer work and charity administration. They couldn't be easily fit into other chapters.

You don't have a moral obligation to be broke

Asceticism can be good for individuals, who voluntarily take vows of poverty and abstinence. For some individuals, it provides spiritual or moral benefit. Many cultures and religions have days where everybody fasts or voluntarily goes without something they enjoy, simply to help them to focus on the things that are important and to fully appreciate the blessings they have. Also, some religions have a group of individuals who dedicate their lives to sevice to the religion and forego things such as employment or significant ownership of private property. Monasteries exist throughout the known world, where Buddhist, Taoist, Roman Catholic, and other religious groups maintain facilities where people seek enlightenment along with the advancement of their faith. Physical poverty is part of the monastic lifestyle, and many religious institutions require their representative priests and nuns to take vows of poverty in order to avoid creating a conflict between their spiritual work and their personal interests.

For the most part, the concept of sacred asceticism has worked. But one of the side effects is the persistent myth that not-for-profit organizations or charities ought to be poor, and that money should not be saved or invested if there's an opportunity to spend it on a program activity. People who think this way also object to spending any money whatsoever on administrative expenses. But this position is just as extreme as the real estate and asset accumulation goal so popular with some churches. It's also just as impractical.

If you have a private operating foundation or endowment fund, you're supposed to have sufficient assets to provide passive income for your activities. If you're a charity large enough to employ people, it's reasonable to have a full year's worth of operating expenses (including salaries) set aside. An extremely large charity that has very few variations in its annual income can set aside a smaller percentage of its overall income, but the smaller your charity is the more vulnerable you will be to unpleasant surprises or "bad" years due to circumstances beyond your control. It's also very practical, and very normal, to buy income producing assets such as stocks, bonds, or investment real estate instead of letting money sit in a checking account.

As I explained earlier in the chapters on cash flow, having savings provides a financial cushion that will allow you to ride out emergencies without stressing your volunteer or donor base. The same unexpected event that might be a crisis for a charity with no savings will be, for you, a minor inconvenience at worst. You will be able to react to emergencies with minimal disruption to your program activities.

Maxim #23: Well-run charities can respond to minor emergencies without disrupting program operations, because they have an emergency fund.

You aren't doing yourself any favors by spending every available cent on program activities. If you run a lean, mean local charity and spend very little on administration (such as if you're a high school booster club), you don't need much in the way of cash reserves because you have no fixed expenses such as rent or wages. But if you do have fixed expenses such as loan payments, utility bills, salaries and contractual payments, you'd better budget for them and set the money aside. Putting it in a savings account is a legitimate way to do that.

If you are involved in charity out of a sense of moral duty, then run your charity in a moral way. Your first duty is not to perform charity: your first duty is to be a responsible and moral person who conducts business in a righteous and appropriate way. If you're cutting corners by paying bills late or short-changing your own employees so as to spend money on charitable program activities, this is false charity. You might be giving to the poor or needy, but you're doing it by taking from one group of people who contracted with you in good faith, who provided goods or services that you requested, and that are relying on you to pay for what you've used.

Spending to the point where you're unable to pay your bills is mismanagement. It doesn't matter whether you're doing it in a personal capacity or as a representative of a corporation or even a government. Likewise, screwing people over by not holding up your end of an agreement is not OK. Acting in the name of a charity does not somehow sanitize it.

Maxim #24: Not paying your bills because you gave away the money is not an example of morality or good stewardship.

If you have to choose between performing charity and running your organization responsibly—if there's no other option, and if for some reason you've painted yourself into a corner where it's no longer possible to run the charity honestly—then I hope you have the strength to choose to be a responsible and honest person.

Where your money comes from is relevant

It's true that you can lose your tax exempt status by retaining "excess" profit from business operations. In fact it's one of the eight crash-and-burn offenses that can cause the IRS to revoke your tax exempt status. If you make more money from business operations (buying and selling things) than you do from donations or fundraising, then if you retain that profit from year to year like a for-profit business might, eventually you may end up in tax court. It's always dangerous to have more than half your income come from business activities that compete with the private sector. Yet whether you retain money isn't the key issue: the key issue is where the money comes from.

Your income might come from donations, investment income, fundraising, and occasionally a business activity where you compete with the private sector. How much of your money comes from which source may influence your tax-exempt classification, or even whether you are tax-exempt at all.

If the vast majority of your money comes from fundraising and donations such as tithes or endowments, you can stash that cash until the day the world ends and the IRS will not even blink. This is why you see so many wealthy churches and museums. Do they operate small for-profit operations such as souvenir shops, or do they rent out unused rooms to the public in exchange for money? Definitely. But the money they make by providing space, pencils, or snow globes to the public is typically less than half the annual budget.

If you are a private operating foundation and most of your money comes from investment income, you can save as much of it as you want. This is why you see so many scholarship foundations and endowments for the arts and humanities. The healthiest foundations can pay a hundred percent of each year's budget out of investment income alone. The IRS has no problem with that. It doesn't particularly matter what services you provide, so long as you serve a charitable class of people or are helping to fund education, ecological conservation, health care, religious instruction, or some specific activity the tax code has designated as "charitable" or for the public benefit. You can, if you like, suspend program operations completely for a year or two while you build up enough assets to continue.

If most of your money comes from fundraising activities like thing-a-thons, park cleanup, or sales of overpriced wrapping paper, you can save as much money as you like provided you don't alienate your volunteers in the process. Generally, people who help raise money expect to have some say in how and when it is spent. So, at your annual general meeting, be prepared to explain why you're choosing to save or invest. Be prepared to justify your decision.

Be careful and open when redirecting money

If you need to redirect money and ask the permission of the people who helped raise it, the worst thing you can expect to have happen is a big argument with disgruntled volunteers: you will not be in trouble with the IRS simply for saving and investing the proceeds of your bake sale unless you've diverted them from the stated or intended purpose. If you had a bake sale "to support the school's model rocket club" and then you decide not to buy the model rockets because you want to invest the money instead, then you've misappropriated assets and tax court is a fitting place for you. But if you had fundraisers that weren't specifically focused on any activity, and you never led your volunteers, donors, or customers to believe you intended their donations for a specific purpose, your organization can keep and invest that money freely. Buy all the index fund shares you like.

Maxim #25: If fundraising competes with something similar in the private sector, it's business activity.

There's a distinction between making money through fundraising and keeping the money you made selling things or competing in the market. The latter may not be tax exempt.

Although retaining "excess" profits from business operations can cause you to lose your tax exempt status. How much you accumulate should depend on the kind of charity you have. If you are classified as a

376

public charity as opposed to, say, a trade union, most of your income is supposed to come from donations from people in your community. Piling up ridiculous amounts of land, assets, and other things beyond what can generate enough income for you to fund your ongoing operations can actually affect a public charity's tax exempt status.

Operating like a private business, and accumulating large amounts of money or paying large salaries to key executives, is another thing that can keep a non-profit from having or keeping tax exempt status. A charitable hospital that sues patients who are unable to pay their bills, for example, is generally regarded as operating like a private business instead of serving the public.

A non-profit that engages in inurement, insider benefit, or running like a private business generally does not qualify for tax exempt status to begin with. If by some chance they obtain tax exempt status and then start operating in a way that would cause their application to have been turned down, a non-profit can easily lose its tax exempt status.

There are a few exceptions, where a booster club serves people who take lessons in a sport or art that is taught through a for-profit business. Such clubs must take steps to ensure that they meet IRS guidelines for charitable behavior, and they must avoid conflict of interest by being organizationally separate from any for-profit organization that might otherwise benefit from them.

Maintain appropriate balance of power

The Board outranks the executive team; the executive team outranks the employees of the charity. This is the normal and appropriate balance of power. Although the Executive Director of a small charity might wield a lot of power over day-to-day decisions and spending, he or she must be accountable to the Board.

Maxim #26: The Board of Directors is the dog, and the executive team and employees are the tail. Never let the tail wag the dog.

One of the biggest dangers is when the Board of Directors becomes lazy and delegates too much authority to employees of the charity. When the church elders can't be bothered to come to meetings or review decisions, the minister starts effectively running the church. This is not out of malicious intent on the minister's part: it's a perfectly reasonable consequence of allowing a power vacuum to exist. In the absence of leadership from the appropriate leaders, human beings will step up and make their own decisions especially when their own financial interests are at stake.

There's a huge problem with letting employees of the charity run the charity: conflict of interest. One of the things not-for-profit companies are required by law to do is to address and mitigate conflicts of interest. Sitting back and allowing an employee, no matter how competent, to run the show and to make decisions related to his or her own compensation is a breach of your fiduciary duty as an administrator. Do not allow it.

I have seen examples of a small charity that was founded by an unusually dynamic, clever, and proactive person who later became the charity's sole employee. Unfortunately, this Executive Director was so socially dominant over the Board that the Board effectively became a rubber stamp that retroactively approved the Executive Director's decisions. Not only was the Executive Director never recused from decisions affecting compensation, but the Board functioned as a glorified rubber stamp and money-dispensing machine. The Executive Director was allowed to make a series of very ill-informed decisions that resulted in a great deal of debt for the charity, which eventually folded when its volunteer pool was unable to raise enough money to pay the service on the organization's debts.

Going out of business is a very predictable result of allowing the tail to wag the dog. If you want to be a charitable leader, then lead. Attend the meetings, take notes, understand the issues, communicate with the other Board members and the employees, and keep yourself informed. Under no circumstances should you join a Board of Directors simply for social purposes.

Conclusion

I hope very much that the information in this book helps you run the kind of charity that can last a hundred years or more. By putting sustainable policies and management techniques, you can ease the pressure not only on yourself but on your successors. Creating a culture of sustainability will produce a rock-solid, reliable program and a healthy donor and volunteer pool. You can also begin a conversation with some of your peers about long-term strategy and succession management.

My goal, with this book, was to provide not just a list of things to do but explicit instructions about how to decide what needs to be done given the kind of charity you have. I've discussed all the major pitfalls related to not-for-profit administration and I've shown what stability looks like mathematically. I've provided several different models for analyzing and calculating limits to what you can, or should, expect your charity to do given the personnel and money you have available.

Because my emphasis was on sustainable management, I deliberately refrained from discussing charitable activities that, while worthwhile, need not be run in a sustainable way. There are some kinds of charitable ventures I deliberately did not address in this book. Campaign fundraising, political action committees, and one-shot charities designed to solve a short-term problem such as disaster cleanup in a specific area, are deliberately not included. However, if you a part of a community that runs lots of these short-term initiatives, the same rules about ethics and social capital will apply to you as they would if you were a formal organization. You will cross paths with the same people repeatedly over the years, and everywhere there's a group of people that knows each other, reputation and social capital matter.

Besides the basic theory of business management and structure, which you will already understand if you have studied it formally, you will have some new quantitative tools that will allow you to measure, calculate, and make intelligent predictions about what your goals should be given the resources at hand. You will also have a better understanding of why donors and volunteers behave the way they do, and this may help you refine or restructure your fundraising activities.

For your convenience I have attached a glossary of terms I have introduced in this book.

Thank you for reading, and good luck in your charitable venture.

R.A. Williams

Glossary

Administrative expense: Any expense related to running or organizing the charity. This includes costs related to advertising, networking, maintaining the Web site, volunteer recruitment, and filling out the annual tax paperwork

Affinity clustering: The extent to which people in a large single-purpose group spontaneously form smaller group clusters, bond emotionally with the people in those clusters, and socialize as a community apart from the main group

Automobile insurance: Two types of insurance, specifically collision liability that protects the insured against claims due to injury or property damage related to the operation of the car, and also comprehensive that covers the cost to repair or replace a vehicle damaged by non-collision accidents such as fire, theft, hail, or vandalism

Bequest: A donation made as part of a deceased person's will or trust, typically a one-time gift of assets

Board of Directors: A group of people that provide the long-term leadership and direction for the corporation, who delegate the day-to-day operations to the executive team

Booster club: A charity set up to raise money for a specific team or school program, such as an athletic team or a school band. Generally composed of parents, alumni, or other people who have ties to the school or the students

Burn rate: The rate at which an organization spends money, generally expressed as a monthly or weekly dollar value

Cash flow: The movement of money or assets into, out of, or through a company

Cash flow problem: A situation in which there is not enough money on hand, or coming in, to cover expenses

Casual volunteer: A person who donates occasional part-time labor, generally for special events or initiative, but who does not expect to have a multi-year commitment to the non-profit

Charitable immunity: An outdated system of laws in which charities were immune from certain kinds of liability claims (no longer exists in the USA)

Charity: A special kind of nonprofit set up to provide some benefit to the public

Commercial General Liability (CGL) insurance: A type of liability insurance to protect the company and the individuals connected to it from claims related to misconduct by an employee or volunteer. May not necessarily include sexual misconduct coverage

Compassion fatigue: When a person is overwhelmed by demands on his or her emotional or financial resources to the point where he or she shuts down and is no longer emotionally capable of giving

Contractual expense: An expense, generally monthly, that is due every month and does not change in size of due date. Generally related to a loan, lease or signed agreement to pay

Contingency: In the context of budgets or business proposals, a portion of the net bid or budget set aside for expenses that are unpredictable but expected

Conversion: The civil term for embezzlement, when a person is being sued in civil court instead of criminal court

Corporation: A type of business structure in which the day-to-day management of the company is done by officers or executives of the company, while the long-term direction of the company is controlled by the Board of Directors. In a for-profit corporation, ownership is distributed among multiple shareholders who do not take an active role in managing the company. A not-for-profit corporation has no shareholders

Credit union: A non-profit dedicated to basic savings-and-loan banking operations, restricted to its membership

Directors and Officers (D&O) insurance: A type of liability insurance to protect the directors, executives, and officers of a company from claims related to the performance of their administrative duties and/or to decisions they made while running the charity

Dividend: A payment made to the shareholders of a corporation, representing each share's worth of profit from the corporation's business activities

Donor: A person who makes a gift of money or goods to a non-profit organization

Donor pool: The set of people that donate, or have donated, to a specific charity

EIN or Employment Identification Number: A unique number issued by the Internal Revenue Service of the United States to all companies or corporations doing business in the USA. Similar to a Social Security Number for individuals

Electioneering: The act of attempting to influence the outcome of an election, such as by publicly endorsing a specific candidate or by providing resources to some candidates for an elected office but not all

Embezzlement: A type of white collar crime in which a person who is entrusted with money or goods steals it or converts it to his or her own use

Endowment fund: A large gift of money or investments that generates income for a non-profit

Errors and Omission (E&O) insurance: A type of liability insurance that protects a company's employees and volunteers from claims related to mistakes they may have made during the performance of their duties

Executive: A person, either a shareholder, partner, or employee, who is empowered to commit the company by signing a contract, taking out a loan, or otherwise create a legally binding commitment on the company's behalf. Also refers to the collective management team or set of officers. See Officer

Fiduciary: a person who is legally obligated to put the company's or charity's interests before his or her own. For example the officers of the charity have a fiduciary duty to that charity.

Firewall: a computer, or software that runs on a computer, to control electronic message traffic into or out of a computer or network

Fixed cost: A cost associated with doing business that does not scale based on the number of units of service

Flexible expense: An expense that will go up or down from one month to the next, and that is more controllable than a fixed expense such that money can be saved by economizing or by postponing purchases. Not to be confused with variable expense or cost

Founder: One of the people who initially set up a non-profit and register it with the Attorney General of the state in which they live

Fraud: Any misrepresentation, in writing or in communication, made with the intent of getting material benefit or money dishonestly. Examples include check fraud, wire fraud, and bank fraud

Fundraising: Any activity intended to raise money for the non-profit. This could include the solicitation of donations, or the sale of merchandise or services

Fundraising expense: Any expense related to raising money for the non-profit. This includes advertising related to a public event, or food for a church bake sale, or the pre-printed forms used to collect pledges or product orders

Grant: A gift of money made by a government agency, charity, or business to a charitable venture, for the purpose of creating a lasting benefit to society or a permanent program expansion

Hedonic adaptation: The human ability to adjust to a new norm in terms of pleasure or discomfort, such that the person's overall happiness level remains constant

Insider: Any person who is involved with the non-profit as a volunteer or employee, or who is closely related to somebody so involved

Inurement: Any situation in which a portion of the money raised is set aside for the exclusive use of a particular individual (paid or unpaid)

Labor union: A group of workers that have organized themselves into a non-profit corporation for the purpose of collective bargaining with their employers

Liability insurance: A type of insurance purchased to protect a company, its employees, and (in the case of a non-profit) its volunteers from claims related to accidents or injuries that occur on the company's property or in relation to the company's activities, if there is bodily harm or property damage

Limited Liability Company (LLC): A type of business in which the legal and financial liabilities are limited to the assets of the company. Designed to protect the assets of the company owners from seizure in the case of a liability suit.

Lobbying: Any act or communication done with the intent of influencing legislation. Includes letter writing campaigns that require communication with legislators

Malpractice insurance: A type of insurance for medical or legal professionals that protects against claims related to incorrect performance of professional duties

Maximum burst: A brief, intense flurry of fundraising activity, lasting no more than two months, designed to raise 130% or more of the normal money brought in during a short period

Misappropriation: Using money or resources that have been earmarked for one task and spending them on a different task or item

Mission statement: A sentence, or sentence fragment, describing the purpose of the non-profit's existence, and what it is set up to do

Mitigation: The process of reducing the impact or risk associated with a particular threat, such as fire or data loss

Negative cash flow: More money is going out than is coming in

Non-Government Organization or NGO: A multinational or global charity that raises money in one or more wealthy nations so as to perform charitable work in a poorer nation or region

Non-profit or not-for-profit: A specially structured corporation that has no shareholders or owners, generally for some public service

Officer: A person, either a shareholder, partner, or employee, who is empowered to commit the company by signing a contract, taking out a loan, or otherwise create a legally binding commitment on the company's behalf. See Executive

One year push: A one-year effort in which volunteers spend 120% of their sustainable effort to do fundraising. See Sustainable effort

Partnership: A for-profit business with more than one owner, often registered as a limited liability company (LLC)

Per unit cost: The amount of money required to perform one unit of service

Positive cash flow: More money is coming in than is going out

Principal: Invested money that produces interest or a return

Private benefit: Excessive payment for services rendered, or other financial or material benefit to an individual outside of the normal program activities

Private operating foundation: a type charity funded and administered by a single individual, family, or privately held business

Professional liability insurance: Malpractice or Errors and Omissions (E&O) insurance designed to protect against financial consequences due to making a mistake during the course of professional duties

Profit: The net gain created by a transaction, fundraiser, or business operation. Calculated as income minus expenses

Program: A generic term for the services or products a non-profit is set up to provide. For example, a food bank's program is dedicated to the collection and distribution of food to the needy

Program expense: Any expense related to actually delivering services or products related to the charity's mission or program. For example, in a youth mentoring charity, mentor training expenses are considered "program", but the fundraising activities are not

Property insurance: A type of insurance to repair or replace property, particularly real estate, in case of fire or other damage. May include coverage for loss of use

Quorum: The minimum number of decision makers present in a meeting for the decision to be valid or enforceable

Recuse: To take yourself, or somebody else, out of a decision making process

Sacred cow: Something so culturally important to an organization that it is treated as being immune from budget cuts, criticism, or change

Self-dealing: a business transaction in which a not-for-profit corporation or charity does business with an insider or decision maker in a personal capacity

Shareholder: A partial owner of a corporation, who has purchased one or more shares

Silent partner: a co-owner of a for-profit business who contributes money or resources toward the business, but who takes no share in the management decisions

Sole proprietorship: a for-profit business with just one owner, who is an individual human being (not a corporation)

Sustainable: Something that is structured in such a way that it could continue operating indefinitely without exhausting the resources upon which it relies

Sustainable effort: The amount of fundraising a volunteer team can do in any given year without burning out

Tax exempt: A non-profit that has received formal written acknowledgement from the IRS, because it meets the criteria for some specific tax exempt purpose such as by being a trade union, or serving a charitable purpose, or being a social club. There is more than one type of tax exemption

Umbrella insurance: A type of catch-all insurance that kicks in when another policy is exhausted, or that covers things not addressed by the specific policy. Examples may include loss of use of a building related to a fire

Unit of service: The means by which you measure a charity's programmatic impact. A unit of service might be one pair of socks handed out to a homeless person, or one meal served at a soup kitchen, or one tree planted in a reforesting project

Variable cost: A cost of doing business that scales with the units of service. Consists of the total of all the per-unit costs

Volunteer: A person who performs work for the non-profit's benefit, but who is not paid or compensated for their time

Volunteer pool: The set of people from whom your organization draws its volunteers

Windfall: A one-time donation or grant, often unexpected, generally received without significant effort

Bibliography

CharityWatch. (2016). *CharityWatch Hall of Shame*. [Online Article].

Gladwell, Malcom. *The Tipping Point: How Little Things Can Make a Big Difference*. (2000) Little Brown and Company.

Goedert, Paula C. (2011) *Tax Issues for Exempt Organizations – A Primer*. Copyright 2011 by Barnes and Thornburg LLP.

Gonzales, Richard. (March 19, 2015) *Blue Shield of California Loses Its Tax-Exempt Status*. NPR Morning Edition. [Radio] Renee Montagne, Host. National Public Radio, Washington, DC.

Kennedy, John F. (1961) *Special Message to the Congress on Urgent National Needs*. [Speech, delivered in person before a joint session of Congress].

Lagnado, Lucette. (Feb. 19, 2004) *Hospital Found "Not Charitable" Loses Its Status as Tax Exempt*. The Wall Street Journal.

Lydon, John. (March 6, 2013) *Nonprofit myths: Many don't pay property taxes—but for many good reasons*. Pittsburgh Post-Gazette.

Oshinsky, Gerold., & Dias, Gheiza M. (2002). *Liability of Not-for-Profit Organizations and Insurance Coverage for Related Liability*. The International Journal of Not-for-Profit Law, 4 (2-3). Online.

Reilly, Peter J. (Sep. 5, 2013) *Parent Booster Clubs: Raising Money For Your Own Kid Is Not Charity*. Forbes.

United States Federal Bureau of Investigation, Philadelphia Division. (1995). *Foundation for New Era Philanthropy*.[Online Archive].

United States Internal Revenue Service. (2016). *Life Cycle of a Public Charity – Jeopardizing Exemption*.

United States Internal Revenue Service. (2006). Notice 1340. *Tax-Exempt Organizations and Raffle Prizes – Reporting Requirements and Federal Income Tax Withholding*.

United States Internal Revenue Service. (2015). *Publication 598, Tax on Unrelated Business Income of Exempt Organizations*.

United States Internal Revenue Service. (2016). *Revoked? Reinstated? Learn More*.